BREAKING THE BACKCOUNTRY

Breaking the Backcountry

*The Seven Years' War in Virginia
and Pennsylvania, 1754–1765*

MATTHEW C. WARD

UNIVERSITY OF PITTSBURGH PRESS

Published by the University of Pittsburgh Press, Pittsburgh, Pa., 15260
Copyright © 2003, University of Pittsburgh Press
All rights reserved
Manufactured in the United States of America
Printed on acid-free paper

ISBN 0-8229-5865-1

First paperback edition, 2004
10 9 8 7 6 5 4 3 2 1

To my parents

Contents

Illustrations follow page 90.

Acknowledgments

THIS WORK HAS BEEN many years in creation, lasting longer than the Seven Years' War itself. Along the way I have moved from Virginia to eastern Scotland and been sidetracked by many other projects and diversions, all of which have allowed my ideas to mature. This time has also allowed many people to offer advice in many different forms. The late John Selby provided inestimable guidance during the project's early stages at the College of William and Mary. The work would also never have developed without the support and encouragement of James Axtell, Jim Whittenburg, and Bill Abbot. Over the years many other colleagues and peers have offered advice and assistance, and on occasion even small comments have prompted a new approach to some of my thoughts. In particular I would like to thank Chris Bartlett, Tony Parker, Judy Ridner, Peter Silver, and John Oliphant. I must also extend my greatest thanks to the two anonymous readers of my manuscript at the University of Pittsburgh Press, whose invaluable comments helped me to focus more clearly. Barrie Blewett, John Williams, and Scott McIntosh gave me equally important assistance by providing accommodation, while Sigrid Clark had the unenviable task of proofreading my manuscript as well as offering much other encouragement. David Aiton has listened to many moans from me and had to endure too many of my mood swings and bouts of despair.

I could also not have completed this book without the assistance of many different archivists and librarians. In particular I would like to thank the staff at the Cumberland County Historical Society in Carlisle, Pennsylvania; the Pennsylvania State Archives in Harrisburg; and the William L. Clements Library in Ann Arbor, who all went beyond the call of duty to assist me. Interlibrary loans at the University of Dundee were also remarkably efficient. I received assistance in answer to often frantic phone calls or e-mails in my hunt for documentary art from James

Kilvington at the National Portrait Gallery, London; Kristen Froehlich at the Atwater Kent Museum of Philadelphia; Stephanie Jacobe at the Virginia Historical Society; Jordan Rockford and Kerry McLaughlin at the Historical Society of Pennsylvania; Jonathan King, James Hamill, and Elizabeth Harbord at the British Museum; Charlene Peacock at the Library Company of Philadelphia; and John Scally at the National Library of Scotland. Carolyn Bain and Gordon Keir at the University of Dundee provided vital technical assistance and expertise in the production of maps.

Perhaps most importantly, this work could never have been completed without the financial support I have received from various sources. In particular, research grants from the British Academy and the Carnegie Trust for the Universities of Scotland allowed me to make extended research trips back to the United States. A summer research fellowship at the Historical Society of Pennsylvania was perhaps the most invaluable support I received. I also received important financial support from the College of William and Mary and the Department of History at the University of Dundee. For too much of this project the most important source of both financial assistance and encouragement has been my parents, without whom this work would never have seen the light of day.

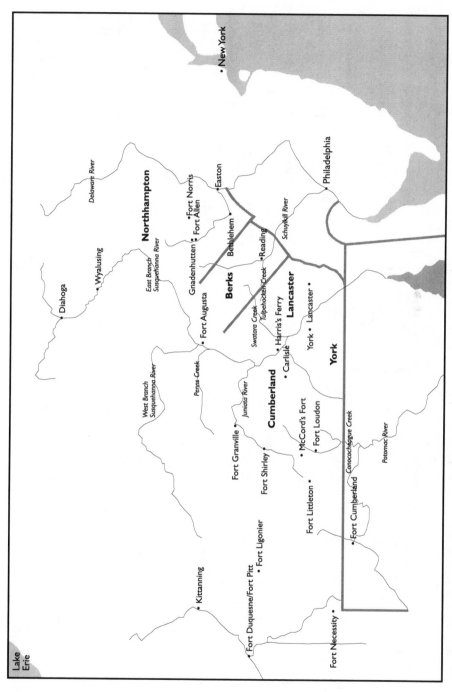

The Pennsylvania backcountry during the Seven Years' War

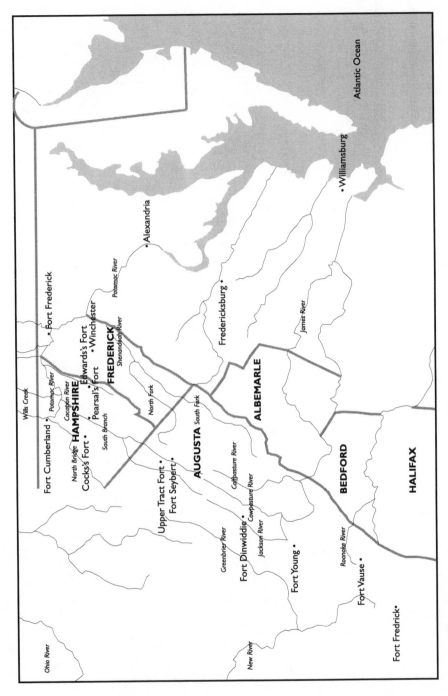

The Virginia backcountry during the Seven Years' War

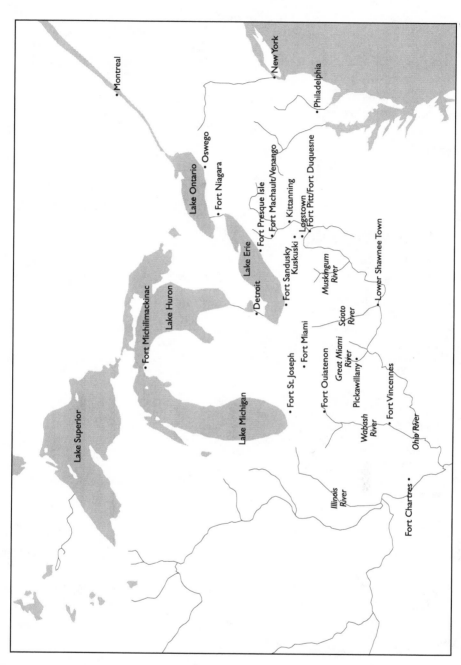

The upper Ohio Valley and the Great Lakes region during the Seven Years' War

BREAKING THE BACKCOUNTRY

Introduction

IN 1754 MILITARY COMMANDERS IN BRITAIN BEGAN PREPARATIONS for a grand expedition against the French Empire in North America. Since the end of King George's War in 1748, tensions between France and Great Britain had increased rather than lessened. Nowhere was friction more apparent than in the Ohio Valley. Here British and French traders had come into direct competition, and the French had responded by building a string of new forts and driving the British from the region. Now Whitehall had determined to take action. Defeat could not be comprehended. As ministers confidently noted, it was "taken for granted, that this . . . Campaign will make Major General Braddock Master of the Ohio."[1]

When Gen. Edward Braddock's expedition was routed, Indian raiders, acting both at French instigation and on their own initiative, launched devastating raids on the frontier and generated a crisis throughout the Virginia and Pennsylvania backcountry.[2] Settlers who did not flee were as likely to prey on one another, or to take advantage of the military crisis, as to cooperate in their own defense. Families and individuals sought safety with little respect for the preservation of the broader community. Efforts on the part of the colonial governments to intervene were hampered by endemic political factionalism, especially in Pennsylvania, which the war only exacerbated. When faced with the slaughter of nearly fifteen hundred settlers, the capture of over one thousand more, the flight of many thousands, and the devastation of twenty thousand square miles of backcountry, the provincial governments finally created military organizations to establish a defensive barrier. However, the provincial soldiers proved as likely to increase the problems of security as to alleviate them and initially did little to stabilize the frontier, halt the flight of refugees, or prevent raids by Indian warriors who were far more proficient in forest and guerilla warfare than most provincial soldiers. It took several years for the British and their colonists to develop a coherent response to the Indians' raids upon the frontier. For most of the war British and colonial troops in the region were few, disorganized, ill treated, and fond of desertion and insubordination. If not for the successes of the Royal Navy, Virginia and Pennsylvania could have suffered a severe social and economic crisis in 1758. It was only the direct intervention of Whitehall in 1758, in the form of Brig. Gen. John Forbes—armed not only with thousands of men and hundreds of thousands of pounds sterling but with sufficient perception to use diplomatic means to detach the Indian residents of the upper Ohio Valley from their French allies—that ended the raids and halted the disintegration of backcountry society. All but miraculously rescued, the colonists proceeded to turn years of disorder and defeat into a source of pride, ultimately seeing themselves as victors in a war in which they had been repeatedly humiliated.

Following the conquest of the Ohio Valley, direction of affairs in the region fell to Gen. Jeffrey Amherst. With Amherst unable, and unwilling, to understand the fears of his former Indian enemies, whose military power remained undiminished, his policies of fiscal retrenchment and reform in Indian diplomacy created friction with the Ohio Indians. Relations were further damaged by the large numbers of settlers who sought to reinhabit old settlements and to expand into new areas now made accessible by the roads that the army had constructed. Amherst's shortsightedness and the settlers' belligerence set the scene for the outbreak of yet another frontier war, "Pontiac's War," which from 1763 through 1764 recreated the misery of 1755–58.

This decade of warfare fundamentally transformed both colonies.

In no other previous decade since their foundation had Virginia and Pennsylvania witnessed such a thorough transformation. Political, economic, social, and military institutions were all changed by the war. In both colonies the assemblies furthered their powers at the expense of the colonial governors and, in Pennsylvania's case, the proprietors. These disputes would, of course, continue with even greater vigor after the war as the imperial crisis instigated by the Stamp Act deepened.

In four critical areas in particular the war transformed the nature of colonial life. First, it greatly increased the powers and activities of the colonial governments. Before the war in both colonies the colonial assemblies had largely contented themselves with setting boundaries for new counties, building new roads, and settling the dates for county courts. For most colonists the activities of the assemblies were remote and not too important. Suddenly the assemblies found themselves responsible for raising and provisioning armies with which to combat the Ohio raiders. They needed to raise taxes, recruit men, and impress wagons and provisions. Almost overnight the actions of the provincial assemblies began to impact the day-to-day lives of Virginians and Pennsylvanians who formerly had had little or no contact with central government. The war allowed the assemblies to develop methods of creating professional military forces with the minimum of social disruption and provided many colonists, most notably of course George Washington, with important military experience.[3]

Second, the war changed forever the relationship between the colonies and Great Britain. Colonists witnessed firsthand the ineptitude of British commanders such as Edward Braddock. Indeed, the British commander who displayed the greatest military ability during the conflict was Henry Bouquet, who was not British by birth but Swiss. The wartime experience of the colonies was to prove central in convincing Virginia and Pennsylvania of their ability to resist British power. Without such confidence the political crisis of the 1760s and early 1770s might have taken a rather different turn in this region. British officials bridled at the reluctance of colonists to defend themselves, their parsimony in providing assistance to the war effort, and worse still their willingness to trade with the enemy. Consequently, after the war each side viewed the other with increased suspicion.

Third, the war decisively changed colonists' attitudes toward their Native American neighbors. Central to the minimization of social discord in the wake of the war was the ability to focus animosity away from the elite and onto the Indian peoples. In the early stages of the war many colonists were suspicious that it had broken out because of the machinations of the Ohio Company, because of Pennsylvania traders, or because of the Penns' maneuverings for land. By the end of Pontiac's War most colonists believed that the war had been caused by Native American duplicity. During the Revolutionary War such feelings of animosity would once more be focused on the Indians as they sided with the Crown or sought to maintain a fragile neutrality.[4] The focusing of animosity upon the colonists' neighboring Native American population had important long-term results. In both Virginia and Pennsylvania mobs of frontiersmen, respectively known as the Augusta Boys and the Paxton Boys, attacked peaceful Native Americans. Never again would either colony be able to return to the relatively peaceful relations they had known before the outbreak of war. As James H. Merrell has commented, "The bloodshed and anguish forever changed the face of the frontier, leaving Penn's peaceful vision little more than a memory."[5]

Finally, the war also served as a turning point in the history of the backcountry. The backcountry of Virginia and Pennsylvania on the eve of the Seven Years' War was a socially fragmented, economically weak, and culturally diverse area that had little in common with the long-settled coastal zones. The war demonstrated the depth of individualism and the importance of the quest for self-improvement in backcountry society. Community ties, fragile before the outbreak of war, were now shattered and only slowly replaced by new ties. Ethnic and social divisions emerged to hamper the conduct of war, while the region's elite found themselves unable to direct the war effort.

The nature and impact of the war in Virginia and Pennsylvania have to a large extent been overlooked because the Seven Years' War was fought across North America and across the globe. The backcountry of Virginia and Pennsylvania has thus seemed comparatively unimportant compared to the campaigns on the St. Lawrence or the Plains of Bengal. There have been several studies of the impact of the Seven Years' War on colonial societies. However, these have focused principally on New England.[6] Broader studies of the war have tended to underplay the importance of the war in this theater and its uniqueness. Military historians have equated the struggle for Canada, not the struggle in the backcountry, with the entire war. John Shy, for instance, has argued that "the Seven Years' War in America was primarily an attack on Canada."[7] The most expansive study of the war, Lawrence Henry Gipson's fifteen-volume study, discusses the war in the middle colonies between Braddock's defeat and Forbes's expedition in a mere thirty-two pages.[8] Even Fred Anderson's recent work, while paying more attention than Gipson to the backcountry and the involvement of the Ohio Indians, focuses principally on the regular campaigns and fails to recognize the unique experience of Virginia and Pennsylvania.[9]

In New England the Seven Years' War was fought outside the region. Massachusetts soldiers served in New York, on the St. Lawrence, and in Acadia and Nova Scotia. They were not involved in a bitter struggle to protect their own homes. The military experience of the region was thus very different from that in Virginia and Pennsylvania. For civilians the difference was even starker. For New Englanders the war brought new jobs, as wartime contracts for army supplies and the demands of the army for laborers pushed up wages. Gary B. Nash has shown how the demands of war affected the residents of the region's port cities.[10] In Virginia and Pennsylvania there were far fewer army and naval contracts, and the early years of war instead brought economic dislocation as Indian raiders laid waste to great swathes of the backcountry. The backcountry suffered devastation comparable to the Revolutionary War and even to the Civil War, hardly events whose impact on the history of these regions could be ignored.[11]

The uniqueness of the conflict in this region also allows the examination of several other issues. The Seven Years' War provides an ideal opportunity to examine the nature of backcountry society under pressure. The Virginia and Pennsylvania backcountry has been identified as a region that was to play a significant role in the development of cultural patterns across much of southeastern America. Even though politically divided, the backcountry settlers of the two colonies shared many common cultural traits and can be regarded as residents of a single region. Thousands of settlers traveled through the region, down the Great Valley from Pennsylvania, through Virginia, and on into the Carolinas, often staying for months or even years in backcountry counties of the two colonies. A study of the region under pressure can reveal much about the nature of this borderland society.[12]

The war reveals clearly the fissures that existed in this fragile society. Turk McCleskey has argued that in Augusta County, Virginia, the local elite of land speculators and surveyors were able to recreate many aspects of eastern society.[13] Yet during the Seven Years' War the elite of the backcountry were not able to draw their community together in a common defense. Perhaps much of the reason for this lay, as Richard R. Beeman has argued, in the elite's comparative lack of wealth. Unlike their eastern counterparts, the elite in the backcountry of both Virginia and Pennsylvania on the eve of the Seven Years' War lacked sufficient wealth and prestige to force their neighbors to accede to their wishes. The progress of the war would demonstrate clearly their inability to cajole their neighbors to support unpopular policies for the common good.[14]

The divisions revealed by the war go even further. During the Seven Years' War backcountry inhabitants displayed an intense individualism. In many ways the community revealed by the tensions of war was more representative of that found by Albert H. Tillson Jr., who has argued for the existence of a separate backcountry political culture that rejected many of the values of the eastern elite. Both the elite and the common settlers were highly competitive, and this in turn heightened divisions in the region. Indeed, Tillson has argued persuasively that the local elite behaved with an "aggressive social and economic conduct."[15] As the Indian raiders descended on the region this competitiveness would rear its ugly head and severely hamper all attempts to defend the region.

While the backcountry has been a focus of much recent historiography, and the backcountry of Virginia and Pennsylvania in particular has received much attention, little attention has been paid to the impact of the Seven Years' War.[16] It would be unthinkable to write a social history of western Virginia and Pennsylvania without discussing in detail the impact of the Revolutionary War and the Civil War, yet the Seven Years' War is given relatively short shrift. For example, detailed social studies such as Peter C. Mancall's study of the Susquehanna Valley and Robert D. Mitchell's study of the Shenandoah Valley make almost no mention of the Seven Years' War.[17] Perhaps the interest of such historians in long-term trends has caused them to overlook what superficially could be seen as a short-term aberration in the history of the region. Yet as Richard Slotkin has demonstrated, the war's impact was deep and long lasting.[18] Similarly, Richard I. Melvoin has argued that "the major force that challenged the frontier was war."[19] Warfare, especially with Native Americans, was a key element of backcountry life and had important implications for the development of backcountry institutions. Violence, or the possibility of violence, fundamentally influenced the way that backcountry communities developed.

If social studies of the backcountry have ignored the role of warfare in shaping communities, ethnohistorical studies of the native peoples of the Ohio Valley have also largely ignored the role of the Seven Years' War in transforming Native American society. The development of ethnohistory over the past two decades has stressed the cultural interaction between Europeans and Native Americans. In recent studies cooperation and communication have replaced hostility and warfare as the primary means of interaction between peoples. Consequently, works such as those of Richard White, Michael N. McConnell, and James H. Merrell, among others, have examined the intricacies of Native American diplomacy and the changing nature of Indian culture in the Ohio Valley. Quite rightly, these studies have stressed the extent to which European settlers and Native Americans created common cultural patterns. However, any reader of these studies could be forgiven for thinking that before the American Revolution warfare played a relatively minor role in shaping the relationship between Europeans and Native Americans, as virtually all studies have ignored the military aspect of the Seven Years' War.[20]

Yet the Seven Years' War reveals the extent to which the Indian peoples developed effective patterns of warfare. The Indian raids on the frontier reveal an awareness of strategy. They targeted military outposts, tried to cut supply lines and communications, and attempted to impede diplomacy. This style of warfare is very different from traditional Native American patterns. The raids reveal not only a new sense of strategy but also a new tactical approach. In particular, Indian raiders consciously waged psychological warfare. During Braddock's march to the Ohio in 1755, Indian parties captured stragglers from the main British column. They then pinned the soldiers' scalps to trees as a warning of what would happen to any other captives.[21] These terror tactics succeeded. When Braddock encountered the enemy near Fort Duquesne his troops were not surprised in an ambush but were thrown into panic when the Ohio Indians began to flank their force. It was the British troops' fear of the Indians that won the battle for the French.[22] Raiders also used psychological war against civilians. Particularly on the northern frontier of Pennsylvania, Indian raiders mutilated the bodies of women and children, displaying them at crossroads or other locations where they would be sure to be discovered. These tactics were largely responsible for the mass panic on the frontier and proved immensely successful in persuading thousands of settlers to abandon their homes. The use of psychological warfare, particularly the mutilation of women and children, is again a major departure from the norms of Indian warfare.

Indian warriors also developed new tactical and strategic sensibilities. By Pontiac's War in 1763 the Indians had developed the capability to defeat European armies in "set-piece" battles, although only on a small scale. They had also realized the potential of frontier raids to neutralize a numerically and technologically superior adversary. When John Craig, a Pennsylvanian captured by the Indian raiders, asked his captor, Delaware war captain Shingas, whether he feared retaliation from British forces, Shingas laughed heartily.[23] He replied that British forces were nothing but "a Parcel of Old Women," for "they could not travel without loaded Horses and Waggons full of Provisions and a great deal of Baggage."[24] Shingas's reaction reveals the extent of Indian confidence in the transformation of their patterns of warfare and the inability of the British and their colonists to respond.

This study places the Seven Years' War in the backcountry of Virginia and Pennsylvania in a broader context. It examines the impact of the war upon the backcountry communities of Virginia and Pennsylvania, upon the Indian communities of the Ohio Valley, upon the political and military organization of these two colonies, and upon the imperial relationship between the colonies and Great Britain. In all these areas the Seven Years' War would prove a major turning point and would transform patterns that had existed for much of the previous century.

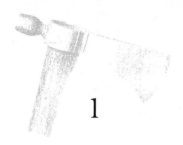

1

The Collision of Worlds

1700–1755

IN THE FIRST HALF OF THE EIGHTEENTH CENTURY THE DISPARATE
worlds of French Canada, the British colonies of Virginia and Pennsylvania, and the Indian villages of the Ohio Valley were drawn into closer
contact and eventually dramatic conflict. The conflict, now most commonly termed by historians the Seven Years' War, would devastate Canada,
the Ohio Valley, and the backcountry of Virginia and Pennsylvania. This
struggle was neither planned nor desired by any of the participants. It
grew out of the developing forces of trade and settlement, which pulled
all sides together.

Between 1700 and 1755 settlers poured into the region from all directions: Indians and European fur traders migrated into the Ohio Valley;
German, Scottish, Irish, and English planters, squatters, farmers, and
merchants moved into the backcountry. As these groups migrated they
drew larger worlds together. Settlers moving into the backcountry of
Virginia and Pennsylvania extended the political boundaries of the
colonies: counties were organized, courts established, churches built.
However, the settlers did not always fully replicate the political or social
structures of the east, and some links remained fragile. The expansion

of the colonies into the backcountry also encouraged settlers to begin to eye land further west across the Appalachians, in the upper Ohio Valley. Some settlers even braved the isolation and threat of Indian attack to cross the Appalachians and establish settlements in the west.[1]

Indians, seeking access to European trade goods, encouraged fur traders to come into the region and drew the French and British into increasing rivalry. As competition for the fur trade increased, so did the interest of the imperial governments in Whitehall and Versailles. When fur traders returned east with reports of the fertility of the upper Ohio Valley, increasing numbers of Anglo-American settlers, and more importantly land speculators, began to take an interest in the region. In 1700 the upper Ohio Valley had been a region of little interest to most settlers and imperialists alike. By 1755 it was viewed as a vital region for both the French and the British Empires. Steadily drawn into the region, by 1755 both Britain and France were pulled into a bloody war, a war in which the backcountry of Virginia and Pennsylvania would be a major theater.[2]

Backcountry Society

Settlers first arrived in what would become the backcountry in the 1720s and 1730s. Over the following years the population grew steadily. As migrants moved into the region they established community and social ties. While many settlers who moved west may have wanted to replicate eastern society, they failed to do so. The social structure of the backcountry remained rather distinct from that of the more established eastern societies. In particular, backcountry society lacked a clearly defined elite. That does not mean, however, that some settlers did not view themselves as members of an elite or believe that they should be part of that elite.

Virginia society east of the Blue Ridge revolved around the world of tobacco, and it was the great planter families, such as the Byrds, Carters, and Lees, who held sway in the Old Dominion.[3] Almost from the inception of Virginia the great tobacco planters had discovered that the ownership of land was as much a route to wealth as was the production of tobacco. By the early eighteenth century, as speculation east of the Appalachian Mountains became more difficult, these wealthy planters began to look to the west for new opportunities. By 1740 members of the eastern elite, including the powerful Fairfax family, had acquired grants to 470,000 acres in the lower Shenandoah Valley, in what would become

Frederick County. Further south, in what would become Augusta County, other settlers received equally large grants of land. Most notably, William Beverley received 118,491 acres, and Benjamin Borden received 92,100 acres.[4]

The process of making such large grants of land met only limited opposition. The main reason for this was that the process appeared to facilitate the settlement of the Shenandoah Valley. The recipients of these land grants encouraged settlers to buy their lands, in particular inviting migration from Pennsylvania and New Jersey. These settlers found purchasing land directly from Fairfax, Beverley, or Borden much easier than surveying and patenting for themselves. As Governor Robert Dinwiddie wrote, the whole process allowed the "poor People that come from other Colonies to the North . . . who cannot bear the Expence of coming down . . . [to Williamsburg] to make their Entries, & other Necessaries in taking up Lands."[5] However, while land speculation formed the basis of the wealth of many Virginians, by the 1750s few of the eastern elite had ventured west of the Appalachians, and they were not the men who dominated backcountry society.

Pennsylvania society was subtly different. While many Pennsylvania fortunes, most notably that of James Logan, owed much to land speculation, the powerful colonial elite was formed not of tobacco planters but of merchants, often Quakers, who traded out of Philadelphia. In the mid-eighteenth century, Pennsylvania was a highly commercial society dependent upon overseas trade, particularly in grain, which was exported both to the West Indies and to southern Europe. Philadelphia had emerged as a major east coast entrepôt, with trading connections throughout the Atlantic world. Merchant families, such as the Pembertons, Allens, and Norrises, dominated the political life of the colony. This mercantile aspect of Pennsylvania society was reflected in the colony's growing interest in the west. Whereas Virginia land speculators eyed western lands greedily, Pennsylvania traders viewed the European and Indian inhabitants of the region as a new market that they could tap. However, as in Virginia, while merchants and traders may have had an interest in the backcountry and the Ohio Valley, few Pennsylvania grandees ever settled in the region.[6]

Backcountry society in both Virginia and Pennsylvania was accordingly not dominated by eastern elites but rather by settlers of middling fortunes. While many historians have portrayed the backcountry as a region of endemic poverty, in the middle of the eighteenth century the most notable feature of backcountry society was not poverty but the vast number of relatively comfortable settlers.[7] In Paxton Township, in Lancaster County, Pennsylvania, for instance, the average farm size was 130 acres. In Berks County in 1767 the mean farm size was 121 acres, and 40 percent of taxpayers owned between 80 and 150 acres of land. What was extraordinary about backcountry society was thus not the number of poor settlers but the number of middling settlers.[8]

In addition to those settlers who legally held land, in both Virginia and Pennsylvania there were many who illegally squatted upon unoccupied land. Indeed, James T. Lemon has argued that in parts of the backcountry "squatters held most of the land." Provincial authorities and landholders such as Lord Fairfax made attempts to turn these squatters off the lands they illegally occupied. In Pennsylvania in 1748 and again in 1750 Richard Peters and Conrad Weiser led expeditions of magistrates to evict settlers from their lands. However, no sooner did the magistrates leave the region than the squatters returned. Indeed, in some ways squatters played an important role in the first stages of settlement in the backcountry, for they cleared the first fields and built the first tracks that would later make the region accessible to other settlers. In addition, the majority of backcountry settlers had little sympathy with the great landholders and tended to support their squatting neighbors. Indeed, in both Virginia and Pennsylvania popular methods of claiming ownership had developed and were widely recognized. These included the right of settlement and cultivation as a basis of ownership, and some backcountry settlers even set up "fair play tribunals" that oversaw claims and resolved disputes between squatters.[9]

The existence of these fair play tribunals suggests a strong degree of antipathy between the "common sort" and their betters. While this cannot be clearly defined as class consciousness or class identity, there were clear elements of what might be termed class distinctiveness in society. Certainly members of the elite felt that they were a class above the middling ranks of yeomen farmers. They attempted to distinguish themselves from their neighbors by their deportment, clothing, and housing. At church and in court they attempted to assert their superiority. However, while the elite may have believed that they were a class above the middling ranks, there is little evidence that the middling farmers believed that they were any different from their slightly wealthier neighbors. Indeed, central to the functioning of backcountry society was a degree of tension between the self-styled elite and those just below them.[10]

Unlike the tidewater elite, the backcountry elite could not create a political climate of deference in the west and lacked the means to coerce the "middling sort" to follow their wishes. Many of them lacked previous political experience and the interpersonal skills to persuade neighbors to support them. The elite were also internally divided. During the 1750s, although ties between the elite families of the backcountry were growing, they had still not created a cohesive social network. While some residents, such as William Preston in Augusta County or Edward Shippen in Cumberland County, had strong ties to the eastern elite, many others did not. The elite were further divided by ethnic and religious differences as Scotch-Irish and Germans, Presbyterians and Quakers moved into the region. In Virginia the growth in support for the "New Light" Baptists challenged the traditional influence of the Anglican hierarchy. In Pennsylvania numerous religious groups settled in each county, and it was rare for one group to have an overwhelming predominance. Although in parts of the backcountry the Presbyterian Church had begun to develop the same institutional structures that the Anglican Church possessed in tidewater Virginia, such organizations were still in their infancy during the 1750s.[11]

Most importantly, the elite lacked substantial wealth with which to impress their neighbors. In Augusta County, on average, justices of the peace owned only 50 percent more land than their neighbors. In Berks County a landowner in the wealthiest tenth of society owned only twice the land of the median landholder. Such an egalitarian society did not automatically produce deference, and the justices' lack of personal authority made them reluctant to enforce any judicial powers that they held. The predominance of middling farmers in the backcountry, and the lack of a clearly defined elite, meant that during times of crisis there was no natural leadership to which backcountry settlers could look for guidance. Men who believed that they had the right to assume leadership often found they had little support from their neighbors, while men who had support from the local community often met with opposition from those members of the elite who had ties to eastern government. During the Seven Years' War the lack of leadership in the region, and the bickering between members of the elite, would become major stumbling blocks to the successful prosecution of the war.[12]

If backcountry society lacked a clearly defined elite, it was also a society where community ties were often fragmented. A principal effect of the geographic, economic, and social structure of the backcountry was to undermine any sense of broader community that might have developed in the region. There were several forces that retarded the formation of broader community structures. Backcountry communities were frequently divided along lines of ethnicity, for the settlers who moved into the backcountry were a heterogeneous mix. The backcountry was not populated by Englishmen, Britons, or even Anglo-Americans, but by a myriad of different ethnic groups, each with their own cultural traditions, ethnic dislikes, and political biases. Not surprisingly, such differences made the formation of any sense of community identity difficult. Many backcountry settlers were recent immigrants who tended to associate within their ethnic groups. The largest single group throughout the backcountry of both Virginia and Pennsylvania were the Ulster Scots, or as they are more popularly known, the Scotch-Irish, but there were also substantial minorities of Catholic Irish, Germans, Scots, Welsh, and English, with smaller numbers of French Huguenots, Swedes, and Swiss. In Virginia the entire frontier was a polyglot mix of ethnic communities. In Pennsylvania the Germans dominated the northern frontier of the colony, while the Scotch-Irish dominated the western frontier. Such ethnic divisions frequently divided frontier communities: language tended to isolate the Germans, religion the Catholic Irish, and Scottish Highlanders arriving in the wake of the brutal suppression of the 1745 Jacobite Rebellion had little sympathy for the English.[13]

The divisions created by ethnicity were echoed closely by those produced by religion. Religion, which had served a major role in the development of community ties in the east, where community members worshipped in the same parish church or Quaker meeting, in the backcountry served only to further divide communities as Mennonites, Presbyterians, Anglicans, Quakers, Baptists, and Roman Catholics all jostled for preeminence. Members of different denominations frequently vied for influence within a particular county and viewed each other with deep suspicion. Religious divisions were further heightened as the Great Awakening took hold and the Baptist Church began to mount a challenge to the Anglican orthodoxy of Virginia. In the Pennsylvania backcountry "New Light" Presbyterians enlightened by the Great Awakening battled with "Old Light" Presbyterians for control of existing Presbyterian congregations. Religion and ethnicity thus created fundamental community divisions.[14]

If religion and ethnicity divided communities, resolving those differences was made more difficult by the very high geographic mobility of frontier settlers. Because the settlement of the backcountry only took place in the first half of the eighteenth century, the inhabitants of the region had fewer social and kinship ties than those in longer-settled regions. In Paxton, Derry, and Donegal Townships, on the frontier of Lancaster County, mobility rates may at times have averaged around 50 percent per annum, half the population either arriving or leaving each year. While many settlers did make permanent homes in the region, and even some squatters remained on the same land for years, many others moved on within a few years or even months.[15]

Mobility rates in the Virginia and Pennsylvania backcountry may have been so high because the region was also a major conduit for settlers moving from the port cities of New York and Philadelphia to the south. The major migration route was through Philadelphia, west to the Susquehanna River, then following the Great Valley southwest, through Cumberland County on to Maryland, and then south down the Shenandoah Valley. Between 1740 and 1760 an average of twenty-two hundred settlers a year passed southward through the Shenandoah Valley, and smaller numbers of settlers moved west along the Potomac and James River Valleys. High mobility thus made it difficult for community ties to develop and was one of the major features that differentiated backcountry society from that of the Virginia tidewater and southeastern Pennsylvania.[16]

Lacking the social and kinship ties that came with a more settled existence, the residents of the Virginia and Pennsylvania backcountry struggled to build communities. However, the institutions that might have bound backcountry settlements together were also weak. Courthouse and meetinghouse, which served as a focus in other communities, only reflected the divisions in backcountry society. Indeed, the only real place where community ties within the backcountry were developed, where neighbors of different ethnic and religious backgrounds could be found together, were the taverns that dotted the region with amazing frequency. The Berks County tax list of 1767 showed thirty-two tavern and innkeepers in the county.[17] In Winchester in 1756 there were at least seven licensed houses for a town that had fewer than two hundred dwellings. Taverns played a central role in pulling communities together, in creating a network of social ties that bound neighbor to neighbor. So important was their influence that many settlements developed around the local tavern. However, while building some social ties, taverns were unlikely to produce a society in which deference to one's superiors was a highly valued attribute. In many ways the ubiquity of taverns is indicative of the individualism and disorder of the region.[18]

Backcountry society in Virginia and Pennsylvania was thus distinctive. Religion and ethnicity divided backcountry communities. The high geographic mobility of backcountry settlers impeded the development of social and kinship ties that could have drawn these communities together. The distribution of land and wealth made this a society dominated by the "middling sort," lacking a clearly defined elite. Local leadership was further weakened because the institutions that provided a framework for leadership in the east, whether the county court or the parish church, were much weaker in the backcountry.

Commercialism and Individualism

The geography and economy of the backcountry were also important in heightening the individualism of settlers. The eastern settlements of both Virginia and Pennsylvania were located mainly on fertile, low-lying alluvial soils. Rivers such as the Schuylkill and Delaware in Pennsylvania, and the James, York, Rappahannock, and Potomac in Virginia, gave settlers in the east relatively direct access to overseas markets. The topography of the backcountry was very different. Although the same rivers penetrated into the backcountry, they were not navigable. The Susquehanna River, for instance, rolled through the backcountry of Pennsylvania. Yet the rapids and shoals that dotted its course meant that it was only navigable by bateaux upstream from Harris's Ferry and that produce could not be shipped to the Chesapeake Bay. The mountains that crisscrossed the region made overland transport even more difficult. In the Virginia backcountry, the Blue Ridge formed a major barrier to movement of settlers and goods. Rising over two thousand feet, breached by only a few high passes and the James River in southern Virginia, and stretching almost unbroken from the Potomac River through what is now North Carolina, it held few passes where a wagon could safely cross. To the north of the Potomac River the chain was more broken, but the

Blue Ridge continued through Cumberland County as the South Mountain and east of the Susquehanna as the Blue Mountain. Beyond the Blue Ridge lay the Great Valley. Composed of several interlinking river valleys, the largest of which was the Shenandoah Valley, and stretching from Harris's Ferry—modern Harrisburg, on the Susquehanna River—to the Cumberland Gap, the Great Valley formed a natural channel for movement and tended to channel settlers in a southwesterly direction.[19]

By the middle of the eighteenth century dense settlement had not penetrated much further than the Great Valley. The region immediately to the west seemed inhospitable and, as British commanders would discover in the 1750s, was extremely difficult to traverse. To the west of the Great Valley lay the Allegheny Plateau or Mountains, a region of narrow valleys separated by flat-topped ridges, such as Laurel Ridge in southwestern Pennsylvania, rising five hundred to one thousand feet above the valley floors. Several large rivers pierced the Allegheny Mountains, and their valleys provided the main arteries of communication. In northern Pennsylvania the Delaware and the east and west branches of the Susquehanna River provided accessible valleys. It was into the lower reaches of these valleys that, in the 1720s, large numbers of Pennsylvanians began to move. By the 1730s settlers were even beginning to cross west of the Susquehanna River north of Harris's Ferry to occupy the Cumberland Valley, and by the 1750s were moving into the Juniata Valley.[20]

Further south, the Potomac River, with two main valleys—the northern and southern branches—penetrated deep into the Allegheny Mountains and provided the easiest access route from the Ohio Valley into northern Virginia and Maryland. This would prove the major approach route for Indian raiding parties during the 1750s. To the south and west of the Potomac the rivers drained not into the Atlantic but into the Ohio River and thus the Mississippi and Gulf of Mexico. In the south the plateau was pierced by the Holston, Clinch, and New River Valleys, which again ran northeast to southwest. By the late 1740s, several parties of Virginians had crossed the Appalachians and settled along the upper reaches of the Monongahela River and as far west as the Holston River Valley, a tributary of the Tennessee in what is now southwestern Virginia. Topography dictated that these settlements on the Allegheny Plateau were very isolated. While they were only a few miles from each other, travel between settlements was often difficult. Strung out along stream courses, from the Potomac River to the James River, settlements did not form a continual line west of the Shenandoah Valley but instead isolated pockets. Indeed, Governor Thomas Pownall wrote of frontier settlers they "are so settled that they have no Connection nor Union amongst each other, scarce of Communion much less of Defence. Their Settlements are vague without design scattered independent."[21]

Even within the Shenandoah Valley settlers tended to congregate in small communities, or "open-country neighborhoods," with farmsteads scattered along rivers and streams about half a mile apart. In both Virginia and Pennsylvania farms and plantations tended to be large, located at approximately half-mile intervals. Low population density alone meant that many settlements were relatively isolated from each other. In Cumberland County the population density averaged fewer than ten people per square mile, and east of the Susquehanna, Berks and Northampton Counties averaged fewer than twenty people per square mile. In addition, rather than settling evenly across the landscape, settlers tended to congregate in small "subcommunities." Paxton, in Lancaster County, for instance, had several small communities: clustered around taverns in the township; around the ferry at Harris's; around local churches and small clusters of artisans such as at Middletown, on Paxton Township's southern border. These subcommunities tended to further isolate settlers from the broader backcountry community.[22]

The isolation of the settlements was also reflected in the relative remoteness of both provincial and local government. Physically the Pennsylvania and Virginia backcountry was far removed from the colonial capitals in Williamsburg and Philadelphia. For a settler in Frederick County, Virginia, or Cumberland County, Pennsylvania, a return journey to the provincial capital could take the better part of three weeks. For many settlers Philadelphia and Williamsburg were thus far removed from their day-to-day lives. In theory local government was a more direct point of contact for these settlers. As the settled area of the colonies expanded into this region, the colonies responded by expanding the political organization of the colonies and establishing new counties to the west. Politically the Shenandoah Valley was divided between Augusta and Frederick Counties, with Hampshire comprising the Cacapon Valley and the branches of the Potomac. North of the Potomac River lay a sliver of Maryland, Frederick County, only a few miles wide, bounded to the north by an uncertain boundary with Pennsylvania. In Pennsylvania the backcountry west of the Susquehanna was contained in York and Cumberland Counties. East of the Susquehanna stretched Lancaster County, while the colony's northern frontier comprised Berks and Northampton Counties.[23]

In both colonies the backcountry counties faced problems older counties in more settled parts of the colony did not. Backcountry counties tended to be much larger than their eastern counterparts. Augusta County, Virginia, at one time included in theory the present-day states of Kentucky, West Virginia, Ohio, Indiana, and Illinois. While Augusta is the most extreme example, all backcountry counties in Pennsylvania and Virginia were larger than their eastern counterparts. Lancaster County in the 1750s stretched from the Maryland line up the east bank of the Susquehanna River for over seventy miles. Distance alone meant that many backcountry settlers were relatively isolated from local community authority. The county court met solely at the courthouse, also the sole location for voting in elections, but this was sometimes many miles from a settler's residence. In the east, county court meetings were not just legal proceedings but great social events for the entire county. Hundreds of residents would gather at the courthouse to watch proceedings and converse with their neighbors.[24] In the backcountry, by contrast, court days were far less important. Most settlers had little contact with the county court, and even many of the justices only attended sporadically. In Augusta County in 1762 only two of the twenty-two justices were present for half or more of the court's sessions, and ten came to less than one-quarter. More isolated from these proceedings, it is little wonder then that backcountry communities were slower to develop.[25]

It was not only distance that tended to retard the growth of community but also the centralized nature of the government of both Virginia and Pennsylvania. Unlike New England, where many government functions were decentralized to town meetings and to the town's selectmen, in Virginia there was no local structure below the county. In the smaller, more densely populated eastern counties this posed little problem; in the backcountry it promoted a sense of isolation. In Pennsylvania there was a government structure below the county: the township. However, the township had negligible autonomy and was merely a convenient subdivision of the county for administrative and tax purposes. Indeed, the only elected officer was the pound keeper, who managed the pound for stray horses.[26]

While the geography and political structure of the backcountry may have led to a sense of isolation, the backcountry's economy promoted a sense of individualism that ultimately stressed the importance of the individual over the community. Backcountry settlers are frequently portrayed as self-sufficient and economically independent farmers who had little contact with outside markets. However, with a few exceptions this was far from being the case. Commercialism was as strong in the backcountry as in the more settled regions of the east. Indeed, the very reason that settlers moved to the backcountry was to seek economic opportunity. Migration was driven by a quest for economic advantage, and once settlers arrived in the backcountry they did not abandon their desire for improvement. The region into which they had moved was one of aggressive commercialism and an emphasis on economic opportunity; by the 1750s it was already tied into the Atlantic market.[27]

While there can be no doubt that the region's economy was commercially driven, it revolved around small-scale agriculture rather than the production of cash crops for export. Most settlers produced small surpluses of wheat that they sold to local merchants, who in turn sold to merchants in Philadelphia for sale overseas. In the Shenandoah Valley some settlers successfully grew tobacco, which they sold to tidewater merchants. However, the cost of transportation meant that profits from wheat and tobacco were reduced. Cattle and hogs were much easier to transport. Many settlers raised cattle. In Berks County in 1767 over four-fifths of families owned cattle, although the majority had only enough for household consumption. Cattle raising was even more important in Virginia. Here many households sold cattle to cattle drovers, who sold to eastern markets. In the Opequon community in the Shenandoah Valley, for instance, the average household owned ten cattle. Indeed, by the 1750s there were frequent cattle drives from the Carolina Piedmont through the Great Valley to Philadelphia.[28]

Cattle were not the only animals that could be raised for sale in more distant markets. Many settlers also kept flocks of sheep. While sheep were less widely held than cattle in the backcountry, more households were likely to raise them for commercial ventures rather than purely for home consumption, selling either the animals or their wool in eastern markets. In Berks County over one thousand residents owned sheep, some possessing substantial flocks.[29] However, in the backcountry economy the most important animals were neither cattle nor sheep but lowly hogs.

Hogs could be allowed to run wild in the woods of the backcountry and required little day-to-day attention, unlike cattle or sheep. All their meat was usable, and they multiplied faster than cattle. They could fend for themselves in the woods and were even known to kill predators who might think them easy prey. They could be butchered easily; their carcasses were smaller and could easily be dried or salted and preserved over the winter.[30]

While agriculture and the raising of livestock and crops were central to the economy of the backcountry, many settlers also practiced a range of crafts. Backcountry settlers engaged in many occupations; they were blacksmiths and gunsmiths, weavers and hatters. Backcountry settlers were thus anything but self-sufficient farmers; they participated in a much broader economy. While most were not deeply engaged in the wider Atlantic economy, they were involved in the provincial economy and in a local exchange economy. The economic structure of the back-country thus produced a commercial society. Settlers sought economic gain wherever possible. The competitive spirit generated was not, however, balanced by a broader sense of community. Indeed, the nature of backcountry community served only to heighten divisions in backcountry society.[31]

There was one other important economic activity for many back-country households, namely the fur and skin trade. Many backcountry families in both Virginia and Pennsylvania participated in this trade. The participation of some households might involve merely the exchange of provisions for furs with passing Indians. Other households participated in a more direct way. Many settlers distilled part of their crops into whiskey, which they then transported to Indian communities on the Susquehanna River or across the Appalachians. Indeed, by 1750 the fur trade in much of the region was becoming dominated by hoards of un-regulated whiskey traders and small-scale peddlers. Almost any settler who had a few pounds to invest could enter the trade.[32] The Pennsylvania authorities made several attempts to regulate traders. In Cumberland County, Andrew Montour led efforts to halt the illegal trade. Several unlicensed traders were brought before the county court and prosecuted. Yet in nearly every case the grand juries found them not guilty, "tho' the Facts be ever so clearly proved." This outcome was hardly surprising, considering that one of the largest illegal traders, John Smith, was also one of the county's justices.[33] It was the fur trade that would begin to draw the communities of the backcountry and the upper Ohio Valley into conflict.

The Struggle for the Fur Trade

The Anglo-American communities of the backcountry and the Indian communities of the upper Ohio Valley had been relatively isolated from the outside and from each other. European wars and imperial conflicts seemed far away from the region. The growth of the fur trade, however, would bring the region's communities into contact with a wider world. In the late seventeenth century, French coureurs de bois had penetrated into the upper Great Lakes region—encompassing principally the modern states of Indiana, Illinois, and parts of Michigan and Wisconsin—which they called the *pays d'en haut* and which the British would later call the "Upper Country." However, they had little reason to travel to the upper Ohio Valley, for it lay largely devoid of human habitation. The original inhabitants of the region had left their homes in the mid-seventeenth century, possibly driven out by Iroquois raids. Because of the lack of human habitation, the woods still teemed with deer and game birds, while the rivers and lakes provided abundant fish and, most importantly, beaver.[34] The comparative wealth of wildlife in the region meant that there were tempting opportunities for the development of the fur trade, as most other regions of eastern North America had by the 1740s been denuded of their fur-bearing animals through overhunting. For the French the fur trade had become a central element of their imperial presence in North America, allowing them to exercise an influence over the native peoples without having a substantial physical presence.[35]

By the mid-eighteenth century, however, not only the French participated in the fur trade. Many hundreds of Anglo-American backcountry settlers supplemented their incomes through trade, although largely in deerskins rather than beaver skins. Pennsylvania fur traders, such as George Croghan, held places of influence in the colony. Many of these traders had amassed considerable fortunes. When the French captured Pennsylvania trader John Patton in 1750, he had in his possession over 750 pounds worth of trade goods. In Virginia the fur trade was less organized. However, many settlers in southwestern Virginia, particularly Augusta County, frequently welcomed Indians passing along the Shenandoah Valley into their homes, exchanging skins and furs for ammunition, cloth, knives, and alcohol.[36]

In the mid-1740s growing British interest in the upper Ohio Valley began to cause concern among French officials. The speed with which Pennsylvania traders penetrated into the Ohio Valley in the late 1740s, and the extent to which they were welcomed by the Indian peoples, were remarkable. Within a few years they had established a string of major trading posts at Pickawillany, Lower Shawnee Town, and Logstown. There were several reasons for this success. While the French had a better understanding of the types of goods most valued by the Indian peoples, British manufactured goods were often of a superior quality as Britain underwent the first throes of the industrial revolution. Metal tools, guns, and ammunition were all in high demand, as was cloth, in particular duffels (coarse woolen cloth, typically red, white, or blue, sometimes striped) and strouds (cheaper cloth made from woolen rags). In the production of all these items the British possessed a significant advantage. In 1749 the intendant of New France, François Bigot, complained to Paris about the poor quality of trade goods sent to Canada. The cloth, he reported, was "frightful; the red cloth is brown and unpressed; the blue of a very inferior quality to that of the English." Bigot predicted that "as long as such ventures are sent, they will not become favourites with the Indians."[37] Not only were British goods of a superior quality, but they were also cheaper because of profiteering by suppliers in France and by the leaseholders of the western posts. Consequently, the Pennsylvania trade boomed. By 1748 there were over twenty Pennsylvanian traders in Logstown alone and a similar number at Pickawillany, the skin and fur trade providing the colony with over one-third of its exports.[38]

The conclusion of King George's War in 1748 intensified competition between the Pennsylvanians and the French. From their trading posts Pennsylvania trade goods spread westward. Soon posts such as Pickawillany were thronging with Algonquian and Iroquoian peoples from across the Ohio Valley—Delawares, Shawnees, Hurons, Potawatomis, and Miamis.[39] The French commander at Fort Miami complained that "the English spare nothing to keep them and to draw away the remainder of those who are here." He was quite clear as to the reason: "The excessive price of French goods in this post, the great bargains which the English give, as well as the large presents which they make to the tribes, have entirely disposed those tribes in their favor. . . . We have made peace with the

English, but in this country they do not cease working to make war on us by means of the Indians and to bring them into a general revolt against the French."[40]

The development of British trade posed such a threat to the French presence because trade goods played a crucial role in Indian diplomacy. Prestige in Indian society was gained not by a conspicuous display of possessions but by the ability to give gifts. Gifts were especially important in the upper Ohio Valley because the traditional ties of kinship and family that buttressed Indian leadership had been shattered by disease and migration. Epidemics had eradicated many traditional leadership patterns. As the survivors of these epidemics moved into the Susquehanna and Ohio Valleys, they moved as individuals, families, or at most village fragments, rather than intact village and tribal groups. Traditional kinship and leadership networks were thus severely disrupted, and by the mid-eighteenth century there was a leadership vacuum in the Ohio Valley.[41] Across the Ohio Valley the ability to provide one's supporters with more prized gifts provided a major route to power. The reciprocal giving of gifts created a sense of obligation and alliance and became an integral part of the Ohio Indians' diplomacy, both among the Ohio Indians themselves and between Indians and Europeans. It also created the basis for a split into those who had access to French goods and traditional kinship ties to the French and those who had developed new ties with Pennsylvania traders. The growth of the Pennsylvania fur trade struck at the heart of the French relationship with the Ohio Indians. The expansion of the fur trade thus proved a major catalyst in promoting Anglo-French tension in the Ohio Valley.[42]

The Ohio Company

While the activities of British fur traders began to raise French concerns in the region, the activities of land speculators began to raise Indian concerns. The British thirst for Indian land was to become the central issue that would alienate the Ohio Indians from the British. The Ohio Indians already had plenty of opportunity to hear for themselves about the perfidy of their Anglo-American neighbors from the Delaware migrants who had moved to the Ohio Valley from Pennsylvania. The expansion of Pennsylvania settlements into the backcountry had steadily pushed the Delawares from their homes. Initially, the Pennsylvanians had sought to establish a trusting relationship with their Indian neighbors. However, in the early eighteenth century Indian relations came increasingly under the influence of less scrupulous men such as James Logan who schemed to acquire lands beyond the agreed purchase lines. By the early 1730s the Delawares had been driven out of their original homelands on the lower reaches of the Delaware River and had moved farther north into the upper Delaware Valley and west into the Susquehanna Valley, into territory that the Iroquois claimed but did not occupy.[43]

The Delawares' settlement on Iroquois-claimed land gave Logan and the Penns an opportunity they could not resist. The Penns were desperately short of funds. Their "fortune" lay in their grant of Pennsylvania, but only a small part had been made available for settlement. The remainder of the land was claimed and occupied by Indians, principally the Delawares, and it was necessary to get a quitclaim before the Penns could sell it. It was far easier for the Penns to recognize the Iroquois as the sole owners of Pennsylvania than to have to deal with the many smaller groups, including the Delawares.[44]

The most notorious fraud began in 1735 when the Penns produced some rough notes of what they claimed was an old Delaware land cession to lands bordering the Delaware River, made in the seventeenth century. A day and a half's walk would determine the boundary of the grant. In 1737, under intense Iroquois pressure, the Delawares agreed to allow the "Walking Purchase." When they agreed to this, the Delawares believed that any walk to determine the bounds of the grant would be done at a normal pace, the walkers stopping "to eat their dinner, [and] after that smoak a pipe." With horror they now discovered that the Penns intended to use trained runners to cover as much ground as possible. The land the Penns thus acquired included a large area along the Delaware River, the heart of Delaware territory. The Delawares protested, but the Iroquois quickly moved to silence them and declared that they were "women" who had settled on Iroquois land and thus had no power to treat directly with the Pennsylvanians. Faced with the combined power of the Iroquois and the British, the Delawares had little choice but to bide their time.[45]

After the Walking Purchase many Delawares relocated to the east branch of the Susquehanna. Then these lands also came under white scrutiny. At the Albany Congress of 1754 Pennsylvania obtained from the Iroquois a cession of these lands. The Iroquois now encouraged the Delawares to move further up the Susquehanna to the Wyoming Valley.

Here they thought they would be safe. However, almost immediately, these lands would become the focus of a group of Connecticut speculators who had formed themselves into the Susquehannah Company.[46]

As numbers of Delawares headed west to new homes on the Allegheny and Muskingum Rivers they took tales of their repeated eviction with them. These tales caused increasing concern among the Ohio Indians as the British began to show a growing interest in their lands. Before the late 1740s British settlers had demonstrated little interest in settling the upper Ohio Valley. The region was too remote to be of any interest. However, as traders and explorers such as Peter Salley, a German immigrant from Augusta County, returned to the backcountry they described the Ohio Valley in glowing terms: it was "well Water'd, there are plenty of Rivulets clear fountains and running Streams and very fertile Soil." Soon the region drew the attention of speculators, who by the 1740s began to consider the possibility of establishing settlements to the west of the Appalachians. Over four years in the late 1740s the Virginia Council issued grants for over two million acres of land in the west to several different land companies.[47]

Initially, the government was willing to make these grants because many Virginia burgesses and councilors, who made the decisions, were themselves involved in land speculation. However, by the 1740s Governor William Gooch was becoming increasingly concerned that these grants in the west "might possibly give Umbrage to the French." In November 1747 and again in the summer of 1748, he wrote to London requesting advice on making any future grants.[48] Nevertheless, while Gooch's reservations increased, so did the power and influence of by far the most important and influential of all the land companies, the Ohio Company of Virginia, established in 1747. With members and supporters—including the Earl of Halifax, the president of the Board of Trade—espousing the company's case at the highest levels of government, the Board of Trade proclaimed that the settlement of the Ohio Valley in this manner was in "His Majesty's Interest, and the Advantage and Security of that and the Neighbouring Provinces."[49] At the same time, the departure of Gooch from Virginia and his replacement first by Thomas Lee, as acting governor, and then by Robert Dinwiddie aided the cause of the company. Both Lee and Dinwiddie were active members of the company and could be relied upon to further its cause. Dinwiddie himself divulged that he had "the Success and Prosperity of the Ohio Company much at Heart." In the early 1750s the activities of the Ohio Company would play a major role in determining Virginia's policy toward the Ohio Valley.[50]

In January 1749 John Hanbury, a wealthy London merchant and leading member of the Ohio Company, presented the Crown with the company's petition for land on the Ohio River. Unlike the other Virginia land companies, the Ohio Company was to receive its grant directly from the Crown, not from the governor and council, for this would give it substantially more power. In February the petition received royal assent, and the company acquired the right to half a million acres on the Ohio, on condition of it "seating at their proper Expence a hundred Familys upon the Lands in Seven Years" and "Erecting a Fort and maintaining a Garrison for the protection of the Settlement."[51] The Ohio Company thus acted as more than just a holder of land for sale to potential settlers. It was actively to be involved in the development of their lands and envisioned settling German Protestants from the Rhineland. This meant that it was essential to negotiate with the Ohio Indians to secure their assent to settlement of the region.[52]

As soon as the company heard of the grant it began to make preparations to exploit it. There were only two obstacles: the attitude of the Ohio Indians and the opposition of the French. In the company's eyes neither seemed a major barrier. Company agents could foresee few reasons why the Ohio Indians would oppose their settlement. They maintained that at a conference in Lancaster, Pennsylvania, in 1748, the Iroquois had agreed to surrender all their claims to land west of the Appalachians. The treaty specified that the Iroquois surrendered to Virginia "the Right and Title of our Sovereign the King of Great Britain to all the lands within the said Colony, as it is now or hereafter may be peopled and bounded by his said Majesty."[53] As Virginia's charter gave the colony a claim to most of North America from the Atlantic to the Pacific, the Iroquois had unwittingly given up any claim of theirs to North America outside Iroquoia. The Iroquois, however, believed that they had ceded no more than a strip of land along the Appalachians, most notably the Shenandoah Valley, to prevent disputes caused by their warriors traveling south along the valley. Amazingly, Ohio Company officials saw no reason to be concerned at this misconception. Nor did they see any reason for concern that the lands they sought were settled not by Iroquois but by Shawnees and Delawares. Equally amazingly, they failed to perceive why the French might oppose their settlement of these lands. As far as the Ohio Company was concerned, the French had shown no previous interest in these lands, and under the terms of the 1713 Treaty of Utrecht they were "rightly" British.[54]

The Ohio Company arranged a conference with the Ohio Indians to attain their assent to the company's proposed settlement. No request could have been more calculated to arouse Indian suspicions. The conference convened at the Indian town of Logstown, ten miles downstream from the forks of the Ohio, at the end of May 1752. Initially, the Ohio Indians believed that the Ohio Company sought permission merely to establish a fortified trading settlement, another Pickawillany. Such a settlement would probably have been acceptable, perhaps even desirable. However, they were soon disabused of this idea. Andrew Montour, speaking for the Virginians, came straight to the point. He informed the Ohio Indians that under the terms of the Lancaster treaty, the lands on the Ohio were part of Virginia. He further informed them that the Virginians now wished "to make a Settlement of British Subjects on the South East side of the Ohio."[55]

The Ohio Indians were worried. The Iroquois headmen who were present floundered in the face of British claims that they had themselves ceded the Ohio Valley without informing its inhabitants. The Iroquois headmen protested bitterly, claiming that they had "never understood . . . that the Lands then sold were to extend further to the Sun Setting, than the Hill, on the other Side of the Alligany Hill." All the Iroquois agreed they would have to consult with the Onondaga Council "so that we can't give you any further Answer now." Referring the matter to the Iroquois Council was not acceptable to the Ohio Company. They could not wait. Consequently, they persuaded métis Andrew Montour "to converse with his brethren the other Sachems in private on the subject to urge the necessity of such a settlement and the great advantage it would be to them as to their trade." Several Iroquois headmen "retir'd for half an Hour" with Montour. In the end they were persuaded to agree to the Ohio Company's plans. Montour may simply have tried to convince them that all that would result was a settlement little different from Pickawillany, from whence seemed to come so much benefit, or he may have applied more pressure, possibly even offering some form of bribe. Certainly over one thousand pounds worth of gifts were distributed at the conference. Whatever happened, the Iroquois, but not the Shawnees or Delawares, emerged from their meeting consenting to the Ohio Company's settlement and guaranteeing its protection.[56]

The Ohio Company now had the deeds they wanted, even though they came without the blessing of the Shawnees or Delawares. While the company's indifference reflected the British position that the Iroquois possessed the Ohio, in practical terms this exclusion of the Ohio Indians was a huge mistake. The Logstown conference merely served to increase Indian doubts about British intentions in the Ohio Valley. By the spring of 1753 villages across the Ohio Valley buzzed with the news that "the Iroquois have sold the Ohio River to the English and that the latter have set about making settlements." This made it easy for French officials to convince the Ohio Indians that their interests would be best looked after by supporting the French and driving out the British.[57]

The Struggle for Control of the Ohio Valley

French officials knew that they had to act quickly to prevent the loss of their influence among the Ohio Indians. However, their early attempts to halt the spread of British influence were feeble and halfhearted. In the summer of 1749 Governor Roland Michel, Marquis de la Galissonière sent a small military expedition, headed by Pierre-Joseph Céloron de Blainville, down the Ohio River to bury lead plates claiming the region for the French. Shortly afterwards a new governor, Pierre-Jacques de Taffanel, Marquis de La Jonquière, arrived in the colony. Initially he had determined to send a large expedition to the Ohio. However, he soon abandoned the project and limited French actions to small expeditions to seize British traders and establish trading posts.[58]

The French, however, soon increased their activity. Over the winter of 1751–52, moving south from Detroit, parties of French regulars and Canadian militia killed several Anglophile Miami warriors. The Miamis appealed to Pennsylvania for arms and ammunition. For years they had presumed that the Pennsylvanians would be only too happy to provide them with weapons with which to fight the French, but the reality could not have been more different. Their request placed Governor James Hamilton in a quandary. He could hardly refuse such an appeal when it was the Miamis' support of the British that had exposed them to the wrath of the French. On the other hand, he realized that the Quaker-dominated assembly would never approve sending arms directly to the Indians. Hamilton therefore instructed Croghan to tell the Miamis that he could not supply them but that he was sure the Virginians would.[59]

However, the French had only just begun their assault on the Anglophile Indians. On June 21, 1752, a party of twenty Frenchmen and over two hundred Ottawas and Chippewas descended on the town of Pickaw-illany. The party had specific orders "to kill all such Indians as are in amity with the English, and to take the Persons and Effects of all such English Traders as they could meet with." They killed one trader, captured six more, and killed many more Indians. Any Indians who survived the attack soon fled. When traders Thomas Burney and William Trent arrived in the town two weeks after the attack, they found it completely deserted. Over the next few months the French sent an additional four hundred troops to Fort Miami and prepared an even larger expedition to descend the Ohio in the spring of 1753. The French show of force succeeded. Across the Ohio Valley British traders decamped and headed east.[60]

The Ohio Indians expected swift British retaliation for the destruction of Pickawillany, but none came. At Governor Hamilton's suggestion, the Miamis now appealed frantically to Virginia for aid. Instead of ammunition, Governor Robert Dinwiddie sent William Trent to the Ohio with an invitation to a planned conference in Winchester the following spring. To the Miamis this invitation seemed ludicrous. They sought action, not words. Trent himself reported that the Miamis were in a "miserable Condition." All the traders had either been killed, captured, or had fled the region. Those Ohio Indians who would not join the French were left to starve.[61] The following spring the newly arrived governor of Canada, Ange Duquesne de Menenville, marquis de Duquesne, established French forts at Presque Isle on Lake Erie and at Rivière au Boeuf and Fort Machault, or Venago, on tributaries of the Allegheny. These would secure the portage to the upper Ohio River, in preparation for the establishment of a fort at the forks. This "invasion" of the Ohio Country still did not provoke an immediate British response. Preoccupied with their own internal bickering, neither Virginia nor Pennsylvania sent aid to their Indian allies.[62]

The years 1752–53 would prove to be a pivotal point in the history of the Ohio Valley. At Logstown and Pickawillany the British demonstrated that they had no interest in the welfare of the Ohio Indians; they cared only for themselves. The British sought land but would offer no protection to their allies. Almost overnight the Ohio Indians came to view the British in a very different light. It was not long before the former "Anglophiles" began to flood back to the French fold. In the autumn of 1752, for instance, Le Gros Bled, formerly one of the most Anglophile head-men, traveled to the French post at Fort Vincennes "to ask pardon" from the French. The son of another rebel leader, La Mouche Noire, abandoned his father to seek French forgiveness. Other Miamis turned on their former allies, killing two British traders and presenting their scalps to the French as evidence of their newfound loyalty. By winter most of the Miamis and Illinois had renewed their allegiance to the French.[63] The sudden change of loyalty in 1752–53, however, does not solely reflect the actions of individual chiefs. Rather, within the villages and clans of the Ohio Valley the balance of power shifted rapidly away from Anglophile chiefs. Unable to supply their supporters with trade goods and weapons, and unable to provide any protection against increasingly aggressive French actions, Anglophile leaders found their power daily eroded. Many cut their losses, swallowed their pride, and returned to the French. Even Tanaghrisson, one of the most Anglophile of all the head-men, approached the French, but he was "received in a very contemptuous manner."[64]

As they saw their influence in the upper Ohio Valley evaporate, both Virginia and Pennsylvania appealed to Whitehall for assistance, claiming that the French presence in the Ohio undermined the security of the colonial frontier. From their new bases on the upper Ohio the French could launch raids on the backcountry of Virginia and Pennsylvania, as they had done for the previous century on New England. The French forts thus posed a threat to the security of the British Empire in North America. Before 1754 neither Britain nor France had exercised substantial military power in the Ohio Valley. In 1754 both sides would resort to the use of arms. French and British officials began to play a game of brinkmanship, each side gambling that the other would not risk a general war over control of the region. They were wrong. By the end of 1755 the largest of the colonial wars had broken out in the "backwoods" of America, a war that would soon become global.

As conflict loomed, Pennsylvania looked to Virginia for military leadership. Of the two colonies only Virginia possessed any military organization that could respond to the French threat; Pennsylvania could provide little more than financial support. In early 1754 Virginia's governor, Robert Dinwiddie, determined that the best course of action would be to construct a fort at the forks of the Ohio. For Dinwiddie this was a desperate action. Indeed, he argued that even if the military significance of the fort was limited, "if we can only erect a Fort or Two as a mark of our Possession, it will be doing something."[65] Dinwiddie also determined that before he could take action he needed to issue a final warning to the French. To deliver this message he needed someone with both western experience and sufficient gentry status so that the warning would carry weight. To send a trader such as George Croghan would have under-valued the weight of the message. To send a wealthy planter such a Lord Fairfax would have exposed Fairfax to the dangers of an arduous journey in the early winter. There was one person who had both gentry status and experience on the frontier as a provincial surveyor, a young man named George Washington. In November 1753 Dinwiddie sent Washington to the newly constructed French forts in the upper Ohio Valley to parlay with the French commanders and demand their withdrawal.[66]

Washington returned with the news that the French had no intention of withdrawing from the region. Dinwiddie presented his report to the House of Burgesses and convinced them to provide ten thousand pounds to fund an expedition. However, the burgesses had concerns about the involvement of the Ohio Company in the growing conflict in the west. Instead of giving Dinwiddie power to dispose of the funds as he saw fit, the burgesses established a committee to oversee disbursement of the funds. This was a highly unusual step, which angered Dinwiddie. At first he would not consent to the bill, complaining that "the People here are too much of a republican Spirit. The Ho. of B. making resolves in dis-pos'g of the King's Money without the Concurrence of the other Branches of the Legislature, is without Precedent." However, if Dinwiddie wanted to construct a fort at the forks he knew that he had to act quickly. Grudg-ingly he approved the bill.[67]

In January 1754 a small party of volunteers, mainly former Indian traders, commanded by William Trent, began construction of the post. The Ohio Company had already chosen a defensible site a few miles downstream from the forks of the Ohio. To reinforce Trent, Dinwiddie drafted three hundred men from the militia and formed them into the Virginia Regiment. Joshua Fry, commander of the expedition, was to assemble the main body of the force in northern Virginia awaiting the arrival of three independent companies that Dinwiddie had persuaded Whitehall to send. Fry's second in command, Washington, was to march a forward detachment to Wills Creek, where he would prepare for the march to the Ohio.[68]

Numerous problems beset Fry and Washington. There were few skilled officers and an abundance of petty disputes over their respective authority, particularly between officers of the independent companies, who had royal commissions, and those of the Virginia Regiment, who had commissions from Dinwiddie. The troops were slow to assemble, for there were few volunteers, and several of the county justices refused to draft men from the militia into the regiment. In addition, the independent companies took much longer than expected to arrive, leaving Fry dawdling in northern Virginia. Finally, a shortage of horses and wagons slowed Washington's progress toward the Ohio.[69]

Trent wrote to Fry and Washington at the beginning of March, pleading with them to hurry their men to the Ohio before the French arrived. Since there was no chance that Trent could complete his fortifications before the French arrived, Washington took the initiative to march a detachment to the forks to reinforce Trent. However, at the forks the Virginian force was growing desperately short of supplies. When the local Delawares refused to supply the force, even though the Virginians offered to pay well for any produce, Trent was forced to return to Wills Creek, leaving behind only a small detachment of forty-one men commanded by Ens. Edward Ward. On April 17 French forces under the command of Capt. Claude-Pierre Pécaudy de Contrecoeur appeared outside the uncompleted post. When Contrecoeur offered Ward the chance to surrender the post, he had little choice but to accept and march his men back to Wills Creek. The French then proceeded to utilize the supplies of lumber Trent had amassed to construct their own fort a few miles upstream at the forks themselves, naming it Fort Duquesne in honor of their governor.[70]

The surrender of the fort threatened to shut the British out of the entire Ohio Valley. Washington, who was now in command of the expedition following the death of Fry, determined to proceed toward the fort to see if there was any chance of taking it by surprise. However, the French had scouting parties out. For several days Tanaghrisson and Scarouady, two Iroquois headmen who accompanied Washington, reported that there were French parties in the vicinity. Finally, on the evening of May 27, they informed him that there was a party shadowing him. Whether this was a diplomatic party sent out to parlay with Washington or a military force sent to intercept him is unclear. However, Washington determined to send out a detachment to ambush the French. In the ensuing skirmish the French commander, Joseph Coulon de Villiers, sieur de Jumonville, and ten other French troops were killed. Who fired the first shot is uncertain. Possibly Jumonville was not even killed in the fighting but was clubbed to death immediately after the skirmish by Tanaghrisson. Whatever the details were, the French reacted quickly. Almost immediately a much larger party, under the command of Jumonville's brother, Louis Coulon de Villiers, set out from Fort Duquesne to intercept Washington.[71]

Surely aware that the French would react, but unaware that the French had sent out a much larger party, Washington continued his advance toward Fort Duquesne. Why he did this is unclear; he must have known that he was outnumbered and could not take the fort. Worrying about what his young commander might do, Dinwiddie sent Washington a message warning him not to be too rash or to "make any hazardous Attempts agst a too numerous Enemy."[72] Washington did not heed Dinwiddie's warnings. On June 28 he halted at Gist's Plantation, a few miles south of Fort Duquesne. Only now did Washington's scouts discover that the French had sent out a much larger force against him. Washington had around four hundred men with him, many of them ill and unfit for duty. Instead of continuing, he chose to retreat, but his troops, weary from their march over the rough terrain, made slow progress. Informed that the French were quickly closing on him, Washington determined to halt his retreat at a spot already prepared for defense, Fort Necessity. The Indians accompanying Washington were disgusted at his temerity and at his refusal to accept their advice despite their knowledge of the terrain. Many felt that throughout the expedition he had treated them with contempt and would later complain that "he took upon him to command the Indians as his Slaves." Consequently, shortly after the arrival at Fort Necessity, Washington's Indian allies abandoned the expedition.[73]

On the morning of July 3, 1754, the French arrived at Washington's camp with about six hundred French and Canadian soldiers and one hundred Indians. They quickly besieged Washington's force. The earthworks surrounding the camp proved little protection from the continual fire of French snipers. The wooden palisade was only seven feet high, and the fort could only shelter sixty of Washington's men. The rest took what shelter they could in hastily made entrenchments outside the fort. One by one, the French picked off Washington's forces. By dusk Washington had lost one hundred men, his soldiers finding that a fierce storm prevented their muskets from firing. With his force surrounded and demoralized, and abandoned by his Indian allies, Washington asked for terms. Unable to read the French in which the surrender document was written, Washington admitted responsibility for the "murder" of Jumonville, acknowledged that the Ohio was French territory—"les Terres du Domain du Roy"—and agreed that the British would evacuate the region. Washington, of course, repudiated the agreement as soon as he was back in Virginia, claiming that he had been unable to read the surrender document clearly in the flickering candlelight of the sodden evening. The French, however, viewed their victory as decisive. Governor Duquesne described it as "a brilliant action . . . such as any soldier will scarcely believe possible in a country where only wars of ambush are known." French officials hoped that the defeat would mark the end of the dispute in North America and that the British would now lose interest in the Ohio Valley. However, Washington's defeat merely encouraged the British to make bolder attempts to recover the region.[74]

NEITHER Britain nor France intended to start a war over the Ohio Country. However, pressures within the region steadily brought both sides to a crisis. The movement of settlers into the backcountry began a process of westward expansion. By 1750 those settlers were beginning to spill over the Appalachians and were eying the fertile lands of the Ohio Valley. In the Ohio Valley itself French and British fur traders, who had moved into the region following their Indian customers, were drawn into increasing conflict. As British trade expanded, the only way in which the French could halt the advance of British influence was to use military force to expel British traders. The British could not accept their expulsion from the Ohio Valley, not only because the Ohio Company had so many influential supporters but also because the French presence posed a threat to the security of Virginia and Pennsylvania. Provincial forces proved unable to dislodge the French. Consequently, the British resorted to the use of the regular army. This decision effectively declared war upon the French in North America. The escalation to war thus had little to do with diplomacy and politics within Europe, but was rather the result of developments in the Ohio Valley and on the frontier of Virginia and Pennsylvania. Over the next seven years a global war would rage. The backcountry of Virginia and Pennsylvania would be a central theater of that war.

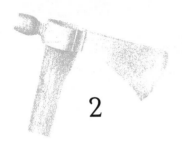

2

War Comes to the Backcountry

THE SETTLEMENT OF THE BACKCOUNTRY AND THE GROWTH OF THE
fur trade had steadily drawn Britain and France into conflict in the
upper Ohio Valley. Neither country had sought confrontation, yet the
British decision to send an army to North America to capture the Ohio
Valley ensured that war would engulf the region. In early 1755 British
officials were confident that they would be victorious and force the
French to evacuate the region. However, they were to reap defeat, not
victory. When Maj. Gen. Edward Braddock's expedition suffered one of
the most decisive routs in British military history, the French were able
to develop a policy to drive back the British and seek an advantageous
peace. Since the British had alienated the Ohio Indians and allowed the
French to construct posts in the upper Ohio Valley, the backcountry of
Virginia and Pennsylvania now lay exposed to attack.

Encouraged and supplied by the French, the Ohio Indians descended
upon the backcountry. Their raids were immensely successful and
wrought damage beyond the expectations of the French. In attacking the
backcountry the Ohio Indians demonstrated the extent to which traditional patterns of Indian warfare had been adapted to counter European

weaponry and tactics. While raiders devastated the backcountry, the Virginia and Pennsylvania assemblies continued to squabble over prerogative and hamstring the governors' attempts to act decisively. More worrying was that the colonies' attempts to develop a military policy to counter the raids proved ineffective. The backcountry lay exposed and vulnerable.

Braddock's Expedition

By the autumn of 1754 the French were in undisputed possession of the Ohio Valley. Washington's force had been routed, yet the colonial assemblies and governors were squabbling. There was only one way that the French could be driven out—through direct intervention by Great Britain. In Whitehall the Duke of Newcastle's administration initially tried to avoid the expense of a conflict with the French and sought negotiations. The French ambassador in London, Charles-Pierre-Gaston-François de Lévis, duc de Mirepoix, proposed the creation of a neutral buffer zone in the upper Ohio Valley, with the Alleghenies marking the boundary of the British colonies and the French boundary running southwest from Lake Erie. However, neither side could agree on exact boundaries, and both demanded the demolition of the other's forts in the region. Each side could have compromised, but neither was willing.[1]

Newcastle remained reluctant to commit forces to a full-scale war. He was concerned about lack of popular support in Britain for a war in North America, for he sensed that "Ignorant People say what is the Ohio to us, what expense is there like to be about it, shall we bring on a War for the sake of a River."[2] French officials were equally reluctant. In the spring of 1755 French officials were informed that "His Majesty is on his side very far from allowing that any invasion be undertaken against his neighbours." They were ordered "to keep strictly on the defensive."[3]

Newcastle, however, was by no means a "dove." From the start he had opposed the Treaty of Aix-La-Chapelle of 1748 because it offered too few advantages. By the fall of 1754 he was convinced that in order to recover British power in the Ohio Valley regular troops would have to be sent to North America. In the same manner that the French had hoped that the British would cut their losses after Fort Necessity and lose interest in the Ohio Valley, Newcastle hoped that the recapture of the forks by British regulars would cause the French to lose interest in the region. While British troops were mounting offensive operations in the Ohio

Valley, British diplomats in Paris could negotiate a settlement that essentially restored the status quo. However, unfortunately for Newcastle, in order to gain political support for his scheme, he had to involve the Duke of Cumberland, favorite son of King George II. Cumberland already had a fearsome reputation as the "butcher of Culloden" for his brutal suppression of the Jacobite uprising in the Scottish Highlands. He soon transformed Newcastle's relatively limited schemes to a much grander plan of operations.[4]

On September 24, 1754, General Braddock received his instructions. He was to take two regiments of infantry, the Forty-fourth and the Forty-eighth, from Cork, Ireland, to Virginia. The colonial governors were instructed to assist him and to ensure that his regiments were recruited up to full strength. With these troops, numbering over three thousand regulars, and accompanied by provincial levies, he would drive the French from the Ohio. Meanwhile, Gen. William Shirley would command the Fiftieth and Fifty-first Regiments and force the French from Niagara. Braddock arrived in Virginia on February 24, 1755. The transports carrying his troops arrived three weeks later. Preparations had already been underway for several weeks. Q.M. Gen. Sir John St. Clair had arrived ahead of Braddock and had already begun reviewing the colonial forces, amassing provisions, and searching for a good route to the Ohio. All along the frontiers of Virginia and Pennsylvania, officials scoured plantations for provisions, wagons, and horses. Braddock's expedition was a major undertaking that would strain the resources of the colonies.[5]

In many ways Braddock and St. Clair were unfortunate choices to lead the expedition. Both were irritable and haughty; both regarded the colonists with a disregard equaled only by their disdain for their Indian allies, which they made no effort to hide. Almost immediately upon his arrival Braddock began to complain about his reception. In particular, he berated Pennsylvania's governor Robert Hunter Morris and Robert Dinwiddie for their failure to provide him with all the necessaries he demanded for the expedition and complained to Newcastle, "I cannot say as yet they have shown the Regard . . . that might have been expected."[6] Braddock's demands and expectations would strain relations among the governors, assemblies, and Whitehall to their limit.

Braddock saw no possibility of failure. He had massed over three thousand troops. The French had fewer than three hundred soldiers and militia and six hundred Indians protecting Fort Duquesne. Governor

Pierre de Rigaud de Vaudreuil saw little hope of victory. He wrote despairingly to Paris, informing the government of the dire straits of the post; it could not possibly withstand a siege, he maintained, because it had not been sufficiently reinforced and supplied. He added, "I dread, with reason . . . the first intelligence from that fort."[7]

In mid-April Braddock summoned Governors James De Lancey of New York, Horatio Sharpe of Maryland, and Dinwiddie and Morris to his camp at Alexandria. There he informed them of his demands. He expected that they would create a general fund of money from all the colonies on which he could draw directly for his expenses without having first to gain the approval of the colonial assemblies. The governors replied that they were sure that their assemblies would never approve of the creation of such a fund. Not only did they counsel against the creation of a general fund, but they also informed Braddock that they would be unable to provide him with any funds at all. To avoid failure, they advised Braddock that he should instead "make use of his Credit upon the Government at home to defray the Expence of all the Operations under his Direction." Braddock was astounded. Not only had the governors refused to create the general fund he needed, but they had also had the audacity to suggest that he should pay all the costs of the expedition.[8]

While Braddock was enraged at the colonial governors in Alexandria, Sir John St. Clair was fuming at the backcountry inhabitants. Braddock had sent St. Clair to Wills Creek to reconnoiter a route to the Ohio and to gather wagons and supplies. St. Clair found, however, that it was much more difficult than he had expected to engage road cutters, obtain wagons, and purchase provisions. Repeatedly rebuffed by the frontier inhabitants, he "stormed like a Lyon Rampant" at the provincial commissioners appointed by Pennsylvania to assist him. He threatened the local planters that "instead of marching to the Ohio he would . . . march his Army into Cumberland County" and would "by Fire and Sword oblige the Inhabitants" to follow his instructions. If they would still not cooperate he would order his troops to "kill all kind of Cattle and carry away the Horses, burn the Houses, &ca." He further suggested to the commissioners that to speed the cooperation of the planters, they should "hang an arse."[9]

The demands of Braddock and St. Clair meant that both Dinwiddie and Morris again had to call their assemblies into session in an attempt to procure supplies. Because of disputes over prerogative, the Pennsylvania Assembly wrangled with Morris over any provision. Eventually, thanks largely to the efforts of Benjamin Franklin, the assembly agreed to provide fourteen thousand bushels of wheat, but no more. Then even this offer became enmeshed in the disputes, both sides refusing to back down. The House of Burgesses in Virginia was little more compliant. While the burgesses supported the expedition, they were annoyed at the lack of support from the other colonies and refused to provide funding unless they were also forthcoming.[10]

Braddock's expedition was thus beset with many handicaps before it was even underway. Indeed, there were some who doubted that the expedition could ever succeed. Braddock's secretary, after touring the camp at Fort Cumberland, wrote to Morris that he was "greatly disgusted at seeing an Expedition (as it is called) so ill concerted originally in England and so ill appointed, so improperly conducted since in America, and so much Fatigue and Expence incurred for a Purpose which if attended with success might better have been left alone." The delays were so long that the expedition was "in Danger of ending in little or nothing."[11] The troops were to rendezvous at Wills Creek—or Fort Cumberland, as the newly constructed defenses on the Potomac River were called. Newcastle had ordered Braddock to bring his regiment to full strength when he reached North America, but finding recruits was difficult. In addition, Braddock was determined to conduct the expedition in European style and march to the Ohio with a large baggage train and heavy artillery to conduct a siege. To move such a baggage train and so much heavy artillery, Braddock required numerous horses and wagons, and the difficulty of obtaining these greatly delayed the advance. Braddock also had to hire hundreds of workers to build the very road along which he intended to march. The scores of camp followers who swarmed around the expedition further delayed progress: sutlers and victualers, whores and washerwomen, wives and mistresses. Braddock's army thus appeared more like a market than a military expedition.[12]

Braddock also delayed to await the arrival of the Indian auxiliaries he expected. Dinwiddie had invited the Ohio Indians to meet in May in Winchester, intending to ask them to join the expedition. However, it should not have been surprising that no Ohio Indians arrived. Dinwiddie had also opened negotiations with the Catawbas and Cherokees to seek their assistance. Governor James Glen of South Carolina, however, objected to Dinwiddie's interference in what he viewed as his colony's exclusive preserve and prevented the Cherokees from attending. Even the

Iroquois were reluctant to send men because of French pressure and the failure of the British to provide a suitable diplomatic gift (due to the inability of Morris and the Pennsylvania Assembly to agree upon a supply). About one hundred Indians eventually assembled at Fort Cumberland, composed mainly of Ohio refugees from George Croghan's plantation at Aughwick but also including some Ohio Indians, like the Delaware headman Shingas, who used the expedition to gather intelligence on British forces and determine Braddock's exact purpose. They received a frosty reception, not the warm welcome they had expected. Braddock repeatedly moaned about their small number and ordered them to send their families home.[13] His lack of consideration disturbed many of the Indians. Several months after the expedition Seneca headman Kanuksusy, or Newcastle, as the British knew him, complained of "the pride and ignorance of that great General that came from England. He is now dead; but he was a bad man when he was alive; he looked upon us as dogs, and would never hear anything what was said to him. We often endeavoured to advise him and to tell him of the danger he was in with his Soldiers; but he never appeared pleased with us, & that was the reason that a great many of our Warriors left him & would not be under his Command."[14]

Braddock's attitude alienated his potential Indian allies as surely as it did the colonists who attempted to assist him. His arrogance toward the Indians who had ventured to his camp may have had an even more profound effect on the outcome of the war. According to a later account, Shingas asked Braddock what he intended to do when he had driven the French from the Ohio. Braddock replied bluntly that "the English Shoud Inhabit & Inherit the Land." Shingas then asked if the Indians who supported the English "might not be Permitted to Live and Trade Among the English and have Hunting Ground sufficient To Support themselves and Familys as they had no where to Flee Too But into the Hands of the French." Braddock replied abruptly that "No Savage Shoud Inherit the Land." This amazed Shingas, who repeated the question. But Braddock merely repeated his reply. Shingas and the other Indians then informed Braddock that "if they might not have Liberty To Live on the Land they woud not Fight for it[.] To wch Genl Braddock answered that he did not need their Help and had No doubt of driveing the French and their Indians away."[15]

It should have been little surprise that Braddock's Indian allies soon deserted him. Even the refugees who had come from Aughwick left in disgust, claiming they wanted to protect the wives and children whom Braddock had ordered home. It is possible that even the British stalwart Scarouady had thoughts about defecting to the French. On June 19 he was "captured" by the French, although he later managed a miraculous escape. He may well have been attempting to ascertain what his reception would be if he were to side with the French. Consequently, Braddock was left with only eight Indian scouts for the expedition, a woefully insufficient number.[16] This did not overly concern Braddock, for he felt that he had little need for Indian assistance and was convinced of the superiority of British regular troops. However, many of his men had only been recruited after his arrival in Virginia. While he tried to drill the new recruits, by the time his expedition departed it was not yet the highly trained and disciplined force he would have liked. In addition, much of the expedition's equipment was inadequate for the task it faced. The flintlock musket was susceptible to damp and was extremely unreliable in the wet Appalachian forests. The soldiers' uniforms provided inadequate protection from the climate and had to be replaced upon arrival in North America because of the "excessive Heat," even though it was only April.[17]

Braddock finally left Fort Cumberland on June 10. His party made a strange sight, "the Knight [St. Clair] swearing in the Van, the Genl curseing & bullying in the Centre, and their Whores bringing up the Rear."[18] The advance was painfully slow because Braddock took with him some of the heavy guns from the warship *Norwich* moored in Alexandria. Yet with the shortage of horses the guns were more of a liability than an asset. It took seven of "the most able Horses" to pull one howitzer and five for each twelve-pounder. When the expedition came to steep hills it was necessary to send horses from the rear of the column to help those in the front pull the guns up the slope. With such obstacles the expedition advanced at a snail's pace, averaging only five or six miles a day and on some days no more than two miles. With a column extending for five miles, the men offered an inviting target for French and Indian attacks.[19]

Lacking Indian scouts, Braddock's expedition moved blindly. The French took full advantage to send out scouting parties to keep track of his advance. The French-allied Indians quickly captured any of Braddock's men who wandered from the camp and left their mutilated bodies along the line of march for their fellow soldiers to find. Several times Braddock's men came across abandoned Indian camps, finding the fires still burning, often roasting assorted body parts, "Threats and Bravados with all Kinds of Scurillous Language" carved into the bark of the trees warning the men of what would happen if they continued. Not surprisingly, Braddock's men became nervous. Rumors spread quickly through the expedition; morale plummeted. At times the flanking troops fired timorously into the woods, believing they had spied the French.[20]

The possibility of an ambush preoccupied Braddock. He had flankers posted during his march to prevent a surprise attack on the column. The most dangerous point was the crossing of Turtle Creek, only a few miles from Fort Duquesne, where the column would be split and the French could attack with a great advantage. On July 7 Braddock's expedition arrived at the creek. Braddock was convinced that the French would attempt an ambush at this point. He spent two days preparing for the crossing. On the morning of July 9 his troops began to ford the creek. By noon the whole party had crossed. Fort Duquesne was only ten miles away. It seemed that nothing could prevent Braddock's success. The plight of Fort Duquesne was critical. Contrecoeur, its commander, decided that it was pointless to attempt to resist a siege and sent Liénard de Beaujeu with 123 soldiers, one hundred militia, and six hundred Indians —Onondagas, Ottawas, Mississaugas, Wyandots, and Potawatomis—to try to halt Braddock's column. At that moment, for the first time on the expedition, Braddock let his guard drop. Having secured the crossing, he had not ensured that he had adequate flankers protecting his column. This gave the French a vital advantage. However, the French attack did not go as planned. Beaujeu had intended to surprise and surround Braddock's troops, but "his ambush . . . failed"; his troops were sighted, and the fighting began just after two o'clock on the afternoon of July 9.[21]

Braddock imagined a heavy attack and sent the colonial troops forward to reinforce the regulars in the vanguard. He ordered his artillery to open fire. The volley wreaked havoc on the French, who reeled back with heavy losses, including Beaujeu himself. The Indians were on the verge of fleeing the field, leaving the British to destroy the remaining French troops and advance unmolested to Fort Duquesne. But Jean-Daniel Dumas, the second in command of the French forces, managed to rally his men and encouraged the Indians to flank the British column. The Indians needed little encouragement. As they advanced around the flanks, "the whoop of the Indians, which echoed through the forest, struck terror into the hearts" of Braddock's troops. They remembered what had happened to their comrades who had been captured. Demoralized by this "psychological warfare," the regulars gave ground, only to find to their horror that they were now trapped between the French and the advancing colonials.[22]

Braddock's troops fought bravely for three hours, but one by one their officers, clearly visible mounted on their horses, were picked off by Indian snipers. Braddock attempted to order his men, but he was unable to form them into their regular ranks in the thick woods and deep ravines. The firing grew more intense. The colonials fired blindly into the melee ahead, but more often than not they hit their own men. The casualties were horrific. Two-thirds of the enlisted men were wounded and three-quarters of the officers. Braddock himself was mortally wounded. Two-thirds of the British casualties had been shot by their own men. Not surprisingly, exposed to this endless fire from all sides, the regulars soon gave way.[23]

Retreat became a rout. Indian warriors pressed in on the terrified column from all sides. Officers tried to rally the men, "but a great Number of them threw away their arms and Ammunition, and even their Cloaths, to escape the faster." The French even discovered Braddock's secret instructions from the Privy Council and his war chest, containing twenty-five thousand pounds, thrown aside to expedite the flight. Braddock himself was hastily buried in the field. It had taken the British twelve days to reach Fort Duquesne from Gist's Plantation; the retreat took them only thirty hours. Colonel Thomas Dunbar was several miles to the rear, near Gist's, with the supply train advancing slowly. He had as many troops as Braddock, his men still outnumbering the French. Dunbar's forces alone were capable of attacking Fort Duquesne. However, panic spread quickly, and soon Dunbar's troops were also in full flight.[24]

Braddock's defeat need not have ended the British offensive. Governor Dinwiddie in particular was in favor of another attempt on the fort. However, Dunbar's men were badly demoralized, and their uncontrolled flight meant that they had lost much of their equipment. Dunbar decided, rather than to launch another assault, to withdraw into winter quarters so that his men could recoup. To protect the frontier he left behind only a few forces. At Fort Cumberland he posted five hundred sick and wounded with a company of Virginia troops to guard them. Not surprisingly, the troops felt they had been left as "a Prey for the Enemy" and deserted. By the middle of August the Virginia and Pennsylvania frontier was almost completely unguarded, an inviting target for the French and their Indian allies.[25]

Braddock's defeat was a terrible disaster for the British. Not only had a major field army been completely destroyed, its equipment lost, and hundreds killed, but the defeat had major political ramifications and influenced Indian relations. It seemed unlikely that the British would ever again exercise any influence in the upper Ohio Valley. Perhaps more importantly, the defeat shattered Indian concerns about the capability of British arms. Braddock's substantial army, which outnumbered his opponents three to one, had been defeated by a force composed principally of Indians. With such an apparently impotent adversary, the frontier offered an inviting target. Indeed, Shingas himself now maintained that the Indians had nothing to fear in going to war against the British, for the British were nothing but "Old Women." Since the British could not find their way to the Ohio towns without Indian guides, if the Indians refused to help them their towns would be safe.[26]

Strategies

Braddock's defeat had provided the French with an unparalleled opportunity. By committing regular troops, the British had in effect declared war on France. The Duke of Newcastle still hoped that the war could remain limited to North America, for "in North America, the Disputes are; And there They shall remain for us; And there the War may be kept."[27] However, Newcastle's hopes were unfounded. A struggle solely limited to North America would place the French at some disadvantage. The French were well aware that the Royal Navy would eventually be able to strangle French trade and supplies, and the British colonies so outnumbered the French colonies that their weight of numbers must eventually tell. Braddock's defeat, however, meant that in North America the French had military dominance, if only temporarily, while in Europe French land forces had an overwhelming superiority. If a war could be fought quickly in Europe, making gains in George II's Hanoverian territories before too many losses were sustained in North America, the French could force concessions from Great Britain.[28]

The raids on the backcountry formed a central part of French military strategy. The British North American colonies dwarfed New France. French authorities lacked essential supplies and faced an enemy who outnumbered them almost twentyfold. The French were pessimistic about the ability of their colonies to defend themselves against a British onslaught. French hopes of victory lay in using Canada's meager resources on the St. Lawrence and Hudson Rivers against the main British and colonial armies, while encouraging allied Indian nations to paralyze the backcountry of Virginia and Pennsylvania. In 1756 Canadian governor Vaudreuil outlined this military policy. He asserted that there was no hope "of managing the English. Their enterprises are carried to excess, and . . . they are making new and greater efforts against this Colony." The only way that the French could hope to halt the British advance, he believed, was "to carry the war into their country . . . [by] sending parties of Indians into the English Colonies." Vaudreuil concluded, "Nothing is more calculated to disgust the people of those Colonies and to make them desire the return of peace." This was the key to French strategy in the early years of the war. The French were thus prepared to equip and provision Indian war parties, hoping to neutralize the British war effort and to compel the British colonies to seek peace rather than to agitate for war.[29]

Using the bulk of their regular troops in the north, on the New York frontier, and on the St. Lawrence, French strategy depended upon the support of their Indian allies. Without this support it would be impossible to paralyze the British frontier. For the French the war in the Ohio theater was thus a distinctive struggle, separate from the struggle to the north. The struggle in the north was a war of regular armies, of set-piece battles in the European style. In the Ohio Valley the war was one of logistics and supplies, of Indian raids and Indian diplomacy. It reflected the patterns of La Petite Guerre, developed on the New England frontier over the previous century. Unable to attack the British colonies directly, the French had encouraged their Indian allies, eastern Algonquian peoples driven from the region after King Philip's War, to devastate the colonial frontier. The construction of new French posts in the Ohio Valley, particularly Fort Duquesne, and the British alienation of all the Ohio peoples enabled the French to attempt this strategy in Virginia and Pennsylvania. In the backcountry this war was to be waged with an intensity not seen before; Indian warfare, La Petite Guerre or La Guerre Sauvage, would be central to the campaigns in the region.[30]

Before the beginning of the war most British colonists had believed that their technological superiority would guarantee victory over Indian raiding parties. However, although reliant on European supplies of arms and ammunition, the Indians had military skills that more than compensated for any technological inferiority, and they appeared to have little reason to be afraid of the British and their colonists. When Pennsylvanian John Craig asked Shingas if he feared retaliation from Anglo-American forces, Shingas, as recounted earlier, laughed heartily and called the British forces "a Parcel of Old Women." [31] The dismissal of the British as "Old Women" carried special significance for the Delawares. The Iroquois' designation of them as "Women" denoted their inability to negotiate directly with the colonies. The Ohio Indians referred to the French in familial terms as Onontio, "The Great Father." Thus their disregard for the British as "Old Women" signifies the absolute contempt in which they now held British and Anglo American forces.

Shingas's disdain was not unfounded. The Ohio Indians recognized that they had little to fear from Virginia or Pennsylvania, for both colonies were unable to launch any meaningful offensive action. Indian raiding parties were able to use their superior knowledge of the environment and the terrain to evade pursuit and engage in battle only when they had some advantage. British commander Col. Henry Bouquet claimed that the strength and endurance of Indian warriors meant that Indian war parties were difficult to locate, for "Rivers are no obstacles to them," while "they can bear hunger and thirst for several days, without slackening." Their stealth and speed allowed them to "fight only when they think to have the advantage" and prevented their being "forced to it, being sure by their speed to elude the most eager pursuit." [32] The commander of the Virginia provincial forces, George Washington, echoed Bouquet, admitting that "the advantageous way they have of fighting in the Woods, their cunning and craft are not to be equalled; neither their activity and indefatigable Sufferings." Unlike the British and provincial troops, who had to take large quantities of supplies with them, the Indians could "depend upon their dexterity in hunting, and upon the Cattle of the Inhabitants for provisions." If the British and provincial forces could neither attack the Ohio Valley nor locate raiding parties, there was little for the Indians to fear. [33]

The raiders took full advantage of their superior knowledge of the terrain and their ability to wage guerrilla warfare. Further, the raids they launched on the backcountry were coordinated to make maximum use of these advantages. A few raids were initiated and planned by the French.

These were generally the larger raids that originated primarily from Fort Duquesne and Fort Niagara. The Indians who participated in these raids were generally from the Great Lakes or Illinois Country: Miamis, Ottawas, Hurons, and Potawatomis, sometimes accompanied by a few Shawnees and Delawares. While the French determined the regions to be raided in the light of their overall military strategy, the Indian participants determined the specific targets. These raids principally attacked regions such as the rear of Fort Cumberland, attempting to cut supply routes. The Ohio Indians themselves initiated many other raids with no French prompting, attacking Augusta, Frederick, and Hampshire Counties in Virginia and Cumberland County in Pennsylvania, while the Susquehanna Delawares raided the Susquehanna Valley and Lancaster, Berks, and Northampton Counties in Pennsylvania. These raids rarely attacked military targets but instead concentrated on isolated frontier plantations.

War offered the Ohio Indians new opportunities to acquire trade goods. Now they did not have to procure these goods through trade but could plunder them from the homes of backcountry settlers. In this manner raiders could acquire not only cloth and metal tools but also more exotic items such as gold and silver jewelry or carved wooden chests. In the world of the Ohio villages, where the distribution of gifts was an important route to political influence, warriors who returned home laden with gifts for their clan and village could rapidly gain status. Raids also provided an important opportunity for warriors to prove their courage in battle, another important route to social status in Algonquian society.[34] Frontier raids therefore appealed particularly to the younger warriors of a village, for they could acquire prestige both through their military exploits and through their redistribution of goods and captives. French calls for their allies to descend upon the frontier thus heightened existing generational tensions on the Ohio. When Indian headmen blamed their "Young men" for the raids on the frontier, they were not just speaking metaphorically. Once the ardor of the younger warriors cooled, as the availability of booty declined and the French were less able to supply them with ammunition, older headmen such as Tamaqua were able to reassert their authority over their warriors and begin negotiations with the British.[35]

For those Ohio peoples who lived further east, closer to the British colonies, particularly the Shawnees and Delawares, there were additional reasons to attack the backcountry, and they needed little French encouragement to launch raids. Their aim was principally to prevent any Anglo-American settlement in the Ohio Valley. Many of their parties had little contact with the French beyond the occasional provision of arms and ammunition. Indeed, the few accounts that trickled in from the upper Ohio Valley claimed that there was a "grand Scheme of the Indians, independent of the French . . . for they apprehended the English extending their Settlements . . . must sometime end in a total extirpation of them."[36] Only if the inhabitants of the British colonies could be convinced that the cost of settling the Ohio Valley was too high could the Ohio Indians hope to retain their homelands.

The Susquehanna Delawares had additional motives for entering the conflict. While they sought to halt the tide of Anglo-American settlement, they also saw the conflict as a chance to get revenge for the Iroquois disposal of their ancestral homelands along the Delaware River and to break free from Iroquois domination. Intelligence received from former Moravian acolytes who had returned to their homes on the upper reaches of the Susquehanna suggested that the Delawares had relatively specific plans and intended, simply with "the assistance of the French," to push back the line of colonial settlement to the South Mountain, about fifty miles from Philadelphia. Once they had done this, "they made no doubt but the English would be glad to make peace."[37]

The motives of any raiding party affected the region that the party raided and the tactics it employed. Canadian ensigns and militia, generally former fur traders, often accompanied Indian raiders from the Illinois Country and the Great Lakes region. Lacking any direct motivation to destroy the frontier, and fighting principally as French allies, they focused chiefly on military targets. In particular, their assaults concentrated on the region around Fort Cumberland and on Cumberland County, Pennsylvania. It was from this region that Anglo-American forces would launch any assault on the Ohio Valley.

The Shawnee and Ohio Delawares' raids concentrated on both civilian and military targets on the exposed western frontier of Virginia and Pennsylvania, particularly Augusta, Frederick, and Hampshire Counties in Virginia and Cumberland County in Pennsylvania. This region was the most accessible from the Ohio and was the source of the settlers who had first crossed into the Ohio Valley. The raids on southwestern Virginia also sought to obstruct Virginia's attempts to acquire allies from among the Catawbas and Cherokees, ambushing any warriors who might venture north to serve alongside the British forces. This was, in many ways, merely a continuation of the sporadic warfare between the Ohio Indians and their traditional enemies in the south that had occurred for much of the eighteenth century.[38]

The Susquehanna Delawares raided Pennsylvania's northern frontier, along the Susquehanna and Delaware Valleys and on the frontier of Lancaster, Berks, and Northampton Counties in Pennsylvania. These raids principally focused on civilian targets, seeking to drive all settlers from the region, as this was the heart of the land the Delawares had once claimed, territory that the Iroquois had "sold" to Pennsylvania. The Delawares sought to empty Berks and Northampton Counties in particular, not only by destroying the settlers' farms and plantations but also by creating widespread panic and hysteria, causing the settlers to abandon their homes ahead of raids.

The specific tactics employed varied according to the targets being attacked. Raiding parties preferred targets where there was little opposition and where they could easily obtain prisoners and booty. Ideally they sought lightly guarded plantations with many women and children. If raiders discovered that the guard was too strong, they might abandon the attack and seek easier pickings elsewhere or wait until many of the garrison were absent, guarding workers in the fields or ranging the frontiers. Indeed, raiders seemed on occasion to know that troops were going to be disbanded or reassigned. For instance, attackers seem to have delayed an attack on Fort Vause in Virginia in June 1756 until the local militia unit had disbanded and most of the garrison were absent. When they attacked Fort Granville in Pennsylvania during the same month raiders waited until the garrison had departed to guard reapers working in the fields nearby.[39]

Any "battle" was typically short. Once the raiders had succeeded in overwhelming the guard, they would quickly set fire to the settlements and seize prisoners and plunder. They would return to the Ohio or Susquehanna driving the settlers' cattle and horses before them, having killed those they did not want. In a typical raid on Cumberland County and along the Potomac River in April 1756, the French reported that "all the oxen and cows having been collected together were killed; a hundred and twenty horses . . . served to carry the large quantity of plunder the Indians got, and in returning they set fire to all the settlements they had left." Virginians reported that the Indians drove away over five hundred cattle after a raid on the Greenbrier River in Virginia in the fall of 1755.[40]

The primary goal of the raiders was surprise. For this reason on many occasions ambushers would use edged weapons rather than guns. Indeed, many of those wounded by raiding parties suffered knife wounds rather than gunshot wounds. When using guns, raiders had a preference for the hunting rifle. While much slower to load than the musket, the rifled barrel ensured that the shot was much more accurate than any musket. Thus it was perfect for skirmishing in the thick forest undergrowth. Indeed, so important were rifles to the Ohio Indians that in 1764 Col. John Bradstreet proposed that there should be a total ban on the their importation into the colonies.[41]

On occasion, raiders would target provincial forts. They rarely directly assaulted even the smallest blockhouse but instead would try to starve out the garrison or set the fort on fire. Often attackers would use cover to get as close to a fort as possible. During the siege of Fort Granville the attackers used the cover of a ravine to get close to the walls of the fort. They then filled the ravine with underbrush that they set on fire. With the walls ablaze the garrison had little choice but to surrender. The reluctance to storm fortified positions was in part a reflection of the reality of combat. Lacking artillery and scaling ladders, the raiders had little chance to seize a fort. However, this reluctance also reflects patterns of traditional warfare, which deemed it better to abandon an attack, even if that attack was likely to be successful, than to suffer heavy casualties.[42]

Having overwhelmed their target, the primary goal of the raiders was to retreat before they could be intercepted. If threatened by a party attempting to rescue captives, raiders would do anything necessary to escape. Children, the elderly, or any wounded captives who could not maintain the pace of travel might be killed. Abraham Miller, captured in May 1757 on the Northampton County frontier, described how his captors killed his mother and a girl with him because of their wounds. Under other circumstances it was highly unusual for the raiders to kill women and children, and for most raiding parties, certainly those from the Ohio Valley, it was much more beneficial to acquire captives than to slaughter the colonial population. Thus, it is ironic that the lives of women and children captured on the frontier were in the greatest danger when parties set out in pursuit in an attempt to rescue them.[43]

The Role of Captives

Between 1755 and 1758 raiding parties seized perhaps as many as 2,000 captives. These captives lived throughout the Ohio and Susquehanna Valleys, in Iroquoia, in the upper Ohio Valley, and in much of the Great Lakes region. British officials believed that there were captives held in nearly every Indian town from the Delaware to the Ohio. This view was supported by captives who escaped or were released. John Baker, who escaped from Kittanning in 1756, estimated that the Ohio Indians held over 100 prisoners in that town alone. In the wake of the "Articles of Agreement" concluded between the British and the Ohio tribes at Fort Pitt in 1764, the Shawnees and Ohio Delawares returned over 260 captives to Henry Bouquet in just six months. Other Indian groups returned large numbers of captives at Easton from 1757 onward, and at various times at Albany, Fort Niagara, and Detroit, while throughout the war the French routinely returned small numbers of captives whom they had purchased from the Indians.[44]

The colonists had lurid notions of what happened to captives, particularly to any women. Adam Stephen, a commander in the Virginia Regiment, insisted that the Indians "Spare the Lives of Young Women, and Carry them away to gratify the[ir] Brutal passions."[45] While backcountry settlers had reason to fear captivity, most captives were not killed, tortured, or raped. The Ohio Indians sought prisoners principally for adoption into their tribes and in most cases treated their prisoners well. Consequently, the most desired captives were women and particularly children, who could be most easily integrated into Indian society.[46] Male captives, particularly men of military age, were viewed with more mistrust. They were less easy to incorporate into Indian society and more likely to be disruptive and threaten the security of a raiding party. If a man did not show the required subservience after his capture, his captors would rarely think twice about killing him. During flight, however, any killing was generally quick and without torture. William Fleming described how, after his capture, Captain Jacobs, the leader of the raiding party, informed him that he "looked young and lusty, [and] they would not hurt me, provided I was willing to go with them." When ordered to do various tasks, Fleming did them with "my usual submission." Fleming was well treated, but soon after he was captured the raiders seized another young man who was more defiant, and he was quickly killed "with several tomahawk blows."[47]

Most prisoners were not killed or tortured but prepared for return to the Ohio or Susquehanna Valleys. To prevent their escape they were bound and often forced to strip. When a raiding party halted for any reason, the captives would be tied up. John Craig reported that when his captors halted, the prisoners "were stripp'd stark naked and their Limbs stretched out to the utmost Extent and tied to a Post and Trees."[48] Raiding parties that divided into smaller groups would arrange to reassemble after several days at an agreed-upon location. There they would divide the prisoners and booty among the different groups. At this point the raiders might kill and ceremonially torture some captives, while others might be painted black for execution upon their return to the Ohio Valley.[49]

When a party finally neared the raiders' village, as was traditional in many northeastern woodlands societies, the captives were whipped and forced to "run the gauntlet" before their adoption into the tribe. Any male captives who had been selected for execution would now be singled out. John Cox reported that during his captivity at Kittanning the war captains Shingas and Captain Jacobs returned to the village with several prisoners. They "made an example" of one of the prisoners. Calling "all the Prisoners to be Witnesses to this Scene," they beat him "for half an hour with Clubs and Tomahawks, and afterwards fastening him to a Post, cropt his Ears close to his Head; after which an Indian chopt off his Fingers, and another, with a red hot iron, burnt him all over his Belly." Eventually they "Shot him full of Arrows, and at last killed and scalped him."[50]

Such torture was not the fate of most captives. Outside the northern frontier of Pennsylvania, where the execution and mutilation of captives were more common, most captives could expect integration into Indian society rather than a cruel execution. Indeed, nearly all the prisoners who escaped or were released agreed that they had been comparatively well treated during their captivity, and most reported that the Ohio Indians had treated them "very kindly." When Christian Frederick Post met with Delaware headmen and war captains on the Ohio in 1758, Shingas assured him that he "was always very kind to any prisoners that were brought in." Others informed Post that "when we take any prisoners from you, we treat them as our own children. We are poor, and yet we clothe them as well as we can, though you see our children are as naked as at the first."[51]

The good treatment captives received reflected their importance in Indian society. Some captives might replace deceased family members, even on occasion acquiring their social status. For instance, a Detroit headman adopted Peter Lewney to replace a deceased relative. Lewney was soon integrated into the Indian family. He was treated as a respected warrior and "was often with them at their Councils with the French, being dressed and painted as the Indians were, and not known by the French but as an Indian, living in every Respect as they did." Others provided much-needed labor in a society that had witnessed continuing population decline for over a century. They often fulfilled an important economic role, being allowed to hunt while the warriors were away raiding the frontier. Indeed, many of the captives who escaped were able to do so because their captors had treated them as full family members and had provided them weapons for hunting.[52]

If village members felt that any captives were not suitable for adoption —if, for example, they were deemed too old—they might ransom them to the French. When the Delawares captured Charles Stewart and his family in Cumberland County in 1755, they took Stewart and his family to Kittanning, where they divided the prisoners among the various raiding groups. There they separated Stewart and his wife from their children. They took the two adults to Detroit, where they sold them to a French missionary.[53]

Because of the good treatment they received and the great length of their captivity, many captives came to view the Ohio Indians as their family and were reluctant to return to the backcountry after the war. David Boyd reported that when he returned to Virginia and his family he was very unhappy, for "he had grown fond of the wild and free life of the forest and was greatly dissatisfied by his new surroundings." He considered escaping to the Ohio and "had to be closely guarded for weeks before he finally abandoned his plan." Thomas Ingles, who returned to Virginia after spending thirteen years among the Shawnees, "became very restless & uneasy" and likewise had to be closely watched. A young girl whom the Susquehanna Delawares returned to the British in 1758 "was obstinate, [and] would neither tell her name nor Speak a Word, and made great resistance to her being delivered up."[54] After the occupation of the Ohio Valley by the British army in 1759, agents sent among the

Ohio Indians to recover prisoners were horrified to discover how many refused to leave.[55] Many "captives" remained permanently with their "captors." Mary Jemison, captured in Cumberland County in 1758, remained with the Senecas until her death in 1833, even though some of her family survived. Several captives rose to prominence in their adopted tribes. George Brown rose to "become one of the chief Men among the Shawnese," and Joshua Renick became a Miami headman.[56]

Captives thus played a vitally important social and economic role for the Ohio Indians. In addition, however, the fear of capture played an important role in generating terror among the backcountry inhabitants and was part of what might be termed the psychological warfare waged by the Ohio Indians in the backcountry. If the desire for the acquisition of captives reflects traditional patterns of Indian warfare, psychological warfare represented a new response to European contact. During Braddock's march to the Ohio, the practice of capturing stragglers from the main column and placing their mutilated bodies along the line of march so terrified the British regulars that when Braddock was attacked, "the whoop of the Indians . . . struck terror into the hearts" of the troops.[57] When Forbes's army neared the forks in 1758 they found the heads of Grant's highlanders, who had recently been defeated outside the post, displayed on stakes; underneath hung their kilts flapping in the breeze. The deliberate mutilation of victims to spread hysteria among the colonists occurred with the greatest frequency on the northern frontier of Pennsylvania. Here the scalping and mutilation of women and children were not uncommon. A report from Northampton County at the end of 1755 described "Men, Women and Children cruelly mangled and Massacred . . . some haggled and covered all over with Wounds."[58] This strategy seems to have been immensely successful. A few weeks later it was reported that the "shocking Descriptions . . . given by those who have escaped of the horrid Cruelties and indecencies committed by these merciless Savages on the Bodies of the unhappy wretches who fall into their Barbarous hands, ha[ve] struck so great a Pannick and Damp upon the Spirits of the people, that hitherto they have not been able to make any considerable resistance or stand against the Indians."[59]

Psychological warfare was thus important in undermining the morale both of regular and provincial forces and of civilians. Fear of capture caused many tens of thousands of settlers to flee their homes and seek safety in the east. Even before news of Braddock's defeat, settlers complained to the Council of Pennsylvania that "their Wives and Children are terrified to death with every . . . most trifling story, and are with difficulty persuaded to stay and do the Duty of their Families." Many families did quit their homes and head to the east, or to North Carolina or New Jersey.[60]

Consequently, when raiders struck, panic swept through the back-country. After the fall of Fort Vause in Augusta County in 1756, William Preston was horrified at "the Confusion and Disorder [of] the Poor People . . . Mothers with [a] train of helpless Children at their heels straggling through woods & mountains to escape the fury of those merciless savages." Covered wagons, loaded with the belongings of families heading for safety, blocked the roads. James Maury reported in south-western Virginia that "from the waters of Potomac, James River, and Roanoke . . . from the side of the Blue Ridge, hundreds of families have, within these few months past . . . deserted their habitations." He added that "by Bedford Court House, in one week . . . near three hundred persons . . . passed on their way to Carolina. And I have it from good authors, that . . . five thousand more had crossed [the] James River . . . at Goochland Court House." Those fleeing were "not the idler and the vagrant . . . but the honest and industrious, men of worth and property."[61]

Not everyone was free to evacuate. The departure of a prominent settler's family might prompt widespread panic. James Burd confided to Edward Shippen in August 1755 that he was thinking of evacuating his wife and children but had "been plagued with the Solicitations of the People in this County not to Carry my Family to Lancaster." After the raids began, Conrad Weiser complained to Governor Morris that "I must stand my ground or my neighbours will all go away and leave their habitations to be destroyed by the Enemy." In May 1756 James Wood, the founder of Winchester, did decide to evacuate his family from his plantation near the town. His decision created a panic in Winchester and "caused many to think their Case desperate."[62]

Life for the refugees was often desperate. They had abandoned their plantations and possessions, their crops and livestock. They had nowhere to live and lodged in what amounted to refugee camps in backcountry towns near military garrisons such as Carlisle, Lancaster, York, and Winchester. The Moravian settlements at Bethlehem and Nazareth alone provided shelter to over three hundred refugees. Here they lived in barns and stables, "Men, Women and Children who had lately lived in great Affluence and Plenty reduced to the most extreme Poverty and Distress . . . and in want of the Common Necessaries of Life."[63] Philadelphia merchant Joseph Turner reported that "Women & Children who Escap'd from Immediate Death [were] in the greatest want of both Covering & Victuals & very great numbers tho' at some Distance from the Scene of action, retiring leaving their Dwellings with what Corn and Stock they had . . . are now in a Starving Condition."[64]

The images of mangled bodies and fleeing refugees created widespread hysteria. The generation of this hysteria was an important aim of the raids. Raiders could only penetrate into the backcountry where population density was relatively low and they could launch surprise attacks, and this limited the regions that could be raided.[65] However, the raids themselves depopulated the backcountry. For many miles into the settled part of the colonies, often far away from the raids, settlers packed up their belongings to escape attack. In November 1756 Washington reported that "the ruinous state of the frontiers, and the vast extent of land we have lost since this time twelve-month[s ago], must appear incredible to those who are not eye-witnesses of the desolation. Upwards of fifty miles of a rich and (once) thick-settled country is now quite deserted & abandoned."[66] In many ways this was a key to the raiders' strategy. A raid would devastate one region, while settlers abandoned the neighboring area. The next raid would thus be able to push on further, causing a new wave of settlers to flee, ad infinitum. In theory, if the raiders could not be halted there was no reason why they should not eventually push the colonists back to the Atlantic. Such an outcome was, of course, highly unlikely. To push the settled areas of Virginia and Pennsylvania back to the Atlantic would have taken several years of intense raids, for which the Ohio Indians had neither the manpower nor the supplies. However, colonists and colonial administrators did not have the assurance of many modern historians that such an attack was impossible. Particularly after the fall of Fort William Henry in New York in August 1757, there were genuine fears that the French army could descend the Hudson River while Indian raiders completed the devastation of the Virginia and Pennsylvania backcountry.[67]

IN THE SUMMER of 1755 Braddock marched to the Ohio confident in his victory. Even the French believed that their chance of holding the forks of the Ohio was slim. However, Braddock's force was routed, and the frontier of Virginia and Pennsylvania was left all but undefended. Supplied and encouraged by the French, but fighting for their own purposes, Indian warriors from across northern Pennsylvania, the Ohio Valley, and the Great Lakes region descended upon the backcountry. War left Virginia and Pennsylvania floundering. Whitehall's decision to send Gen. Edward Braddock to the forks of the Ohio and escalate the conflict in the Ohio Valley seemed, at the end of 1756, to have been a dreadful mistake. French strategy had succeeded in paralyzing both colonies.

Indian raiders demonstrated an awareness of tactics and strategy in the devastation of the backcountry. The targeting of vulnerable groups and the acquisition of booty and prisoners in raids were traditional features of warfare for the northeastern woodlands Indians. However, the use of psychological warfare, particularly on the northern frontier of Pennsylvania, to destroy civilian as well as military morale, the interception of important supply routes, and the siege and even capture of isolated frontier posts were tactics that played no role in traditional Indian warfare. The raids that devastated the Virginia and Pennsylvania frontier from 1755 to the end of 1756 were thus a combination of traditional Indian warfare and European strategy. The raids were conducted in a particularly Indian manner, emphasizing the taking of captives and booty. However, they also reflected a broader sense of strategy: the desire to paralyze the enemy and the need to disrupt enemy communications and supply routes. Indian warfare had been transformed to counter European warfare, and the Ohio Indians had proved their worth. The extent of the damage wrought by the raiders, the number of captives and refugees, created political and social problems for the two colonies, in addition to the military crisis. These problems would not easily be overcome; it would take the colonies several years to find a solution.

3

"Dissatisfact'n, Discontent and Clamours of All Ranks"

The Breakdown of Backcountry Society, 1755–1758

FOR OVER TWO YEARS FOLLOWING GEN. EDWARD BRADDOCK'S defeat, raiding parties laid waste to the backcountry of both Virginia and Pennsylvania. However, the damage caused by these raids was not just in the abandoned settlements that littered the backcountry and in the streams of refugees who fled east; the raids also opened up deep rifts within backcountry society. By simultaneously offering new opportunities and new dangers the war heightened divisions that had been scarcely visible in peacetime. In particular, the war highlighted the insubstantial nature of the elite's influence over backcountry society.

When faced with the Indians' onslaught, backcountry inhabitants were not prepared to accept unquestioningly the leadership of the eastern elite who attempted to organize the defense of the backcountry. On issues such as the drafting of troops from the militia, the harboring of deserters, and the impressment of wagons and supplies, backcountry settlers plainly demonstrated that they would not accept the dictates of the elite. Ethnic and social disputes emerged as neighbors sought safety and refuge. The strength of these disputes forced local elites to acquiesce to the demands of their neighbors, rather than to follow instructions from Williamsburg, Philadelphia, and London, and seriously hampered the colonies' conduct of the war.[1] In Virginia such disputes tended to emerge as social conflict between the "lower sort" and the elite. In Pennsylvania, by contrast, these struggles more often surfaced as ethnic or religious clashes between Germans and Scotch-Irish, and Presbyterians and Quakers. In the manner in which the war generated internal disputes, its progress was fundamentally different from that seen elsewhere in the British colonies, notably New England.

The progress of the war greatly dismayed those settlers who remained in the backcountry. They bitterly reproved the provincial authorities for their failure to protect them. After the first raids upon Pennsylvania, Conrad Weiser was lucky to escape death from a mob of angry settlers who swarmed around his home. He wrote that "some of the people threatened to shoot me. . . . The Crie was the land is betrayed & sold. The Comon people, from Lancaster County, were the worst." They wanted powder and believed that Weiser "had it in my power to give as much as I pleased. I was in danger of being shot to death. . . . There is no doing with the People."[2] When the Pennsylvania Assembly delayed authorizing a defense bill, a mob of seven hundred backcountry settlers descended upon Philadelphia demanding protection. In Virginia Colonel Dunbar's flight produced the greatest outpouring of wrath. The bitter sentiments of the backcountry settlers horrified Governor Robert Dinwiddie, who informed Gen. William Shirley that he could not "in strong enough Colours represent to You the Dissatisfact'n, Discontent and Clamours of All ranks of People here."[3]

The Descent on Virginia: July–October 1755

The raids had begun even before Braddock marched toward the Ohio. In July 1754 and again in the early spring of 1755, there were sporadic attacks on the Holston River in Augusta County. These raids aimed to break communications between Virginia and the colony's Indian allies, the Cherokees and Catawbas in the Carolinas.[4] The Ohio Shawnees and Delawares also launched a few isolated raids on Cumberland County, Pennsylvania. However, the raiding parties were small and the damage limited. As Braddock advanced toward Fort Duquesne, the first large-scale raids commenced upon the frontiers. These raiding parties were composed of a wider range of France's allies, including not only Shawnees and Delawares but also Ottawas, Miamis, and Potawatomis. The raiders targeted the rear of Braddock's column and wrought particular devastation on the settlements at Patterson's Creek, Virginia, twelve miles east of Fort Cumberland. From Patterson's Creek the raiders fanned out into the rest of Frederick and Hampshire Counties and into Cumberland County in Pennsylvania, killing fifty settlers and capturing about thirty more.[5]

These early raids demonstrated Virginia's lack of preparedness for war and, in particular, the limitations of the militia. The commander of the Frederick County militia refused to march outside the county's boundaries. Some men refused to leave their own families, while others fled from the frontier. Even when the men could be persuaded to muster, they often lacked weapons. When raiders struck Augusta County, descending upon settlements on the Holston and New Rivers, the militia once more proved a sorry lot. In two engagements the Indians killed several Virginians, including the commander of one party and a respected Augusta gentlemen, James Patton, while suffering no casualties themselves. By the end of July raiders had penetrated as far as Smith's Mountain in Halifax County, deep into the settled parts of Virginia, inflicting heavy casualties. Indeed, the French reported that the Miamis and Potawatomis alone had killed or captured 120 settlers. From the French perspective the raids had the desired effect. The inhabitants deserted large areas of the backcountry behind Braddock, rendering the acquisition of supplies for the expedition increasingly difficult. Those who had not fled refused to bring provisions to the army without an escort and forced Braddock to divert men to provide a guard. Fleeing settlers clogged the roads with wagons heading east, hindering communications between Braddock and his rear.[6]

With raiders already harassing the frontier, when news of Braddock's defeat arrived in Williamsburg it was clear that decisive measures needed to be taken to defend Virginia's exposed backcountry. Dinwiddie hurriedly summoned the House of Burgesses. The burgesses approved the formation of a twelve-hundred-man Virginia Regiment. Following the Fort Necessity debacle, the regiment had been broken down into independent companies, and George Washington had resigned his commission rather than be reduced in rank. He had served with distinction in Braddock's expedition, but as an aide to Braddock, not as a member of the Virginia forces. However, he clearly had the greatest military experience of any Virginian, and the burgesses took little time in selecting him to command the new regiment. To fill the ranks the House authorized a draft of single men from the militia. However, those drafted could avoid service by paying a ten-pound fine or finding a substitute. This allowed the wealthy to escape service while forcing the poor into the regiment. The law would prove a disappointment. The bounty remained too low to attract sufficient volunteers, while drafting men proved unworkable, as justices were reluctant to draft their neighbors.[7]

The creation of the Virginia Regiment had little effect, for the raids continued unabated into the fall. However, they increasingly targeted the region around Fort Cumberland. This was now the British post closest to the French on the Ohio and the most likely base for any future assault on the Ohio. In early October Adam Stephen, the fort's commander, reported that about 150 raiders had crossed the Appalachians and then "divided into Small parties." One party descended on settlements on the Greenbrier River in Augusta County, and another attacked the settlements on Patterson's Creek east of Fort Cumberland and then pressed on down the Potomac to Town Creek, Maryland. A third party, composed principally of Delawares, commanded by Shingas, descended on the south branch of the Potomac. This raid so terrified a detachment of the Virginia Regiment stationed there that they abandoned their positions and hastily retreated toward Edwards's Fort on the Cacapon.[8]

The October raids once more threw the Virginia backcountry into chaos and inflicted heavy casualties. Of equal concern, there seemed to be no military response. Washington hurried to Winchester, where he "found everything in the greatest hurry and confusion by the back Inhabitants flocking in, and those of the Town removing out." He urged the settlers to remain and seek protection in the many blockhouses that the Virginia Regiment had thrown up. A few did, but most were intent on fleeing as far as possible and warned Washington that if he made any attempt to stop them they would "blow out [his] brains." He tried to maintain morale by rushing forces to buttress the frontier defenses, but many of the new recruits were still in Fredericksburg for rudimentary training. When Washington ordered them to force-march to Winchester, they deserted in droves.[9]

When Washington attempted to bring in other reinforcements, they were unable to move owing to "the Crowds of People who were flying" down the roads. The panic also bred wild rumors that made it difficult for Washington to make the most effective disposition of his troops. On October 11 he received a report that a large party of Indians had attacked only twelve miles from Winchester and was advancing quickly on the town. The townspeople were terrified and were "flying in the most promiscuous manner." In desperation Washington sent out a company in a brave attempt to intercept the raiders. What the company found, however, was not a large raiding party but "a Mulattoo and negro seen hunting" and three drunken soldiers "carousing, firing their Pistols, and uttering the most unheard of Imprecations."[10]

The October raids had revealed the weakness of Fort Cumberland. Washington now believed the garrison was too exposed to resist an attack and sought to withdraw his men to blockhouses and forts further east. When the fort had been constructed in 1754 it was located on the outer limits of settlement, but now, following the summer and autumn raids on Hampshire and Frederick Counties, it was many miles beyond the furthest settlement. Garrisoning it drew men from other areas without offering any protection to the settlers, for incoming raiding parties could bypass the fort with ease. Simply supplying the fort was difficult and provided a major drain on manpower. The withdrawal of Virginia forces seemed a logical move. However, Washington faced intense opposition both from Governor Dinwiddie and from General Shirley, which compelled him reluctantly to maintain the fort as a supply base for a future attack on the Ohio.[11]

The October attacks also revealed many of the critical weaknesses in Virginia's new military system. The procedures for conducting courts-martial were at best slow and at worst impossible to operate. Mutiny and desertion were endemic in the force, and when Washington attempted to round up deserters, they were hidden and protected by local civilians, including county justices. Some civilians even encouraged the men to desert, offering them protection in return for some pilfered ammunition or other supplies. Fortunately for Virginia, following the raids in October the Indians did not launch another attack on the colony until the following April, as their focus shifted to the even more exposed frontier of Pennsylvania. Over the winter of 1755–56 it would be the backcountry of Pennsylvania that would bear the brunt of the Indian assaults.[12]

The Descent on Pennsylvania: October 1755–February 1756

In Pennsylvania news of the raids on Virginia had created considerable concern. Even before the full brunt of the raids fell on Virginia, the first reports of Braddock's defeat had thrown the western frontier into chaos. In Cumberland County the settlers were "in general in great Trouble and Confusion," and the "Back Settlers are in general fled, and are likely to be ruined for the Loss of their Crops and Summer's Labour."[13] In Philadelphia Quaker assemblymen had acquiesced in the funding of a volunteer force, and it looked as if governor and assembly might overcome their disagreements. They now descended, however, into another, even more bitter dispute over the taxation of proprietary lands. Across the province their squabbling caused consternation. Several leading Pennsylvanians even offered to pay the proprietors' tax if the assembly and governor would compromise. Both sides refused. This refusal reflected their belief that Pennsylvania could not experience the same fate as Virginia. Most Pennsylvanians believed that the Ohio Indians could not attack east of the Susquehanna unless the Susquehanna Delawares were "drawn off." The defection of the Susquehanna Delawares was impossible, the commonly held wisdom maintained, as long as the Iroquois remained allies of the British, for the Delawares remained at the bidding of the Iroquois. When at the beginning of October rumors began to circulate of the Delawares' defection, concern began to rise.[14]

In early October messengers arrived on the Susquehanna carrying a message from Governor Vaudreuil informing the Delawares that those who were reluctant to fight the Pennsylvanians should "go where I cannot hurt you." They should move to the Ohio Valley or at least farther up the east branch. This threat threw many Susquehanna Delawares into panic. They had no ammunition to defend themselves against the French, and thus they offered no resistance, either moving away or allowing the French and their Indian allies to move through their territory unmolested to reach the unprotected Pennsylvania frontier. Many even joined their Ohio compatriots and prepared for war. Their numbers would mount quickly as the Pennsylvanians proved their inability to protect themselves.[15]

In the middle of October the Susquehanna Delawares summoned Andrew Montour to the "Great Island" on the west branch of the Susquehanna to warn him that they were preparing to go to war against the

British. John Harris, who visited the Great Island at the end of October, reported that he found the Indians all painted in black and ready for war. It was apparent that many Susquehanna Delawares had "defected" to the French. Conrad Weiser warned William Allen, "I think all our Indians are gone off with the French, or rather joined them because they could not stand their Ground." Yet despite all these warnings, when the raids on the frontier finally began, Pennsylvania officials seemed stunned.[16]

On October 16 a party of Ohio Indians, accompanied by a few Susquehanna Delawares from the west branch, descended upon the settlement of Penn's Creek on the west side of the Susquehanna, a few miles south of Shamokin, destroying it. A party that set out from Harris's Ferry to bury the dead was itself attacked on October 24. The raiders then crossed the Susquehanna and attacked in Lancaster County, coming within five miles of Harris's Ferry and leaving a trail of destruction along the Susquehanna.[17] The final realization that the Susquehanna Delawares had deserted their former allies caused alarm. Alarm turned to panic as the raiders pressed deeper into the settled parts of Pennsylvania, east into Paxton Township in Lancaster County, and on into Berks County. Here Conrad Weiser attempted to organize defense and halt the flow of refugees. However, the inhabitants "did not care to fight if they could avoid it," and their anger soon turned against the local Quakers. A report from Reading declared that "the people exclaim against the Quakers, & some are scarce restrained from burning the Houses of those few who are in This Town."[18]

Worse was yet to come. At the beginning of November Shingas's party, consisting of about one hundred Ohio Indians who had been raiding around Fort Cumberland, crossed into Pennsylvania and descended upon the Great Cove in Cumberland County. The party then divided into smaller parties to ravage the Little Cove and Conolways. Pennsylvania now faced two major incursions, one on the western frontier and one on the northern frontier.[19] Other smaller raiding parties attacked the increasingly isolated settlements on the Juniata River and in Sherman's Valley before returning to the Ohio laden with booty. On the northern frontier the raids also spread. On November 16 a combined force of Ohio Indians and Susquehanna Delawares descended on the northern frontier. A large raiding party attacked the settlements at Tulpehocken and Bethlehem in Berks and Northampton Counties. The party then divided into two groups. One group advanced southwest into Berks

County, while the other attacked southeast toward the Delaware River. On November 24 the latter party descended upon the Moravian settlement at Gnadenhütten with surprising ferocity, perhaps reflecting their anger at the Moravians' influence among some Susquehanna Delawares. The raiders looted the settlement before burning it to the ground and killing most of the Moravian brethren there, including one party that they burned alive in the garret of one of the settlement's houses.[20]

One reason why the attacks on the Pennsylvania backcountry met with little opposition was that Pennsylvania had no military organization at all with which to oppose the raiders. Following the first attacks on Pennsylvania, some settlers attempted to organize themselves to make a stand, but they lacked arms, experience, and authority. The justices of Berks County wrote desperately to Governor Robert Hunter Morris from Reading, informing him that "we are all in uproar, all in Disorder. . . . We have no authority, no commissions, no officers practised in War." They warned Morris, "If we are not immediately supported we must not be sacrificed, and therefore are determined to go down with all that will follow us to Philadelphia, & Quarter ourselves on its Inhabitants and wait our Fate with them."[21] Morris replied that if they would organize themselves into volunteer companies he would do all he could to provide them with supplies and weapons. Some did this. Others built their own blockhouses. However, these ad hoc defense units and frontier blockhouses were inadequate protection. The blockhouses were small and often offered an inviting target to the raiders. The volunteers quickly disbanded if they perceived it was more in their interest to flee or protect their families.[22]

As the onslaught continued, a new assembly met in Philadelphia. Throughout October it wrangled over the creation of a militia and the passage of a new supply bill, but governor and assembly remained deadlocked over matters of prerogative and privilege. Many backcountry settlers were horrified at the deadlock. When the assembly pointed out the dangers to the colony's liberties of yielding to the demands of the proprietors, many backcountry settlers seethed, claiming that "they did not know that their Liberties were invaded, but they were sure their Lives & Estates were."[23] Faced with widespread unrest in the backcountry, the assembly finally passed a supply bill and agreed to create a volunteer military force. However, the assembly was not prepared to give officers any powers of coercion over their men. The men could not be compelled to perform duties they objected to. Indeed, Governor Dinwiddie regarded the Pennsylvania law as "a Joke on all military Affairs." Yet for a colony that had a strong pacifist tradition, it was a major development, and indeed the war was to prove that volunteer forces were much more effective than the traditional militia.[24]

Despite the assembly's approval of a volunteer force, the raids on Berks and Northampton Counties continued throughout December. Numerous parties raided isolated settlements and picked off refugees as they ventured back to their homes to recover their possessions. Weiser reported to Morris that "the Country is in a dismal Condition: Believe me kind Sir, that it cannot hold out long. Consternation, Poverty, Confusion, Parties is everywhere." William Parsons warned that even the inhabitants of the town of Easton on the Delaware River were preparing to evacuate. The number of casualties was horrific. Across the Pennsylvania backcountry, nearly five hundred settlers had been killed or captured.[25] A report painted a gruesome picture: "There may be seen horror and desolation, populous Settlements deserted, Villages laid in Ashes, Men, Women and Children cruelly . . . Massacred, some found in the Woods very nauseous for want of interment, some just seeking after the hands of the Savage Slaughterers, and some . . . covered all over with Wounds, which look like so many Mouths crying for Vengeance against their Murderers, and yelling at the negligence & insensibility of the Administration, to whose inactivity there are so many Sacrifices."[26]

Over the winter the backcountry continued to suffer sporadic raids. On January 27 a raiding party led by Shingas attacked the few remaining settlements on the Juniata River in northern Cumberland County, Pennsylvania, and pressed on southward, attacking first the Conolaway in southern Cumberland County and then McDowell's Mill. Meanwhile, other small parties harassed the entire western frontier. Some skulked around the newly constructed provincial forts, making supply difficult; others looted and burned deserted plantations. Although comparatively few settlers were killed (many had already abandoned their plantations, and those who remained were on their guard), the raids continued the panic and left settlers more discontented with the government's failure to protect them. They continued throughout February and March, and by the end of March raiders were pushing deep into Berks County, reaching to within a few miles of Reading. In the spring, however, some of the volunteer parties began for the first time to offer resistance. In Cumberland County one company pursued a raiding party for several miles, forcing them to abandon some of their booty and one of their captives.[27]

The Overwhelming of Provincial Defenses: Spring and Summer 1756

In Virginia the winter saw the number of raids decline sharply. Dinwiddie attributed the decline to the success of the Virginia Regiment, but in reality it was probably due more to bad weather and the availability of more tempting targets in Pennsylvania, for in the spring large-scale raids recommenced. Jean-Daniel Dumas, the commander of Fort Duquesne, sent out several parties with orders "to observe the enemy's movements back of Fort Cumberland," "to harass their convoys," and where possible to attack stores and destroy forts.[28] The French sensed a weakness in the British strategy of constructing small and isolated fortresses as a barrier: when they proved too strong for a raiding party, they could easily bypass them; when their garrisons were too weak to resist, they could surround and destroy them. From mid-March until the end of July, the French encouraged their Indian allies to launch repeated attacks against the forts. In four months they attacked nine forts and destroyed five.

Toward the end of February two large raiding parties rendezvoused near Fort Cumberland. The raiders spent several days scouting around the fort, collecting intelligence for the French, and killed or captured several stragglers from the garrison. One of the parties pressed southward into Virginia and attacked and destroyed a blockhouse known as William's Fort, killing thirty-three out of the thirty-five men in the fort. For the next few weeks this party harassed the upper reaches of the Potomac River, attacking Ashby's Fort on Patterson's Creek and then Cocks's Fort a little further up the river. The second raiding party pressed northeast into Pennsylvania, destroying McCord's Fort in Cumberland County, Pennsylvania.[29]

These assaults worked perfectly. At the beginning of April Washington reported to Dinwiddie that all communications with Fort Cumberland had been cut off and that "the roads between [Winchester] and Fort Cumberland, are much infested."[30] His concerns became greater when, on April 7, a party of Cherokee warriors and Virginia Regimentals skirmished with one of the raiding parties, killing the French commander of the party and discovering his orders from Fort Duquesne. These detailed the attacks on Fort Cumberland's supply routes and the intention to isolate the fort from its supply sources before a larger attack could commence. Despite this information, Washington was unable to strengthen his position. He attempted to enlist local inhabitants to foray routes that raiders were expected to use. Only fifteen men appeared for service. By the end of April the inhabitants had abandoned all of Hampshire County and most of Frederick County. There were no settlers west of the Shenandoah except for isolated pockets upon the south branch and near Edwards's Fort on the Cacapon. Those who remained cowered in forts with little food or ammunition.[31]

As raiders descended upon Frederick County and pushed toward the Shenandoah Valley, Washington had only forty regimental troops at his disposal. The rest of the regiment was on garrison duty while Washington awaited the arrival of new recruits. Upon receiving Washington's first reports of the raids, Dinwiddie hastily ordered out half the militia of the northern Virginia counties, but the Frederick County militia refused to muster and other militia units, more removed from the action, deliberately delayed their muster. On the frontier despair at the failure of the provincial defenses mounted. At the end of April Washington reported that some settlers even talked about "capitulating and coming upon terms with the French and Indians."[32]

It was nearly a month before Washington received sufficient numbers of militia to relieve the regimental troops from garrison duty and commence a more vigorous defense. Sensing the arrival of the militia the raiders now moved to other more exposed parts of the frontier, to Pennsylvania and western Augusta County, where they had equal success. On June 25 the raiders captured Fort Vause in Augusta County, which was crowded with people seeking protection. In the wake of its capture terrified settlers abandoned much of Virginia's frontier. While Washington attempted to stabilize the Virginia frontier, Pennsylvania's western frontier continued to endure heavy raids. Throughout May and early June raiding parties terrorized Cumberland County and continued the strategy of attacking blockhouses and forts. On June 11 a party destroyed Bigham's blockhouse at the junction of the Juniata and Tuscarora Rivers. Like Fort Vause, this fort was crowded with settlers from the surrounding district who had sought protection. On July 30 the raiders took their greatest prize, Fort Granville in Cumberland County, Pennsylvania.[33]

While the larger parties concentrated on destroying the forts and blockhouses along the frontier, smaller raiding parties concentrated on attacking more exposed parties of settlers. In particular raiders targeted those who ventured out into the fields to harvest their crops or who attempted to carry supplies to any of the increasingly isolated forts. On July 20 one raiding party attacked soldiers guarding reapers near McDowell's Mill in Cumberland County and pressed on down the Conococheague while another went down the Potomac toward Maidstone and on into Frederick County, Virginia. Further north a series of smaller raids, conducted by Susquehanna Delawares, devastated Bethel Township in Lancaster County and parts of upper Berks County. Throughout the summer the raids on the frontier continued unabated, particularly on Lancaster and Cumberland Counties, leaving backcountry settlers thoroughly demoralized.[34]

For over a year Virginia and Pennsylvania, two of the most populous colonies in North America, had suffered devastating raids at the hands of just a few hundred Indian warriors. They had contributed nothing to the war effort in the north, and their cries for help had resounded loudly through the corridors of Whitehall. For most contemporary observers their failure was all but inexplicable. In scenes not dissimilar from the Vietnam War two centuries later, raiding parties penetrated deep into the heart of settled areas, "lurk[ing] in the Woods till they have an Opp't'y of surpriz'g unguarded Settlers."[35] Meanwhile British and colonial forces had retreated into fortified encampments, considered evacuating civilians to defensible villages, and suffered repeated humiliating defeats. By the end of 1756, across the Virginia and Pennsylvania backcountry, raiders had killed over a thousand settlers and troops and had taken a similar number of prisoners.[36]

The Impact of the War

Crucial to French strategy in paralyzing the backcountry was creating sufficient discontent so that the colonists would seek an end to the war. The success of the raiders fueled widespread popular resistance to the war among the colonial population. Some backcountry inhabitants provided the French with important intelligence, and some settlers were so disheartened that they considered coming to terms with the French. In June 1756 Governor Vaudreuil reported that he had been doing his "best to multiply as much as circumstances permit" the raiding "parties of Indians [sent] into the English Colonies . . . [for] Nothing is more calculated to disgust the people of these Colonies and to make them desire the return of peace. My labor in this regard has not been in vain."[37] Washington reported to Governor Dinwiddie that frontier settlers were holding "Councils and Cabals to very dishonourable purposes. . . . Despairing of assistance and protection . . . they talk of capitulating and coming upon terms with the French and Indians."[38] Similar reports came to Canadian ears. Governor Vaudreuil claimed that groups of Pennsylvanians had tried to protect themselves from raiding parties by declaring that "they had never done them any harm, that they were so tired of the cruel war being waged against them that they could not but sue them for peace, and that they intended to make the same plea to the French."[39]

The northern and western frontier of Pennsylvania was particularly hard hit, with Cumberland and Northampton Counties suffering heavy losses. However, there were notable regional differences in the impact of the raids. In southern and western Virginia more captives were seized than settlers killed; in Northampton County over four times as many settlers were killed as taken captive. These figures reflect the particular ferocity of the war in this county, representing a substantial loss to backcountry society. As early as April 1756 Governor Morris had written Sir William Johnson informing him that it was difficult to "conceive . . . what a Multitude of Inhabitants, of all ages and both sexes they have carried into Captivity."[40] In June 1756 one raiding party returned to Fort Duquesne with over sixty captives. By August of that year French officials on the Ohio were estimating that the Ohio Indians alone had taken over three thousand captives. While the latter estimate may be rather high, it reflects the sheer scale of the calamity, as the total colonial population of Virginia and Pennsylvania numbered around three hundred thousand.[41]

In Virginia raiders attacked as far as Bedford, Halifax, and Albemarle Counties, while in Pennsylvania they penetrated as far as Reading, only forty miles from Philadelphia.[42] Settlers abandoned a vast area of the backcountry, including the entirety of Hampshire County, Virginia. The county court did not meet from mid-1755 until the end of 1757, and the House of Burgesses even considered amalgamating the county with Frederick County, from which it had been formed in 1752. Settlers deserted an area from the Delaware River to the Roanoke River, a distance nearly four hundred miles long and between fifty and one hundred miles wide. The population of Augusta County, Virginia, fell by nearly half from 1754 to 1758 and did not recover to prewar levels until 1764.

The population of Frederick County, Virginia, fell by almost a third, although it recovered to prewar levels by 1760. Bedford and Halifax Counties in Virginia, neither of which was a "frontier" county, both lost population in 1756 and 1757. Other backcountry counties found their previously high population growth stalled as existing settlers moved out at the same rate that new settlers arrived. A similar area of the Pennsylvania frontier was evacuated. At times Cumberland County was all but deserted, with Carlisle and Harris's Ferry on the Susquehanna River left as isolated outposts. By the end of 1757 Col. John Armstrong of the Pennsylvania Regiment estimated that Cumberland County settlers had abandoned nearly one thousand plantations. Settlers evacuated most of northern Lancaster, Berks, and Northampton Counties, north of the South Mountain.[43]

These figures must be viewed in perspective to comprehend their full importance. The casualties suffered by the colonies, although they may seem small in comparison to modern warfare, were significant in relation to the colonial population. The war saw nearly 1 percent of the total population of Virginia and Pennsylvania killed or captured—nearly 4 percent of the population of the backcountry counties. Such figures are comparable to those in the Revolutionary War or even the Civil War and are much higher than casualties in other "Indian wars."[44]

The war also damaged the colonial economies. Collateral damage was extensive. Raiders destroyed property, burning farms and crops, and took back to the Ohio an assorted range of booty including a substantial quantity of livestock. French reports claimed that in the summer of 1756 alone over thirteen hundred horses were driven back to the Ohio and that "the houses and barns . . . have been burnt, and the oxen and cows . . . have been killed wherever found."[45] Even in areas of the backcountry untouched by raids settlers abandoned their farms, leaving behind their crops and livestock. Philadelphia merchants who had dealings with the backcountry found their customers at best unable to pay their debts, at worst vanished or killed. By the fall of 1757 Joseph Turner claimed that many Philadelphia merchants were on the verge of bankruptcy due to the "great Losses by persons Liveing in the back parts."[46]

The war also damaged the economies of Pennsylvania and Virginia in other ways. French privateers disrupted the colonies' overseas trade. In the fall of 1756 twenty-four French privateers operating out of Guadalupe captured over sixteen British and American merchantmen. By the summer of 1757 some of these privateers had taken station off the Delaware Capes, and Philadelphia merchants complained that their waters were "Infested with French Privateers."[47] The privateers' attacks sent insurance rates soaring, and by the end of 1756 the cost of insurance alone made trade in some items unprofitable. As overseas trade declined, so did the prices that backcountry planters received for their produce. This affected planters not only in the backcountry of Pennsylvania but also in western Virginia, for the settlers of western Virginia shipped their surplus produce not to the Virginia tidewater, but to Pennsylvania. In addition, tidewater planters found their profits from the tobacco trade severely dented in the early years of the war, as drought reduced production at the same time that insurance rates increased shipping costs.[48]

These economic problems were made worse by the embargo on trade with neutral ports, imposed at the start of the war. In particular, the embargo destroyed the grain trade from Pennsylvania to southern Europe and meant that the West Indies became the British colonies' sole market. Not surprisingly, West Indian markets soon became glutted. While merchants would later ignore the embargo and smuggle cargoes to more profitable ports, in the early years of the war merchants were unwilling to chance smuggling, for they could not insure such voyages against privateers. Because of the rise in insurance rates, the loss of European markets, and the glut in the West Indies, the price of Pennsylvania produce fell steadily. In August 1755, for instance, farmers were selling flour in Philadelphia for 14s. 6d. per bushel and corn for 2s. 4d. per bushel; by the end of 1757 flour had fallen to 10s. 6d. and corn to only 1s. 6d.[49]

The Fruits of War

The Seven Years' War and the Indian raids on the backcountry caused widespread destruction in the early years of the war. However, it is easy to overlook the impact of the early stages of the war, because as well as wreaking havoc the war opened new opportunities. In many parts of America it provided a boost to the colonial economy. The demand for men and arms propped up sometimes lagging provincial economies, particularly in New England. However, it was not until 1758 that Virginia and Pennsylvania would begin to benefit from the war as the demand for military supplies picked up, with increased numbers of British troops stationed in the colonies, while the destruction of the raids simultaneously declined. Even then the benefits reaped by these colonies were fewer than those reaped by New York or the New England colonies. The account books of storekeeper John Harris reveal how the early stages of the war devastated the economy around Harris's Ferry. In 1753 and 1754 Harris was completing fourteen or fifteen major transactions a quarter. For a year following Braddock's defeat Harris made a total of only eight transactions, less than a seventh of his previous total. Only in late 1757 as British troops came into the region did Harris's business begin to recover.[50]

For other settlers, however, the war created new opportunities. For every settler who fled, another was ready to move in and occupy their land. Indeed, this is the major reason why wartime population losses are so difficult to assess. As soon as the raiders withdrew from a region, profiteers would move in. There was a multitude of new opportunities for those brave enough to venture into the backcountry. Livestock dealers, millers, and laborers all found their services in great demand. Demand from provincial and British forces caused prices for many commodities to rise steadily from 1757 onward. In the Virginia backcountry beef was selling for ten shillings per hundredweight in September 1755. By August 1760 it had reached fifty shillings. These new opportunities were crucial to the production of wartime tension. In the commercial, competitive, and individualistic environment of the backcountry, settlers scrambled for advantage. One settler's misfortune was another's good fortune. Simultaneously fearing attack and questing for profit, elements of backcountry society began to break down under the strains of war.[51]

One new opportunity was to open an "ordinary" or tavern, taking advantage of the seemingly insatiable demand of the troops for liquor. Even if settlers lacked the means to open an ordinary, they could still take liquor directly to the troops. Sutlers flocked to military encampments, with the result that there was often more liquor available than food. In the spring of 1757, although the soldiers at Fort Augusta were starving and cut off from the rest of Pennsylvania by raiding parties, sutlers still managed to smuggle large supplies of liquor to them. When soldiers had no money to purchase liquor, sutlers sold it on credit. When the men finally received their pay, the sutlers collected their debts, leaving the men penniless. Matters were particularly bad in Winchester, Virginia, the headquarters of the Virginia Regiment. Between 1754 and 1763 the county court licensed an average of fourteen ordinaries a year in and around the town. With so many opportunities for legal drinking, and even more for illegal drinking, it was little wonder that drunkenness was common among the troops. In October 1757 Washington wrote dejectedly to Governor Dinwiddie that he "cou'd give your Honor such instances of the villainous Behaviour of those Tippling-house-keeper's, as wou'd astonish any person . . . it is impossible to do that Service with a garrison thus corrupted by a sett of people, whose conduct looks like the effect of a combination to obstruct the Service."[52] To curry favor with their neighbors, local justices frequently protected those accused of selling liquor illegally. In Cumberland County, Justice Allen Gillespie even promised local residents that they would be given licenses to sell liquor to the provincial forces. Military garrisons did not provide the only opportunity for settlers to sell liquor. Conferences between the Indians and the British provided an all-too tempting chance for settlers to turn a profit. Easton in particular provided a market for the liquor trade, and colonial officials worried about the impact of drunkenness on Pennsylvania's Indian diplomacy.[53]

Pilfering military supplies provided another opportunity for profiteering. In 1756 a Maidstone merchant persuaded several men of the Virginia Regiment to provide him with flour in return for liquor. He then sold the flour back to the army. Other merchants persuaded troops to part with their clothing, equipment, and even arms in return for liquor. When not pilfering supplies, backcountry farmers and planters found other ways to profit from wartime demand. They provided sick or old animals for military service. Col. Henry Bouquet described the horses supplied to Forbes's expedition as "nags who were unable to drag themselves along," while the cattle were "small, lean, and poor as they could be."[54] Food the settlers provided was often inedible. In 1755 Thomas Cresap, one of the most respected Maryland frontiersmen, supplied Braddock's expedition with beef so rotten that it had to be buried. Of the 140 barrels of pork collected for Forbes's expedition, only 60 were fit for consumption. Even when the produce was edible, civilians might use fraudulent weights and measures. In the summer of 1758 one of the commissaries was discovered using weights that were light by 12.5 percent. Such opportunities were widespread, for soldiers demanded a wide range of supplies and services from the local inhabitants. To try to regulate such exchanges a market was established at Harris's Ferry in 1757 and another at Carlisle in 1758; settlers were allowed to sell their produce to the troops, although they were forbidden from carrying liquor to the soldiers.[55]

Even if a settler had no provisions to sell, the army needed laborers of all kinds. While Bouquet was unable to hire wagoners to haul supplies to Raystown, even though he offered fifteen shillings per day, the wagoners were only too willing to haul goods all the way to the Ohio, since their profits were greater. The army also required blacksmiths and farriers, "Carpenters, Joyners, Bricklayers, Masons, Oven Makers, Sadlers, Millrights, Coalmakers, Coopers, Tin Men, Sawyers, [and] Mealmakers," all well rewarded. It lured large numbers of camp followers who served as nurses, cooks, and washerwomen. Indeed, so great were the opportunities for these women that both provincial and regular forces were compelled to issue repeated orders limiting the number of women present in army camps and at frontier posts.[56]

However, backcountry settlers went even further than taking advantage of the presence of the army to profit from the war. Civilians also took advantage of their neighbors' misfortune. In October 1755, after the Penn's Creek raid on the northern frontier of Pennsylvania, many of the local inhabitants began "plundering the Houses, & mak[ing] the best of other people's Misfortune." Elsewhere frontiersmen even disguised themselves as Indians on occasion so that they could ransack neighboring plantations with impunity. Indian disguise could also provide other unforeseen opportunities. During 1758 several settlers successfully received presents designed for the Cherokees.[57]

The Seven Years' War opened new opportunities for those who were prepared to brave the risks of remaining in the backcountry. The decision to remain while others fled was a desperate gamble in the quest for economic advantage, and for this reason settlers paid little attention to the greater needs of the army and their province. They had gambled their very lives to move to the frontier to further their economic interests; the opposition of local justices and military commanders was not going to stop them pursuing that quest. The activities of embezzlers and profiteers merely reflect this individualism; such settlers were unable to see how their benefiting from the war could be so iniquitous. In 1756 Governor

Dinwiddie complained that the backcountry inhabitants "appear to me to endeav'r to make Money unjustly from the Distress of the Co'try." His opinions were echoed two years later by Henry Bouquet, who commented that "no one in this country can be relied on. At all times, private interests outweigh the general welfare."[58] These characteristics of individualism and the desire for self-improvement made it difficult, if not impossible, for provincial and imperial authorities to govern and control backcountry settlers. Throughout the war military and civilian officials struggled to organize defense in the backcountry yet found it difficult to bring backcountry settlers to accept any outside interference or advice that might hinder their progress. The quest for profit rapidly brought backcountry settlers into conflict with civil and military authorities who sought to maintain order and wage war as effectively as possible.

The Breakdown of Civil Authority

The tensions generated by war in the backcountry were most apparent among the elite. War threatened the influence of the backcountry elite over their local community and made it necessary for them to curry favor whenever possible. This was particularly noticeable among justices of the peace in both Virginia and Pennsylvania. Unlike the tidewater and eastern elites, the leaders of backcountry society could not create a political climate of deference in the west. In a relatively egalitarian society they lacked the wealth required to generate deference from their neighbors, and the justices' lack of personal authority made them reluctant to enforce any judicial powers they held.[59]

Because most members of the backcountry elite were not clearly differentiated from their neighbors by wealth, they had to listen to the wishes of their poorer neighbors, for they were the people who voted them into offices such as membership in the House of Burgesses, which was one route to local influence and prestige. As Dinwiddie wrote to the Board of Trade in 1756, "From the number of our Inhabitants it may be suggested that we may easily raise a pretty little Army. But the case is otherways; for most of the People are Freeholders [and] on course have votes for choosing Assembly Men."[60] Nowhere was the weakness of the local justices of the peace more obvious than in their failure to enforce unpopular wartime measures. In Virginia this meant enforcement of the draft of men from the militia into the Virginia Regiment; in Pennsylvania this meant the impressment of supplies, particularly wagons and horses, for the army.

When it became apparent in the fall of 1755 that insufficient volunteers would be forthcoming to fill the ranks of the Virginia Regiment, the Virginia House of Burgesses ordered local justices of the peace to draft men from the militia until the required number was met. In the spring of 1756 the House of Burgesses tightened the conditions for drafting men from the militia. Aware that many justices were refusing to enforce the law, the House authorized fines of up to five hundred pounds for refractory officials and closed various loopholes that had allowed justices to exempt certain men, most notably those they described as slave overseers, justices defining such "overseers" as anyone owning slaves. In many counties justices simply refused to enforce the draft. When finally compelled to draft men, those they drafted were generally vagrants and other undesirables who had no link to the county. Indeed, this was a principal reason for the weakness of the Virginia Regiment in the early years of the war. Justices were constantly compelled to make decisions about whether to prosecute their neighbors under these laws. Between 1755 and 1762, for instance, 675 men from Frederick County were charged with 1,330 separate offenses relating to military service.[61]

Pennsylvania justices were not compelled to draft men into the armed forces but were supposed to encourage men to enlist into both the provincial and regular forces. However, one Pennsylvania justice even went as far as actively discouraging all men brought before him from enlisting in the Royal American Regiment. Whereas in Virginia justices failed to cooperate in the war effort by refusing to draft men, in Pennsylvania justices refused to impress supplies or offered terms far better than those offered by military commanders. Military operations in the colony were severely hampered by the refusal of justices to provide transportation. In 1755 General Braddock found it almost impossible to acquire wagons. Only Benjamin Franklin's timely intervention assured that his expedition was able to move its men and supplies. Gen. John Forbes's expedition in 1758 found it equally impossible to acquire transportation. Only repeated solicitations, and the ability to offer inflated prices, enabled the expedition to move. In addition, Pennsylvania justices found a new way to circumvent the direct wrath of their neighbors; they would simply offer them much better terms for their goods and wagons than military officers had authorized. When military commanders refused to pay the terms the settlers had been offered, they blamed the officers and not their local justices. Henry Bouquet became particularly aware of such practices in Pennsylvania. After he discovered leading Pennsylvanian Edward Shippen participating in such a scheme, he wrote ruefully to General Forbes that "the truth of all this is that everyone wishes to be popular, and build his career at the expense of the government."[62]

The elite's failure to engender support for the war went far beyond justices refusing to draft men and impress supplies. Local civil authorities played a major role in consolidating frontier resistance to military authority and in protecting civilians from retribution from military authorities. Indeed, the primary reason for the military's complete failure to suppress the illegal liquor trade was that the civil courts refused to prosecute offenders, while the military authorities had no right to take direct action against civilians. When there was a direct conflict between civil and military authority, justices almost universally gave precedence to civil authority. In 1758 county justices in York County, Pennsylvania, arrested some troops in Forbes's army for brawling with civilians. When their commanders attempted to obtain their release for the campaign against Fort Duquesne with the promise that the army would punish them, the York County justices refused to release them and held them for a civil trial.[63]

Civil and military authority most frequently clashed when military authorities attempted to halt the widespread profiteering and pilfering that seemed to swallow up much of the military effort. When military authorities attempted to stop the pilfering of supplies, local justices routinely refused to issue warrants allowing them to search private homes and storehouses. When pressed to issue warrants, many magistrates warned merchants that their premises were going to be searched, allowing them ample opportunity to dispose of any illegal supplies. County justices refused to draft men, to punish deserters, to impress needed equipment and supplies, and to enforce military authority over civilians. Some even offered to defend deserters in court. Perhaps the most notorious incident occurred when George Washington discovered John Hamilton, the Virginia Regiment's quartermaster general, selling provincial supplies to the residents of Winchester. Washington immediately sought permission to search the cellars and warehouses of several of the local merchants who were believed to have been in cahoots with Hamilton. He approached the local justices—including Thomas Swearingen, who had defeated him in the campaign for burgess of Frederick County in December 1755—for search warrants. However, the justices examined several witnesses but refused to proceed any further. Eventually Washington was able to obtain a warrant from another local justice, Thomas Speake, probably because Speake himself had sought a commission in the Virginia Regiment.[64] But now the constable, Thomas Wood, refused to execute the search warrant. No one in the town would assist in the search. Eventually a local merchant, Alexander Wood, volunteered to assist Washington; several houses were finally searched and many of the missing items recovered. This was still not the end of the affair, however. The culprits were brought before Justice Speake. Fearful of the popular reaction if he was severe to the culprits and of Washington's reaction if he was lenient, he refused to act without the presence of Justice Swearingen. Finally, the two justices decided that the culprits could only be tried at the next session of the county court, several weeks away. Washington was horrified: they did not demand bail from the suspects or make any attempt to stop them from leaving town. In disgust, Washington wrote to Dinwiddie that it was "impossible to maintain that discipline and do that Service with . . . the Laws made for the punishment of such gross offences, trifled with by the Majistrates." The only remedy he suggested was ordering "those majistrates to be brought to Justice, and appointing others from whom more can be hoped."[65]

In many ways the activities of the justices of the peace reflected the broader sentiments of both backcountry society and provincial society as a whole. In both Virginia and Pennsylvania there was a surprisingly strong current of antimilitary feeling. Especially in Pennsylvania, relations between the military and civilians were often very tense. When Henry Bouquet arrived in Philadelphia in December 1756, he reported that "while entering the city on horseback at the head of the battalion, a farmer rogue mounted on a nag lashed at me with his whip, which missed me fortunately for him. He was at once beaten up and taken to prison." Bouquet added that the incident by itself was not particularly remarkable but that it was "the third incident of this kind to occur." Bouquet for his part denounced the civilian population of Pennsylvania as "riff-raff" and added, "I hope we shall succeed in inspiring them with fear of the red coats. Everything most abominable that nature has produced, and everything most detestable that corruption can add to it, such are the honest inhabitants of this province."[66]

Conflict was most apparent when civilians and troops were in close quarters. When civilians worked alongside provincial or regular forces, they were subject to martial law, yet attempts to compel civilians to obey army officers proved impossible. In 1757 a party of Pennsylvania bateau-men was drawn into conflict with Lt. James Hyndshaw of the Pennsylvania Regiment, who was commanding a convoy up the Susquehanna River. The bateau-men abused Hyndshaw and "shewed a very mutinous Turbulent Behaviour." They quarreled with the Pennsylvania troops who accompanied them and at night were "noisy & troublesome till near twelve O'clock."[67] Such scenes were repeated across the Virginia and Pennsylvania backcountry. Where troops and civilians were crowded cheek by jowl into small blockhouses, tensions often became violent, frequently occasioned by a night of heavy drinking in a local tavern.

At one Pennsylvania fort the commander was drawn into an altercation between two women. When he begged the women to calm down, one turned her attention to him instead. He ordered his sergeant to "bring in some of the Guard, to take her to the Guard House." However, the soldiers "did not yearn to use force" on an old woman. The woman's son now intervened and tried to drag his screaming mother away from the troops. Fuming at their inaction, the officer "damned his men, and said he would sho[o]t a Bullet through their Body, if they would not obey him immediately, and take the said Woman to the Guard House." Eventually the two women escaped from the fort and took shelter in a neighbor's house.[68] Such altercations were not unusual, but not all civilians had such lucky escapes. In Fredericksburg, Virginia, Thomas Frazier, a Maryland post rider, was killed in a brawl with a soldier of the Virginia Regiment. And sometimes these disputes went much further than brawls. In Winchester in 1757 Mary Hinch testified that William Coffland, a soldier in the Virginia Regiment, in the middle of the night "came into her House while she was asleep & came to her Bed & waked her & said that he must have Part of her Bed." When she attempted to throw Coffland out of her house, "he abus'd her much, refus'd to quit the House & said that he wou'd abuse her much more tomorrow Night."[69]

Close quarters almost inevitably drew settlers and troops into conflict. In New England such conflict occurred between civilians and regular troops stationed in their towns, or between provincial troops serving alongside the regular army and regular troops. However, few provincial or regular forces were permanently stationed in New England, for they campaigned in the Hudson Valley or Nova Scotia. In Virginia and Pennsylvania provincial and regular troops were stationed in the backcountry alongside civilians for most of the war, and the conflicts were as often between provincial troops and backcountry inhabitants as between regular troops and civilians. Consequently, these disputes cannot be dismissed as simply a result of dislike of the haughty behavior of regular troops, or of British misunderstanding of colonial conditions; they stemmed from a deeper animosity.

Backcountry settlers did have very tangible reasons to dislike the provincial troops stationed in their midst. Like their civilian neighbors, troops sometimes made use of the confusion on the frontier to acquire abandoned property. The horses and cattle at deserted plantations offered a particularly tempting opportunity. Civilians repeatedly complained that the garrison at Fort Augusta was pilfering their cattle and horses. In the fall of 1756 several settlers claimed that the garrison "dishonourably drove from their Walks . . . a Number of Horses & Mares said to belong to the poor Scatter'd Inhabitants."[70] Not only did provincial forces make use of the chaos of war to acquire property from abandoned plantations, but on occasion they plundered occupied farms and homesteads. In October 1755 Washington received several complaints about his troops "pilaging and plundering . . . Houses" on "all the Roads they have marched."[71] The following year he received further complaints "from the people that the Soldiers plunder and rob their Gardens, and destroy their Fowls, & every thing they can lay their hands on." Matters were no better in Pennsylvania. During the winter of 1757 troops in Northampton County, short of provisions, took to attacking the local inhabitants to force them to provide supplies.[72]

Conflict between military authorities and civilians also had much deeper causes than the close quarters in which troops and civilians found themselves. There were two issues that in particular generated discord between the military and civilians: quartering and the impressment of supplies and wagons. Military authorities failed to comprehend the roots of the conflict between military and civilian officials. American colonists demanded the right to be treated as full British citizens, yet there were no British precedents to guide the conduct of war among a civilian population. Britain had not seen a major foreign invasion since 1066, and only during the Civil War in the mid-seventeenth century had civilians been in close contact with campaigning armies. The only near parallel was in the Highlands of Scotland following the Jacobite Uprisings of 1715 and 1745, but here the members of the local population were viewed as rebels, and there were few scruples about imposing military authority. Elsewhere in Britain the government had not been forced to resolve problems of impressing supplies and equipment. Troops could be lodged in barracks without inconvenience; supplies could be obtained from contractors without dispute.[73] In the backcountry of Virginia and Pennsylvania this was far from being the case. The recalcitrance of the settlers infuriated Braddock, Washington, Bouquet, and Forbes. However, to backcountry settlers the demands of the army seemed unreasonable.

The quartering of troops remained an issue that could not be resolved. When Dunbar retreated to "winter quarters" in Philadelphia in August 1755, the assembly extended the clauses of the British Mutiny Act relating to quartering to Pennsylvania. However, the city refused to provide them with quarters, stressing that the British Mutiny Act expressly gave civilians the right "to refuse to quarter any soldier or soldiers, notwithstanding any demand, warrant or billeting whatsoever." Only the removal of Dunbar's force to New York resolved the problem. However, the issue did not totally disappear, for in July 1756 the Pennsylvania act was ruled unconstitutional. Quite specifically, the Crown ruled that the rights of British citizens did not apply in the colonies during time of war.[74] This ruling was to cause many future disputes.

The arrival of regular troops in Pennsylvania in the fall of 1756 raised the issue once more. Many of the British troops were sick with smallpox, but the colony refused to provide them with barracks. Initially the assembly sought to quarter the troops in taverns, but there was insufficient space. For several weeks the assembly and governor squabbled over where the troops should be billeted, while the troops endured weather so cold that the Delaware River froze. However, the assembly still demanded that all men be billeted in inns and taverns. In desperation Henry Bouquet wrote: "These gentlemen know just as well as we do, that these houses absolutely cannot admit and lodge all these men. . . . In such weather it is cruel to encounter such poor hosts." With both sides at loggerheads there were soon rumors that Bouquet intended forcibly to billet the troops on the city's inhabitants. Although the assembly eventually relented and allowed the troops to be billeted in the city's hospital before completion of barracks in the city, the scene had been set for future conflicts with the civilian population over quartering.[75]

Lancaster and Cumberland Counties in Pennsylvania were also centers of opposition to quartering of both provincial and regular forces. In 1757 backcountry settlers complained to Governor William Denny that Conrad Weiser was billeting provincial troops in their farmhouses and barns, even though these troops were being used to protect the very farms in which they were quartered. On returning from Forbes's campaign on the Ohio, British and provincial troops were disgusted to find that there were no quarters available for them. They pressured the magistrates of Lancaster and Cumberland Counties to provide winter quarters. When they refused the officers resorted to "Menaces and other illegal Methods to extort Billets . . . for Quartering Soldiers on Private Houses, but failing of their Purpose have proceeded to open Violence, and thereby forced Numbers of his Majesty's Troops into the Dwelling Houses of the Inhabitants, taking their Beds and other Necessaries from them for the use of the Soldiers." When Governor Denny complained to Gen. Jeffrey Amherst, he merely replied, "If . . . the Magistrates refused them Billets, they could not do less than make their Quarters good, which is an old Practice wherever the seat of War lies."[76] Matters were little better in Virginia, where the Virginia Regiment was forced to billet some of its troops among the townspeople in Winchester in particular, but also at other remote settlements. The quartering of troops among civilians generated much tension, caused not least by the behavior of the troops. In Virginia Jesse Pugh complained to Washington that the troops billeted at his plantation had "killed his Fowls, pulled down one of his Houses for firewood; turned the Horses into his Meadow and corn; destroyed them and his Fences."[77]

If the quartering of troops was one issue where local justices refused to support military authorities, the impressment of supplies was another. Throughout the war it proved very difficult to acquire the wagons and draft animals needed to transport supplies to the west. Braddock's decision to march his army over the Appalachians with a full supply train drained the backcountry of horses and wagons. Over the next three years military authorities made repeated attempts to acquire desperately needed supplies, but the local justices repeatedly hindered their activities. When Conrad Weiser attempted to impress wagons in Lancaster County, one of the local justices questioned Weiser's authority. He asked if Weiser "was an Officer of the Army? Where is your Contract with the General? What Authority have you to demand Waggons?" He then snatched the impressment order and threw it on the floor.[78]

Both Pennsylvania and Virginia passed laws compelling justices of the peace to assist officers in impressing wagons and horses for the western campaigns. However, justices frequently refused to compel their neighbors to hand over their wagons. Consequently, officers became increasingly irritated. During Forbes's campaign officers were accused of behavior that "terrified, abused, and Insulted the Inhabitants."[79] Bouquet berated the local justices, saying that "by want of Sufficient numbers of Carriages, I am obliged to Stay here, and to . . . [waste] a precious time, that I could employ in Securing our Frontiers; This is very hard for me, and I do not know how your People will answer for the Consequences."[80] Officers such as Bouquet made the greatest noise about their inability to impress supplies, but officers of the provincial regiments faced the same problems. In Virginia Washington complained that he was compelled to resort to force to acquire supplies for the Virginia Regiment, for "without this, a Single horse, for the most urgent occasion cannot be had, to such a pitch has the insolence of these People arriv'd."[81]

Washington begged Dinwiddie to increase military authority over civilians in order to enable him to counter the Indian onslaught. In October 1755 the governor approached the House of Burgesses seeking to increase military authority. He complained bitterly to the house "of the great Obstruct's given to the Service by many of the Magistrates and other civil Officers, some of whom have even given Protect'n to those who have shamefully deserted with their Arms . . . and others with an unparrallel'd and most criminal Undutifulness to their Country have discouraged and prevented the Enlist'g [of] Men, tho' to protect themselves." Much to Dinwiddie's surprise, however, the House of Burgesses refused to increase military authority. Dinwiddie thus resorted to issuing new commissions of the peace, attempting to dismiss those justices he felt were most at fault for the collapse of civilian authority. However, the new justices proved no more compliant than their forebears.[82]

The pressures of war revealed the weakness of the elite's authority in the backcountry. Whether impressing supplies, finding wagons or quarters, or prosecuting embezzlers and sutlers, the backcountry elite refused to support either the provincial or regular forces over their neighbors.

The enforcement of order had all but broken down in the backcountry. In despair Washington complained to Dinwiddie that "no orders are obey'd but what a Party of Soldiers, or my own drawn Sword Enforces."[83]

Social and Ethnic Conflict

The war in the backcountry generated deep conflicts between civilian authorities and the military, whether the British army or provincial forces, but it also generated a crisis within civilian society. Faced with demands for action from Whitehall, Williamsburg, and Philadelphia, the backcountry elite were forced to impose unpopular measures on their neighbors. When justices refused to enforce these measures, it was not always simply because they "wished to be popular" but because they feared for their social position and in some cases their lives. Backcountry settlers often responded with violence to attempts to impose outside order on their society. This violence expressed itself most clearly at election time. The elections for the Virginia House of Burgesses in 1755 and for the Pennsylvania Assembly in 1756 witnessed often violent disputes over the conduct of the war. Washington himself was attacked with a club at the polls in Fairfax County in December 1755 and was decisively beaten in the election in Frederick County, gaining only 40 votes, compared to over 270 for the winning candidates, one of whom Washington later dismissively referred to as "a man of great weight among the meaner class of people."[84] The largest riot came during the 1755 election in Augusta County when the local sheriff refused to let votes be cast. The courthouse was soon reduced to a shambles as backcountry settlers—including, even led by, members of the local gentry—brawled in public. In the same month in Pennsylvania a mob of seven hundred settlers from Lancaster County descended on Philadelphia demanding protection and denouncing the assembly's refusal to compromise with the governor.[85]

In some ways these conflicts could be regarded as class conflicts. The Seven Years' War generated clear tensions between the elite and the "middling" and "lower sort." However, in most ways these conflicts cannot be considered true class conflicts. Only the elite seemed to demonstrate a clear sense of their social status in their attempts to separate themselves from the remainder of society. There is little evidence that small farmers saw themselves as being different in any substantial way from their wealthier elite neighbors. Indeed, the development of any class consciousness in the backcountry was inhibited by the very deep ethnic and religious divisions that existed in backcountry society. Backcountry small-holders simply did not see themselves as a class apart.[86]

The Seven Years' War served to heighten the existing ethnic and religious tensions that divided society. This development was most apparent in Pennsylvania, where Conrad Weiser wrote, "There is always some National Jealousy among the meaner Sort of people."[87] Even before the outbreak of war many Pennsylvanians had felt uneasy at the presence of so many non-British and non-Protestant settlers in the colony. With the threat of war on the frontier looming, some Pennsylvanians, not surprisingly, questioned the loyalty of their German and Roman Catholic Irish neighbors. William Smith, in his bitter invective on the progress of the war in Pennsylvania, *A Brief State of the Province of Pennsylvania,* dismissed the Germans as no more than a "Body of ignorant, proud, stubborn Clowns."[88] Smith and Benjamin Franklin both proposed the curtailment of the liberties enjoyed by Pennsylvania's German population, most notably the right to vote in the provincial elections, unless they were fluent in English. Smith went even further, demanding that "all Bonds, Contracts, Wills, and other legal Writings [be declared] void, unless in the *English* Tongue" and that "no News-Papers, Almanacks, or any other periodical Paper, by whatever Name it may be called, be printed or circulated in a foreign Language."[89] While attempts to legislate against the Germans failed, Franklin and Smith did found a society for establishing English schools among the Germans. The society received substantial support from the proprietors and their supporters, who hoped that if the Germans were properly instructed they would "be capable of using their own judgment in matters of Government . . . [and] would no more be misled by Acts of a Quaker preacher."[90] Not surprisingly, both the Quakers and the Germans generally opposed the society; its actions may have even served to cement relations between the Quakers and the Germans.

While some Pennsylvanians were concerned about the Germans, the Germans themselves complained bitterly about the Irish Catholics who lived in their midst. At the start of the war Conrad Weiser persuaded the justices of Berks County to petition the assembly to disarm all Catholics living among them. The justices maintained that "all our protestant Inhabitants are very uneasy at the Behaviour of the Roman Catholicks, who are very numerous in this County. . . . We know that the People of the Roman Catholic Church are bound by their Principles to be the worst

Subjects and Worst of Neighbours." So great was the paranoia of these justices that they even believed that their Catholic neighbors were traveling to Fort Duquesne to supply the French with important intelligence.[91]

As the war progressed, the Quakers became the focus for opposition in the colony. In particular, they were accused of hampering all the colony's defense measures. Governor Morris claimed that the assembly's reluctance to provide for Pennsylvania's defense was solely due to the Quakers. He maintained that "all the Quaker preachers and others of great weight were employed to shew in their publick Sermons, & by going from House to House through the Province the sin of taking up Arms."[92] Many backcountry settlers soon turned against local Quakers. A report from Reading in November 1755 declared, "The people exclaim against the Quakers, & some are scarce restrained from burning the Houses of those few who are in This Town."[93]

Because of these deep divisions, members of different ethnic and religious groups were often reluctant to fight alongside each other. Edward Shippen wrote that in Lancaster in October 1755 the local German population immediately formed their own defense bands and set out to join their fellow countryman Conrad Weiser. As the war progressed, tensions between different groups in Pennsylvania grew worse. In August 1756 mutiny broke out at Fort Allen when troops from the German and Irish companies stationed there refused to rank with each other. These tensions extended beyond the rank and file to the officers and were so great that German captain Jacob Orndt and an Irish lieutenant ended up in a violent brawl. Orndt was quite clear of the cause: the lieutenant was a "wery heard Roman Catholic." Capt. George Reynolds wrote in his defense that Orndt was "using his utmost Endevour to make things worse on the Lieutenant's Side than it is."[94] Five months later Reynolds and Orndt were themselves involved in a bitter squabble. Orndt accused Reynolds and his men of being a "Company [of] Dirty Idle [fellows]" and maintained that when he was posted to Fort Allen he "found it something nasty, at least not so clean as they used to keep Fort Norris." Ethnic tensions also surfaced at Fort Granville and may have played an important role in hastening the fort's capture by a raiding party in August 1756.[95]

Because of these repeated disputes, Pennsylvania commanders found it easier to keep different ethnic groups apart, and Pennsylvania forces were at least partially segregated by ethnicity. These tensions were to some extent recognized by the British army. The creation of the Royal American Regiment in 1756 was designed specifically to diffuse some problems by allowing foreigners to serve in the regular army under their own foreign officers. As soon as the regiment was created, German officers were sent to try and drum up recruits in Lancaster County.[96] In Virginia ethnic tensions were less divisive, in part because there were fewer Germans and Irish Catholics in the colony's backcountry than in Pennsylvania. This does not mean that such ethnic tensions did not exist. Indeed, upon hearing of the creation of the Royal American Regiment, Governor Dinwiddie commented, "I much fear the Provincials will be very uneasy to be Com'd'd by Foreigners and [there will be] great Difficult's in recruit'g."[97] After some reflection he added, "W't they may do in Pensylvania, where [there] are many Germans, I know not, but here we have very few foreigners, and I have found it difficult to raise Men under the Off's appointed by me."[98] Indeed, he wrote to Lord Loudoun suggesting that only British officers should be sent to recruit in Virginia explicitly because the colony held so few foreigners.[99] This does not mean that the German population of the Virginia backcountry was immune from suspicions during the war. Indeed, they were widely suspected of providing information and supplies to the raiding parties.

In particular, the "Dunker" settlement of Germans Samuel, Joel, and Gabriel Eckerlin was suspected of providing the raiders with intelligence and supplies.[100] Washington wrote to Dinwiddie in the fall of 1756 that he believed "that the Dunkers (who are all Doctors) entertain the Indians who are wounded here."[101] After they had been under suspicion for several years, in the fall of 1757 Dinwiddie finally sent orders to Washington that "as the Peopl are uneasy with them, believing th'm to be Spies, it was resolv'd you Should send a Party out to bring [them] in . . . with their Cattle and Horses and every thing they have that they can conveniently bring with th'm."[102]

Virginia's small Quaker population, located mainly in the Shenandoah Valley, also found itself the target of much hostility. In part, this stemmed from the refusal of the Quakers to serve in the militia. Because of their refusal to partake in any military activity, even when offered work on the defenses of Winchester and other frontier posts, some Quakers suffered the worse fate of being drafted out of the militia into the Virginia Regiment. When they refused to obey orders, Washington had them confined to the jail in Winchester.[103] Despite Washington's threats, "they chose rather to be whipped to death than bear arms, or lend us any assistance whatever upon the Fort, or any thing of self-defence."[104] Only when their neighbors sent a deputation to Dinwiddie in Williamsburg, "pray'g they may not be whipped," was Washington finally persuaded to relent and free them.[105]

THE BREAKDOWN of civil society and civil authority in Virginia and Pennsylvania during the Seven Years' War was notable. The wartime experience of the region was quite different from that of other regions of North America, in particular New England. In New England the primary tensions of war were seen in conflict between the provincial forces and British regulars and did not threaten the social order in the region. In Virginia and Pennsylvania the widespread conflict between provincial forces and civilians cannot be dismissed as anti-British sentiment or as opposition to standing armies. More importantly, discontent permeated civil society. The pressures of war divided backcountry society in particular and revealed the deep fissures within backcountry communities. While the war did not generate true class conflict, perhaps because of deep ethnic and religious divisions, it did generate other equally divisive tensions. In particular, it revealed and heightened the competitive nature of backcountry society. By simultaneously threatening the lives of backcountry settlers and opening new prospects for advancement, it created a ferment of competition. Gentlemen competed for commissions in the militia and the army; farmers competed for lands abandoned by their former occupants and for lucrative contracts with the army; laborers and tenants sought higher wages through auxiliary service in the army or enlisting in the provincial forces or regular army. At the same time all settlers were engaged in the ultimate competition: the quest to stay alive when raiding parties descended on the region to wreak havoc and mayhem.

"Henry Bouquet receiving captives from the Ohio Indians," from Benjamin
West print. Benjamin West was born in Pennsylvania in 1738 and was resident
in the colony for much of the Seven Years' War before departing for Europe
in 1759. This engraving was published to illustrate *An Historical Account of the Expedition against the Ohio Indians in the Year 1764. Courtesy of The Trustees of the National Library
of Scotland.*

"Henry Bouquet negotiating with the Ohio Indians," from Benjamin West print. West was perhaps most popularly known for his 1771 depiction of the death of Gen. James Wolfe and for his realistic portrayals of Indians, for which he assembled collections of artifacts to use as studio props. This engraving, completed a few years earlier, shows West's interpretation of Indian diplomacy in the Ohio Valley. *Courtesy of The Trustees of the National Library of Scotland.*

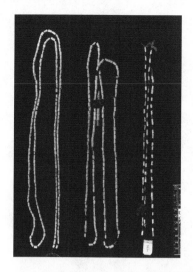

Wampum strings, eighteenth century. Eastern woodland Indians. These wampum strings are typical of those exchanged as part of the protocol of eighteenth-century Indian diplomacy. The acquisition of wampum beads for conferences on the Pennsylvania frontier was one of the major activities of the Quaker Friendly Association. *© Copyright The British Museum.*

Wampum belt, eighteenth century. Eastern woodland Indians. Such belts of wampum were typically used to convey important messages from one Indian village to another or to symbolize a historic agreement or treaty. The belts were constructed of many strings of small cylindrical beads. The black beads were made from the shell of the quahog clam, and the white beads from univalve whelks. *© Copyright The British Museum.*

Eighteenth-century Delaware pipe tomahawks. Pipe tomahawks were manufactured by Europeans for Indian use in both war and peace making. Their function was both practical—they could be used to kill an enemy—and symbolic. In West's "Henry Bouquet negotiating . . ." an Indian at the bottom right can be seen smoking a pipe tomahawk. *© Copyright The British Museum.*

Tiscohan, by Gustavus Hesselius. Delaware headman of the 1730s. Tiscohan was one of the Delaware headmen involved in the negotiations that surrounded the Walking Purchase of 1737. His dress is typical of a Delaware headman of this period. *Courtesy of The Historical Society of Pennsylvania Collection, Atwater Kent Museum of Philadelphia.*

Iroquois warrior, eighteenth century. From *Encyclopédie des Voyages,* by J. Grasset. This engraving, probably from the late eighteenth century, reflects the Iroquois' combination of traditional warfare, reflected in the wooden club in the warrior's right hand, and European warfare, signified by the gun—possibly a rifle—slung over his shoulder. Although they were fearsome warriors in the seventeenth century, by the eighteenth century it was their diplomatic skill that preserved Iroquois influence in Indian affairs.

"An Indian of ye Outawas Tribe & his Family going to War," by George Townshend, fourth Viscount and first Marquess Townshend. George Townshend was renowned in Britain for his caricatures of leading members of British society. He accompanied Gen. James Wolfe on the 1759 expedition that captured Quebec, where he completed this sketch of an Ottawa warrior and his family. This sketch reveals a British officer's view of Indian warriors. *By courtesy of the National Portrait Gallery, London.*

Northeastern woodlands Indian scalp. This is a photograph of an eighteenth-century scalp dried and stretched on a wooden hoop. After stretching, the scalp was painted red with a face, now barely visible, perhaps reflecting the person from whom it was taken. The scalping of victims was a traditional element of Indian warfare. However, the Seven Years' War saw combat on both sides become more brutal as Indians on occasion deliberately mutilated their victims' bodies to spread terror and provincial authorities offered scalp bounties to encourage colonists to take up arms. © *Copyright The British Museum.*

Canadian militiaman, by Henri Beau. This twentieth-century depiction of a Canadian militiaman in the Seven Years' War reflects the ways in which Canadians, more than any other troops of European descent, adapted their uniform to suit frontier conditions. Canadian militia on occasion even accompanied Indian raiding parties as they crossed the backcountry of Virginia and Pennsylvania. *Beau, Henri / National Archives of Canada / C-000630.*

"Officer and Serjeant of a Highland Regiment," from *Military Antiquites,* by Francis Grose. This late eighteenth-century depiction shows the uniform of a soldier serving in a Highland regiment. Highland troops formed a major part of Gen. John Forbes's army in 1758. Forbes and Henry Bouquet both admired their ability to traverse difficult terrain, and they often formed the basis of raiding and skirmishing parties, such as the one led by Maj. James Grant against Fort Duquesne. *Courtesy of The Trustees of the National Library of Scotland.*

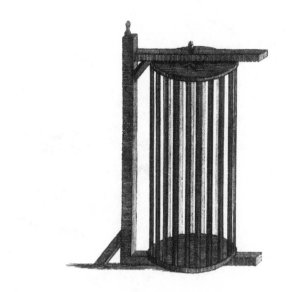

"Military Punishments," from *Military Antiquities*, by Francis Grose. The British army had numerous forms of punishment for recalcitrant troops, most of which made it easier to inflict a brutal flogging. Such forms of punishment were also often adopted by the provincial forces as they struggled to maintain discipline in their ranks. Punishments that were both painful and humiliating, such as straddling the horse, were especially popular. *Courtesy of The Trustees of the National Library of Scotland.*

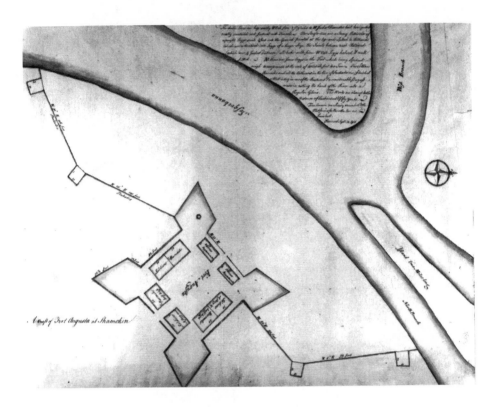

The Plan of Fort Augusta. Fort Augusta was one of the largest, and perhaps the most important, of Pennsylvania's provincial forts, guarding the junction of the east and west branches of the Susquehanna River. Its plan is representative of many of the larger provincial and British forts constructed along the frontier. *Courtesy of The Historical Society of Pennsylvania.* The Plan of Fort Augusta, *Logan Family Papers, Box 359.*

George Washington. Charles Wilson Peale engraving. An engraving of
the earliest known portrait of George Washington, painted in 1772.
Washington played a crucial role in shaping the development of the
Virginia Regiment; in turn his experiences during the Seven Years' War
made him uniquely qualified to command the Continental Army two
decades later. *Courtesy of The Virginia Historical Society, Richmond, Virginia.*

Robert Dinwiddie, 1693–1770. This portrait by an unknown artist depicts
Scotsman Robert Dinwiddie. Dinwiddie was already an experienced colonial
administrator before he became governor of Virginia in 1751. During his tenure
in office he played an instrumental role in shaping Virginia's policy toward
the Ohio Valley and in directing the colony's affairs in the early portion of the
Seven Years' War. His support for Washington was important in launching the
latter's career, although by 1757, when Dinwiddie left the colony, their relationship had become more strained. *Courtesy of The Virginia Historical Society, Richmond, Virginia.*

Sir William Johnson, by C. Spooner after T. Adams. Johnson's pride in acquiring his title is reflected in his pose in this 1756 portrait. From 1755 onward he served as superintendent of northern Indian affairs and jealously guarded his position. His attempts to enhance his status and to maintain his special relationship with the Iroquois often brought him into conflict with Pennsylvania and caused the Delawares to look upon him with particular distrust. *By courtesy of the National Portrait Gallery, London.*

Sir Jeffrey Amherst, 1717–97. During the early 1760s Sir Jeffrey Amherst directed British policy in the upper Ohio Valley. His attempts to limit the costs of Indian diplomacy, necessitated by the parsimony of Whitehall but also driven by his own view of the Ohio Indians, would dash hopes for peace in the region. This image shows him in a classical pose with a suit of armor, perhaps reflecting his own notion of the role of a military commander. *Courtesy of The Virginia Historical Society, Richmond, Virginia.*

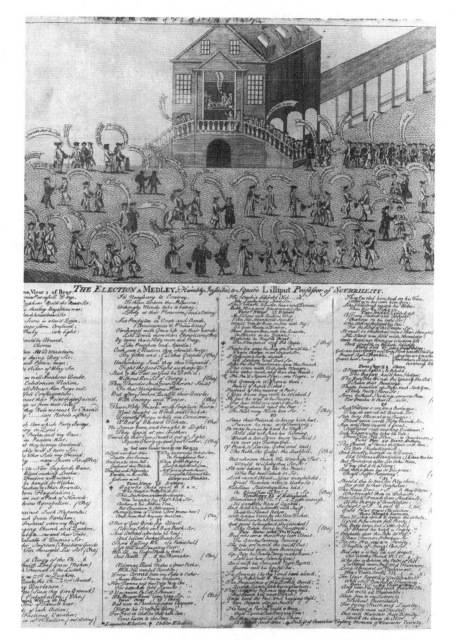

"The election, a Medley Humbly Inscribed . . . ," probably after Henry Dawkins. This depiction of the Paxton Boys and the election of 1764 reflects the disorder into which Pennsylvania politics and society were thrown by the pressures of the Seven Years' War and Pontiac's Uprising. *Courtesy of The Library Company of Philadelphia.*

The first house in Bethlehem. The Moravians were one of the first groups to commence settlement of Pennsylvania's northern frontier. This engraving depicts one of the earliest structures in Bethlehem and is typical of much German domestic architecture of the northern Pennsylvania frontier. *Courtesy of the Moravian Archives, Bethlehem.*

4

"An Extream Bad Collection Of Broken Innkeepers, Horse Jockeys, & Indian Traders"

The Provincial Forces

THE SOCIAL UNREST THAT PERMEATED THE VIRGINIA AND Pennsylvania backcountry during the Seven Years' War stemmed, at least in part, from the failure of the provincial forces to protect the region. Backcountry settlers fumed at the inactivity of the Virginia militia and the Virginia and Pennsylvania Regiments. They were not alone in disparaging the military effectiveness of these forces. When reviewing the Virginia and Pennsylvania forces who had assembled under his command in the summer of 1758, British general John Forbes derided the provincial officers as "an extream bad Collection of broken Innkeepers, Horse Jockeys, & Indian traders." The ranks, he maintained, were even worse, no more than "a gathering from the scum of the worst of people in every Country, who . . . are more infamous cowards, than any other race of mankind."[1] Forbes's comments were extreme and reflect the frustration and ethnocentricity of a British officer. However, there is also a grain of truth to them. The social status of the provincial forces in Virginia and Pennsylvania was very different from that of other provincial forces, notably those of New England, and this would influence the conduct of the war.

When war came to the backcountry of Virginia and Pennsylvania in 1755, it came to a region that had witnessed little previous conflict. Since Bacon's Rebellion in 1676 and the Iroquois victory over the Susquehannocks in the following year, there had been little warfare in the region.[2] Virginia had had little contact with its Indian neighbors following Bacon's Rebellion, while Pennsylvania's leaders had, at least initially, attempted to pursue an equitable relationship with their neighbors and had avoided the conflict that so often dominated the early settlement of other colonies. Because of these long years of peace, unlike the New England colonies, which had witnessed repeated conflicts with both their French and Indian neighbors and consequently had something of a martial tradition, neither Virginia nor Pennsylvania was equipped to wage war. The Virginia militia, which had been honed into the colony's principal defense force in the seventeenth century, had by the middle of the eighteenth century become more of a social institution than a military force. The pacifist Quaker founders of Pennsylvania did not even feel the need to establish a militia to defend the colony, which remained without any form of defense force from its founding until the Seven Years' War. For both Virginia and Pennsylvania, creating, recruiting, and maintaining provincial armies would prove a major task.[3]

The Failure of the Militia

Virginians initially expected the militia to form the backbone of their defense. At the beginning of the war Governor Robert Dinwiddie mustered the militia and ordered the companies to engage incoming raiding parties and protect the frontier from attack. However, the militia soon proved itself inadequate for such a demanding task. Eighteenth-century militia musters had become social events rather than opportunities for inculcating military discipline. Local gentry sought ranks in the militia as a symbol of their social status, rather than as an opportunity for proving their martial prowess. Consequently, county militia captains were reluctant to risk their lives during Indian assaults. During the first major raid on the Virginia frontier, in October 1755, one militia commander refused to summon his troops, maintaining "that his Wife, Family and Corn were at Stake, so were those of his Soldiers, therefore it was not possible for him to come."[4] When Dinwiddie ordered the Frederick County militia to protect their county from Indian raids, they too refused to muster, causing Dinwiddie to lament that he had "found the Militia were a cowardly People, or seiz'd with such Pannick as not to resist the Insults of the Enemy."[5]

On occasions when the militia could be persuaded to muster, it neither hurried to its station nor remained in service for any length of time. In the summer of 1755 one detachment took twenty-two days to march six miles. As the militia normally expected to be on duty for only one month at a time, when units arrived at their posts they often felt that they had served long enough and would disband immediately. In May 1756, for example, Dinwiddie called up the northern Virginia militia to defend Frederick and Hampshire Counties against an intense Indian attack. Many of the men deserted en route. The few who arrived at their post refused to serve any longer, claiming that they had done their duty merely by marching to the frontier. On several occasions entire militia companies decided that they had served a sufficient time and abandoned their posts, leaving important positions unmanned. Similarly, the militia refused to march out of their home counties. The Frederick County militia refused to march into Hampshire County, even though raiders were passing through Hampshire to get to Frederick. The House of Burgesses further increased the difficulty by specifying that the militia could not march more than five miles beyond the furthest settled part of the colony, a restriction that prevented it from garrisoning the advanced frontier posts.[6]

Even if the militia could be marched to the scene of an attack, it still proved of little use. Because the militia was largely untrained, the men lacked basic military proficiency. British officers had presumed that backcountry settlers would possess important skills that would make them good soldiers. However, despite the myth of the backcountry woodsman, or the importance of "gun culture" in early America, most backcountry settlers did not make good soldiers. Instead of ranging stealthily through the woods in an attempt to surprise the enemy, they would dash "hooping" and "hallooing," warning any nearby raiders of their presence.[7] Few militiamen seem to have been familiar with the use of guns. Although by law all members of the militia were supposed to provide their own weapons, fewer than half the militia who mustered possessed any sort of arms. Many of those who carried arms had weapons that were too ancient for use or of different bores, which made the provision of ammunition all but impossible. Even if they had weapons that could be supplied with ammunition, few militiamen were experienced marksmen. Governor Dinwiddie repeatedly complained of the militia's "Ignor'ce of Arms and Cowardly Disposit'n."[8] George Washington stressed that when recruiting in the backcountry "great Care should be observed in choosing active Marksmen; the manifest Inferiority of inactive Persons unused to Arms . . . [compared] to lively Persons who have practised hunting, is inconceivable."[9] William Parsons similarly complained that the Pennsylvania frontiersmen were "generally as much afraid to fire them [their guns], as they would be to meet an Indian."[10]

The militia officers were the source of many other problems. The militia elected their officers, and as a result officers were reluctant to execute an order that might prove unpopular. As the election of an officer was more a reflection of social status than military prowess, militia officers were especially sensitive about rank, and Washington complained several times that "every petty Person must assume Command, direct and advise."[11] Even the ranks were conscious of their status. When Washington attempted to use the militia to construct defenses at frontier posts, the men refused to do such service unless they received additional pay. When finally offered additional pay, they still refused to lower themselves to such menial work. Many militia officers saw their commissions more as opportunities for profit than as a service to their country. They presented the House of Burgesses with inflated accounts of their costs and requested pay for more men than had served, pocketing the difference. They also aided their friends and neighbors when impressing provisions by leaving the valuation to their "ignorant and indifferent neighbours . . . [who] exact high prices."[12]

The weakness of the militia became apparent even before Braddock's defeat. At the end of June 1755, a raiding party attacked the Holston and New River Valleys in southwestern Augusta County. Dinwiddie hastily called out the militia, but although the raid was small the militia was in such disarray that it could not repulse the attack. Initially, few militiamen would muster. Dinwiddie complained bitterly to the county commanders that "if the Militia w'd only in small Numb's appear with proper Spirit, the Banditti of Ind's w'd not face them; but it appears to me that the inhabit'ts of Augusta have been siez'd with a Pannick in allowing a few Ind's to bully all that Co'ty."[13] The complete failure of the militia disgusted Dinwiddie as he received repeated complaints from frontier settlers who found themselves unprotected and were forced to flee. He wrote despairingly to an officer of the Augusta militia: "If Y'r People will dastardly give up their Families and Interest to a barbarous Enemy, with't endeavour'g to resist them, they cannot expect to be protected." He added ominously, "If they will run away from themselves and desert their Int[eres]ts[,] those that y[e]t rema. to defend the Co[un]ty may hereafter be tho[ugh]t worthy of enjoying their Platat[ion]s."[14]

Although it had proved of little worth, Dinwiddie continued to try and muster the militia, primarily because it had one large advantage over regular forces—it cost the provincial treasury little money. He attempted to circumvent the weaknesses of the militia by posting militia units with regular forces. However, the Virginia militia and regular forces detested each other. In particular, the militia felt that the regiment was a collection of debauched scoundrels. In May 1756, when the militia from the Piedmont was mustered in Winchester, the men "made use of every mean's to treat not only the Private Soldiers but the Officer's of the Virga Regt ill." Washington ordered one of the militia members arrested and held in the guardhouse overnight for his behavior, but the militia officers gathered their men, attacked the guardhouse, and released the prisoner.[15] Worse still, when militia units were posted alongside regular units, "the spirit of Desertion was so remarkable in the Militia, that it had a surprising effect upon the Regiment, and encouraged many of the Soldiers to desert."[16] By the summer of 1756 it had become quite apparent that little reliance could be placed upon the militia to assist in the colony's defense. The colony would have to develop a professional military force, the Virginia Regiment.

The Creation of Provincial Armies

For the first year of the war Virginia struggled to find a military policy to defend the backcountry. However, Virginia at least had some experience in such matters, and the militia could provide a basis for the development of a more effective military body. Pennsylvania, in contrast, had no such force and little prior experience of raising troops. The province's substantial Quaker and Mennonite population had prevented the creation of any previous military establishment, although small volunteer units had served during King George's War as frontier "guards." The task of forming a military organization in a colony where many inhabitants considered even the provision of funds for military purposes to be a violation of their religious scruples was thus a major endeavor. Any attempt to impose compulsory service, as in neighboring Virginia, was unthinkable. Both colonies from the start of the war had to find means of creating substantial military establishments with the minimum of social and political unrest. It was several years before they managed to develop adequate methods for doing this.

Pennsylvania faced two fundamental hurdles in creating a military force: the colony's substantial pacifist minority and the political deadlock between the governor and the assembly. Although many Quakers had decided not to seek office and others made few efforts to campaign, the assembly still had a substantial Quaker presence, "so strongly were the Publick disposed to have Friends for their Representatives." Indeed, in the early stages of the war many Pennsylvanians, not just Quakers, feared that Governor Robert Hunter Morris intended to create compulsory militia service. In the fall of 1755 Conrad Weiser reported to Richard Peters that one of his neighbors, Jonas Seely, had been running for sheriff of Berks County. It seemed at first that he had widespread popular support. However, his opponents went around "to all most every man and reported that Jonas Seely was a Governors Man . . . and that he would Certainly bring things about that they must all take up a Musket and Exercise, which our foolish Germans did belief." As a result Seely was decisively defeated. A similar pattern was repeated throughout the colony.[17]

In the wake of the Penn's Creek raid the governor and assembly continued to debate the creation of a military force. Backcountry settlers, however, flooded the assembly with petitions demanding that it should take action and "either enact a Militia Law, or grant a sufficient Sum of regular Troops as may be thought necessary to defend our Frontiers."[18] This dissatisfaction was not limited to the backcountry. The mayor and aldermen of Philadelphia came before the assembly demanding action to provide "legal protection to your bleeding Country, which ought to be the chief object of all Government." They warned that it would "not be possible to preserve the peace and quiet of this City, nor of the Province itself much longer, if some effectual Methods are not speedily taken for their general Defence and Security." Almost as if on cue, a mob of seven hundred frontiersmen descended on the city denouncing the assembly.[19]

Faced with such mobs, assemblymen finally found a way of overcoming the pacifist scruples of many Pennsylvanians by creating a purely volunteer force to defend the backcountry. The act passed by the assembly in November 1755 provided a general framework for the formation of military units. It simply allowed "such people as are desirous to be united for military purposes" to form their own volunteer units. There was no compulsory military service, officers were elected by the rank and file, and there was no way to enforce discipline.[20] Across Pennsylvania independent companies mustered and paraded, but under no overall command. In Philadelphia rival companies backed respectively by the Penns and by Benjamin Franklin all but clashed with one another. Not surprisingly, these independent companies were of only limited effectiveness. In January 1756, for instance, a raiding party descended on the settlement of Gnadenhütten, defended by a provincial detachment. While raiders destroyed the settlement, the men cowered in a blockhouse, offering no protection to the Moravian village's women and children. The assembly's opponents were quick to lay the blame for this failure on the militia act. Richard Peters, provincial secretary and bitter opponent of the act, commented, "Perhaps there was never such a Farce acted as this . . . Militia Law, and from first to last never was seen a greater Scene of Hypocrisy and Dissimulation."[21] By the spring of 1756 it was clear that the Militia Act of the previous year had failed to provide adequate protection to the backcountry. The assembly thus passed a new act, which once more provided for a voluntary force but tightened military discipline. However, it still did not apply the full rigor of the British Mutiny Act to Pennsylvania forces. Only in the fall of 1756 did the assembly finally extend the British Mutiny Act to Pennsylvania forces and thus create a truly professional force.[22]

Like Pennsylvania, Virginia resorted to the creation of a professional military force, the Virginia Regiment. The Virginia Regiment had its origins even before Braddock arrived in North America, but following his defeat the House of Burgesses expanded the regiment and put its establishment on a more regular footing. Dinwiddie initially hoped that volunteers lured principally by patriotism and the quest for adventure would fill the ranks, for the colony at first resisted the payment of a bounty to new recruits. Patriotism, however, was not by itself a sufficient attraction to lure men to enlist. In the three months following the creation of the regiment, its officers recruited only five hundred men, half the required number. For the officers themselves this provoked a crisis.

They needed to obtain a specific number of recruits before the governor would confirm their commissions. This had unforeseen consequences; some officers created phantom companies. Washington informed Dinwiddie that many officers had produced "a list . . . of sundry persons who are willing to serve under them, one part of those, it is said, are fictitious names another, the names of persons who never saw the list and the remainder are persons drawn into it by fallacious promises."[23]

With such a shortage of recruits, in the spring of 1756 the House of Burgesses extended the provisions for drafting single white men from the militia. A new act ordered the county lieutenants and justices of the peace to seek volunteers among all able-bodied single men in the county. If there were insufficient volunteers, they were to draft men by lot until one in twenty of the single men were in the regiment. To ensure compliance, the House of Burgesses authorized fines of up to five hundred pounds for refractory officials. Not surprisingly, these measures proved very unpopular. In many counties across Virginia there were protests and even draft riots. Consequently, local justices refused to draft men into the regiment unless they were vagrants or undesirables who had no link to the county. Even on the occasions when the justices enforced the draft, most men could avoid service by hiring a replacement or paying a ten-pound fine. Thus, most of the men drafted into the regiment were both too poor to pay the ten-pound fine and had too few community ties to be able to place pressure on the local justice. Indeed, this situation was even recognized by the House of Burgesses, which specifically authorized the impressment of vagrants and in August 1756 even considered drafting convicts.[24] The impressment of vagrants created new problems for the regiment: "Compelling these abandon'd Miscreants into the Service, who only waited time and opportunity to effect their escape, gave loose to all their vicious Principles, and [they] invented the most unheard of stories to palliate Desertion and gain Compassion," wrote Washington.[25]

A solution was finally found in 1757. In February William Pitt wrote to the governors of the "southern colonies" (which included Pennsylvania), promising to pay the burden of the costs of recruiting provincial troops. Determined to win the war at any cost, Pitt felt that the only successful strategy he could pursue was to bankroll the war and use Britain's superior financial resources to defeat the French. In Virginia this news allowed the House of Burgesses to increase the bounty paid to the Virginia troops to ten pounds, twice the rate of Pennsylvania. The high bounty resulted in an increased number of voluntary recruits, and for the rest of the war Virginia was able to rely on volunteers lured by the bounty to fill the regiment's ranks.[26]

Pennsylvania, like Virginia, encountered problems recruiting troops. The colony initially offered of a bounty of one pistole, about sixteen shillings, to all new recruits. However, few men came forward, and throughout 1756 the provincial forces remained under strength. Pitt's decision to fund the war and reimburse the colonies for their expenses allowed Pennsylvania to raise the bounty and exploit a potential pool of recruits, indentured servants. Initial moves to recruit indentured servants provoked intense hostility, but as the war dragged on the assembly began to consider this option. In part, this came about because of moves by the British army. In January 1756 William Shirley of Massachusetts, who initially replaced Gen. Edward Braddock as commander in chief, ordered his officers to accept indentured servants into the ranks if they offered to enlist. The British army's recruitment of servants created "the greatest Consternation, and . . . most violent Commotions throughout every Part of the Province."[27] The Pennsylvania Assembly immediately begged Governor Morris to seek an end to the practice and urged him to allow "Masters to rescue their enlisted Servants."[28] However, Shirley refused to end the practice, asserting that "his Majesty's Service must suffer at this very critical Conjuncture if they were restrained from enlisting such as voluntarily offer themselves." He maintained that he could not see how "the Distress arising from the enlisting a few Servants can be any thing like what the President and Council seem to apprehend."[29] Enlisting servants did prove immensely successful. In April 1757 Benjamin Franklin provided Lord Loudoun, Shirley's replacement as commander in chief, with a list of 612 servants who had enlisted in the British army, a list Franklin still described as "very imperfect."[30]

With the British army recruiting servants with such success, in the spring of 1757 the Pennsylvania Assembly abandoned its opposition and allowed servants to enlist in the provincial forces. This was possible because Pitt's promise to refund all recruiting expenses allowed the assembly to recompense masters for their loss. The compensation that masters received was not large, averaging only around six pounds per servant, while a new servant cost around fourteen pounds. However, not only did masters receive a sum upon their servant's enlistment, but they also continued to receive half of the servant's pay for as long as he remained in the army.

Thus, compensation could easily repay the servant's cost. As the early stages of the war had dislocated Pennsylvania's overseas trading network, causing the prices of many agricultural products to drop sharply, the return from a servant's labor was minimal. This servant's enlistment in the provincial forces, however, could offer his master a guaranteed source of income. With masters abandoning their opposition, indentured servants provided an important pool of manpower for the Pennsylvania Regiment.[31]

Additional potential recruits began to come forward in 1757 as the Pennsylvania bounty for recruitment was increased: former servants who had recently completed their indentures. As servants came to the end of their indentures, their economic prospects in 1756 and 1757 were especially bleak. More than three-quarters of servants indentured during the mid-eighteenth century were forced at some time to rely on public assistance, and the war made their economic prospects even worse. Consequently, one Pennsylvanian reported that "hardly able to maintain themselves . . . [many] have lately Enlisted."[32] By raising the bounty Pennsylvania was able to attract many of these men into the provincial ranks. By 1757 both Virginia and Pennsylvania had discovered that by providing a high bounty and high pay and by identifying the elements of society who would serve in their provincial forces, they could fill the ranks of their regiments.

Provincial Strategy

Having created regular forces, Virginia and Pennsylvania needed to develop a strategy that could be used to halt the raids. The success of the raiders in the spring and summer of 1756 was made possible, in part, because of the difficulties the colonies faced in developing an effective strategy in the backcountry. From the start of the war provincial and British officials knew that the only truly effective strategy would be offensive. In Pennsylvania the provincial commissioners argued that the only way to wage war was "to carry the warr into the Enemy's Country and hunt them in all their Fishing, Hunting, Planting, & dwelling places."[33]

Initially, however, British strategy was primarily defensive. Both Virginia and Pennsylvania hastily threw up a cordon of provincial forts to protect the frontier. Most of these forts were no more than log stockades, but some, such as Fort Augusta on the Susquehanna River, were more substantial constructions of log and earth ramparts. In theory, provincial forces scouted between the forts and intercepted raiding parties before they could attack the backcountry. In practice, there were insufficient men to range the country between the forts effectively. Even on the rare occasions when ranging parties did intercept raiders, it was usually after they had already attacked the backcountry. Typically manned by a garrison of no more than fifty, and in many cases only ten or twelve men, these forts were supposed to protect an exposed frontier nearly five hundred miles in length, from the Delaware River in Pennsylvania to the Roanoke River in Virginia. Not surprisingly, as a defensive barrier the forts were a dismal failure. When individual forts possessed large garrisons, raiders could simply avoid them. If the forts were lightly garrisoned, they offered tempting targets.[34]

In addition to serving as bases from which troops could range the frontier, these forts served another important purpose: providing protection for civilians. Consequently, to encourage settlers to remain on their plantations, the colonies built forts often with more regard paid to protecting valuable settlements, such as the south branch of the Potomac, than to military strategy. In addition to these provincial forts, many settlers built their own forts, and county militias constructed blockhouses for the protection of local inhabitants. By the end of 1756 there were at least sixty-eight nonmilitary fortified posts on the Virginia frontier; Pennsylvania had almost fifty such posts. Some of these were even constructed under the auspices of county authorities. In Cumberland County in 1755 a mass meeting of the inhabitants decided to build five forts across the county to provide a refuge for their families.[35] When local authorities did not construct forts the settlers might fortify their own farms, turning them into strongholds, such as Henry Enoch's plantation and Job Pearsall's in Hampshire County. These smaller blockhouses posed a conundrum for the provincial authorities. Forcing settlers to abandon them caused great dissatisfaction, but defending them drew away valuable troops and resources. Many of the small blockhouses were too weak to offer substantial defense against raiding parties, instead providing tempting targets. To further complicate the development of an effective strategy, many of the forts, which had been constructed at the outer limits of settlement in 1755, were by 1757 many miles from the nearest settlers. Fort Cumberland, in particular, had become dangerously isolated. If these posts were maintained, the logistical efforts of maintaining supply routes drained provincial resources. However, abandoning them seemed to signify accepting the permanent loss of rich settlements. There may have been another reason for retaining some of these more isolated frontier forts. These forts at some distance from the frontier may have distracted Indian raiders from attacks on more valuable settlements, leading them instead to concentrate their efforts on these military outposts. Pennsylvania authorities, in particular, seem to have constructed posts beyond the limits of settlement to protect the frontier. This was more difficult in Virginia, where the outer limits of settlement were more dispersed.[36]

The construction and defense of these forts preoccupied Virginia and Pennsylvania throughout the early stages of the war. However, there was another reason why the colonies followed such a defensive policy: offensive operations in the backcountry were hindered by overwhelming logistical problems. In both Europe and North America the activities of armies were limited by the ability to supply them. In the northern theater, in New York and along the St. Lawrence River, supplies could be moved by sea or river. On the Virginia and Pennsylvania frontier the movement of supplies was much more problematic. There were no rivers providing easy access into the interior. Even the Potomac and Susquehanna were only navigable for parts of their length, and they did not penetrate far into the interior. Then there was the problem of moving men and supplies across the Appalachians. The densely wooded ridges of the Appalachians, rising two thousand feet above the valley bottoms and stretching for many miles, provided an almost impenetrable barrier for the movement of European wagons. Even packhorses made slow progress. By comparison, Indian warriors traveling on foot found the mountains much less of a barrier.

Even in the backcountry moving supplies posed major logistical problems. The roads in Virginia and Pennsylvania were abysmal and were incapable of handling the volume of traffic required to supply and move the provincial forces, let alone the British army. Col. Henry Bouquet warned that the poor roads would cause delays in simply marching the troops from Philadelphia to Lancaster, the most important provincial town in the backcountry. Roads out of the backcountry toward the frontier were yet worse. Heavy rains made them a quagmire and swelled the rivers until they were all but impassable. In May 1758 it took three days to ferry just thirty wagons across the Susquehanna River.[37]

The poor condition of the roads also destroyed the army's supply wagons, which themselves proved very difficult to acquire. Nearly half of the wagons that arrived at Fort Lyttelton on the Pennsylvania frontier in 1758 could continue no farther, and the roads were "strewn with broken wagons."[38] It proved difficult to repair these wagons because there were few craftsmen in the backcountry with the necessary skills. The destruction of the wagons, not unnaturally, increased the reluctance of backcountry farmers to provide wagons for the service, and the severe shortage of transport hampered operations. Moving from the frontier toward the Ohio was even worse. New roads had to be cut through the forest, streams had to be bridged, and supplies had to be shifted hundreds of miles. The distances from colonial supply depots further exacerbated these difficulties. The distance from the last major Pennsylvania outpost at Carlisle to Fort Duquesne was over two hundred miles, yet most of the raiders lived many miles west of Fort Duquesne. On the Virginia and Pennsylvania frontier merely building roads to transport supplies entailed the employment of hundreds of laborers. When officers in desperation attempted to use provincial troops for this task, they refused to work and on occasion even mutinied when forced to do so.[39]

All these impediments meant that to undertake a campaign in the west the army needed to be self-sufficient and had to take with it both the supplies and all the skilled laborers it would need. This was the principal cause of the massive baggage trains that Shingas so derided. Bouquet himself bemoaned the fact that the army's baggage trains created yet "another unavoidable incumbrance . . . for which a road must be opened, and bridges thrown over rivers and swamps." He continued, "[This] weakens our line of march, and keeps the troops tied to a convoy which they cannot lose sight of."[40] Braddock's column, for instance, stretched for five miles. Forbes's expedition in 1758 moved even more slowly. Forbes sought to move his army forward detachment by detachment and to secure his supply lines by building forts and magazines as he advanced. Such a plan required a major logistical effort, which all but condemned the expedition to failure as it was delayed by the shortage of laborers and transport.[41]

Facing such logistical problems, it was little wonder that the provincial forces, and even the British army, found it difficult to mount an offensive in the Ohio Valley. Many colonists, however, failed to perceive these difficulties. Increasingly the colonists expressed dissatisfaction with the performance of their military forces. The Virginia Regiment in particular endured bitter attacks for its failure to protect the frontier. In the late summer of 1756 the *Virginia Gazette* carried an editorial venomously attacking the regiment:

> They lie skulking in Forts, and there dissolving in Pleasure, till alarmed by the Approach of the Enemy, who could expect to find them no where else; when instead of searching out the Enemy . . . and preventing their Incursions, they tempt them by their Security and Laziness, to come in Quest of them, and attack them in their Fortifications.—When this is the Case, how wretchedly helpless must a Nation be? What useless Lumber, what an Incumbrance, is the Soldiery. . . . But when Nothing brave is so much as *attempted* . . . when Men, whose Profession it is to endure Hardships, and encounter Dangers, cautiously shun them, and suffer their Country to be ravaged . . . then certainly, Censure cannot be silent, nor can the Public receive much Advantage from a Regiment of such dastardly Debauchees.[42]

The unrest and dissatisfaction of colonists forced both Virginia and Pennsylvania to take offensive operations. Virginia was the first to act offensively, in early 1756. The Virginia offensive was made possible because Governor Dinwiddie had managed to woo a number of Cherokee auxiliaries to guide the Virginians to the Ohio. For the Cherokees service on the Virginia frontier offered a new avenue to trade goods. Instead of spending the winter hunting to acquire skins to be sold to South Carolina merchants, they could now obtain these goods directly from Virginia as payment for their services. With the Cherokees, Dinwiddie could consider offensive operations. He ordered William Preston and John Smith to draft 350 men from the Augusta militia and appointed Andrew Lewis, one of the most prominent settlers in southwestern Virginia, to command the expedition. Preparations were complete by the beginning of February 1756, and the expedition set off on February 19 from Fort Frederick in Augusta County to travel down the Big Sandy River to the Ohio River and thus attack the Ohio Indians' towns.[43]

The Sandy Creek expedition was beset with problems from the outset. Many of the officers were barely on speaking terms. John Smith and Obadiah Wilson both believed their experience meant that they deserved command, rather than the relatively inexperienced Lewis. In addition, all the officers took an immediate dislike to the Indian trader Richard Pearis, to whom Dinwiddie had given a commission because of his influence with the Cherokee warriors accompanying the expedition. The expedition was also poorly planned. The strategy urged by the Cherokees was to attack the Shawnee bases on the Scioto. The Cherokees expected the Virginia forces to travel light and live off the land, as they did. However, the Virginia troops were incapable of marching such a distance over the rough terrain. Heavy rains made fording streams difficult. The expedition "had no tents, nor Indeed hardly any other Necessaries for such a Journey." The February and March weather was cold and wet, and exposed to the bitter weather, many of the provincials fell ill. The expedition had insufficient packhorses, and with no fodder en route many of these died. The men also went hungry, as the commissaries had provided only fifteen days' worth of provisions for the three-hundred-mile march, expecting the men to hunt and provide much of their own food. Despite the myth of the frontier hunter, the men proved singularly inept at locating and killing game, and on March 2 Lewis put them on reduced rations.[44]

The expedition moved slowly. Not surprisingly, there was soon unrest among the forces. William Preston reported that "the Men Murmured very much for want of Provisions & numbers Threatened to Return home." Lewis was able to persuade the troops to stay, but they were "faint & weak with hunger and could not Travel the Mountains nor wade the Rivers." By the middle of March there was open mutiny among the men. Large numbers deserted and sought their own way home: "Hunger & Want was so much Increased that any man in the Camp would have Ventured his Life for a Supper." On March 13 Lewis called the men together. He told them that he believed they would soon find good hunting grounds. He reminded them of the importance of the expedition and asked "all that was willing to share his Fate to go with him[.] All the Officers & some private men not above 20 or 30 Join'd him." The rest returned home. With only thirty men remaining Lewis was also forced to return to Virginia.[45]

The Sandy Creek expedition had been a complete fiasco. Peter Hog, a captain in the Virginia Regiment, blamed the failure on "the Disobedience of Men Undisciplined, & Subject to no Military law, a too Smal Store of provisions; & the most Impassable Route that Ever was Attempted." The House of Burgesses established a committee to investigate the disaster. The committee largely agreed with Hog's assessment, with the exception that they also blamed the "refractory and mutinous Behaviour" of Captains Obadiah Wilson, John Smith, and John Montgomery.[46] The failure had major repercussions that affected the frontier throughout the rest of the war. In Augusta County a legacy of unrest and dissatisfaction remained between the men and the officers who had commanded the expedition. More importantly, the failure distressed the Cherokees. In the same manner that Braddock's reliance on a heavy wagon train had disgusted his Indian auxiliaries, the Cherokees now observed firsthand the inability of the British to march beyond the frontier without vast quantities of supplies.

However, attacking the homes of the Ohio Indians remained the most likely way of ending the descent upon the frontier. Despite the failure of the Virginia expedition, in April 1756 a Maryland party under the command of frontiersman Thomas Cresap made another attempt to attack the Ohio Indians. The party set out on April 23 from Fort Cumberland but had even less success than the Sandy Creek expedition. Without Indian auxiliaries, the expedition was unable to detect enemy parties. In addition, at the start of their journey, Cresap was killed in a skirmish. Lacking a strong leader, many members of the party mutinied and drifted back to Fort Cumberland. The expedition only marched twenty-one miles beyond the fort before turning back.[47]

Pennsylvania also attempted offensive operations with its new provincial forces. In August 1756 a colonel in the Pennsylvania Regiment, John Armstrong, came up with the plan of launching a raid upon the Indian town of Kittanning on the Allegheny River, about twenty miles upstream from Fort Duquesne. The town was the home of Shingas and Captain Jacobs, believed to be the chief instigators of the raids on western Pennsylvania. It was also rumored to hold a large number of prisoners, many of whom had been taken a few weeks earlier with the capture of Fort Granville. Armstrong thus proposed what amounted to a "rescue mission," and Governor Morris himself commented that the attack "will be of great use to the Publick as it will raise the spirits of the People and serve to remove that dread and Panick which has seized the generality."[48]

The Kittanning expedition set off from George Croghan's plantation, Fort Shirley, on August 30. Although a lack of competent guides proved a great hindrance and the force followed an atrocious route, Armstrong did manage to reach Kittanning and attack. The Pennsylvanians burned much of the town and killed many Indians, including Captain Jacobs, but freed only seven prisoners, many fewer than Armstrong had hoped. On their withdrawal the expedition became divided and was ambushed by several Indian parties, who managed to kill seventeen of Armstrong's men, wound thirteen, and capture another nineteen, far more than the number of prisoners freed.[49] At best Armstrong had won a Pyrrhic victory. However, so great was the need for a boost to the colony's morale that the rout was trumpeted as a great colonial victory, even being celebrated in poetry! Despite its popular representation, the Kittanning expedition, and the similar failure of Virginia's Sandy Creek expedition, proved that the colonies remained incapable of undertaking serious offensive measures against the Indians. Even with the creation of military forces, Virginia and Pennsylvania still remained unable to wage war effectively.

The Problems of Command

Virginia's and Pennsylvania's forces were handicapped not only by problems of defining an effective strategy that might win the war, or at least end the raids on the frontier, but also by problems of maintaining discipline in the ranks of the provincial forces. In the fall of 1756 the *Virginia Gazette* carried a stinging piece of doggerel attacking the Virginia Regiment's conduct of the war:

> But Soldiers differ; some will shed their *Blood,*
> And some drink *Bumbo*—for their Country's Good.
> Some in the Field will nobly risque their Lives;
> Some Hero Like, will *swear,* or play at *Fives.*
> Some shew themselves the genuine Sons of *Mars;*
> Some brave in *Venus'* or in *Bacchus'* Wars
> Can shew their *letcherous* and *drunken* Scars.[50]

This bitter attack reflects the widespread belief in Virginia and Pennsylvania that the colonies' forces were morally corrupt and militarily ineffective, for the Virginia and Pennsylvania forces both experienced a substantial breakdown in discipline. This breakdown can perhaps best be summarized in three broad categories: mutiny, desertion, and insubordination. Mutiny was the most serious action, involving coordinated group action and threatening the integrity of units. Desertion was more of an individual action, although it could also involve groups of soldiers. Desertion did not pose a direct threat to the integrity of units except through the diminution of the ranks. Insubordination was the least serious, and most common, of the actions and could involve actions by individuals or groups, such as failure to follow commands, questioning of commands, and profiteering from service.

Full-scale mutinies were rare on the Virginia and Pennsylvania frontier. While officers often accused their men of mutiny, the only mass actions that approached mutinies occurred at isolated frontier posts and most often took the form of mass desertions. In March 1757 soldiers comprising most of the garrison at Fort Augusta handed in their arms en masse and refused to do duty, claiming that their terms of enlistment had expired. However, after much cajoling the fort's commander, James Burd, managed to convince them to remain in service until fresh reinforcements arrived. More seriously, following Dunbar's retreat from the frontier after Braddock's rout, nearly half the Virginia forces garrisoning Fort Cumberland deserted. Only the failure of the French and their Indian allies to launch an immediate attack saved the post. In August 1756 there was a mutiny of troops at Fort Norris. The garrison attacked several of their officers before breaking into the storehouse.[51] These incidents of mutiny, however, were small and posed relatively little threat to the overall war effort. Certainly when compared to major mutinies, such as the "stoppages mutiny" of British troops in Canada in 1763, these mutinies were of very small scale. In addition, in the first two cases the troops who mutinied had good reason for so doing: those at Fort Augusta had been left short of supplies and beyond their terms of enlistment; those at Fort Cumberland felt abandoned to the wrath of the French by the regular officers, who had retreated to the safety of Philadelphia. At Fort Norris the mutiny was more the result of freely flowing rum and a commander frequently absent on business than of any deep-seated grievances.

Desertion was a much more common action and seems to have been more serious in the Virginia and Pennsylvania forces than in other units, for example, the New England forces studied by Fred Anderson. It is impossible to provide desertion rates for the forces, but at times as many as 30 percent of some units may have deserted, leaving frontier posts frequently seriously undermanned.[52] Several circumstances encouraged mutiny and desertion. Because of the wrangling between the governors and the assemblies, both Virginia and Pennsylvania often lacked the funds to pay the troops. Men also deserted when they discovered that the conditions under which they were serving were different from those they had been led to expect. Officers, desperate to recruit men into their companies, frequently encouraged them to enlist under false pretenses. Several officers informed potential recruits that they would serve only until the end of the war, stressing that it was bound to come within a few months. When the war showed no sign of ending, the men grew restless and eventually headed home. Washington connived in such practices and dismissed them as "nothing more than one of those little subterfuges which, from the disagreeable nature of the Recruiting service, has, at some junctures been considered necessary." Other officers used more direct means to coerce men to enlist. The most infamous case was that of Denis McCarty, who was discovered "forcibly taking, confining and torturing those, who would not voluntarily enlist."[53] In Pennsylvania in 1757 one recruiter discovered that he could only enlist German settlers by guaranteeing that they would not do garrison duty at Fort Augusta and that they would not "do any kind of work but to range & scour the Woods continually." He had no authority to do this. However, he was unconcerned at his deceit, since once recruited the men ceased to be his responsibility, and he was able to recruit many Germans. Not surprisingly, their new commander, Edward Shippen, reported that the recruits were "a parcel of mutinous Dutch Rascalls."[54]

Desertion was perhaps most widespread among those troops drafted into the Virginia Regiment from the militia. Each county was given a specific quota of men to provide for the regiment. The county lieutenant would muster the militia and call for volunteers. If sufficient volunteers were not forthcoming, the lieutenant would draft men from the militia. The men most frequently chosen were either those with few ties to local society—local "undesirables"—or those who had not presented themselves for the muster. It is little surprise that both these groups were reluctant to serve in the regiment. Butts Roberts, for instance, was absent in Maryland on business for his father when his local militia was mustered. Unable to attend the muster, Roberts found himself drafted into the Virginia Regiment. Not surprisingly, Roberts refused to serve. Some troops viewed military life as so appalling that they would risk all to avoid service. In 1758 John Catlet, convicted of stealing a horse, was offered the opportunity to serve in the Virginia Regiment "to free himself from a nauseous Goal and the Sentence of Death which hung over him." No sooner was he freed and handed over to the regiment than he deserted. When recaptured he claimed that "the Mercy extended to him appeared more terrible to him than Death itself[,] and he chose rather to Run the Risque of Suffering an ignominious Death by living with his Wife and Children than to embrace that Mercy which was to deprive him of every Blessing which made life dear to him."[55]

While desertion may have been common, insubordination was rampant and seems to have spread into every aspect of the provincial forces. The pilfering of supplies, for example, was endemic. Following Braddock's defeat in 1755 troops purloined supplies that had been abandoned in the flight and later sold them to unscrupulous settlers. In 1758 there was an orgy of looting of military supplies in all the Pennsylvania forts. One commander complained to Bouquet that it was impossible to protect the stores from "the plundering Hands of unjust & ungratefull Men, who receive the King's Pay to guard & protect the very Effects, they Steal & embezzle: Nothing is spared, Horses, Saddles, Waggons, Provisions, Hay, Planks, all these & many other Articles, are every Day, Night, & Hour, Stolen." At Fort Ligonier the men even looted the officers' baggage.[56]

Troops were also repeatedly drunk. Across Pennsylvania and Virginia soldiers missed duty or performed duty while drunk. At Fort Allen in the summer of 1756 the whole garrison celebrated the arrival of Teedyuscung by heavy drinking. The men, who had been isolated in the garrison for several months, soon "got ajoking" with the women Teedyuscung had brought with him and "behaved very undecently with them the whole night." They then took the "Rum & Water, and washed their parts with it, for fear of getting some distemper of the Squaws." The commander, who himself was drunk, attempted to stop the proceedings. He threatened to shoot the men, but they "began to lay on him with sticks." Another group, worried by the chaos, decided to set out for help, but they were too drunk to get far and soon returned. The behavior of the garrison paralyzed the fort during a period of many raids and jeopardized important Indian diplomacy.[57]

Disorder could also take more practical forms that could be just as devastating to military operations. The men were reluctant to shave and keep clean and had to be ordered to wash themselves and their clothes. When they did wash, they used the same springs and streams from which the drinking water was taken. Such behavior forced Forbes to issue standing orders that "Cleanliness in Camp is particularly to be taken Care of, by sweeping the Streets and Communications twice a day." Sweeping the streets was especially important as the street cleaners had to ensure "that the Camp is kept clean & free off all Dead Carcasses & Deseased Horses." However, the refuse exuded by the army was still so great that the army attracted packs of wild dogs, forcing Bouquet to issue orders that each camp's provost should track and kill all the stray dogs that he could find.[58]

The greatest source of disease was the excrement of the troops themselves. Provincial troops, unused to military necessity, were reluctant to use the "necessary houses." Bouquet issued standing orders that "no Man [should] presume to ease himself any where near the Camp, but in the House of Office." James Burd reissued the order the following year to the Pennsylvania Regiment, adding that "the Sentries [are] to call upon the Guard[,] who is to Confine those the[y] See Disobeying this Orders." Even when the men used the necessary houses, there were problems because they were often built too close to the camp and allowed to overflow. In 1759 James Burd had to issue explicit orders that the necessary houses be built at least one hundred yards from the camp, threatening to court-martial any officer who disobeyed the order.[59]

The general disorder reflects the poor discipline apparent across the provincial forces. This poor discipline meant that the provincial forces were all but incapable of coordinating any attacks or maneuvers essential to effective combat against insurgent forces such as the Ohio Indians. Upon reviewing the Pennsylvania forces for Forbes's expedition in 1758, for instance, Bouquet lamented: "It is impossible to make any plan or accomplish anything with these troops. . . . I find their battalions in utmost confusion."[60]

General disorder among colonial forces was not just restricted to Virginia and Pennsylvania. Disorder and a reluctance to accept the discipline of the regular army were also features of the Massachusetts forces, studied by Fred Anderson, and those of Connecticut, studied by Harold E. Selesky.[61] However, in Virginia and Pennsylvania the breakdown of discipline and order seems to have been particularly severe, especially in the early years of the war. In part, this was due to the reluctance of the colonial assemblies to pass stricter Mutiny Acts. This was most apparent in the provincial forces established by Pennsylvania in the fall of 1755. The lack of organization and discipline among these early companies meant that their impact was limited, and they proved all but incapable of protecting the frontier. The 1755 act stressed that the force created was a "voluntary militia of freemen" and not "mercenary standing troops." As a result, officers had no means to force men into service they did not want or to compel them to stand and fight against a determined enemy. In April 1756 the assembly acted to strengthen the Mutiny Act, allowing the officers to hold courts-martial and extending the British Mutiny Act to Pennsylvania forces. However, all sentences had to be approved by the governor, and the British Mutiny Act only applied when Pennsylvania forces were stationed alongside regular troops. The April act was an improvement, but discipline remained lax. Only in November 1756 did the assembly finally extend the British Mutiny Act to the colony's forces at all times.[62]

Washington also attributed the disorderliness of the Virginians to the lack of punishment for insubordination. He complained that the lenity of the laws punishing deserters resulted in the "growing Insolence of the Soldiers, the Indolence, and Inactivity of the Officers, who are all sensible how confin'd their punishments are, in regard to what they ought to be." At the start of the war the Virginia House of Burgesses proved extremely reluctant to provide for the harsh punishment of Virginia's forces. Only following pleas from Washington to impose harsher penalties did the burgesses reluctantly agree to provide for the death penalty.[63]

Unlike Massachusetts, which by the middle of the eighteenth century had gained much experience waging war both on the colony's frontier and through expeditions sent "overseas," such as the 1745 expedition against Louisbourg, Virginia and Pennsylvania had no prior military experience. Initially both maintained an idealized view of the recruits they hoped to lure into their regiments. Because neither colony had previous experience in creating a professional military force with which to defend themselves, at the start of the war they believed that the men who would volunteer to serve would be motivated more by patriotism than by the promise of monetary rewards. Such men, they felt, should not face the full wrath of military discipline. The New England colonies, however, with a long tradition of raising provincial armies to fight in the colonial wars, were aware that many of the troops who would serve in their forces would be motivated more by greed than patriotism. As Virginia and Pennsylvania came to realize the true nature of the forces they were creating, as reflected in the rising pay and bounties, they also accepted the need to impose military discipline on their forces.

By 1757 Washington did have the power to execute troops when necessary. The officers of the Massachusetts provincial forces never had such power. Generally, the punishments Massachusetts's officers inflicted were very lenient, the most common punishment being a public whipping that never exceeded thirty lashes. Other offenders were forced to straddle the "wooden horse," two planks of wood nailed together in an inverted "V."[64] Compared with these punishments, those imposed on Virginian and Pennsylvanian troops were severe. The penalty for desertion was death, although many executions were commuted at the last minute to other forms of punishment. However, in July 1757, in an attempt to halt mass desertions from the provincial forces, Washington chose to hang some of the deserters on a forty-foot-high gallows in the camp at Winchester because "it conveyed much more terror to others; and it was for example sake, we did it." Even the Pennsylvania authorities resorted to hanging deserters as a deterrent.[65] Troops could also be executed for other offences, most notably cowardice. In 1756 Washington had Sgt. Nathan Lewis executed in front of the Virginia Regiment for cowardice after he ordered his men to retreat during a skirmish with a raiding party. Washington purposefully delayed his execution until the new recruits had arrived in the camp so that "all of his way of thinking will take warning from his death."[66]

Only a few of the many deserters were finally executed, but those who had their sentences commuted were still severely punished. A court-martial in the summer of 1756 gave deserters punishments ranging from 250 to 1,000 lashes. While offenders did not always receive their entire sentence, most still suffered severely. Adam Stephen apprehended two men attempting to desert in July 1756. He "wheal'd them 'till they pissd themselves and the Spectators Shed tears for them." Indeed, Washington specifically ordered that offenders should "receive as much of their punishment as the Surgeon (who must attend upon this occasion) shall judge they are able to bear."[67] By 1757 Virginia and Pennsylvania commanders could inflict the full wrath of military justice upon their troops. However, the disorder among the colonies' troops did not disappear, for it was not simply the lack of punishments that caused so much disorder in the ranks of the Virginia and Pennsylvania Regiments.

The Composition of the Provincial Forces

Central to creating disorder was the composition of the forces themselves. The Virginia and Pennsylvania Regiments were composed of men from rather different backgrounds from those of other provincial forces, particularly the New England forces. The New England forces were in the main a mirror of provincial society, including largely the sons of farmers waiting to receive their "portion" when their father's estate was divided at his death or when old age forced him to rely on his children for support. Until they received it—and after that if they were younger sons and received only a small portion—these men had insufficient funds to establish an independent household. They joined the New England forces to accumulate a lump sum with which to begin their independent lives. They were typically young. Although they represented in some ways a "surplus population," they were not permanently poor, or permanently in surplus supply, and were not part of an "agricultural proletariat."[68]

Virginia and Pennsylvania forces, by comparison, were not so representative of society as a whole. Virginia recruited convicts, deserters, and vagrants. Pennsylvania recruited indentured servants. Part of the reason for the difference in the composition of the forces lies in the different opportunities that the army offered. In New England joining the provincial forces was, in Anderson's words, "a reasonably lucrative proposition, providing cash income to hasten . . . [the] attainment of independence."[69] With few prospects at home, Massachusetts men viewed a term in the provincial forces as attractive. They could expect to serve for one campaign (about eight months); receive a generous bounty upon enlistment, which would provide for them during the campaign; and at the end of the campaign receive their pay, which averaged one pound twelve shillings per month, giving them a sum of around eight pounds with which to return home.[70]

In Pennsylvania and Virginia joining the provincial forces was comparatively less attractive. While the pay of the troops was comparable to Massachusetts, allowing for differences in colonial exchange rates—Pennsylvania privates received two pounds per month and Virginia privates about one pound—Virginia and Pennsylvania troops received smaller bounties; had to pay for their uniforms; and received their pay monthly (at least in theory), which allowed them to fritter it away on liquor and gambling. In addition, for much of the war Virginia and Pennsylvania authorities were well in arrears with pay for their men. As a result, recruits could not expect to leave the army with a large lump sum. Still more importantly, in these colonies from 1756 onward men enlisted for at least three years, not just a summer's campaign as in Massachusetts. The length of service, as much as the lower bounties, explains the reluctance of "respectable" yeoman farmers to enlist in the Virginia and Pennsylvania forces. For many New England recruits a season's service was a chance to see the world, an adventure. For Virginia and Pennsylvania recruits, with a bitter war being fought within their own colonies, enlisting would mean several years of often tedious garrison duty, interspersed with periods of terrifying combat. It was little wonder that the "respectable" sort were loath to volunteer for service.[71]

The most telling difference between these troops and those of New England was their place of birth. Four out of five troops in Massachusetts were born in the Bay Colony, while Selesky estimates that a similar percentage of the Connecticut forces were born in the colony.[72] Less than half the Virginia Regiment and only one in six of the Pennsylvania Regiment were born in their respective colonies.[73] Even more telling, nearly half the Virginia Regiment, and nearly three-quarters of the Pennsylvania Regiment, were born in Europe. Forty percent of the troops in the Pennsylvania Regiment were born in Ireland and almost 20 percent in Germany. Twenty-two percent of the Virginia Regiment were born in England and 16 percent in Ireland. These varying backgrounds served to break down cohesion in the regiments. Like backcountry society the Virginia and Pennsylvania Regiments lacked binding ties of origin to create a military community; the regiments were initially communities of strangers. Ties of origin were further strengthened in New England, on the other hand, because most of the troops in each regiment came from a relatively small area, just one or two counties. Massachusetts's troops knew one another before recruitment, and such ties played an important role in the recruiting process. Virginia and Pennsylvania forces were recruited from all over the colonies and from neighboring colonies, and the troops were more likely to be strangers to one another.[74]

There was also a degree of ethnic segregation in both the Virginia and the Pennsylvania Regiments. While no companies were entirely composed of one ethnic group, different groups of immigrants did cluster in specific companies. In the Pennsylvania Regiment half the German recruits were found in just three of sixteen companies, and half the Irish recruits were found in just five companies. More particularly, the Germans were clustered in German officer Captain Weatherholt's company, 85 percent German, and the Irish in Captain Singleton's company, 94 percent Irish, and in Captain McClung's company, 75 percent Irish.[75]

The Virginia Regiment shows slightly less clustering of immigrant groups, although German recruits were found in only nine of twenty-one companies and 83 percent of German recruits were concentrated in just five companies.[76]

If there was a substantial difference in the ethnic origins of recruits, there was also a difference in preenlistment employment.[77] Nine out of ten of the Pennsylvania forces described their preenlistment occupation as some manual craft or simply as a "Labourer," an unusual circumstance for such an agricultural society. There were also many artisans among the Pennsylvania forces: fifty-four, or 8.2 percent, described their preenlistment occupation as weaver; twenty-six, or 3.9 percent, as carpenter; and twenty-five, or 3.8 percent, as shoemaker. There were also many craftsmen with rather more esoteric skills, including a "fiddle-maker," a "linen painter," and a "peruke or wig-maker."[78] The large number of skilled artisans in the Pennsylvania forces reflects the status of many recruits as indentured servants or former servants. Indeed, the highest number of skilled artisans were found among foreign-born recruits, whereas the lowest number were found among those born in other colonies. Nearly two-thirds of recruits born in neighboring colonies were unskilled laborers, undoubtedly men attracted into the regiment from New Jersey, New York, Virginia, and Maryland by the lure of pay and the bounties. These men were typically the poorest and least skilled of all the recruits.

The Virginia forces included large numbers of planters, hardly surprising given the nature of Virginia society, but 38.0 percent of recruits could also be categorized as artisans, surprising for such an agricultural colony. Indeed, 124, or 8.6 percent, of Virginia Regiment recruits described their occupation as carpenter; 93, or 6.4 percent, as shoemaker; and 76, or 5.3 percent, as tailor. Like Pennsylvania's recruits, Virginia's also included many craftsmen with more esoteric skills, including an armorer, 2 coach-makers, 2 glass-makers, and 4 book-binders. Virginia's recruits, like Pennsylvania's, did not reflect the social structure of the colony as a whole.

In terms of age, the Virginia and Pennsylvania Regiments more closely resembled the New England forces. The men who enlisted in the Pennsylvania and Virginia forces were on average slightly older than their New England counterparts—or rather there were fewer younger men and fewer older men in the Pennsylvania and Virginia forces. In Massachusetts nearly one in four of the troops was under twenty; in Pennsylvania the figure was one in seven, and in Virginia it was only one in ten. Of the Massachusetts forces, 11.7 percent were forty or older, compared with 10.1 percent of the Virginia Regiment and only 3.5 percent of the Pennsylvania Regiment.[79] The lack of younger men reveals the presence of indentured servants, particularly in Pennsylvania, some of whom had already served several years indenture. The mean ages of the troops, however, were not that different: twenty-five years, nine months, in Massachusetts; twenty-five years, two months in Pennsylvania; and twenty-six years, seven months, in Virginia. The compression of ages perhaps accounts for a small part of the lack of cohesion in the ranks, diminishing the deference found between younger and older men coming from the same community.

There were thus some important differences between the New England recruits and those who served in the Virginia and Pennsylvania Regiments. These differences explain some of the difficulties encountered by Virginia and Pennsylvania. Most significantly, the New England forces represented the communities they came from, and the ties of kinship and authority in those communities were transferred to the army. Officers in New England were often local community leaders, and the respect they enjoyed in their home communities was also evident in the service. The Virginia and Pennsylvania forces did not represent the communities that recruited them. Consequently, the officers were strangers to their ranks. In both colonies the officer corps had to earn the respect of the men who served under them. The officers had neither the overwhelmingly higher social status of the officer corps of the British army, which could intimidate the ranks, nor the familiarity of the New England officer corps.

In the early stages of the war the officer corps did little to earn the respect of the ranks. Officers had little military experience and in many cases seemed more concerned about social rank and preferment than about military operations. There was thus a deep rift between the officer corps and the ranks that was not evident among the New England forces.[80] In Virginia and Pennsylvania officers were extremely reluctant to lower their style of living even when campaigning on the frontier. Washington repeatedly complained that despite the shortages of supplies it was impossible to get officers to restrict their consumption. Indeed, Washington himself was accused of living a luxurious lifestyle in the substantial house that he rented in Winchester.[81] In Pennsylvania the most notorious case was that of William Clapham, the commander at Fort Augusta. Edward

Shippen described dinner with him: "We generally had choice Beef, both Roast & Boiled. . . . We had Good Table Beer et une boteille ou deux d'excellent Vin." After dinner "the Collo[nel] ordered three Musicians (his own Soldiers) to stand under a Tree at a Proper Distance & Play us a few Tunes on the Claronette, Violin and Fife." This excess occurred at the same time that many of the men in the fort were malnourished because of a shortage of supplies.[82]

Officers were reluctant to restrict their lifestyle because they viewed conspicuous consumption as a symbol of their social status, about which they were exceptionally conscious. From the start of the war Virginia gentlemen had besieged Washington with requests for commissions in the Virginia Regiment. When gentlemen received commissions, they frequently complained that they did not have the rank they deserved, causing Dinwiddie to remind them that were they in the British army they "might have served twenty Years before . . . [they] had a Co[mpan]y, and then, with a large Purchase."[83] A result of this pressure for commissions was that the Virginia Regiment was top-heavy with officers. Each company had a captain, a lieutenant, and an ensign, as in the regular service. However, at full strength each company would have contained only sixty men, whereas a company in the British army typically numbered around one hundred. Because of slow recruitment, the companies had even fewer men compared with the number of officers. As the expenses of the war mounted, some Virginians began to raise "Great Clamours . . . ag'st the many officers in Commiss'n to command so few Men."[84] In May 1757 the House of Burgesses finally intervened. "Having consider'd the great Expence the Virg'a Regim't has cost the Country from the No. of Companys it has consisted of, and those Companys not half compleat in proportion to the vast Charges of Officers," the House reduced the number of companies to seven, with an accompanying decrease in the number of officers. This reduction forced several officers to resign their commissions to avoid the insult of demotion and deeply embittered many others.[85]

Because of their extreme sensibility to rank, most officers were reluctant to submit to any order that might be construed as inappropriate, and disputes over command were frequent. Washington complained in 1757 that if an officer was not consulted "he takes huff[,] thinks his wisdom and merit affronted, and so Marches off in high Indignation, and great contempt of every Social Law." In Pennsylvania James Burd likewise complained about the "paultry Behaviour of some of the Officers." He added, "I can't help taking notice that their Self Sufficient Opinion of themselves only tends to expose their Folly, and it is with Regret that I see them too wise to be taught."[86] Washington himself, however, was just as guilty as his officers. He frequently tried to bypass Governor Dinwiddie by appealing directly to the House of Burgesses through the speaker, John Robinson. In August 1756 Washington directly appealed to Robinson to secure more funding for the regiment from the assembly. In November he appealed to Robinson for help to enforce the articles of war. In December he wrote complaining of Dinwiddie's decision to reinforce Fort Cumberland. Not surprisingly, his actions frustrated the governor; by the fall of 1756 Dinwiddie had largely lost patience with his commander and accused him of hampering the war effort by his deliberate obstructions. General Forbes echoed Dinwiddie's concerns. When Washington publicly questioned his motives in selecting a Pennsylvania route to the Ohio, Forbes wrote to Bouquet lamenting that Washington's "Behaviour about the roads, was no ways like a Soldier."[87]

The cohesion and esteem of the officer corps were further undermined by disputes among officers and between the officers of the different colonial forces. The officers of the Virginia militia and of the Virginia Regiment detested one another and frequently quarreled.[88] The different colonial forces bickered even more frequently. At Fort Frederick, Maryland, the officers of the Virginia and Maryland forces repeatedly disputed command. The command of Fort Cumberland was even more contentious. The fort was located on the Potomac River in Maryland, and several Maryland officers had received commissions in independent companies from the Crown. The Maryland officers therefore claimed that they had precedence over the Virginia officers and thus had the right to consume Virginia's stores and supplies as they saw fit. However, over three-quarters of the forces in the fort were from Virginia, which had constructed and supplied the fort. The Virginia officers refused to cooperate and countermanded any orders of the Maryland officers. During the height of the Indians' assault, internal bickering paralyzed this key frontier post. Disputes between officers of the British regular forces and provincial officers were equally bitter. Henry Bouquet described the provincial officers as "without knowledge & Experiences. . . . They are all a cruel Incumbrance upon us." For their part, provincial officers constantly sniped at Bouquet and complained of the haughty and imperious behavior of the British officers.[89]

The development of an effective officer corps was further hindered because many of those who sought a military career wanted commissions not in the provincial service but in the Royal American Regiment. Many colonists saw service in the Virginia and Pennsylvania Regiments as miserable and unrewarding. The officers lacked skills and were often very aware of their inadequacy to command. None of them had military experience before 1754. Instead, they had to rely on military treatises, most notably *A Treatise of Military Discipline,* by Humphrey Bland, who had served under the Duke of Marlborough. Known to officers as "Old Humphrey," Bland's work, published in 1727, had run to nine editions by 1762. However, by 1755 Bland's treatise was already dated and had almost nothing to say on guerrilla warfare.[90]

Over time, however, the influence and effectiveness of the officer corps increased. In 1755 and 1756 both Virginia and Pennsylvania struggled to create an officer corps who could command the respect of their men. By 1757 the officer corps had developed, as resignation, death, and removal of officers allowed men with experience and ability to be promoted into the officer corps. Many of those being promoted had served several years in the provincial forces as volunteers before acquiring a commission. Many of these men served as "cadets" in the Virginia Regiment, without rank and usually on a private's pay. Washington recognized their service and experience by insisting on giving the volunteers preference when an ensigncy in the regiment became available. By the end of 1757 most of the officers in both regiments had gained their commissions through merit and had the experience to earn at least some respect from the ranks.[91]

Washington himself had gained experience and an awareness of the demands of command. By 1757 he was conscious of the need to cultivate a good relationship with the governor and was assisted in June 1758 by the arrival of a new Virginia governor, Francis Fauquier, which allowed him to recommence his relationship with the governor with a clean slate. He was also aware of the need to maintain a sound relationship with civilians and attempted to halt some of the worst excesses of impressment and quartering. By 1758, and his involvement in Forbes's campaign, Washington had succeeded in creating a more effective officer corps and thus a more effective regiment. It was not without justification that Capt. Robert Stewart later wrote to Washington, "I think without vanity we can assert that there never was and very probably never will be such another Provincial Regiment."[92]

Similarly, among the ranks increasing numbers of men had served in the regiments for several seasons. Beginning in 1756 Virginia and Pennsylvania both recruited men not just for one year or one campaign but for three years. Thus, the absence of kinship and familiarity caused by the diverse origins of the recruits was steadily replaced by new ties of friendship and camaraderie wrought over several years of hard service. The Virginia and Pennsylvania Regiments were not totally transformed from a disorderly and disorganized rabble into an efficient and effective fighting machine. However, by 1757 the problems of disorder and disobedience were declining. By the end of 1757 both regiments were substantially more effective and more disciplined than they had been at their creation, although British officers still balked at their disorder when serving alongside them.

BETWEEN 1755 AND 1757 Virginia and Pennsylvania slowly and painfully created military forces with which they could oppose the Indian onslaught on the backcountry. Although Virginia had more military experience than Pennsylvania, it took both colonies several years to refine methods of recruiting to fill the ranks of their regiments with a minimum of social discord. Both colonies struggled to deal with problems of indiscipline in the ranks. Men deserted, mutinied, and embezzled supplies; officers quarreled and bickered over their social status. Such problems never disappeared, but they were notably reduced by the end of 1757. At the start of the war both Virginia and Pennsylvania struggled to recruit men into the provincial regiments; by the end of 1757 both colonies had perfected the means of recruiting by attracting specific recruits, extending the length of service, and increasing bounty and pay. The forces they created were unique in colonial America and very different from those of New England. They were not composed of the sons of middling farmers, but contained a much higher percentage of the poor and landless, lured into the provincial forces by the bounty and wages offered. Indeed, in many ways the ranks of the provincial forces had become much more representative of the British army than the New England forces. After 1756 they served not for one campaign but for several years and were becoming, in effect, a professional military force. By 1757 both Virginia and Pennsylvania had thus created provincial military forces that could fight with some degree of effectiveness. However, the creation of these military forces did not bring an end to the war any closer. Neither colony had yet discovered a way to end the Indian raids upon the frontier and bring peace to the backcountry. It would take a substantial diplomatic effort and the involvement of large numbers of regular troops to accomplish this.

5

Wars and Words

Political Conflict and the Diplomatic Offensive

THE SEVEN YEARS' WAR WITNESSED CONFLICT NOT ONLY IN THE backwoods of Virginia and Pennsylvania but also on the floors of the colonies' assemblies. Both colonies suffered bitter political disputes that on occasion even spilled into physical violence as the war unleashed competition for power and patronage. As both colonies raised troops and procured supplies, political disputes focused not just on the war itself but on the raising and spending of provincial funds. This resulted in a contest over the powers and privileges of the assemblies and the rights of the governors.

Political disputes in turn affected the diplomacy of both colonies. With the military deadlock in the backcountry, both Virginia and Pennsylvania turned to diplomacy as a means of winning the war. Part of this diplomatic offensive involved the acquisition of Indian allies who could attack the homes of the raiders. To this end Virginia began to make overtures to the Cherokees and Catawbas in North and South Carolina. In Pennsylvania the diplomatic offensive focused on attempts to negotiate a peace with the Indian raiders, in particular the Delawares living upon the upper reaches of the east branch of the Susquehanna River. Unfortunately, diplomacy soon became entangled in the disputes between the assembly and the proprietors.

The Roots of Political Conflict

The political disputes in both colonies had their origins before the war. In Virginia Governor Robert Dinwiddie's attempts to collect a fee of a pistole for the registering of land patents caused a bitter dispute with the assembly in the early 1750s. In all other colonies the governor was allowed to collect a fee for registering land. When, with the council's support, Dinwiddie attempted to introduce such a fee in Virginia in 1751, he started a heated dispute that continued for several years. Eventually, in October 1754, the Privy Council finally upheld Dinwiddie's right to collect the fee but ruled that it was not to be retroactive.[1] While this settled the immediate issue, the dispute would continue to undermine relations between Dinwiddie and the House of Burgesses as the war in the backcountry commenced.

Indeed, it was not long before the pistole fee and Dinwiddie's attempts to conduct war became enmeshed. Upon receiving news of Washington's defeat at Fort Necessity, Dinwiddie called the House of Burgesses into session. The House agreed to provide 20,000 pounds. However, a group of burgesses tacked a rider onto the supply bill authorizing the payment of 2,500 pounds to Peyton Randolph, who was then in London arguing the assembly's case in the Pistole Fee Controversy.[2] Dinwiddie was mortified. He rejected the bill and promptly prorogued the assembly. When Dinwiddie summoned the House the following spring to provide funds for Braddock's expedition, the House was more compliant. However, the burgesses would only raise funds by issuing paper money, to be paid off with the proceeds of future taxes. With the French firmly established at the forks of the Ohio, Dinwiddie felt that he had little choice but to accept the paper, or else risk not being able to defend the backcountry. Having begun to issue paper money, the House now pressed for even greater emissions. Following Braddock's defeat, several burgesses used the emergency to press for the establishment of a loan office to issue the much larger sum of 200,000 pounds in paper. Dinwiddie knew that such a large sum would be totally unacceptable to Whitehall. When several burgesses continued to press their cause, Dinwiddie was forced to dissolve the House and issue writs for a new election. However, when the House reassembled in the spring of 1756, the burgesses continued to press for paper money, and with the backcountry laid waste by raiding parties, Dinwiddie had little choice but to agree. Over the next eighteen months the House would issue a total of 135,000 pounds in paper.[3]

If in Virginia disputes between the governor and burgesses hampered the war effort, they were of little consequence compared to those in Pennsylvania. There the political impasse between governor and assembly also had its roots long before the outbreak of war. The assembly had been given substantial powers by William Penn's Charter of Privileges in 1701 and was determined to protect these privileges, the most important being the power to levy taxes and control the disbursement of funds. The Penns meanwhile gave their governors strict instructions to ensure that proprietary estates were exempt from taxation and that the governors controlled the distribution of any funds raised. In addition, they chose as governor men like Robert Hunter Morris, who in his career as chief justice of New Jersey had already gained a reputation for protecting proprietary interests. Finally, they forced all governors to provide a bond as guarantee that they would follow their instructions.[4] Not surprisingly, governor and assembly were soon drawn into an impasse.

Braddock's expedition caused the conflict to begin in earnest. In December 1754 Governor Morris sought funds to assist the expedition. However, as in Virginia, the assembly would only issue paper money and demanded the right to control the disbursement of the funds raised. Not surprisingly, Morris refused to accept the bill. There followed weeks of wrangling: the assembly would not abandon its desire for paper money (in part because it was widely felt that there was a shortage of specie in the colony); Morris would not abandon his instructions. Braddock grew furious at the impasse and complained to Morris, "I cannot help expressing the greatest Surprise to find such a pusillanimous and improper Behaviour in your Assembly, and to hear of Faction and Opposition where Liberty and Property are invaded."[5]

Because the issues involved in the dispute were so fundamental—the rights of the governor and the assembly—it soon spread across the Atlantic. In February 1755 Anglican clergyman William Smith, provost of the College of Philadelphia, published in London a stinging invective against the behavior of the assembly. He claimed that the assemblymen, and the Quakers in particular, were "Possessed of such unrestrained Powers and Privileges, they seem quite intoxicated; are factious, contentious, and disregard the Proprietors and their Governors . . . [and] have employed themselves in grasping after Power."[6] Smith's words soon drew an equally bitter response. Probably penned by Joseph Galloway, and published in London in the fall of 1755, the response claimed that the proprietors, for their part, were seeking to destroy the liberties and rights of all Pennsylvanians. Galloway stressed that the assembly had not refused to grant money for Braddock but had simply tried to ensure that all money raised was spent "to answer the public utility, for which it was voted; and not to be sunk in the pockets of venal Lieutenant-Governors." He emphasized that the sole reason that Morris and the Penns had not accepted the supply bill was because they did not have "disposal of the money . . . poor gentlemen . . . who does not pity their deplorable case? who would not gratify their longings to finger the public money but such hard-hearted men as the Assembly."[7]

The dispute between the governor and the assembly, between supporters of the proprietors (or the proprietary faction) and supporters of the assembly (or the antiproprietary faction), had thus been simmering for some time before the descent of the Indians upon the frontier. The devastation of the backcountry, however, greatly complicated the state of affairs. The need to raise funds for defense was now more desperate than ever. Pennsylvania had to take decisive action, but the pacifism of the Quakers who controlled the assembly meant that any act establishing a provincial military force would have to be carefully worded. In addition, political lobbying in London, which in normal times would have made little impression, now carried additional weight. War thus offered an opportunity for both the proprietors and the assembly to silence their opponents if each could convince the Board of Trade and the Privy Council that the other was responsible for the devastation of the backcountry. Thus began a bitter war of words on both sides of the Atlantic.[8]

Following Braddock's defeat, the assembly approved a 50,000-pound supply bill, not to be funded by paper money but by a tax on all estates in the province. However, included in the tax were the estates of the proprietors. Morris rejected the bill. Following the Penn's Creek raid on Pennsylvania's frontier, the assembly once more tried to tax proprietary estates. And Morris again rejected the bill. When Indian raiders extended their attacks to Pennsylvania's northern frontier, it was Morris who gave ground, agreeing to the taxation of proprietary estates as long as he had a voice in the appointment of the commissioners who were to assess the rates. The assembly, however, refused to make any concessions and rejected the amendments to their supply bill, claiming that "one of the most valuable Rights of *British* Subjects, [is] to have their Bills granting money to the Crown accepted without Amendments." The constitutional deadlock at a time of such distress in the backcountry alarmed many Pennsylvanians, and several council members pressed Morris to compromise further, stating that "the lives of the people are not to [be] plaid with nor thrown away because the two parts of the Legislature differ." However, neither Morris nor the assembly would come to terms. Only following a "gift" of 5,000 pounds from the proprietors, which the assembly viewed as their share of the tax, was a temporary compromise achieved; the assembly finally agreed to raise 55,000 pounds without taxing proprietary estates.[9]

In addition to squabbling over the ways of raising funds for the war, the assembly and governor were also deadlocked over the formation of a permanent military force in the colony. In the autumn of 1755 the assembly passed a militia bill. However, Quaker assemblymen would not support any bill that established compulsory military service. For pacifist Quakers and Mennonites any military service was unthinkable, but exempting them from a compulsory service that applied to everyone else was equally unacceptable to the remainder of the population. In addition, Quaker members were reluctant to allow the full rigor of the British Mutiny Act to be extended to the province's forces. These limitations severely hampered the ability of the colony to defend itself.[10]

The assembly's failure to raise funds for the war and its reluctance to establish a militia or to extend the Mutiny Act were soon the subject of attention in London. Early in 1756 the Board of Trade received a petition from Pennsylvania drafted by Chief Justice William Allen, a leading member of the proprietary faction, blaming the Quakers for all the disputes and seeking their formal exclusion from the colony's government. Allen argued that the presence of pacifist Quakers in the government made it impossible for the colony to defend itself. In March 1756 the board sent a report to the Privy Council attacking the Pennsylvania assembly for its pacifist stance and suggesting that Quakers should be permanently barred from holding office or sitting in the assembly because their pacifism was inconsistent with the province's defense.[11]

The possibility that the Penns might succeed in barring Quakers from politics brought a swift backlash. The antiproprietary faction, which was now led by Benjamin Franklin, quickly organized itself. In the summer of 1756 it commenced a pamphlet war on both sides of the Atlantic mobilizing opposition to the proprietors. The antiproprietary faction claimed that Allen's petition "under the plausible pretence of providing for the Publick Safety aims at nothing less than the Subversion of the present Constitution of Pennsylvania."[12] Franklin's position was strengthened when the London Quakers persuaded many of their Pennsylvania brethren not to stand in the elections for the assembly in the fall of 1756. The new assembly that met in October had only twelve Quaker members out of a total of thirty-six, whereas previously it had contained twenty-eight. This allowed Franklin to defend the assembly from charges of pacifism, for he was anything but a pacifist. It also shifted the debate from the pacifism of the assembly back to the restrictions and constitutionality of the proprietors' instructions.[13]

The withdrawal of most of the Quakers from public life fueled hopes that the assembly and governor could now cooperate. These hopes were furthered when a new governor, William Denny, arrived in Philadelphia in August 1756. All sides hoped for a rapprochement between governor and assembly. Indeed, the prospects for compromise looked good. While bound by the same instructions as Morris, Denny was prepared to approach them with some flexibility. One of his first actions was to lay the instructions relating to financial affairs before the assembly so that they could frame their bills accordingly, an act Morris had always refused.[14]

However, the relationship between Denny and the assembly soon began to sour and take on an all too familiar tone. When Denny pressed the assembly for a supply bill, the assembly demanded the right to both issue paper money and control the disbursement of the funds. Like Morris before him, Denny refused. Over the winter of 1756–57 relations between Denny and the assembly deteriorated further as they entered into new squabbles over the quartering of British troops in the colony and continued to argue over the taxation of proprietary estates. In January 1757 the assembly passed another supply bill taxing proprietary lands. Of course, Denny rejected the bill. In desperation the assembly agreed to send Franklin to London to argue their case in front of the Board of Trade. The bickering in Pennsylvania would now get a full airing in London. The decision to send Franklin to London raised the stakes in Pennsylvania. While the proprietors continued to seek a formal removal of the Quakers from all public offices, the antiproprietary faction sought nothing less than the royalization of the colony and the end of the proprietors' privileges.[15]

The political wrangling between the governor and assembly in Pennsylvania was not significant solely because it hampered the raising of funds for the war effort and the passing of a militia bill. The disputes had much broader ramifications. Because both sides had reached deadlock, the only way they could see of breaking that deadlock was the removal of the other side—barring the Quakers from public office or royalizing the colony. Both sides needed ammunition for this struggle, and the search for ammunition led the disputes to spill over into the colony's diplomacy.

The Role of the Quakers

Indian diplomacy offered a perfect opportunity for each side to find ammunition and level accusations of treachery against the other. For the antiproprietary faction it was easy to accuse the proprietors of causing the war through their shady land dealings. For the proprietors it was just as simple to accuse the Quakers of meddling in government affairs and hindering Indian diplomacy. Indeed, the Quakers did play a central, and probably unconstitutional, role in Pennsylvania's diplomacy with the Delawares. Diplomacy was of vital significance to the Quakers because they sought any possible way to end the conflict by pacific means. The raids on the backcountry had generated deep divisions within the Pennsylvania Quaker community. Some Quakers refused to compromise their pacifism at all and would not tolerate any involvement of the colony in warfare, while others were prepared to allow the expenditure of the colony's funds on nonmilitary supplies. A final group, the "defense Quakers," was prepared to support defensive measures as long as they were not compelled to fight themselves. For all Quakers, ending the war by pacific means, through diplomacy, was the best possible outcome.[16]

Unlike many other Pennsylvanians, the Quakers saw the Delawares not as foolish savages but as rational human beings. They felt that there must therefore have been some sound reason for them to attack the colony. If that reason could be ascertained and the source of Delaware discontent remedied, war could be avoided. Many Pennsylvanians believed that the most likely source of Delaware dissatisfaction was some underhand acquisition of Delaware lands. Such suspicions of underhand land dealings brought the Quakers into direct conflict with the proprietors, who alone in the colony were able to purchase lands from the Indians. The disputes between the proprietary and antiproprietary factions in the assembly thus soon became mirrored in the colony's Indian diplomacy.[17]

The Quakers' quest for an investigation into the causes of the war began as soon as the Indians descended upon the frontier. On November 7, 1755, a group of Quakers sent an address to the assembly begging them to uncover the causes of the attack. The Quakers based their appeal upon Governor Morris's own words, for at the beginning of the session he had informed the assembly that the French had won over the Delawares "under the ensnaring pretence of restoring them to their Country." To many Quakers this suggested that the Delawares still considered the backcountry to be their land, whereas most Pennsylvanians believed that the Delawares had sold these lands. The implication was clear: for some reason the Delawares regarded the sale of their lands as invalid. If this issue could be resolved, perhaps the Delawares would halt their raids. The Quakers thus demanded negotiations with the Delawares and persuaded the assembly to establish a commission to inquire into their alienation.[18]

The opening of hostilities had not ended all communication between the Susquehanna Delawares and Pennsylvania. Sporadic communication, particularly via the Moravians and their converts, continued. Intelligence from these communications suggested that some Delawares desired to make peace. Indeed, some of the Wyoming Indians sent warnings to the Moravians of raiding parties about to descend on the frontier. Many Delawares had relations among the Indians in the missions, and others had themselves spent time among the Moravians. However, the raids of other Delawares upon the northern Pennsylvania frontier undermined their efforts toward peace. The raids prevented them from communicating with Pennsylvania, and any messengers they did try to send were intercepted and detained by Francophile parties. Their inability to contact Morris, many feared, would be interpreted as signifying open hostility. The Moravians' sporadic contacts, however, convinced Morris that there were sufficient grounds to believe that some Susquehanna Delawares remained pacific and to invite them to a conference at Harris's Ferry in January 1756. Here he would attempt to formulate a diplomatic solution to the crisis. While a few Susquehanna Delawares may indeed have desired an end to the conflict, with the French ascendant on the northern frontier and with few signs of Pennsylvania's being able to dislodge them, they dared not openly speak their minds. Not surprisingly, few Delawares came to Harris's Ferry in January.[19]

The Quakers still did not abandon all hopes for a diplomatic solution. Instead they pinned their hopes on the intervention of the Iroquois. However, news from Iroquoia was not encouraging. As late as the fall of 1755 the Iroquois had branded simply as "false" any accounts that the Delawares had joined the French. Sir William Johnson attempted to prompt the Iroquois into action and warned headmen that unless they asserted their authority they would lose any control they had over the Delawares. When Iroquois headmen reluctantly agreed to discipline the Delawares, it soon became apparent that in reality Iroquois power was nonexistent.[20]

The lack of conclusive evidence for the existence of a Delaware "peace party," and Iroquois impotence, finally convinced Governor Morris that a negotiated end to the conflict was impossible. At the beginning of April 1756 he announced that he was preparing to issue a formal declaration of war against the Susquehanna Delawares. He delayed the official proclamation for several days as the Quakers made last-ditch efforts to prevent war. In seeking to postpone the declaration of war, the Quakers commenced a campaign that would prove central to Pennsylvania's war effort and would place them in bitter opposition to the proprietors. However, the Quakers' pleas for peace were drowned out by the clamor for action from the backcountry. Backcountry settlers protested the assembly's failure to take decisive action. Outraged, the protestors planned a mass meeting on April 16 in Lancaster, from which they intended to march on Philadelphia. Immediately on hearing of their plans, Morris issued a proclamation banning their meeting but also sending commissioners to meet with and attempt to appease them. Toward this end, on April 14 he issued a formal declaration of war.[21]

When the Quakers heard of the declaration of war they sent one of their most prominent members, Israel Pemberton, with a final plea to the provincial council to send a message to the Delawares. Pemberton maintained that if they could inform the Delawares that the Pennsylvanians were still prepared to investigate their complaints, at least some Delawares might sue for peace. The council reacted with some surprise and maintained that private individuals should not intervene in Indian policy, but suggested inconsistently that if the Quakers wanted to open negotiations with the Delawares they could do so under their own auspices rather than under the colony's.[22] The Quakers offered to pay all the costs of any diplomacy, and this offer may have convinced the cash-strapped Morris to accept their intervention. Meanwhile, the Quakers hurriedly drafted a letter to Sir William Johnson urging him to accept their mediation, claiming that their reputation for fair dealing would surely mean that the Delawares would accept them as mediators in the dispute. The Quakers found in Johnson a surprising, although temporary, ally. Morris's decision to declare war on the Delawares without his approval had jeopardized Johnson's power and, more importantly, further threatened Iroquois influence over the Delawares. While accepting the Quakers' mediation was a recognition of his weakness, a negotiated peace might restore Iroquois power and see Morris's control over Indian affairs in his own province undermined.[23]

The Quakers immediately arranged to meet with a few Anglophile Indians. In a series of private meetings with, among others, Scarouady, Newcastle, Jagrea, and William Lacquis, the Quakers discussed the means by which peace could be restored. They decided to send Scarouady, Newcastle, and Jagrea with a message to the Susquehanna Delawares to let them know that "there are a people risen in Philadelphia, who desire to have peace restored" and invite them to come to Pennsylvania to discuss the causes of the current crisis. Quaker influence was thus central in the commencement of Pennsylvania's negotiations with the Delawares.[24]

Negotiations Commence

The Susquehanna Delawares, while wary of opening negotiations with the Pennsylvanians, had pressing reasons for doing so. For them the winter of 1755–56 had been one of fear for the future, rather than jubilation at their recent success. Having witnessed the attacks upon the Pennsylvania frontier, they lived in dread of reprisals. In addition, provisions were running low. Fear was thus sharpened by the pangs of hunger. Many Delawares began to migrate to the upper reaches of the west branch of the Susquehanna, closer to the French, or even to the Allegheny and Ohio Rivers. In the heady days of November 1755, when the Delawares first descended on the frontier, there had been rumors of the French building a fort at the forks of the Susquehanna, at Shamokin, to protect them. By the spring of 1756 the Pennsylvanians instead occupied Shamokin and were building their own formidable fortress, Fort Augusta. Meanwhile the Iroquois had sent demands that the Delawares lay down their arms. While the Iroquois remained comparatively impotent for the moment, the Susquehanna Delawares still felt isolated and vulnerable, but as long as the French were prepared to offer support, some were willing to oppose the British. However, in case French support should suddenly evaporate, some Delawares prepared to open negotiations.[25]

Scarouady and his companions arrived on the Susquehanna in March 1756. There they informed the Delawares of the Quakers' wish for peace and met with the leader of the Wyoming Delawares, Teedyuscung. He had been a resident of the Moravian mission at Gnadenhütten in the early 1750s, but in 1753 he had been chosen as headman by the Wyoming Delawares. The following year, accompanied by a fellow Delaware, Shabash, he had led a schism of the Gnadenhütten Indians and encouraged a sizable part of the Moravian congregation to leave the mission to live with him in the Wyoming Valley. He was not unknown to Scarouady, for he had met him the previous winter when he made clear his opposition to the British. He had then seemed ill disposed to making peace. Now, however, Teedyuscung seemed unsure. He was desperately in need of supplies. The Quakers' offer sounded tempting, but he wondered whether he could he trust other Pennsylvanians. Teedyuscung decided to play both sides. He sent the messengers back to Philadelphia, saying that he was prepared to talk. At the same time, however, he hurriedly sent a deputation to Niagara to assess the willingness of the French to supply him. Teedyuscung's messengers found the French welcoming, but much to their horror they discovered that the French garrison at Niagara was almost as short of provisions as they were. There could be little hope of obtaining future supplies from the French.[26]

Morris was heartened by the news of Teedyuscung's willingness to talk and immediately proclaimed a cessation of hostilities to the east of the Susquehanna. He sent Newcastle back to the Delawares to encourage them to come down to the province. At daybreak on June 21, braving the threat from French raiding parties and the even greater threat from the settlers who had set out to intercept the raiders, two bedraggled Indians, Nicodemus and his son Christian, forerunners for Teedyuscung, arrived in the Moravian settlement of Bethlehem. They had come to inform the Pennsylvanians that the Wyoming and Diahoga Indians were ready for negotiations. On July 15 Teedyuscung, having been assured by Nicodemus and Christian that he was safe, arrived at Fort Allen.[27]

Newcastle informed Morris of Teedyuscung's arrival. The time had come for Pennsylvania to negotiate with the Delawares. However, it was not just Morris whom Newcastle informed. He also visited the homes of several leading Quakers, letting them know that since the Quakers had initiated the peace proposals it was vital for them to attend the forthcoming conference. The next evening, July 20, at a hastily convened meeting, the Friends decided that they must organize an association to promote the work of peace and specifically to raise a subscription to provide gifts for the conference. The group would in December finally adopt the name the "Friendly Association." The association immediately showed its potential by raising twelve hundred pounds for these gifts in less than a week.[28]

Meanwhile, Teedyuscung awaited the arrival of the Pennsylvanians at Fort Allen. The local settlers around the fort were uncertain how to treat his deputation. Timothy Horsfield wrote to the governor that the local people "are not sure whether they are Friends or Enemys . . . [and] hope that your Honour will not expose them like Sheep to the Mouths of the Wolves." Morris himself was not quite sure of the Delawares' intentions and invited them to Easton where he could post a better guard, "in case they should not be so friendly as they Pretend."[29]

Easton was an unfortunate location in many ways. The local inhabitants were suspicious of their former enemies and were "very ignorant & indiscreet" in their comments around the Delawares, many of whom understood English. The local magistrates, charged with keeping order in the town during the conference, informed Morris that they were "apprehensive that the whole Body of the Country People will come and with some of the Town, force the Indians away." The magistrates also feared that the inhabitants' "Curiosity, especially when in Liquor, will lead them to go & see the Indians with whom they will either quarrel [or] if it is possible . . . give them Liquor and make them drunk." The conference thus opened in an environment of considerable mistrust.[30]

Sensing the importance of the negotiations, the Privy Council sent some of their most prominent members, James Logan, Richard Peters, Benjamin Chew, and Thomas Mifflin. However, it was not the eminent councilors, or even Governor Morris, who were the linchpin to the negotiations, but rather Teedyuscung, the "King of the Delawares." Born on the New Jersey side of the Delaware River, Teedyuscung was well versed in Anglo-American ways. Contemporaries described him as "near fifty years old, a lusty rawboned Man, haughty and very desirous of Respect and Command." Conrad Weiser described him as "well inclined" and noted that "he talked in high terms of his own Merit, but expressed himself a Friend." He had a short temper and was desperately jealous of any threat to his authority.[31] Teedyuscung had come to Easton to see what the Pennsylvanians could offer in return for peace. He sensed that the French could not sustain the Delawares and that they would be unable to resist a combined assault from the British and Iroquois. By the summer of 1756 Pennsylvania was reeling under the onslaught of Indian raids and was desperate for peace. The time seemed ripe to push Delaware claims of political independence from the Iroquois, to attempt to recover lost territory on the Delaware River, and to gain guarantees for the territory they still held. The Quaker offer of mediation seemed to provide the possibility of obtaining a just settlement.

Governor Morris arrived at Easton on July 25, but he postponed negotiations for several days to await the arrival of provincial interpreter Conrad Weiser. The delay provided an opportunity for Teedyuscung to meet face-to-face with the Quakers. Teedyuscung publicly "expressed his Regard for and confidence" in them and added that "Newcastle had told him of the Quakers, and that they would come to meet him." The Quakers believed that this demonstration of faith offered an unparalleled opportunity to resolve the conflict. Governor Morris, however, was angered at these direct talks, seeing them as a threat to his authority, and immediately issued orders that "no Person should speak with the Indians, and a Guard was sett near their Lodgings to prevent it."[32] However, despite Morris's orders Teedyuscung slipped past the guard and that night "came uninvited & supp'd" with the Quakers. This was the final indignity for Morris, who sent a haughty message to the Quakers that "he should treat them as his Majesty's Enemies if they held any more Conference with the Indians on any matter relating to the Government."[33] These encounters were unfortunate, for although from Quaker accounts it appears that little of substance occurred, any future complaint or request that Teedyuscung made could be dismissed as a Quaker creation.

When the conference finally convened, Teedyuscung made few specific demands. He had come merely to open negotiations with the Pennsylvanians and to discover their disposition toward peace. Morris, for his part, seemed prepared to recognize both Teedyuscung's claim to speak for the Delawares and his claim that the Iroquois had renounced their overlordship of the Susquehanna Delawares. However, Morris asked for more time before concluding a formal peace and demanded that the Delawares return all their prisoners. Teedyuscung replied that he too would need time to collect prisoners and added that he also believed that he could broaden the peace process by including his brethren on the Ohio, and possibly even the Shawnees and the Francophile Senecas. Both sides thus promised to return to Easton in two months. For the first time Teedyuscung held out the prospect of a general peace that would end the raids on the backcountry. However, Teedyuscung had greatly overestimated his own diplomatic weight. He did not have the influence among the Ohio Indians to bring them into the peace process. Only the presence of a British army in the region would do that.[34]

The Pennsylvanians, for their part, tried to cement their friendship by providing a lavish assortment of gifts for the Delawares. Fortunately for Morris, the Quakers had brought with them a large assortment of Indian goods, for it turned out that the provincial present was rather paltry. The provincial gift and the Friendly Association's were presented to the Delawares together with a simple announcement that "a part of this Present was given by the People called Quakers." However, the Quakers skillfully appended a list of all the presents they had supplied, leaving Teedyuscung in no doubt as to who his main benefactors were.[35]

After the conference Teedyuscung dallied for over a month at Fort Allen, despite his promise to return in two months with more Indians. Rumors claimed that he had remained in Pennsylvania only to talk to the Moravian Indians at Bethlehem and inform them of a plot to attack the colony so that they could make their escape. Other reports claimed that the Delawares had burned all their presents in disgust and were now determined to continue the war. Neither of these rumors was true, but they do reflect the fears of the backcountry settlers about the Delawares' intentions. Teedyuscung, for his part, was equally suspicious of the Pennsylvanians. When he finally reached Wyoming, he heard rumors that the Pennsylvanians now intended to capture him, and he delayed his return for several weeks. He sent messengers ahead who reported that he would be safe, but many of his men were still reluctant to continue. He was forced to leave them behind and continue to Easton with only a small retinue. Negotiations finally resumed on November 8.[36]

Following the rumors of the Delawares' disgust at the small size of the presents distributed at Easton in July, the Quakers determined that at any future conference suitably large presents should be distributed.

These would both demonstrate the colony's esteem for those with whom they were negotiating and allow the Quakers to participate actively in support of the colony's war effort without compromising their principles. They were also hopeful that the change of governor would provide added support for their activities. They had grounds for this hope, for after his arrival "Governor Denny . . . in several Occasional Conversations appeared well disposed to our Design." Unfortunately, he soon changed his mind and would not even meet face-to-face with Quaker representatives, demanding that all future business be conducted only by letter. The Quakers had no doubt where the blame for his sudden change of heart lay—with the proprietary faction, for they "were afterwards informed [that] this was occasioned by some Misrepresentations made to him and his Council by Secretary Peters."[37] Nevertheless, the Quakers were determined to press on. After a hurriedly called meeting at Israel Pemberton's house, they sent an address to Governor Denny stressing that the Delawares had placed "great Confidence in the Continuance of our Endeavours." If they were now suddenly banned from the negotiations, the Delawares might become suspicious about the colony's intentions. They asked Denny to allow their representatives to attend the upcoming meeting and to give their presents of clothing to the Delawares. Denny finally agreed that the Quakers could participate. The Quakers may have convinced Denny that Peters had lied to him about their intentions. However, the governor almost certainly also had other motives for changing his mind. He was aware of the rumored dissatisfaction of the Delawares with the previous presents, but his continuing disputes with the assembly meant that he remained desperately short of cash. His need for cash quickly overcame any reticence, and he replied that he would happily include the Quakers' gift with the provincial present. If he was to accept their substantial present, he had little choice but to inform the Quakers that he would also "be glad to see them at Easton."[38]

The First Treaty of Easton

The conference that met in Easton in November 1756 was fraught with disputes even before the proceedings officially commenced. These disputes had at their heart the conflict between the assembly and the proprietors, for it was the proprietors' acquisition of lands that would soon become the focus of the negotiations. The Quakers were determined to discover the causes for the Delawares' defection. At their previous meeting in July Teedyuscung had not made clear the reasons for the estrangement of the Delawares. The Quakers and many of the assemblymen who attended the conference were now determined that he should reveal the full causes of the war so that these could be quickly rectified. Richard Peters, a staunch supporter of the Penns, feared that such a revelation might disclose some underhand dealings of the proprietors. He therefore attempted to postpone any direct questioning of the Delawares about the causes of the war, claiming rather lamely that Johnson had already uncovered the cause, which was quite clearly the intervention of the French. In his quest to divert the negotiations he was backed by another supporter of the Penns and the provincial interpreter, Conrad Weiser, who also "endeavor'd to divert the Governor from putting the Question about Frauds and Grievances pretending it not to be the proper Time for it and that the Indians are not used to give Answers off hand." Despite the efforts of Peters and Weiser, the Quakers and assemblymen pressed on. There followed a "warm Debate" between the Quakers and the proprietary supporters in which Peters and Weiser were forced to submit to the Quakers' demands, although they were successful in obtaining an agreement that the Delawares would be asked "no leading Questions, as whether the Proprietor ever wronged them." There would be no specific question about land fraud.[39]

When the conference finally opened on November 13, Denny asked Teedyuscung outright: "Have we the Governor or People of Pennsylvania, done you any kind of Injury? If you think we have, you should be honest and tell us your Hearts."[40] Teedyuscung was, not unnaturally, worried about being too frank and would only say vaguely that "some things that have passed in former times, both in this and other Governments, were not well pleasing to the Indians." The explanation was insufficient, and Denny once more pressed Teedyuscung for a full answer. Finally, Teedyuscung complained that the root of the Delawares' alienation lay in the province's fraudulent acquisition of their lands. He continued: "I have not far to go for an Instance; this very Ground that is under me . . . was my Land and Inheritance, and is taken from me by fraud. When I say this Ground, I mean all the Land lying between Tohicon Creek and Wioming, on the River Susquahannah."[41]

Teedyuscung's claim was a bombshell, for Easton was on land acquired in the 1737 Walking Purchase. Richard Peters pretended to be so confused that he stopped taking minutes, hoping rather naively that if the official minutes contained no reference to this statement it might be passed over. Unfortunately for Peters, Denny noted that the Quakers' clerk, Charles Thomson, was still taking notes; he stated that he "desired him to proceed therein & signified that he should consider his Notes as the most Perfect." The following morning Peters stormed in on the Quakers and demanded to see the notes. He bellowed that "Mr. Thomson has got it that the Proprietaries were greedy of purchasing Lands and had bought of them that had no right to sell which was Mr Franklins Interpretation to blacken the Proprietaries and support a Party—that the Proprietaries could not be charged therewith nor had Teedyuscung said any such thing." He accused the Quakers specifically of "putting things in the Indians Heads."[42]

Peters's claim of Quaker interference was not totally groundless. After Teedyuscung had made his accusation, several Quakers met with Moses Tatamy to discuss the complaint. It was in this meeting that attention first focused directly on the Walking Purchase.[43] In the open conference Teedyuscung had made no specific reference to this purchase. He had merely referred to the "very Ground that is under me," and Easton was located on lands acquired in the Walking Purchase. This was more a rhetorical technique than a specific reference, and Teedyuscung did not mean to suggest that the Walking Purchase was the sole cause of the Delawares' alienation. The borders he mentioned included far more territory than Pennsylvania had acquired by this one purchase, and Teedyuscung went on to elaborate a series of other grievances, including the alteration of deeds after the fact, the fraudulent enlargement of boundaries covered in deeds, and the purchase of lands from Indians who had no claim to them. Most significantly, the Delawares complained that the Iroquois, especially the Mohawks, had used their overlordship to sell land against the Delawares' wishes. In essence, this was the crux of Teedyuscung's complaint: the proprietors had acquired lands from the Iroquois and not from the Delawares. However, for the antiproprietary faction a focus on the Penns' misdoings rather than simply on the acquisition of lands from the Iroquois provided ammunition in their long-running battle. Instead of focusing their attention on the role of the Iroquois in the disposal of Delaware lands, they focused on the misconduct of the proprietors.[44]

Teedyuscung thus had accidentally directed attention to the Walking

Purchase, and the focus on this issue would eventually sink the Delawares' cause. The proprietors were only too aware of the unscrupulous nature of the purchase: they had dredged up at best only the ancient draft for a deed, at worst an absolute forgery, and then conducted the "walk" for the purchase with a trained runner.[45] While the antiproprietary faction remained unaware of the details of the fraud, the sensitivity of the proprietors and their supporters on this issue suggested that here was ground where they could launch a fatal attack. If they could prove that the proprietors' actions had caused the war, Whitehall would have little choice but to end the proprietors' government and royalize the colony. Thus, unfortunately for the Delawares, the issue immediately assumed a much broader importance in colonial and imperial politics.

Indeed, while Teedyuscung was making his claims in Easton, in London the Privy Council and the Board of Trade were already hearing arguments about the royalization of the colony. Those who opposed the proprietors quickly leveled Teedyuscung's charges directly against the Penns. The first petition presented to the Privy Council by the antiproprietary faction in the fall of 1756, before Teedyuscung even made his claim, had claimed that alienation of the Delawares was the result of "some Suspicions in His [Penn's] Manner of dealing with the Indians."[46] Charges against the Penns also came from another direction—Sir William Johnson. Pennsylvania's negotiations with the Delawares threatened Iroquois influence over the tribe. Johnson thus sought to halt them at all costs. In the fall of 1756 he wrote to the Board of Trade attacking the proprietors and claiming that the Delawares had been alienated solely by Pennsylvania's land purchases and the stationing of troops on the Susquehanna. The Penns were horrified and in turn tried to deflect blame to Virginia's land purchases on the Ohio.[47]

On his return to Philadelphia Denny asked the council to examine proprietary dealings with the Indians, particularly the Walking Purchase.[48] The proprietors' supporters began their campaign to deflect attention from the issue of land fraud. Both Conrad Weiser and Richard Peters stressed that the Delawares had only alleged that land fraud was, in Denny's words, "the cause why the Blow came the harder on us." They claimed that the accusations of land fraud had encouraged the Delawares to attack the colony with ferocity once the fighting had commenced but were not the cause of the war.[49]

Weiser and Peters pursued separate strategies. Weiser claimed it would be difficult, if not impossible, to determine Teedyuscung's claims, as any Indians who might have been defrauded were "either dead or gone . . . to other places." He pointed out that the Delawares had previously brought their complaints before the Iroquois, who had dismissed them. He also advised Denny against promising Teedyuscung a government investigation of his complaint, since "such Promises had frequently been made . . . by the Governors of other Provinces and not performed, and these people might consider them now as made with a Design to evade giving them redress."[50] Avoiding any commitment would, of course, also mean that the government would be under less pressure to examine Teedyuscung's claims in detail.

Peters attempted to discredit Teedyuscung's claims by arguing that the motivation for them came from elsewhere. While the Francophile Indians had initially "corrupted" the Delawares, Peters claimed that it was the Quakers who had fabricated the charge of proprietary land fraud in order to have ammunition against the proprietary government.[51]

The Delawares' cause would have to wait for future conferences to be determined, but Peters and Weiser were already pursuing strategies that would make it very difficult for them to receive justice. Nevertheless, until Pennsylvania could find a more effective way of defending its frontiers, the colony needed to continue negotiations.

Virginia's Indian Diplomacy

While Pennsylvania was seeking a diplomatic solution to end the war with the Susquehanna Delawares, Virginia was engaging in a rather different diplomatic offensive. Unlike Pennsylvania, which sought to make peace with the Indians, Virginia hoped to find Indian allies with whom the colony could wage war against the Ohio Indians. In the spring of 1756, in the wake of the Sandy Creek debacle, Governor Dinwiddie sent Andrew Lewis to Chota, one of the Cherokees' main towns, to build a post among the Cherokees, Fort Loudoun. Dinwiddie hoped that this fort would secure an alliance with the Cherokees and encourage them to send more warriors to aid Virginia. The governor did not intend to garrison the fort with a large number of men; rather, he intended it to serve as a place of retreat for the warriors' families while they were away. The Cherokees welcomed the fort because they believed trade with Virginia would soon follow, lessening their dependence upon South Carolina. However, the traders did not come, and for the next eighteen months Virginia's relations with the Cherokees fluctuated wildly. Virginia continued to send many diplomatic missions to the Cherokees, and several Cherokee deputations visited Williamsburg, but when Virginia traders did not flock to Fort Loudoun many Cherokees grew restless at the existence of the British outpost in their midst. Others were suspicious at settlers who had fled the Virginia frontier, settling on Cherokee hunting grounds in the Lower Cane Valley. The activities of Carolina traders further heightened Cherokee misgivings. Jealous that the gifts of Indian diplomacy might lessen the demand for their trade goods, and more importantly that Virginia traders might destroy their livelihood, the Carolinians spread rumors of Virginian plots and encouraged the Cherokees to break their relations with the colony.[52]

The French also made efforts to undermine Virginia's relations with the Cherokees. By the summer of 1756 the French had gained the support of many of the neighboring Creeks and through them sent envoys to the Cherokees. French influence was particularly strong in the westernmost Cherokee town, Great Tellico, and during the summer of 1756 many Cherokees threatened to join the French. In an attempt to strengthen the Francophile faction Governor Vaudreuil even invited a party of Cherokees to Detroit to negotiate. Vaudreuil did not need to do much to weaken Virginia's alliance with the Cherokees, for the greatest threat to the alliance came from the Virginians themselves. During the autumn of 1756 increasing numbers of Cherokee warriors who had served on the frontier returned home with tales of the colony's dishonorable behavior. In entering the conflict Cherokee warriors were not motivated by an altruistic desire to protect the Virginians from the Ohio Indians, although their traditional enmity may have been some incentive. Instead they were lured principally by Virginia's promises of payment. They were well aware that their service was invaluable to the colony, and they expected equal compensation, particularly "Cloaths, Arms, and Ammunition."[53]

Virginia's funds soon ran short, the supply of trade goods available in the colony dried up, and Dinwiddie found it increasingly difficult to reward the Cherokees as they expected. Even Virginia's closest allies grew restless. The Anglophile leader the "Swallow" protested that it was specifically the "Promise of great Rewards from the Governour that engaged his young Men to come in, and that the Govr had now made him a Liar amongst his own Warriours." The Virginians thought that they could satisfy the Cherokees with the normal gifts that accompanied diplomacy, but having decided to wage war for economic reasons, the Cherokees wanted, and needed, more.[54]

Fighting on the Virginia frontier prevented the Cherokees from hunting for skins with which to trade. In addition, the uncertain conditions on the southern frontier kept traders from venturing to their towns. As a result the prices that the Cherokees had to pay for trade goods rose. They were caught in a trap: they were unable to hunt, while the prices for the items they needed increased. Dinwiddie had assured them that they would be rewarded handsomely for their services, and thus the colony's failure to provide adequate gifts caused deep dissatisfaction. When upon their arrival in Virginia the Cherokees heard that the colony's presents had not yet arrived from London, they were disgusted, and some warriors resorted to attacking and looting the frontier settlements they passed. Not until the end of September 1756 did the Cherokees receive any of the goods they had been promised the previous spring.[55]

The reports of growing Cherokee dissatisfaction disturbed the House of Burgesses. In the fall of 1756 the House granted two thousand pounds worth of goods for the Cherokees and allowed Dinwiddie to draw on other small sums that they had previously raised but that had not been used to support his Indian diplomacy. When the House of Burgesses met again in April 1757 they once more attempted to strengthen the Cherokee alliance. Realizing the importance of trade to winning the goodwill and allegiance of the Indians, the House hurriedly passed another act, providing for the establishment of an Indian trade to supply the Cherokees "with the goods and other necessaries for their support upon reasonable terms."[56] However, the House misunderstood the nature of the immediate crisis, for the act was designed to encourage private traders to develop the colony's relationship with the Cherokee nation, not to meet the needs of the hundreds of warriors who were heading north. The crisis remained unresolved.

Despite the dissatisfaction of many warriors who served on Virginia's frontiers, substantial numbers of Cherokees, accompanied by smaller numbers of Catawbas and Nottaways, continued to arrive on the frontier. The presence of Cherokee scouts, guides, and warriors enabled the Virginia Regiment to launch offensives of its own. Several combined parties of Indians and provincial troops set out from Winchester to patrol the frontier and intercept incoming raiding parties. Some parties, composed almost exclusively of Indians but sometimes including provincial observers, even launched raids around Fort Duquesne and harassed French supply routes, killing several French soldiers and, most importantly, distracting the Ohio Indians from their raids on the Virginia frontier.[57]

The success of the Virginians in wooing so many parties to the frontier, however, sowed the seeds of future disaster. Not only were Indian trade goods in very short supply, but the direction of Indian affairs was in chaos. Whitehall had appointed Edmund Atkin the southern superintendent for Indian affairs, and his jurisdiction included Virginia. Sir William Johnson, on the other hand, was supervisor for the northern colonies, including Pennsylvania. Atkin arrived in Williamsburg from South Carolina in April 1757 to coordinate Virginia's diplomacy with the Cherokees. The Virginia council immediately entrusted him with all supervision of Indian affairs on the colony's frontier and provided him with gifts for the Cherokees. Instead of hurrying to the frontier to meet the troubled Cherokees, Atkin dallied in Williamsburg dealing with personal business and did not arrive in Winchester until June 2, almost two months after his arrival in the colony. His absence left Indian affairs in Winchester in turmoil.[58]

Circumstances improved only slightly when he did arrive. The delay had caused some Cherokee parties to despair of receiving supplies from Virginia and to head north to seek support from Pennsylvania and Maryland. Several groups met Johnson's representative George Croghan in early June. They protested "that they did not think themselves sufficiently rewarded for their Services" in Virginia and complained that "after promising us a great deal of Goods . . . [the Virginians] have not given us Cloths for Ourselves, tho' we have been five Months in their Country."[59] Croghan's talks with the Cherokees infuriated Atkin, who, not unlike Johnson, was "very tenacious of his Power." He forbade Croghan from undertaking any further negotiations and ordered Pennsylvania not to make any more gifts to the Cherokees, a most unfortunate order at a time when the Cherokees already felt slighted by the paucity of their rewards. Atkin also instructed the Cherokees not to head north to Pennsylvania. However, this action seemed to the Cherokees no more than an attempt to prevent them from accessing another source of trade goods, and it merely increased their hostility. Problems grew yet worse when Atkin, who lacked an adequate interpreter, suspected French spies among the Cherokees and threw several warriors into the Winchester jail.[60]

The largest Cherokee group to arrive on the frontier in the spring of 1757 was led by Wawhatchee, from the eastern Lower Cherokee settlements around Estatoe. From the outset his party encountered problems. Wawhatchee came by a more easterly route than the Virginians had expected, passing through Lunenburg and Halifax Counties, where there were no gifts awaiting him, as Dinwiddie had arranged for the party's gifts to be assembled at the Bedford Court House. Angered, Wawhatchee and his party soon began ransacking local farms and plantations, placing Dinwiddie in a quandary. Although reluctant to punish the Cherokees too severely for fear of discouraging them from intervening against the French, Dinwiddie needed to mollify the Halifax and Lunenburg inhabitants. He ordered Clement Read, a Halifax justice, to round up the Cherokees "in a mild Method," while instructing the county lieutenants to have the militia ready if needed. Read then hurried Wawhatchee's group on to Winchester, promising that presents awaited them there.[61]

When they arrived in Winchester the gifts were not ready. This was the final insult, and many of Wawhatchee's warriors stormed off in disgust. Their discontent soon spread to other groups. George Mercer warned Washington that the Cherokees were "all wavering." They had told him that "the Govr knew not how to treat Indians; that the French treated them always like Children, and gave them what Goods they wanted." Wawhatchee himself had warned that if he was no given sufficient reward he "would come & fight, and if he did not get it . . . he would turn back and take every thing from the Inhabitants as they went along, and maybe . . . scalp some of them too." By the beginning of August 1757 most of the warriors had quit Virginia's service and returned south, leaving the frontier once more dangerously exposed.[62]

The Decline of Frontier Attacks: The Winter of 1756–1757

The use of Cherokee and Catawba warriors and the commencement of negotiations with the Delawares seemed at first to bear fruit. The number of Indian raids on the backcountry declined sharply over the winter of 1756–57. Yet the decline in raids was not simply due to activities of the British. Initially, heavy snows made crossing the Appalachians difficult as the winter was unusually bitter. One French officer reported that it had been "the most severe winter, during which the snow has been as much as ten or twelve feet deep."[63] Following the thaw in the spring the raids were renewed, but not with the same vigor. Indeed, from the fall of 1756 until the summer of 1757 there were only two small raids on the Virginia backcountry. One reason for the decline in the Ohio Indians' enthusiasm lay in the onset of a fierce smallpox epidemic. During 1755 and 1756 a major smallpox epidemic had swept through Canada. Those Indians who served alongside the French on the Ohio or on the St. Lawrence returned home carrying the disease with them. While the epidemic did not spread much further west than Fort Duquesne, it made many Indians reluctant to travel east in case they contracted the disease. Another reason for the lack of raids was the involvement of many raiders in the French campaign against Fort William Henry. Nearly one thousand Indians from the Ohio Valley participated in the campaign over the summer, lured by the prospect of captives and booty. With such rich pickings elsewhere, the devastated Virginia and Pennsylvania backcountry was less enticing.[64]

Over the winter the French encouraged what raiding parties they encountered to attack Pennsylvania's northern frontier in the hope of disrupting Pennsylvania's negotiations with the Delawares. During the negotiations at Easton in November 1756 small groups of Delawares, opposed to Teedyuscung's peace endeavors, raided nearby Lancaster and Berks Counties. At the beginning of December other Delaware parties attacked Berks and Northampton Counties. On the western frontier the Ohio Indians continued to conduct raids on Pennsylvania, though not Virginia. The winter raiders were predominantly Ohio Shawnees and Delawares, most of whom had been sent out from Fort Duquesne, for the French sought to maintain pressure on the British while using diplomacy with the Susquehanna Delawares to prevent their concluding a separate peace. Raiders continued to harass the region to the rear of Fort Cumberland, and several small parties forayed around the fort itself and along the Potomac River.[65]

When spring arrived the Indians continued their attacks upon Pennsylvania. A large party of Ohio Shawnees and Delawares, reinforced by Potawatomis and Ottawas, attacked near Chambersburg and pressed on to ravage the Conococheague Valley. Several smaller parties scouted around Fort Cumberland, killing several guardsmen. Simultaneously a large party of Francophile Senecas and Cayugas attacked Northampton County.

From there they pressed west into Berks County and in early May raided Swataro Creek. The raiders soon advanced into the Susquehanna Valley, where the Senecas and Cayugas coalesced with a group of Ohio Indians under French commander Chauvignerie, attacking from the west. In June yet another raiding party assaulted Cumberland County, penetrating as far as the Great and Little Coves. The raids devastated a large area along the Susquehanna, and settlers who had drifted home during the winter lull in raids once more abandoned much of the region north and west of Harris's Ferry.[66]

Over the winter Virginia had been spared the worst attacks, but in the summer of 1757 the assault on the Virginia backcountry recommenced. At the beginning of June over two hundred Ohio Indians gathered at Fort Duquesne. The French intended to launch a major raid on Virginia and to attack and isolate Fort Cumberland. If nothing else, Washington would be forced to concentrate substantial forces on the fort's defense and would waste valuable manpower and supplies keeping the supply routes open. This would leave the remainder of the colony's frontier exposed. If Washington failed to reinforce the fort, it might be possible to destroy it. Washington received advance intelligence of the raid from a scouting party. However, he had so few men available for service that he was unable to take advantage of this news. His position was desperate. Over 200 of his men, under the command of Adam Stephen, had been sent to South Carolina, where there was fear of a Spanish attack. Due to desertion and the slow pace of recruitment, Washington had only 384 men fit for duty, and some of those were over two hundred miles away, on the Augusta County frontier. With so few men, Washington pondered how he could possibly protect the frontier. Fort Cumberland was exceptionally exposed. Since 1756 Maryland had refused to provide any men or resources for the garrison, arguing that it protected Virginia more than Maryland. With no Maryland troops and with the Virginia garrison no more than a skeleton, Washington and his commanders agreed that the fort "must inevitably fall into their hands." Fort Cumberland's fall, especially were the French to capture the substantial magazine there, would imperil the entire frontier, and Winchester would surely soon fall.[67]

Washington called his officers to an emergency council of war. They agreed that it was hopeless to defend the fort and that they should make a final stand at Winchester. To facilitate the defense of the town it was imperative to recall the men stationed on the south branch, Patterson's

Creek, and the Cacapon. All but seven of the frontier posts would be abandoned. Without the protection offered by the troops, civilians would be exposed to French and Indian raids, and thus the evacuation meant accepting the loss of many valuable settlements. It was a terrible decision that demonstrated how little progress had been made in defending the frontier.[68] If these settlements were to be abandoned, the civilians must be warned and removed, and Washington thus ordered Andrew Lewis to supervise the evacuation of civilians "before it may be too late."[69] Fortunately for Washington, the French commander of the raid, Montisambert, fell ill and was forced to return to Fort Duquesne. Lacking a commander to coordinate their activities against the fort, the raiders split into small groups. Instead of massing to attack Fort Cumberland, they sought booty in the now largely abandoned settlements of the south branch. The Virginia frontier was spared further devastation, and Fort Cumberland remained in British hands.[70]

While the focus of the summer raids was on northern Virginia, other smaller parties of Ohio Indians recommenced attacks on Augusta County in an effort to interdict communication between Virginia and the Cherokees. In mid-July a raiding party attacked southern Augusta County, penetrating deep into Bedford, Halifax, and even Lunenburg Counties. The attacks caused chaos that was heightened by the actions of some of the local militia commanders, in particular Col. David Stewart, who at the first sign of raiders panicked and began "raising false Alarms, terrifying the People, and refusing to act as becomes an Officer."[71]

The raids continued through the summer. In mid-August a raiding party attacked the south branch. The raiders pressed on to the Cacapon and then to Cedar Creek and Stony Creek, tributaries of the Shenandoah River. A month later a large party, numbering over one hundred warriors, attacked settlements along the Potomac River and temporarily severed communications between Winchester and Carlisle. Similar raids continued until the end of November, causing settlers to abandon a large part of the northern Shenandoah Valley.[72] The renewal of raids in the summer of 1757 revealed that Virginia's release from the wrath of the French and their Indian allies had been only temporary. As the Cherokees grew increasingly disenchanted with their former allies and quit the colony's service, Virginia once more lay open to attack. Despite the diplomatic efforts of both colonies, an end to the devastation of the backcountry still seemed remote.

In Pennsylvania the continuation of the raids, despite the commencement of negotiations with the Delawares, increased demands that the government seek a military rather than diplomatic solution. They also provided an opportunity for those opposed to Teedyuscung to disparage him. At the beginning of December 1756, for instance, Richard Peters openly claimed that it was Teedyuscung's followers who were raiding the frontier. Governor Denny, however, was determined to continue negotiations. He proposed holding a general conference in March 1757 with the Susquehanna Delawares and the Iroquois and Ohio Indians. This conference, Denny hoped, could hammer out a diplomatic solution to the war. He sent George Croghan to Harris's Ferry to persuade some of the Anglophile Conestogas who lived there to send messengers to the Ohio Indians, inviting them to the conference. He also wrote to Sir William Johnson begging him to use his influence to persuade as many Iroquois as possible to attend.[73]

While many Pennsylvanians hoped that the forthcoming conference would lessen, if not halt, the raids, there were soon signs of problems. Within Pennsylvania the battle between the proprietary and antiproprietary factions continued to rage. In January 1757 several representatives of the Friendly Association approached Richard Peters for permission to search the minutes of the council for all records of land transactions to try to ascertain the exact causes of the Delawares' alienation. Peters refused the Quakers' request, but the association pressed on. In February, supported by the assembly, the association decided to assemble all the papers and records it had found relating to land purchases. This activity intensified the animosity between the association and the proprietors and even caused the Penns themselves to intervene. They ordered Peters to take care that "our malicious opponents may not take this opportunity of furnishing the Indians beforehand with more of their false suggestions" and to be "very careful who you take along with you to the Enquiry, that the Indians may not be poisoned by false Notions, to be instilled into them."[74] For all sides Teedyuscung's accusations had become a central element in their conflict. Such deep animosity within the government would hamper the progress of negotiations.

Denny and Sir William Johnson hoped to conclude negotiations with the Delawares at a grand council to be held with the Susquehanna

Delawares, the Ohio Indians, and the Iroquois at Lancaster in the spring of 1757. However, the Lancaster meeting proved to be anything but a grand council. The Iroquois arrived at the end of March and impatiently awaited the arrival of the other participants. It soon became apparent that few Ohio Indians would attend. The only Shawnees and Delawares present were a few refugees who had been living at Aughwick, George Croghan's plantation on the Juniata River. The Ohio Indians were not the only ones who failed to attend. By the middle of April Teedyuscung had still not appeared. Rumors circulated that he would not arrive for several weeks. The only message from him was a request that food and provisions be prepared for his arrival, but he gave no hint of when that would be.[75]

The end of April arrived, and the Iroquois grew restless. They threatened to leave, complaining that "we have been here a great while and the Spring is coming on Fast [and] it is Time for us to think of going Home to Plant."[76] The Pennsylvanians were horrified. The commissioners hurried up to Lancaster before the Iroquois delegates could leave, arriving on May 9. Still hoping that Teedyuscung would appear, they made hurried preparations for a meeting between Denny and the Iroquois. The Iroquois were not prepared to wait any longer. Many of their warriors had contracted smallpox and were dangerously ill. Scarouady, perhaps the staunchest British ally, died of the disease. The remaining Iroquois headmen were now desperate to leave as soon as possible.[77]

On May 12 the conference finally convened without its main participant. The reasons for Teedyuscung's absence soon became apparent. As soon as the conference opened, the Iroquois set about dismantling Teedyuscung's case point by point, even his right to speak for the Susquehanna Delawares. Instead, the Iroquois reasserted their right to negotiate on behalf of the Delawares and proceeded to brush aside all the Delawares' assertions of land fraud.[78] Denying any role in the Delawares' alienation, they claimed that it was the Pennsylvanians who had been "Covetous of Land, [and had] made Plantations" on the Delawares' land and had "spoiled their Hunting Grounds," thus driving them into the arms of the French.[79] Despite these claims, the Iroquois sought to avoid a public test of their authority over the Delawares, for they knew that they lacked the power to enforce it. Instead, they advised the Pennsylvanians that it would be better to "give up some Points to them than to contend." If the Pennsylvanians would restore some lands to the Delawares, perhaps they would cease their hostilities. Thus the Delawares could be compensated, but not for any specific lands. This formula would eventually become the basis of both the Iroquois' and the proprietors' attempts to conclude a peace.[80]

The Lancaster conference was a bitter disappointment for many Pennsylvanians. The Iroquois had publicly questioned the right of the Delawares to negotiate and thus thrown Pennsylvania's Indian diplomacy into confusion. By suggesting that the colony should compensate the Delawares, they had also alienated the proprietors. The conference had pleased no one. While Croghan and Denny were meeting with the Iroquois at Lancaster, Teedyuscung himself remained on the Susquehanna at Diahoga, afraid to confront the Iroquois, especially the Mohawks, with his accusations. Despite his promises to the Pennsylvanians, Teedyuscung had kept his options open. In the fall of 1756, after the conference at Easton, Delaware messengers had met with François-Marie Le Marchand de Lignery, the commander at Fort Duquesne, and informed him that they were "firmly resolved to abandon the English forever." So firm did their resolution appear that the French doubted the initial reports of the negotiations at Easton.[81] As soon as the French received confirmation of these negotiations, Vaudreuil attempted to bolster Delaware support for the French by sending wampum belts to Diahoga, reminding the Delawares of their former friendship and promising that if they would resettle in the vicinity of Presque Isle they would be well supplied with trade goods. Vaudreuil's belts may have had some effect, for the French continued to receive reports that the Delawares were deeply divided over the prudence of negotiating with the British, and many Delawares continued to attack the Pennsylvania frontier despite the onset of negotiations. Teedyuscung himself journeyed to Niagara and sent messages to Governor Vaudreuil, promising to send some warriors to aid in the French attack on Fort William Henry, although there is no evidence that he ever did so. He also sent representatives to the Senecas, the most Francophile of the Six Nations, seeking their support.[82]

While many Delawares may have been inclined to continue to support the French, the French were unable to provide them with much-needed supplies. By the summer of 1757 Canada itself was extremely short of provisions. Louis-Joseph, marquis de Montcalm-Gozon de Saint-Véran, feared that "the extreme scarcity we are suffering, only too severely, in the interior of the Colony, will not fail to make itself felt . . . on the

Beautiful River [the Ohio]."[83] During 1757 the French were able to secure supplies for the Ohio Country from Illinois and Louisiana, and from the captured garrison at Fort William Henry, but their own situation for 1758 was uncertain, and provisions for their Indian allies were all but nonexistent. Without ammunition from the French, not only were the Delawares unable to maintain their assaults on the frontier, but they could not hunt for skins and meat. Convinced that the French would never be able to meet the Delawares' needs, Teedyuscung pressed on with negotiations with the Pennsylvanians. When it was clear that the Iroquois had left the colony, Teedyuscung appeared in Easton at the end of June.[84]

Denny immediately sought to limit any influence that the Friendly Association might have in the forthcoming negotiations with the Delawares. He informed the Quakers that the Earl of Halifax had sent him strict orders that he was to allow no "Body or particular Society in Pennsylvania to concern themselves in any Treaty with the Indians."[85] He warned them that they would thus "do well to decline appearing at the ensuing Treaty in a Body."[86] However, aware of the substantial gifts that the Quakers had made available for the colony, he hinted that they might attend the conference as individuals rather than as representatives of the Friendly Association. The Quakers for their part assured Denny that they had the interests of Pennsylvania at heart and that Teedyuscung himself had "repeatedly inform[ed] us of the Necessity of our Personal Attendance" at Easton and had "express[ed] his Regards for & Confidence in the Quakers & declare[d] he would not proceed to any Business unless we were Present." However, they informed the governor that their attendance as individuals would be acceptable.[87]

The presence of the Quakers, however, once more provided an opportunity for the proprietary faction to dismiss the Delawares' complaints as a Quaker fabrication. Ironically, the proprietors received help from Teedyuscung himself. As the conference convened, Teedyuscung refused to rely on the provincial secretary, Richard Peters, who was of course a staunch supporter of the proprietors, and demanded his own clerk. Too often, Teedyuscung felt, records of such meetings had been distorted or changed, and he desired a separate account. To keep his record, he chose Charles Thomson, the master of the Quaker School in Philadelphia. His selection of a Quaker as clerk provided wonderful ammunition for the proprietary faction, who were now able to dismiss all Teedyuscung's claims as simply "dictated . . . by Charles Thompson, who was known to be under the Directions of the Quakers."[88]

The conference finally started at the end of July 1757. Teedyuscung's complaints focused around two issues. First, the proprietors had bought lands from Indians who "had not a Right to sell, and to whom the Lands did not belong." Second, when the Delawares had agreed to a sale, the proprietors had, "contrary to agreement or bargain, taken in more Lands than they ought to have done." Likewise, he had two objectives in negotiating. He sought compensation for the lands that the Delawares had lost and a guarantee of future Delaware possession of lands at Wyoming.[89] Teedyuscung asked the Pennsylvanians to examine their records in order to recompense those Delawares who had lost their lands. This was a clever ploy, as Croghan observed, for if the Pennsylvanians agreed, the Delawares could demonstrate that many of the lands had been sold by the Iroquois and not by the Delawares.[90] Still, many Pennsylvanians remained unable to understand how their purchase of lands from the Iroquois could be fraudulent. Denny asked Teedyuscung to clarify his complaint. Teedyuscung finally stated explicitly that they felt "the Proprietaries had made fair purchases of the Lands from the Six Nations; but these . . . were not the rightful owners of these Lands." Consequently, they would not recognize "any Deeds made by the Six Nation Indians to be good" and demanded an investigation of all deeds ceding Delaware lands to the colony.[91]

Richard Peters now stepped into the fray. He informed Teedyuscung that an investigation of the province's acquisition of Delaware land was impossible, for he had received instructions from the Penns not to open the files while Sir William Johnson investigated the matter. Any claims of fraud would have to be resolved by Johnson, not by the province. This was a serious blow to the Delawares. Teedyuscung asked the conference, "Why should we be obliged to go to Sir William Johnson to have the Proof of Lands and Deeds examined by him, when there is nothing in the way . . . [of] our making a League of Friendship?" He reminded the Pennsylvanians that he could have no hope of receiving a fair hearing from Johnson, for he was influenced by "some of the Nations . . . that have been instrumental in this Misunderstanding in selling Lands in this Province, having in former Years taken us by the Foretop and throw[n] us aside as Women."[92]

For the proprietors to retain any hope of hiding their unscrupulous land dealings, they knew that any complaint had to be investigated by Johnson. An open hearing of the proprietors' Indian affairs could mark disaster. Peters refused to provide the conference access to the deeds. Much to his horror, however, the provincial commissioners appointed by the assembly announced that they had brought copies of the deeds that they would now show the Delawares. Denny, too, was aghast. He attacked the commissioners for interfering in the negotiations and invading the proprietors' prerogative. The commissioners agreed that control of Indian affairs and particularly the purchase of Indian lands had been given to the proprietors. However, they added that they did not claim the power to make war and peace but that it was in their interest to attempt to prevent their fellow citizens from being murdered. On August 3 Denny again addressed the Delawares. He had little choice but to inform them that they could now examine the deeds. Their findings would be passed on to Johnson, and he in turn would pass on any complaints for the Crown to judge. This announcement was a masterful stroke, for it kept Johnson in the process while being sufficient to appease the Delawares. Teedyuscung thought that he had all but won his way. The Pennsylvanians had agreed to examine his complaints of land fraud. However, the proprietors knew that it would be years before his case was heard in Whitehall.[93]

The treaty negotiations finally concluded on August 7. Teedyuscung had achieved some of his goals. He had gained a pledge from Pennsylvania to examine his claims of land fraud; he had gained a guarantee of land at Wyoming and a promise from Pennsylvania to assist in the construction of a settlement there. He had also in theory gained a degree of independence for the Delawares. The conference had demonstrated that the Pennsylvanians were prepared to negotiate directly with the Delawares. As the conference concluded, Teedyuscung proclaimed: "I was stiled by my Uncles, the Six Nations, a Woman . . . and had no Hatchet in my Hand, but a Pestle or Hominy Pounder; But now . . . my Uncles have given me the Tomahawk, and appointed and authorized me to make Peace with a Tomahawk in my Hand. I take that Tomahawk and turn the edge of it against your Enemies, the French." He would now claim a role in the Covenant Chain.[94]

In reality, however, the conference had achieved little, for most of Teedyuscung's gains would be wiped away the following year. Still, what was immediately clear was the need for diplomatic efforts to be spread more widely and for Delaware warriors to assist Pennsylvania. Despite the negotiations, raiding parties had continued to harass the frontier throughout the summer and fall of 1757. Many of these parties were composed of Delawares who were opposed to Teedyuscung's negotiations and had joined with Ohio Indians sent by the French to disrupt them. The raids concentrated on Pennsylvania's northern frontier and hit the area east of the Susquehanna particularly hard. Edward Shippen warned that all Paxton Township would soon once more be abandoned, while a report in the *Pennsylvania Gazette* maintained that "there has been nothing but Murdering and Captivating . . . by the Indians."[95]

As the harvest approached, settlers in the open fields again offered a tempting target to raiding parties. Learning from their experiences of the previous year, some Cumberland County residents organized themselves into large reaping parties for protection. However, these parties proved to be more of a target. On July 18, for instance, the raiders attacked a party of twenty reapers outside Carlisle. The raids continued well into the fall, but as French supplies diminished, the raiding parties became smaller and the damage they inflicted was less. However, they continued to create panic among the settlers. Some of the smaller parties scouted around and spied upon the frontier posts in Northampton and Berks Counties, arousing fears of a large-scale assault. The raids achieved their primary purpose. Many settlers grumbled that they had thought that after peace had been made with Teedyuscung they could return home in safety, but now they had been forced to flee again. Why, many wondered, should they continue with negotiations when they yielded so few tangible results?[96]

The misery caused by the raids was heightened by a smallpox epidemic throughout the colony. The epidemic was probably started by the British troops who had arrived the previous winter. Now it spread. As settlers fled from the devastated frontier, they spread the disease. In Cumberland County the situation was especially dire. Many of the inhabitants were "afflicted with a sever Sickness and die fast; so that in many places they are neither able to defend themselves when attacked, nor to run away." Smallpox also ravaged many of the Pennsylvania Regiment's garrisons, lowering morale and the number of men fit for duty. In the fall of 1757 the Pennsylvania backcountry was still in a dismal state.[97]

HAVING FAILED to achieve a military victory, both Virginia and Pennsylvania turned to diplomacy to turn the tide of war. However, political concerns obstructed both colonies' diplomacy. In Virginia squabbles between the colony and South Carolina and between George Croghan and Edmund Atkin threatened the Cherokee alliance. More worryingly, the inability of the colony to provide gifts and rewards for Cherokee warriors caused growing dissatisfaction. Unhappy Cherokees, who made no secret of their displeasure to backcountry settlers, caused unease among settlers in southwestern Virginia. In Pennsylvania competition between the colony and Sir William Johnson equally hampered attempts to negotiate peace. However, more importantly, the broader dispute between the proprietors and the assembly significantly distorted the negotiations. The Delawares' claims were dismissed by the proprietary faction, both in Pennsylvania and in London, as a fabrication of the Quakers. Meanwhile, for their part the Susquehanna Delawares showed little evidence that they would be able to broker a wider peace with their Ohio brethren.

Military failure fueled social and political unrest in both Virginia and Pennsylvania. Imperial and political intrigues hindered the attempts of diplomacy to end the war. Negotiation with the Susquehanna Delawares failed to end the Indian raids on the backcountry and instead led to bitter accusations about Quaker intrigues. By the fall of 1757 the war still seemed far from being resolved. In October 1757 Washington despondently wrote to Dinwiddie that "nothing but vigorous offensive measures (next campaign) can save the Country . . . from inevitable desolation."[98] Unless the military tide of war could be turned, the future looked very gloomy. However, the Indians' success was already ebbing away.

6

Turning Point

The British Drive to the Ohio

IN THE BACKCOUNTRY OF VIRGINIA AND PENNSYLVANIA THE
fortunes of war changed very quickly. For the first years of the war,
Britain and her colonists had reeled from defeat upon defeat. However,
in 1757 affairs slowly began to change. In 1758 British fortunes would be
transformed. The commitment of regular forces in the region allowed
the British to undertake major offensive operations in the theater for
the first time since 1755. However, the British army that assembled on
the frontier in 1758 was very different from that assembled by Maj. Gen.
Edward Braddock. Brig. Gen. John Forbes, who commanded British
forces in Virginia and Pennsylvania, had control of an essentially multi-
national force. Regular troops recruited in England and Ireland served
alongside Scottish Highlanders and Royal Americans recruited in North
America and Germany. Accompanying them were large numbers of men
from Virginia and Pennsylvania. This was possible largely because by 1758
both Virginia and Pennsylvania had perfected the means of recruiting
troops, financed by a new administration in London willing to provide
the necessary funds to bankroll the regiments.

Forbes was also different from Braddock in that he did not intend to rely solely on the discipline and training of his troops in fighting his way to Fort Duquesne. He understood the importance of Indian diplomacy and of Indian warriors acting for the army. Throughout 1758 he encouraged Pennsylvania to continue correspondence not only with the Susquehanna Delawares but also with their Ohio brethren. On the Ohio this diplomacy began to undermine the willingness of some of the Indians to support the French.

Preparing the Campaign

Central to the fortunes of both the British and the French in the Ohio Valley was their ability to supply their troops and their Indian allies with supplies. By 1758 the British had a distinct advantage. In 1755 the Royal Navy had begun seizing French merchantmen around the world. By the end of that year, even before an official declaration of war, the navy had captured nearly three hundred French merchantmen, including sixteen provision ships bound for New France, and over eight thousand French mariners. By 1757, despite a string of French military victories on land in Europe and North America, Canada was desperately short of supplies. In Quebec the French were unable even to feed the students at the city's seminary, which they were forced to close.[1]

Scarcely able to feed their own civilians, the French could not provide for their Indian allies. European supplies were essential for the Ohio Indians, since the war had destroyed their traditional trading networks. Raiding parties required guns and ammunition that only the French or British could supply. Warriors raiding the frontier could not hunt to provide their families with food and required French provisions. Francophile war captains demanded gifts and tributes to redistribute among their villages in order to retain support. Initially, raiding parties could acquire many of these goods from abandoned plantations in the backcountry. However, as the devastation of the backcountry increased, locating fruitful targets became more difficult. As the French became unable to supply these needs, Indian enthusiasm for the war decreased. In addition, the French seemed to be making greater demands of their supporters without repaying them with the traditional gifts of diplomacy. Following their participation in the summer raids of 1757, many war captains began to express their unhappiness with the French, who were unable to reward their allies with supplies. Some even resorted to firing upon their former allies in disgust and seizing cattle and supplies from the French garrison at Fort Duquesne.[2] Increasingly the raiders included only France's closest allies, particularly Ottawa and Huron warriors. Not only did this decrease the number of Indians prepared to raid the backcountry, but it also increased logistical problems, as the Ottawas and Hurons had to traverse much greater distances to reach the frontier.

In the backcountry 1757 also marked the beginning of a change in fortunes for the colonies, which would become apparent in 1758. This shift was due to several unrelated factors. In Whitehall the creation of the Pitt-Newcastle ministry in June 1757 saw a decisive change in national policy. William Pitt saw the importance of the conflict in North America to the whole British Empire. Following the humiliation of the Convention of Klosterseven, where the Duke of Cumberland had removed his army from the field and effectively handed over control of Hanover to the French, Cumberland's influence and that of his supporters in Whitehall had declined precipitously. Pitt now assumed unopposed direction of the war. This allowed him to develop a new military policy. He was determined to hold the French at bay in Europe, providing subsidies to his German allies while launching an offensive against the French colonies around the globe, from India and Africa to North America. He was thus prepared to subsidize the conflict in North America in order to ensure success and persuaded Parliament to reimburse the colonies for their expenses in waging war. Pitt decided to commit two thousand regular troops to the Pennsylvania frontier, posting the first battalion of the Highlanders, the Seventy-seventh Regiment, and the second battalion of the Sixtieth (the Royal Americans) on the colony's frontier. These regular troops were to be joined by substantial numbers of provincial troops. Virginia was to provide two thousand men, garrisoning the frontier forts with militia units and allowing all Virginia forces to be deployed on the Ohio. Pennsylvania was also to provide two thousand men, although some of those would be posted in the province's forts. Forbes, however, feared that the colonies would be unable to raise such numbers and fretted that in Pennsylvania continuing disputes between the governor and assembly would surely hinder recruitment.[3]

For once, Forbes's fears were unfounded. British subsidies allowed both Virginia and Pennsylvania to increase bounties and pay. With Pitt promising to reimburse the colonies, both were prepared to spend lavishly. The approach worked. Sensing the importance of the campaign, the Pennsylvania Assembly quickly agreed to provide a five-pound bounty and a seven-pound advance for new recruits to encourage enlistment. Masters of indentured servants were now being recompensed for their loss, opening a new pool of recruits. Not surprisingly, the officers soon reported that they were "recruiting fast." Similarly, in Virginia the House of Burgesses approved the raising of two thousand men and created the Second Virginia Regiment, under the command of William Byrd. To encourage enlistment the Virginia bounty was doubled to ten pounds per person, and with such a high bounty the regimental ranks were filled relatively painlessly. Within just a few weeks both regiments' ranks were full.[4]

Pitt himself determined the details of the campaign to be waged in 1758. Gen. Jeffrey Amherst was to lead the attack on Louisbourg, Gen. James Abercromby was to assault Lake Champlain, and Forbes was to assault Fort Duquesne.[5] Three years after Braddock's defeat the British would make another attempt to drive the French from the forks of the Ohio. Forbes planned to collect his forces at Fort Loudoun, at the head of the Conococheague Valley on the Pennsylvania frontier. He would then assault the Ohio in the summer. This was to be a very different campaign from that waged by Braddock. Unlike Braddock, Forbes determined to secure his route by establishing defensive posts as the army advanced. This would allow him to keep his substantial supply network safe and to ensure that the army was well fed and well equipped. More importantly, it would allow him to maintain his army at the forks after his men had captured Fort Duquesne. To this end he needed to construct a series of fortified posts, hundreds of miles of road on which to transport his supplies, and thousands of bridges.[6]

Not only was the strategy different from Braddock's, but the caliber of British commanders and their knowledge of how to wage war against the Ohio Indians had also increased dramatically. No one could have been better equipped to shoulder the responsibility of forming an army for this task than Col. Henry Bouquet of the Royal American Regiment. Bouquet had wide experience in Europe and had fought in the Sardinian army, which used guerrilla units and irregular tactics in order to counter the superior strength of their French adversaries. Perhaps the biggest problem facing commanders was preparing their men for such a struggle. British regulars had been trained for European battlefields. They spent much time in complex drills to ensure that in the heat of battle their ranks would not break. Sharpshooting was considered so unimportant that each man was provided with only four balls of lead per annum with which to train. Commanders had, however, already made some modifications to the regulation of their troops in response to conditions in North America. Provincial governors had from the start of the war been arguing that the army needed to adapt to North American conditions. In 1755, following Braddock's defeat, Governor Robert Hunter Morris had written to Sir Thomas Robinson arguing that "American Irregulars are the best Troops that can be employed against Indians & in the Woods but they are not to be depended upon for any length of time, or in the attack of any fortress, but seem absolutely necessary to Accompany Regular troops in a Country Circumstanced as this is."[7]

British officers had been somewhat slow to accept Morris's ideas, but by 1758 traditional tactics and dress were being transformed. In 1758 Lt. Col. Thomas Gage raised a corps of five hundred Anglo-American woodsmen. Gage ordered these men to cut and brown their muskets and to train as light infantry who would have the mobility of rangers but the status of regular troops. The importance of Anglo-American recruits who would be familiar with some of the problems posed by the environment was also recognized with the creation of the Royal American Regiment, which was composed largely of Anglo-American recruits. Bouquet and Forbes were both very enthusiastic about the possibility of using provincial troops as light skirmishers. The members of the Second Virginia Regiment, commanded by Byrd, were soon dressed in Indian garb and employed as scouts. Indeed, Forbes wrote to Bouquet, "I must confess in this country, wee must comply and learn the Art of Warr, from Ennemy Indians or anything else who have seen the Country and Warr carried on in itt." The British army that assembled on the Pennsylvania frontier in 1758 was thus a very different creature from that of 1755.[8]

While Forbes may have had a much broader understanding of the nature of warfare in the Appalachians, he still faced many of the same problems as Braddock. In particular, like Braddock and Washington, Forbes faced the problem of encouraging backcountry settlers to provide his army with supplies and labor. As Forbes assembled his army he needed not only troops but also auxiliaries. To conduct a campaign with an army of this size in the backcountry of western Pennsylvania and the forests of the Appalachians the army would need to be largely self-sufficient, and Forbes set out to recruit a vast array of craftsmen and laborers.[9] The greatest need was for wagoners to haul the army's supplies to the forward posts. While the provinces were more successful than in previous years in providing troops for the campaign, and were able to pay the higher costs demanded by backcountry settlers to acquire provisions, Forbes still remained desperately short of wagons. In mid-May he placed advertisements throughout Pennsylvania appealing for wagons and offering to pay fifteen shillings per day for a wagon, team, and wagon master. Despite such offers few people came forward, and the shortage retarded Forbes's preparations. Forbes soon resorted to issuing veiled threats. At the end of May he informed the inhabitants of Cumberland County that the sheriff had provided Bouquet with a list of all the people who had wagons and horses but had not come forward with them. Forbes advised them to come forward immediately "in order to prevent any Damage that might happen on acco[un]t of Soldiers being turn'd loose amongst y[o]u."[10]

Forbes's threats had little effect. A few days later, after spending four days procuring only four wagons, Bouquet reported to Forbes that "Civil Authority is . . . completely nonexistent in this County."[11] He had approached the local magistrates to impress wagons, but they had refused. In anger, he berated Lancaster County justice Edward Shippen that "I must have waggons without delay, wither by contract, or impressing."[12] In order to encourage their neighbors to provide wagons without resorting to impressment, justices offered them lucrative contracts. These contracts, however, were not approved by the army. When the wagoners joined the army and discovered the real terms, some turned their wagons around and left, spreading tales of the army's unreliability instead of blaming their local justices. The problems of acquiring wagons greatly delayed the start of the expedition, although by the beginning of June the threat of impressment and the exhortations of many local justices managed to exact sufficient wagons for preparations to commence.[13]

Indian Diplomacy

While Forbes was handicapped by the failure of the backcountry settlers to provide wagons, this was partly offset by the attention he paid to overcoming the logistical problems posed by an attack on the Ohio. Even more important was his awareness of the value of Indian support. While he disliked what he perceived as the fickleness of Indian allies, he was well aware of their importance to the army and also believed that the diplomatic offensive had to be continued to blunt Indian support for the French. Unlike Braddock, he was quite prepared to negotiate directly with the Ohio Indians. Indeed, he was prepared to go much further and personally supported a diplomatic offensive designed to bring the Ohio Indians into the peace process. In doing so he risked provoking the anger of Sir William Johnson (whom he personally disliked), but despite this he pressed on. To conduct his diplomacy, at the end of May Forbes approached the Friendly Association to see if they might be able to encourage some of the Wyoming Delawares to carry news of the peace negotiations to the Ohio.[14] The association dispatched Charles Thomson and Moravian missionary Christian Frederick Post to the Susquehanna Valley. At Wyoming they discovered that several Ohio Delawares, including Pisquetomen, had already heard rumors of the peace negotiations and had come to Wyoming to find out if the reports were true. The presence of Pisquetomen was especially encouraging to the Pennsylvanians because he was the brother of Tamaqua and Shingas, the two most feared leaders of the Ohio Delawares. Indeed, over the next few years Pisquetomen was to prove an important voice for peace.[15]

Post and Thomson returned to Philadelphia accompanied by Teedyuscung and Pisquetomen. Hurriedly they arranged to meet the governor. For the first time it was apparent to the Pennsylvanians that some of the Ohio Indians sought peace. However, the Pennsylvanians were hesitant to act, fearing the wrath of Sir William Johnson, who had warned the province not to conduct its own Indian diplomacy. However, Forbes now encouraged the Pennsylvanians to continue. Forbes himself had already protested to General Abercromby about Johnson's inactivity, and Abercromby had responded by specifically giving Forbes permission to conduct his own Indian diplomacy, although Abercromby's consent was directed toward Cherokee affairs rather than broader diplomacy with the Delawares. Forbes pointed out that Johnson had made little previous effort to conduct the province's diplomacy or negotiate a final peace with the Delawares. He was well aware of the need to continue negotiations, and thus, he argued, the province had every right to press on. Encouraged by Forbes, Governor William Denny and the council decided to send Post to accompany Pisquetomen to the Ohio to ascertain the stance of the Ohio Indians and to encourage them to become involved in the peace.[16]

Forbes was not alone in welcoming the possibility of directly engaging the Ohio Indians in the peace process. For the proprietors such a policy had hidden benefits: it would lessen the need to placate the Susquehanna Delawares and might allow some of Teedyuscung's claims to be ignored. However, the machinations of the proprietary faction continued to hamper some aspects of the negotiations. In particular, the proprietary faction attempted to ignore all references to land fraud in their negotiations with the Ohio Indians. Indeed, the details of the peace negotiations at Easton that Denny provided to Pisquetomen to be carried to the Ohio carefully ignored any mention of Teedyuscung's complaints of land fraud, while the issue of defining a clear boundary between lands acquired by Pennsylvania and lands still held by the Delawares was only "repeated in very general and uncertain terms." To ensure that these terms were not explained to the Ohio Indians, Denny specifically refused to send Quaker interpreter Charles Thomson to the Ohio.[17]

Post and Pisquetomen set out for the Ohio from Philadelphia on July 15 and in less than a month had arrived at the town of Kuskuski. There they found the Delawares confused and divided. Most Delawares welcomed news that there could be a peace, as supplies were running desperately short. However, they retained deeper suspicions about the British. Shingas claimed that the British had planned "to drive us away, and settle the country or else why do you come to fight in the land that God has given us?" The Shawnees were even more Anglophobic, and many would not even travel to Kuskuski to hear Post, forcing him to travel, at great personal risk, to their camp outside Fort Duquesne. Despite Post's strongest assurances, it was apparent that most of the Indians near Fort Duquesne still held suspicions about British intentions. While many Indians desired peace, none was prepared to accept a British presence in their midst, and this would remain a central feature in relations between the British and the Ohio Indians over the next few years. Perhaps most worryingly for Pennsylvania, the Ohio Delawares quickly disassociated themselves from any agreement made with Teedyuscung on the Susquehanna. They stressed to Post that they never "had any thing to do with *Teedyuscung*" and told him to "lay aside *Teedyuscung,* and the peace made by him; for that they had nothing to do with it."[18] Here was manna for the proprietors.

Despite their concerns, many of the Ohio and Susquehanna Indians felt that they had little choice but to seek peace, for by the summer of 1758 they were desperately short of trade goods. While some headmen boasted to Post that "they get a great deal of goods from the *French;* and that the French cloath the *Indians* every year . . . and give them as much powder and lead as they want," it was equally clear that the French could no longer maintain this supply. Post's mission succeeded in persuading some Francophile Delawares to cease their raiding, although it did not stop other Shawnee warriors from joining the French forces at Fort Duquesne and attacking Forbes's column as it advanced slowly toward the forks. The presence of Forbes's army on the frontier was also important in convincing many of the Ohio Indians to support negotiations; fortuitously, the slow advance of the army allowed these negotiations to get well under way. While Post could not persuade the Ohio Delawares to send aid to the British, as Forbes had hoped, they did agree to send Pisquetomen with Post to attend the forthcoming treaty at Easton and ask that they might return to the Ohio with news of the negotiations.[19]

It was not only in realizing the importance of Indian diplomacy that Forbes differed from Braddock. Unlike Braddock, Forbes was also aware of the importance of Indian auxiliaries to the army. He sought the service of Catawba and Cherokee warriors to act as scouts and guides and to harass Indian villages on the Ohio. In the early spring he sent William Byrd to Cherokee country to encourage Cherokee support. Byrd's expedition was fraught with problems. Sir Edmund Atkin, superintendent for Indian affairs in the southern colonies, who was supposed to accompany Byrd, fell ill and remained behind. Unfortunately, he also kept all the presents, so that when Byrd arrived in Cherokee country he found himself without any gifts with which to reward any headmen who might listen to his appeals. Byrd's intervention, however, was still successful. Having heard of Virginia's offer of trade goods in return for further assistance, over five hundred warriors traveled north, despite the problems of the previous year.[20]

The French were aware of the importance of these auxiliaries to Forbes's expedition. From their base at Fort Toulouse, at the confluence of the Coosa and Tallapoosa Rivers, they encouraged the Chickasaws to raid Cherokee towns, hoping that this would make Cherokee warriors reluctant to leave their homes. Any reluctance was increased when some Cherokee shamans suggested that the nation would suffer disaster if they joined the British. As a result of their shamans' warnings and the threat of Chickasaw raids, the flow of Cherokees joining the British army ceased.[21]

The French also sponsored another series of raids by their Indian allies on southwestern Virginia, hoping that such activity would hamper communications between Forbes's army and the Cherokees. Raiding parties descended on the Virginia frontier in April and devastated a large area, killing or capturing over sixty settlers in Augusta, Bedford, Halifax, and Albemarle Counties. Hundreds more fled in panic. Their panic was heightened when on April 27 the raiders destroyed Upper Tract Fort and then on the following day descended upon Fort Seybert. Believing they would be allowed to return to Virginia, the garrison surrendered. However, the Indians seized the garrison, killing sixteen and taking the remaining twenty-four into captivity.[22]

The French succeeded better than they could have hoped in frustrating Anglo-Cherokee relations. Since some of the Ohio Indians claimed to be Cherokees, and since the settlers were incapable of distinguishing between their allies and their enemies, the raids caused settlers to be suspicious of any Indian party. Backcountry inhabitants viewed Cherokee parties journeying through Virginia with intense distrust. One militia commander accused the Cherokees of "vilinously Robing & stealing Plundering houses Puling men of[f] their horses striping & whiping Beating with tomahoaks & stoning many People." The Cherokee parties became alarmed at the hostility displayed toward them, and by mid-May the Cherokees and the Virginians had clashed in several skirmishes.[23]

The cessation of new arrivals would not have been such a problem if Forbes's expedition were already well on its way and if the Catawbas and Cherokees who had previously joined the army were content. Unfortunately, the expedition made slow progress. Washington was concerned that the inactivity of the British would encourage the Catawbas and Cherokees to quit, and "no words can tell how much they will be missed." In mid-May he warned that "unless they see the Troops assemble soon, it will be very difficult . . . to retain any number of the Cherokees."[24]

Not only were the Catawbas and Cherokees alienated by the endless delays, but they were also incensed that once more they had received no gifts for their services. Now serving in Pennsylvania, they came under the jurisdiction of Johnson, not Atkin. However, Johnson made little effort to supervise diplomacy with them. In April Washington had written to Gen. John Stanwix, asking him to ensure that the army secured "a supply of proper Goods" for the Catawbas and Cherokees, to prevent the problems that had dogged Virginia's diplomacy the previous year. Stanwix ordered Forbes to apply to the Pennsylvania provincial commissioners for money to buy goods and presents. However, the commissioners informed him that they had insufficient funds and could not help.[25] Forbes desperately attempted to get gifts and wampum elsewhere, but his problems were exacerbated because no one accompanying his army had the necessary authority to control and reward the Catawbas and Cherokees. He protested that he had "no mortal of Consequence" to oversee the Indians, for neither Atkin nor Johnson had "come themselves, nor have they sent any one person to look after those Indians, altho repeated applications have been made to both those gentlemen." Indeed, he felt unable "to account for the behaviour of Sir W[illia]m Johnston and Mr Atkin upon so Criticall and urgent an occasion as this is."[26] When pressed by Forbes to supervise the Cherokees, Johnson wrote to the commander in chief, General Abercromby, claiming that he could "see little advantage from my sending Mr Croghan or any other Person thither."[27] Forbes was outraged at Johnson's refusal and his bickering with the Pennsylvanians. He wrote to Abercromby, "I am afraid the animositys here have been carried on with too great heat, to cool soon, or produce any real good to the publick, but I shall leave no stone unturned on my part, to palliate Circumstances on both sides."[28]

As the Catawbas and Cherokees grew more discontented, Forbes and Bouquet made a final attempt to bring them into order. Frustrated and impatient, they deliberately withheld the few gifts that they did have. This action had the opposite of the intended effect, and many of the Catawbas and Cherokees stormed away from the army in utter disgust. By early June Washington's worst fears became reality: the Cherokees remaining in Winchester informed William Trent that they intended to return home because they had not received any gifts. Indeed, they warned Trent that if he did not immediately give them a "large Present to Carry home with them they would Rob all the English Houses they met with in their way home." By October only about thirty Indians, mainly Catawbas, continued with the expedition. The loss of Indian auxiliaries left the expedition dangerously exposed to surprise raids and incapable of launching diversionary raids into the Ohio Valley.[29]

Frustrated at the failure of Johnson and Atkin to conduct diplomacy with the Cherokees, Forbes wrote bitterly to General Abercomby requesting advice. Abercromby responded by specifically giving Forbes permission to conduct his own Indian diplomacy, although Abercromby's consent was directed toward Cherokee affairs rather than broader diplomacy with the Shawnees and Delawares. However, Forbes's concerns went much further than simply maintaining Cherokee allies, as he also sought to gain intelligence of French strength in the Ohio Valley and to persuade many of the Ohio Indians to halt their raids on his exposed column. Forbes thus took Abercromby's consent as justification for conducting much wider Indian diplomacy than Abercromby had intended.[30]

Forbes did not seek to bypass Johnson completely. Indeed, he hoped that Johnson would assist his attempts to gain allies among the Ohio Indians. However, Johnson was increasingly preoccupied with requests from Abercromby to obtain Iroquois assistance for his attack on Ticonderoga. As Johnson failed to provide the support he had promised, his influence was temporarily diminished. Johnson's surrender of his duties in Pennsylvania and his eclipse allowed Forbes to make his own entrée into both diplomacy and politics. Forbes intervened in two crucial areas. First, he encouraged the Pennsylvanians to continue their diplomacy with the Delawares, despite Johnson's heated opposition. Second, he took his own initiative to open negotiations with the Shawnees and Delawares inhabiting the upper Ohio Valley. Here he directed British Indian policy in new directions, where the concerns of Pennsylvania's Indian neighbors might be heeded. In doing so he would gain the most unlikely ally for a British military commander, the pacifist Quaker Friendly Association.[31]

The Problems of Wilderness Warfare

While Forbes was directing diplomacy, circumstances were conspiring to hamper preparations for his advance. Forbes discovered that many of the newly recruited provincial troops had no arms, and it proved difficult to acquire more. Forbes approached Governor Denny to provide some light arms from the provincial magazine. Denny refused, fearing it would leave the provincial forces still guarding the frontier east of the Susquehanna without weapons. Only after considerable pressure from the general did the governor relent. Forbes also approached John Blair, president of the Virginia Council and acting governor following the departure of Robert Dinwiddie in December 1757, suggesting that while the colony awaited the arrival of their new governor, Francis Fauquier, he might be able to use the arms decorating the entrance hall in the governor's palace in Williamsburg. Blair refused, but the council did agree to pay a special bounty to men who enlisted with their own weapons and promised compensation if the rigors of war damaged them. However, the bounty attracted few additional arms, and those mostly of poor quality.[32]

The provincial forces lacked not only arms but also other essential equipment. The Pennsylvania forces had no blankets. The Virginia forces lacked uniforms, "arms, tents, and other sorts of Field Equipage." Any attempt to begin the campaign with the soldiers so poorly equipped would have been disastrous. Forbes also required a mass of other equipment to construct the road and fortify the camps. He needed "Falling Axes, Broad Axes, . . . and Augers—Brass Kittles, Crescent Saws, hand saws, Trowels, Addges, Hinges, hammers and Gimbletts, Locks File saw sets and sundry other things." Consequently, he delayed while Bouquet and Sir John St. Clair scoured the backcountry for supplies and equipment.[33]

When Forbes finally began to assemble the troops, he faced a new problem: his men, particularly those in the provincial forces, deserted in huge numbers. Some left because they had previously absconded from the provincial troops to join the Royal Americans and were concerned that when the forces joined their former officers would discover them. Desertion for this reason was so extensive that Bouquet offered a pardon to all men who came forward and confessed to their crime. Twenty did so immediately. Forbes extended this amnesty and threatened that if the men had not returned to camp by June 12 he would have them hunted down and tried "without Mercy."[34] The expedition was also delayed when outbreaks of smallpox and dysentery swept through the army. Dysentery overwhelmed Forbes himself so badly in July that he was not "in a Condition, either to write, or think." He never fully recovered and would die of complications in the spring of 1759. Bouquet fretted to Forbes that "sickness has weakened the army so much that I do not see how you can furnish the necessary escorts nor guard the communication."[35]

However, despite these misfortunes, at the beginning of June the expedition finally began its advance. Since Bouquet had already established an advance post at Raystown, Forbes sent out detachments to begin building a road to move supplies from Lancaster, through Shippensburg and Fort Loudoun, to Raystown. At the end of June Forbes finally assembled the Pennsylvania forces in Raystown, withdrawing the men from the frontier posts and leaving behind skeleton garrisons composed largely of the sick and wounded. Peter Burd lamented that the garrison at Fort

Augusta "cuts a drole Figure to what it formerly did" and added that the new troops "look more like a detachment from the dead than the Liveing." As the Pennsylvania forces assembled at Raystown, the Virginia Regiments began their march from Winchester to Fort Cumberland. Washington then began construction of a road forty miles long, from Fort Cumberland to Raystown. By early August both Virginia Regiments were in Raystown.[36]

Moving the troops forward proved a painfully slow business, because of the need to construct or improve roads to move the army's supplies. Bouquet warned Forbes that there would even be delays in marching the troops from Philadelphia to Lancaster because the roads were unable to handle the volume of traffic. Roads out of the backcountry toward Fort Loudoun were even worse. John Armstrong complained that his march from Shippensburg to Fort Loudoun had been "tedious, and Subject to One tryfleing Accident & another." He added that the wagons were so decrepit that he had "never met with any thing like it & too much pains cannot be taken to get them forward." The problems grew worse when heavy rains made the roads a quagmire and swelled the rivers.[37]

Besides slowing the progress of the expedition, the poor roads also destroyed the wagons that had been so painfully acquired. Nearly half of the wagons that arrived at Fort Littleton, only halfway between Fort Loudoun and Raystown, could continue no further; Bouquet described the roads as "strewn with broken wagons."[38] The army lacked the skilled craftsmen to make the necessary repairs to the wagons once they were broken. At the beginning of July, Lewis Ourry, the commander at Fort Loudoun, complained to Bouquet that he had "neither Blacksmiths, Farriers, nor Waggon Makers nor Tools for either, and every Day Waggons breaking to pieces, & Horses wanting Shoes."[39] Many of these problems stemmed from Sir John St. Clair's inefficiency and incompetence. Forbes complained that St. Clair had not "taken the smallest pains, or . . . made the least inquiry" into assessing the problems that the army faced in crossing the Appalachians. He had failed to make adequate provision for forage for the horses along the route, and where forage was available in abandoned plantations he made no effort to gather it. Of even more concern, he had paid little attention to surveying and selecting the best route for the road. Several times workers had already cleared a section of road over the rough terrain when a substantially better passage was discovered nearby. He paid no more attention to the construction and location of the fortified posts. At Loyalhanna, the most advanced of the posts along the route, St. Clair approved the location, and construction began. When Bouquet arrived, he discovered that a hill overlooked the site and rendered it indefensible. The work had to be started afresh.[40]

St. Clair also managed to alienate many of the other officers, in particular the provincial officers, generating much tension. Some officers complained that he gave orders "in a very Odd Manner." Others complained of "his imperious & insulting manner of communicating his intention." On one occasion when St. Clair heard of the officers' discontent, "he bellow'd out Mutiny; & appearing to be in the greatest dilemma roard out what shall I do; shall I fire upon them!"[41] The most infamous incident occurred when St. Clair lost his temper with Lt. Col. Adam Stephen of the Virginia Regiment. St. Clair threw Stephen into jail, claiming that he was trying to incite "a genl mutiny amongst both Officers and Men of the Virginians." This action mortified Bouquet, who warned St. Clair that he would "have a good deal to do to justify the necessity of Such a violent measure against an officer of his Ranck."[42] Indeed, Forbes was eventually forced to write to General Amherst, urging him to tell St. Clair that as quartermaster general he had no power to give orders to troops; "this fancy tho never so absurd is not to be removed by me. . . . I beg . . . that you will set him right as to this affair."[43]

Disputes among his officers were not Forbes's only concern as he awaited the surveyors' reports on the terrain that lay ahead. He had still not determined whether the army should advance to Fort Duquesne on the road cut in 1755 by General Braddock or on a new route to be cut directly from Fort Loudoun to Fort Duquesne. While Braddock's route had already been blazed, it was considerably longer than the Pennsylvania route, crossed many rivers and creeks, and had three years' growth of underbrush to be cleared. The Pennsylvania route, however, had to be constructed over rougher and more uncertain terrain and had to cross the barrier of Laurel Ridge. Toward the end of July the surveyors reported that they had discovered a route across Laurel Ridge. Bouquet and Forbes finally concluded that the advantages of the Pennsylvania route now outweighed its disadvantages. The Virginians were horrified, for they were aware that after the war the road would serve as a route for settlers and merchants traveling to the Ohio and would bring great profits to traders and land speculators alike. They claimed that the surveyors' reports were false and launched a bitter attack on the Pennsylvanians, claiming that they had acted "without regard to the common interest," concerned merely with "advancing their private fortunes" and motivated by "a Selfish & Sordid principle." Forbes saw circumstances rather differently, commenting that "I . . . cannot Conceive what the Virginia folks would be att, for to me it appears to be them, and them only, that want to drive us into the Road by Fort Cumberland." Washington in particular refused to accept the decision. In early August, supported wholeheartedly by the Virginia Council, he sent a formal representation to Forbes protesting the choice of route and claiming that there was now no time to build a new road.[44]

The failure to use the Virginia route embittered Washington against the entire expedition. He had been an ardent supporter of the expedition, but at the beginning of September he wrote to John Robinson, the Speaker of the House of Burgesses, attacking both Forbes and Bouquet. He told Robinson that "we seem then—to act under an evil Geni—the conduct of our Leaders . . . is tempered with something—I don't care to give a name to—indeed I will go further and say they are d[evil]s or something worse . . . to whose selfish views I attribute the miscarriage of this Expedition."[45] Washington's peevishness over the issue was so great that it caused Forbes to lament that "his Behaviour about the roads, was no ways like a Soldier."[46] Indeed, at the end of the campaign he would resign his commission and retire to Mount Vernon.

While Forbes edged his army forward, raiding parties again struck the backcountry. In particular, they took advantage of the weakness of the posts on the Virginia frontier that were now manned by militia units rather than the Virginia Regiment, hoping to force the recall of some of the Virginia Regiment's forces accompanying Forbes. At the end of June a party attacked Hampshire County, crossed the south branch, and pressed on into Frederick County and the Shenandoah Valley, raiding around Masanutten Mountain. In early July the raiding party turned south and headed down the valley, spreading chaos. This raid in particular hindered preparations for Forbes's expedition, as settlers fled or refused to venture far enough from their plantations to provide the army with supplies and wagons.[47]

Despite the raids, Forbes continued to assemble his army. By August Forbes had finally massed over twenty-five hundred men in Raystown. The force included regiments from Britain, Virginia, and Pennsylvania; four companies from Maryland; and three from North Carolina.

Forbes had also overseen the construction of a road to Loyalhanna, only fifty-six miles from Fort Duquesne, over difficult terrain. Constructing it had been a great logistical achievement. However, the quality of the road was considerably poorer than Forbes had hoped. When Bouquet finally traveled to Loyalhanna in September he described the road as "abominable." He added that "no trouble had been taken to go around the hills, to remove or break the stones, and the bridges are worthless." When the weather deteriorated in early October, streams flowed along some of the roads and washed-out bridges. Bouquet commented, "To my great regret it is a job which must be done over." The construction of the road had taken considerable time. Watching the days pass, Bouquet fretted to Forbes that the expedition looked doomed to failure. The first frost could come in late September and "destroy the grass on which our cattle feed, and if we have no pork, on what shall we live?"[48]

The atrocious state of the road had also caused the destruction of many of the wagons, and by September the expedition once more had too few to move the army's supplies forward. Bouquet asked Forbes to attempt to secure more, but Forbes could only inform him that "the Magistrates . . . all agree in the great difficulty of getting fresh Waggons or Horses, saying the Farmers complain their Horses were starved for want of forage." He added simply that "we must make the best of what we have." Bouquet warned Forbes that the army had only a month's provisions and "little certainty of getting enough wagons to sustain us and to push ahead." He asked if they should now consider abandoning their attempt to reach the forks and concentrate instead on improving the route, strengthening their posts, and preparing to make an assault the following spring.[49] Bouquet believed that the army should push on, for it would force the French to maintain their Indian allies over the winter, depriving them of much-needed supplies; if the army were successful, it would immeasurably strengthen their hand in negotiating a peace with the Ohio Indians. Bouquet was also worried that the army was becoming "visibly bored and impatient." He added that "their ardor is cooling, and I am afraid that the discontent may very soon be followed by murmurs and other annoying consequences."[50]

Bouquet soon had other concerns to occupy his mind. The French were aware that the British were mounting a major assault but were initially unsure of the exact route. Bouquet sought to maintain their confusion. He ordered Washington to send parties back and forth along

Braddock's road to mislead the French into thinking that the army was advancing by that route. Yet at the beginning of August a raiding party discovered the main army and attacked one of the supply convoys. Bouquet soon reported that "the Woods about us are full of little Partys of Indians." Having identified the location of the army and its route to the Ohio, the raiders began to concentrate on disrupting its supply routes, forcing Bouquet to strengthen the escorts he provided for the convoys, diverting men from the task of constructing the road and fortifying the camps. Several parties attacked the Virginia forces around Fort Cumberland, cutting off the supply routes from Virginia to the army. Another raiding party attacked near Shippensburg in Cumberland County, threatening the tenuous supply line to Pennsylvania. As August progressed, the intensity of the raids increased. By the beginning of September Forbes was concerned that the raiders were now so numerous that the French might attempt a direct assault on one of the army's advanced posts.[51]

To protect the advancing column, Bouquet asked Washington to organize an attack on the Indian villages on the Ohio. Bouquet felt that if Washington could threaten an attack on the Indians' homes it would be "a great inducemnt for them to provide for their immediate defence and leave to the french their own quarrels to fight." Washington informed him that he had been trying to keep small parties out to harass the enemy. However, the defection of the Cherokees meant that using a larger raiding party was impossible, because the French and the Ohio Indians would detect it before it could get to the Ohio. Without Indian auxiliaries, Francophile Indians could easily surround the party and defeat it.[52]

Washington's fears for the safety of raiding parties soon proved well-founded. By the beginning of September Forbes had massed enough men at the forward base at Loyalhanna to consider preparing for his assault on Fort Duquesne. However, Bouquet, without consulting Forbes, decided to send an advanced party under the command of Maj. James Grant to reconnoiter the fort and destroy supplies, outbuildings, and an Indian camp outside its walls. If Grant could destroy the supplies at the fort, he might force the Ohio Indians to return to their homes. Grant left Loyalhanna on September 12 with 750 men, composed of a party of Highlanders and some Pennsylvania and Virginia troops. He arrived outside Fort Duquesne under the cover of night and consequently caught the garrison by surprise. However, Grant did not press his advantage; instead, he sent Andrew Lewis with a detachment of Virginia provincials to attack some of the outbuildings while he remained behind covering the retreat.[53]

Lewis had a great opportunity to destroy the fort's crucial supplies before the French were aware of his presence. However, his men advanced through the woods shooting and hollering, and the French were soon alerted. Knowing that the French must now be preparing a counterattack, Lewis and his men became nervous. He ordered a retreat before his men had done more than set fire to a few barns and outhouses. Grant made no secret of his displeasure with Lewis for retreating so hastily and attempted to organize another assault. However, as he was trying to regroup his men, the garrison counterattacked. The sortie threw Grant's force into complete confusion. Fearing capture by the Indians, the Pennsylvania troops guarding the flanks fled to save their scalps. Grant later informed Forbes that "in less than half an Hour all was in Confusion. . . . Fear had then got the better of every other passion & I hope I shall never see again such a Pannick among Troops." The French routed Grant's force. British losses were heavy. The French and Indians killed or captured over 20 officers, including Grant himself, and 271 men —over a third of the force. Another 40 returned to Loyalhanna seriously wounded.[54]

Grant had lost almost as many men as Braddock had three years earlier. The flight of the survivors was just as chaotic. Still, Bouquet was no Dunbar, and the rout did not seriously weaken British morale. Bouquet himself commented, "Contrary to my expectation, the troops do not seem at all depressed by this setback, and if everything were ready, moreover, they would be more disposed than ever to go forward." Joseph Shippen agreed with Bouquet, noting that the rout had made the forces desire revenge upon the French.[55]

Grant's defeat did, however, cause Bouquet and Forbes much consternation. It revealed that the garrison at Fort Duquesne was strong and underlined the need for the army to secure its supply lines in case the fort could not be captured before the onset of winter. It also created some mistrust between Forbes and Bouquet. Forbes had not approved the attack. Indeed, it was, he argued, "in every article directly contrary to my own opinion and my orders." Grant had previously approached Forbes for permission to lead a reconnaissance expedition to the fort, and Forbes had specifically forbidden him from undertaking such a mission. Why had Bouquet now allowed him to proceed? Forbes's greatest worry, however, was that the defeat would convince the Ohio Indians of the weakness of his army—that, like Braddock's, his force was no more than a collection of "Old Women."[56]

The French may also have been aware of this advantage, for they quickly decided to follow up on their success. On October 12 a large French and Indian party attacked the forward camp at Loyalhanna. It forced the British forces to retreat into the fortified post, inflicting heavy losses, and then plundered the camp outside the fortifications, seizing much of the army's supplies and cattle and destroying many wagons. After a fierce two-hour assault, the attackers finally withdrew. The British lost sixty-two men and five officers. Exact French and Indian casualties are unknown but were certainly light. Because the attackers departed and did not take the post, some British officers tried to present the battle at Loyalhanna as a victory, but at best it was another Pyrrhic victory. Bouquet commented ruefully: "A thousand men keep more than 1500 blockaded, carry off all their horses, and retire undisturbed with all their wounded and perhaps ours, after burying their dead. This enterprise which should have cost the enemy dearly shows a great deal of contempt for us, and the behaviour of our troops in the woods justifies their idea only too well."[57]

The expedition was at a critical juncture. Although finally within attacking distance of Fort Duquesne, the British were dangerously short of horses and wagons, and if the weather turned inclement they could lose most of their munitions and supplies. The French garrison seemed strong and capable of resisting for some time. However, there were many reasons to press forward. Not least was the unwillingness of the colonies to supply another expedition should this one achieve nothing. Governor Fauquier doubted whether the Virginia House of Burgesses would continue to support the campaign into 1759 because their enthusiasm had been "a little stifled by the inactivity of this Campaign." He informed the Board of Trade that the Virginians were very critical of Forbes's campaign and that "this Inactivity as it is here call'd, and the long Delay before they set forward, has raised a Doubt whether the Attack can be attempted this year which has so much soured some of the Members of the assembly that they are unwilling to grant any more Money towards carrying on the Expedition."[58] So disturbed were the burgesses that they ordered the First Virginia Regiment to return to Virginia to protect the backcountry by December 1, stating that otherwise the colony would cease to pay for it. Criticism of the expedition was widespread not only in the

House of Burgesses. Within the army itself, officers began to complain sharply about the campaign's slow progress.[59]

On November 6 Governor Denny received a depressing letter from General Forbes, still encamped at Raystown, detailing the misfortunes of the expedition, recommending steps that the colony should take to garrison the frontier over the winter, and suggesting that Pennsylvania should provide twelve hundred men for garrison duty. Dismayed, Denny called the assembly to meet on November 15. He informed the assemblymen that it appeared doubtful that Fort Duquesne would be captured before the onset of winter and acquainted them with Forbes's requests for troops for the winter.[60]

While the assembly pondered what it should do, Bouquet and Forbes also considered the future of the expedition. On November 11 Bouquet called his leading officers to a council of war at Loyalhanna. He asked the officers whether the army should continue toward Fort Duquesne or set about fortifying and securing its position for an assault the following spring. The council weighed the advantages of taking the fort—"justifying the expenses of the expedition and the hopes of our Colonies"—against the risks involved, especially the possibility of losing the ordnance in the bad weather and the depletion of provisions. Most officers agreed that "the risks being so obviously greater than the advantages" the expedition should halt. General Forbes, however, was unwilling to abandon the expedition just yet. He had just sent Christian Frederick Post with a message to Tamaqua and Shingas and was convinced that they would not actively help the French. Guides had informed him that the route from Loyalhanna to Fort Duquesne was easy after the first few miles, and he ordered Bouquet to send a party of scouts toward Fort Duquesne to investigate the terrain and see if an assault might be possible before the expedition prepared for the winter. Forbes's decision was fortuitous.[61]

Following their decisive victory over Grant and the debacle at Loyalhanna, the French believed that Forbes would be unable to press on with the expedition as winter approached. They had inflicted a defeat on his army comparable to that inflicted on Braddock. As a result of Braddock's defeat the British army had retreated into winter quarters in July. Why should Forbes behave any differently? With the approach of winter, dangerously short of supplies, the French believed that "Fort Duquesne is safe for this autumn and winter, and that the enemy will also think of going into winter quarters, and content themselves with preserving their new establishment." Consequently, they sent many of their regular troops and the Louisiana militia who had been garrisoning the fort to Illinois, where supplying them would be easier. The Indians at the fort were also allowed to leave to hunt. Suddenly Fort Duquesne lay dangerously exposed.[62]

The Treaty of Easton

Affairs on the Ohio hung in the balance, but what finally swung the situation was Indian diplomacy and the conference that was convening in Pennsylvania. In mid-October a conference convened at Easton to conclude peace. Although he was absent from the proceedings and incapacitated by illness, Forbes's shadow hung over the proceedings. In part, Forbes himself was responsible for the treaty convening. He had encouraged the Pennsylvanians to continue their negotiations despite Johnson's opposition. Not only that, but he had also urged them to concede to many of the Delawares' demands, claiming that "the Indians demands were but few, and to me seemingly not unreasonable."[63] He wanted the Quakers to remain involved in the diplomatic process despite the combined opposition of Johnson and the proprietors, arguing that the Quakers, unlike their opponents, were motivated solely "by the publick good and the preservation of these provinces."[64] Throughout the summer and fall of 1758 Forbes kept up a private correspondence with the Friendly Association, offering support and guidance.[65] His intervention was central in keeping the Quakers involved in the negotiations at Easton. At previous meetings with the Delawares the governor had attempted to keep them apart from the Quakers. Governor Morris had even warned the Quakers that "he should treat them as his Majesty's Enemies if they held any more Conferences with the Indians."[66] During the negotiations in 1758, however, there were few such attempts, and the Quakers and the Delawares seem to have been able to converse relatively freely.

While Forbes's intervention ensured that the meeting at Easton convened, he was many miles away, supervising the army, and could not guarantee that events would unfold smoothly. The meeting faced the problem of reconciling three conflicting and contradictory aims: the Iroquois sought to recover their lordship over the Delawares; the Susquehanna Delawares sought guarantees of their tribal territory from encroachment by anyone; and the Ohio Indians desired peace with a guarantee that the British would not settle their lands. The unfolding of the meeting reflected the shifting power balance in Pennsylvania. As Forbes pressed farther west and the French exhausted their supplies, Teedyuscung and the Susquehanna Delawares discovered that their negotiating position had grown weaker. The conference would finally prove how far the proprietors were prepared to go to dismiss the Susquehanna Delawares' claims of land fraud, but it would also demonstrate the need to conciliate the Ohio Indians.

The conference was further complicated by the numerous conflicting desires of the Pennsylvania delegates. The proprietors sought to isolate the Delawares from the Quakers, whom they viewed as their greatest enemies. This was in deep contrast to Forbes, who greatly admired the Quakers' efforts for peace. Indeed on the eve of the conference Forbes wrote to Israel Pemberton congratulating him on the "promising aspect of our Indian negociations, and as I am convinced that no person understands them better or [is] more zealous to bring them to a speedy and happy conclusion than you are." However, Forbes warned Pemberton that "a jealousy of the Quakers grasping at power, had perhaps taken place in some peoples minds; you have now a very critical time of showing that you are activated only by the publick good and the preservation of this province."[67] The Quakers, however, would soon find that they were to be excluded from any substantial involvement in the proceedings.

The disputes that would surface at the conference were not simply between the proprietors and the Quakers. Representatives of the assembly also sought to uncover any proprietary misdeeds. Meanwhile, George Croghan, representing Sir William Johnson, sought to preserve Johnson's authority in Indian affairs, threatened by Pennsylvania's increasing diplomacy. Even among the Indians present, there were bitter disputes. In 1757 Teedyuscung had avoided a direct confrontation with the Iroquois. Now he was not so fortunate. Over five hundred Indians from thirteen different nations attended, with the Iroquois forming the largest body. Before the proceedings officially convened, the Iroquois and Susquehanna Delawares spent two days in private council, where the Iroquois tried to persuade Teedyuscung to retract his earlier accusations and accept a compromise with the Pennsylvanians. According to Charles Thomson, "the Subject in Debate these two Days, [was] Whether what Teedyuscung has done shall stand, or they are to begin anew." However, in "warm" debates, "Teedyuscung, and his People, absolutely refuse[d] to retract any Thing they have said."[68]

Denny deliberately delayed the opening of the conference to allow these debates to take place, putting increasing pressure on Teedyuscung to withdraw his accusations of proprietary fraud. Indeed, Israel Pemberton commented to Benjamin Franklin: "The Business was shamefully delayed from Day to Day . . . it [is] well known to us who attended, that the Time was spent in attempting Teedyuscung's Downfal, and silencing or contracting the Complaints he had made." He wrote to Forbes that he was horrified "that the honour of our King and Country is so little consider'd."[69] In these negotiations Denny agreed with the Iroquois to return part of the lands acquired at Albany in 1754. This cession included all lands west of the Alleghenies and served to reassure the Ohio Indians that the Pennsylvanians had no immediate designs on their lands. However, when Denny formally returned these lands at the conference he gave them not to the Susquehanna Delawares but to the Iroquois. The return of the lands was thus a tacit acceptance of Iroquois lordship over the Delawares and a blow to Teedyuscung's cause.[70]

Teedyuscung soon found his negotiating position deteriorating further. As the conference convened and Teedyuscung came face-to-face in public conference with the Iroquois for the first time, they openly questioned his authority to speak for the Delawares. On October 15 Nihas, a Mohawk headman, informed the council: "You all know that he [Teedyuscung] gives out he is a great Man, and Chief of Ten Nations. . . . Now I, on behalf of the Mohawks, say we do not know he is such a great Man. If he is such a great man we desire to know who made him so."[71] Teedyuscung realized that his position was fast deteriorating and made a final attempt to secure the Delawares' lands at Wyoming. He turned on the Iroquois, storming, "You have placed us at Wioming and Shamokin. . . . Now I hear that you have sold that Land to our brethren the English." He pressed the Iroquois to provide the Delawares with a deed for the land at Wyoming and a guarantee that the Delawares would be able to remain there. The Iroquois prevaricated. Teedyuscung turned to Denny for support, but Denny washed his hands of the matter. He merely informed the conference that "the Proprietaries are desirous to do Strict Justice to all Indians, but it cannot be supposed they can know in which of you the Right was vested." He then dismissed the matter, simply saying, "It is a matter that must be settled among yourselves."[72]

On October 21 Teedyuscung met the Iroquois in private session. Several Quakers attended "at this particular Request of the Delawares."

Teedyuscung agreed to cede to the Iroquois "the Lands beyond the Kittocktinny Hills," but in return he asked for a deed to the lands at Wyoming. Having realized that the Pennsylvanians were determined to hand over control of all lands to the Iroquois and not to the Delawares, Teedyuscung accepted that he would have to press the Iroquois for a guarantee of possession. Therefore, it did not make sense to antagonize the Iroquois any further. Indeed, Pemberton confided to Franklin that Teedyuscung confirmed the purchase specifically "to engage the Six Nations to confirm the Wyoming Lands to him and his People." Teedyuscung's hopes would be dashed, for "such Measures were pursued by our proprietary Managers, to prevent it, and to set the Indians at variance with each other, that all our Arguments, Persuasions and Presents were scarce sufficient to keep them from an open Rupture."[73] In bitter and acrimonious debates, the Iroquois refused to guarantee Delaware possession of Wyoming. Thomas King, an Oneida, simply told the Delawares that "we have no power to convey Lands to any one." In the meantime, he instructed the Delawares, they must "make use of those Lands in Conjunction with our People, and all the rest of our Relations."[74] However, such statements were possibly misinterpreted to Teedyuscung, presented as a clear promise of Delaware ownership of Wyoming, for from his later behavior in 1760 Teedyuscung seems to have believed that a deal had been struck. It had not.

Teedyuscung also pressed the Pennsylvanians for compensation for lands that they had not returned to the Iroquois, the lands "between Tohiccon Creek and the Kittochtinny Hills," including mainly lands acquired in the Walking Purchase.[75] Teedyuscung pressed Denny for a discussion of these lands, but Denny refused. Such a discussion would of course open up the issue of fraud. He merely informed the Susquehanna Delawares that they would have to deal with the Iroquois. Increasingly Teedyuscung realized that he had been tricked. He turned on Denny, accusing him of duplicity in his dealings. He informed the conference that the Pennsylvanians had promised that "they would take Care for the future, but healed no wounds. In short when they speak to us, they do it with a Shorter Belt or String than that which we spoke to them with. . . . I fear they only speak from their Mouth and not from their Heart."[76] Having made his case, he left the conference and stormed back to Wyoming, knowing that by handing control of the affair over to the Iroquois the Pennsylvanians had betrayed him.

The time for Teedyuscung to triumph had passed. The Seven Years' War had offered the Susquehanna Delawares a window of opportunity, when they could have pressed for compensation and a fair airing of their grievances. By October 1758 there was little reason for Pennsylvania to listen to Teedyuscung's complaints. His influence had waned. As Forbes's army marched to the Ohio and the French ran out of supplies, the Susquehanna Delawares no longer posed a threat to the colony. While some of the proprietary faction, such as Richard Peters, may have sought to silence the Delawares in order to cover claims of proprietary fraud, for many other Pennsylvanians it had simply become less important to appease the Delawares than to placate the Iroquois. Moreover, since the few Ohio Indians who attended the conference intimated that they had no wish to see Teedyuscung speak in their name, it had become clear that Teedyuscung's influence with his Ohio brethren was more limited than he had claimed. Britain's traditional allies, the Iroquois, seemed more likely to be able to bring peace than the ineffectual Susquehanna Delawares.

On October 24 the conference met for the final time. After four days of discussion Conrad Weiser, Richard Peters, and the Iroquois agreed on the "Limits" of Pennsylvania, and the colony provided the Iroquois with a deed of release that recognized a formal boundary between the colony and the Iroquois. From this agreement would stem future attempts to define a "boundary" between Indian and white lands. After two weeks of negotiations "the Conferences were concluded with great Joy and mutual Satisfaction."[77] Only the Susquehanna Delawares had failed; the Iroquois and Ohio Indians seemed to have much to celebrate.

Victory at the Forks

As soon as the conference concluded, Forbes sent Pisquetomen and Post back to the Ohio with news of the negotiations, hoping that this might be sufficient to persuade some of the Indians to abandon the French. In the meantime, he continued to ponder whether he might still be able to assault Fort Duquesne. While he considered the task ahead, at dusk on November 12 another large raiding party, numbering over two hundred men, descended on Loyalhanna and attacked Forbes's cattle guard. In the confusion British troops fired upon one another, inflicting several casualties. It seemed like yet another miserable defeat. However, the skirmish was not all bad news for Forbes. Several prisoners were taken, from whom Forbes managed to acquire much-needed intelligence on the state of Fort Duquesne's defenses. They informed him that most of the garrison had been evacuated and that the Indians had left. Forbes was surprised and overjoyed. He wrote to Abercromby that if these reports were true he believed that even this late in the season he might still be able to take the fort. If Post's and Pisquetomen's mission succeeded, the French would have few men with whom to defend Fort Duquesne.[78]

A week later, on November 20, Bouquet set out with a large party from Loyalhanna toward Fort Duquesne. François-Marie Le Marchand de Lignery, the French commander, was horrified to discover that the British still intended to attack the fort so late in the season. He realized his mistake in dispersing his forces and permitting the Indians to retire to hunt. The weakened garrison would be unable to resist any British advance. In desperation Lignery sent a messenger to the Delawares at Kuskuski, asking for support. However, Pisquetomen and Post had already arrived at the town and had managed to convince many of the Delawares to abandon the French cause. The Delawares now dismissed Lignery's pleas for assistance. The shortage of supplies on the Ohio, Forbes's slow but constant advance, and news of the negotiations with the Susquehanna Delawares had all convinced them that the time was right to abandon their former ally. The Kuskuski Delawares bluntly informed Lignery, "We have often ventured our lives for him; and had hardly a loaf of bread when we came to him; and now he thinks we should jump to serve him." They would not assist in the defense of the fort.[79] Lignery was aghast. With his garrison dispersed, his Indian allies hunting, and the local Delawares refusing to assist him, he had little choice but to evacuate and destroy the fort to prevent it from falling into British hands. On the evening of November 24 scouts from Bouquet's column reported that "they had discovered a very thick smoak from the Fort extending in the bottom along the Ohio." The following morning advance units of Forbes's expedition came in sight of the fort. They found it burned to the ground. That afternoon units of Forbes's army finally occupied the forks of the Ohio. After four and a half years the British again had a presence on the Ohio River.[80]

The British "victory" on the Ohio had been won, in part, thanks to French misfortune and miscalculation. However, the victory also reflected the determination and skill of Forbes. His faith in Indian diplomacy,

his attention to the minutiae of logistics, and his belief in his commanders, most notably Henry Bouquet, all contributed to British success.
Unlike many other British commanders, he understood some of the intricacies of provincial politics and the importance of Indian allies. Only
a few weeks after the capture of the forks and just a month before his
death, aware that life was slipping away from him, he wrote his last letter to Jeffrey Amherst: "The State of the Indians all along the Ohio[,]
Shawnese and Delawares, is Im afraid not generally understood o[r] if
understood, perverted to purposes serving particular ends, Nor can I
conceal from you my opinion, That I have all along thought, that the publick measures and the private interested views of Sir William Johnstone
. . . have never once coincided in my time. . . . I beg . . . that you will
not think trifflingly of the Indians or their friendship; when I venture
to assure you that twenty Indians are capable of laying half this province
waste, of which I have been an eye witness."[81]

The death of Forbes was a major blow to the British. Had Forbes lived,
and been healthy enough to continue his command, he may have been
able to direct policy on the Ohio in a different direction and to allay
many of the Indians' fears. He understood the need to provide the Ohio
Indians with trade goods and the demands of diplomatic protocol. He
saw the victory on the Ohio as a means of "securing the Indians, our real
Friends, for their own Advantages," not as a means of exploiting the region for the advantage of the British.[82]

Unfortunately, other people saw the victory in a different light. It had
been bankrolled by Pitt's administration in Whitehall, which saw the
victory as part of a greater global British strategy against the French.
However, for the previous three years the brunt of the war had been felt
by the backcountry of Virginia and Pennsylvania, and the two colonies
had provided many of the men who fought in Forbes's campaign. Virginians and Pennsylvanians thus saw the victory on the Ohio as a victory
for themselves. The *Pennsylvania Gazette* informed its readers, "Blessed be
God, the long look'd for Day is arrived, that has now fixed us . . . in the
quiet and peaceable Possession of the finest and most fertile Country of
America." The conquest of the Ohio "lays open to all his Majesty's Subjects a Vein of Treasure."[83] Virginians and Pennsylvanians alike expected
that in return for their sacrifices of the previous three years they would
now be rewarded with access to the Ohio Valley. Indeed, many of the
provincial troops had been promised land as part of their enlistment

bounty. The contradictions among the hopes of the Ohio Indians, the plans of British administrators, and the desires of colonial settlers would play out over the next four years with catastrophic consequences.

THE YEAR 1758 witnessed a complete transformation of the war in the Virginia and Pennsylvania backcountry. For the first (and last) time the two colonies were able to raise substantial numbers of troops to assist the war effort. Three years of experience had taught them much about waging war, and now they raised relatively effective armies. British officers had come to understand much more about the intricacies of handling provincial affairs and waging war in the Appalachian forests and mountains. Forbes thus organized and commanded a British army very different from that commanded by Braddock three years earlier. He also better grasped the importance of Indian diplomacy than Braddock had in 1755. Indeed, the diplomatic outlook had been transformed as much as the military. Where Braddock had dismissed the Indians and belittled their concerns, Forbes sought to heed their concerns and involved them in diplomacy. However, now diplomacy would concentrate on the Ohio Indians, rather than the Susquehanna Delawares. Now the central issue would be protecting the backcountry by winning over the support of the Ohio Indians. Unfortunately, in the wake of Forbes's death, British officials would not be able to win their long-term support or even their neutrality. The years following the capture of the forks would be dominated, on both sides, by attempts to establish a new and secure peace in the Ohio Valley. With Forbes gone, and with Virginia and Pennsylvania demanding the fruits of victory, these attempts would ultimately fail.

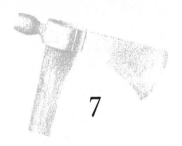

7

The Quest for Security

1759–1763

FROM 1759 TO 1763 BOTH THE BRITISH AND THE OHIO INDIANS had to develop new policies to cope with the realities of North America without the French. For both the period was shaped by their experiences during the war in the backcountry. Many Virginians and Pennsylvanians now saw the Ohio Indians as defeated and the upper Ohio Valley as opened up to trade and settlement. The Ohio Indians, on the other hand, viewed themselves as anything but a conquered people. The war in the backcountry had demonstrated their military superiority, not their inferiority. Indeed, it was the French who had been defeated. The Ohio Indians now sought only two principal goals: the security of their lands and the restoration of traditional diplomatic protocols.

The inherent contradiction between British and Indian perceptions of the progress of the war was further complicated by other developments. As the tide of global war against the French turned in favor of the British, officials in Whitehall became increasingly parsimonious and sought ways to cut back expenses, including not only subsidies for the provincial forces but also the provision of gifts for native allies. Meanwhile, Virginians and Pennsylvanians became increasingly preoccupied with securing the return of "captives" still held by the Ohio Indians and demanded that provincial authorities take more action in this regard. At the same time the Penns continued their quest to conceal the frauds committed in the acquisition of Delaware lands and to place the blame for such accusations upon the Quakers. Finally, throughout this period there was no one individual, or even group of people, coordinating British policy. The death of George II in October 1760 greatly weakened Pitt's influence and caused instability in Whitehall. This lack of coordination, and the mass of conflicting policies, would unravel the victories the British had won, and by 1763 the backcountry would once more be broken apart by Indian raids.

Anglo-Indian Relations in the Ohio Valley, 1759–1760

The fall of Fort Duquesne in November 1758 marked the start of a new stage in the Seven Years' War, for it ended any major raids on the backcountry. In part this was due to simple geography: raiding parties now had further to travel from their supply bases to the colonial frontier and had to bypass the new British post at the forks of the Ohio. Fort Duquesne had also served as the center where the French had distributed ammunition to the Ohio Indians and marshaled their raiding parties. Its fall removed a key component in the organization of the raids. In addition, the increasing shortage of ammunition and weapons among the Ohio Indians played a crucial role. Active Indian support declined once the French were unable to provide their allies with supplies. Indeed, the extent to which they had come to rely on Indian support with little to offer in recompense caused some formerly Francophile headmen to complain, "'Tis not the French who are fighting, 'tis we."[1]

Not only did the fall of Fort Duquesne mark a decline in the Indians' ability and desire to raid the colonial frontier, but it also marked a shift in French strategy. As the military balance in the region shifted in favor of the British, the French encouraged their remaining Indian allies not to paralyze the war effort of Virginia and Pennsylvania but rather to blunt the British onslaught on the Ohio Valley and, most importantly, on New France itself. Any French-supported and -instigated raids would now focus not on the backcountry but on Fort Pitt itself and on British supply lines.

The end of 1758 marked a turning point not just on the Ohio. The Seven Years' War had become a global conflict. As France lost its imperial possessions in North America, new campaigns were being waged in Africa and Asia. In Africa British forces conquered the French outposts in Senegal and Gambia. In the West Indies a new campaign was launched against Martinique and Guadalupe. In Europe British land forces were committed to the protection of Hanover, subsidies lavishly bestowed on Frederick the Great to help him continue his war effort despite heavy losses. From the perspective of Whitehall the war was far from over, and pressure had to be kept upon the French.[2]

In the Ohio Valley the first task for the British was simply to maintain their precarious presence. This was no straightforward matter. The British army needed both to overcome the logistical problems of supplying a force on the Ohio, far removed from its supply sources, and also to win the acquiescence of the Ohio Indians. Indeed, these two issues were inextricably linked, for the Ohio Indians had it in their power to disrupt the precarious flow of supplies to Fort Pitt if they so wished. Brig. Gen. John Forbes had driven the French from the forks of the Ohio, but holding this strategic location was a different matter. The French had destroyed most of the fortifications, and the winter weather meant that little work could be done on refortifying the site. Forbes had also left only a small garrison at Pittsburgh, concerned about the logistical effort required to supply a large garrison across the Appalachians over the winter. Shortages of supplies and isolation encouraged desertion, while sickness further sapped the garrison's fighting power. Hugh Mercer, the commander at the fort, sent Forbes and Col. Henry Bouquet repeated reports of its precarious condition; a concerted assault could bring its fall.[3]

As he organized the coming campaigns, the commander in chief, Gen. Jeffrey Amherst, could expect little support from Virginia and Pennsylvania in holding the upper Ohio Valley. Virginians, frustrated at the decision to cut a new road to the Ohio from Pennsylvania, felt that Pennsylvania would reap the benefits of the conquest of the Ohio Valley. In disgust, Washington had resigned his commission and retired to Mount Vernon with his new bride, Martha. Washington was not alone in feeling disillusioned with the war. The House of Burgesses would approve only one regiment of one thousand men, not the two of the previous year. In addition, it was hesitant to fund the summer's campaign and lowered the recruitment bounty. As the bounty had been a principal means of attracting recruits, they became, not surprisingly, thin on the ground; in mid-June Governor Francis Fauquier had to direct the new commander of the Virginia Regiment, William Byrd, to begin buying up convicts who were being shipped to the colony.[4]

Pennsylvanians, by contrast, welcomed the burgeoning supply contracts that accompanied the presence of the army. However, such feelings could not resolve the conflicts between assembly and governor. William Denny and the assembly continued to squabble over the taxation of proprietary estates. Only when Amherst wrote brusquely to Denny ordering him to "wave your Proprietary Instructions" did Denny finally accept the assembly's supply bill.[5] While Amherst was relieved, the Penns' supporters in the province were horror-struck. Richard Hockley immediately resigned from the post of provincial secretary and in a farcical scene refused to hand over the provincial seals to the governor, fearing that he "might do some other dirty thing."[6] The action placed the final nail in the coffin of Denny's administration, and upon hearing of it the Penns decided to recall him and replace him with James Hamilton. Hamilton came from a trusty pedigree. His father, Andrew, active in Pennsylvania politics in the 1730s, had been a strong supporter of the Penns. James himself had served in the assembly and had already been governor from 1748 to 1754, when he had staunchly defended the proprietary interest. He was further tied to the proprietary faction through the marriage of his daughter to William Allen, one of the leaders of the proprietary faction.

Denny's political suicide was all but in vain, for despite the supply bill recruiting proved difficult. Because of the British army's demands for supplies and equipment needed for campaigning, and the increased economic opportunities that came with the new security in the backcountry, Pennsylvania's economy was entering a boom; consequently the economic incentives for joining the Pennsylvania Regiment declined, and new recruits proved hard to find. Although the assembly had agreed to raise over three thousand men, throughout the spring and early summer Pennsylvania's recruiters found few willing to join the provincial forces. Meanwhile, Amherst fretted about his ability to retain the forks.[7]

The shortage of provincial troops made it difficult to provide an escort to Fort Pitt, and throughout the winter and spring raiding parties continued to harass convoys. Several were captured or forced to return to Pennsylvania, and Fort Pitt remained short of supplies. Upon his arrival at Pittsburgh in May 1759, Adam Hoops was horrified to find the garrison "in such Extremity."[8] The attacks increased the reluctance of backcountry settlers to provide wagons and horses to haul the supplies, the shortage of wagons creating an additional shortage that in turn further impeded supply efforts.[9]

The British hold on Fort Pitt was precarious, and the French had high hopes that they could retake the forks and turn the tide of the war in the upper Ohio Valley. In June and July several hundred Wyandots, Ottawas, Twightwees, Potawatomis, and Delawares assembled at the French fort of Venango. They were joined by seven hundred French troops, many of whom had been in the former garrison of Fort Duquesne and had detailed knowledge of the region. With a force of such size and accomplishment the French commander François-Marie Le Marchand de Lignery could have taken Fort Pitt, and the war in the backcountry could have resumed. However, events elsewhere sealed the fate of the French in the upper Ohio Valley.[10]

Lignery had received reinforcements from Fort Niagara in early July. The fort's commander, Capt. Pierre Pouchot, convinced by late June that the season was too far advanced for the British to launch an offensive against the post, especially as his Indian allies had brought him no news of preparations for any such expedition, dispatched twenty-five hundred men from the garrison to help defend the west. When on July 6 a major British force commanded by Brig. Gen. John Prideaux landed near the fort, Pouchot had a garrison of fewer than five hundred men with whom to mount a defense. He rushed off a dispatch to Lignery, urging him to hurry to his aid. By the time Lignery's men arrived at the fort the British were already well dug in. In a futile attempt to lift the siege, Lignery ordered a frontal assault on the British line, in which the French suffered crippling losses and Lignery himself was killed. On July 25 Pouchot surrendered Fort Niagara, cutting French supply and communication routes between Canada and the Ohio Valley and the Mississippi. News of the fort's loss threw the remaining French troops on the Ohio into "the utmost confusion." Confusion soon turned to panic when the order was given that all women and children should be evacuated from Detroit to the Scioto River, ready to be taken to Louisiana. Almost overnight French military power on the Ohio had disappeared.[11]

For the Ohio Indians this sudden collapse of French power was completely unexpected. For almost a century the French had maintained a substantial presence in the region. Now that presence was fast disappearing. Having lost Fort Niagara, the French suddenly prepared to evacuate the rest of their forces. They abandoned and burned Forts Le Boeuf and Venango and prepared for a siege in Detroit. The collapse of French power in the region made it clear to most Ohio headmen that they had no choice but to seek an accommodation with the British, even though they remained deeply suspicious of British intentions. At Fort Pitt James Kenny reported that news of the French withdrawal greatly disturbed the Indians. They seemed "more sober, [and] their practice of singing & dancing was remarked to have ceased."[12] In only nine months the balance of power in the region had been transformed. Now the Ohio Indians would have to adapt to the new conditions.

There were two ways in which the British could gain acceptance from the Ohio Indians. First, the British could provide assurances of the security of the Indians' lands and ultimately withdraw from the forks, but any withdrawal from the forks was unthinkable for the British commanders. Second, the British could open up the fur trade to meet the Ohio Indians' needs. Here also they seemed unwilling to meet expectations. Unable to supply their own troops, the British, not surprisingly, also had a severe shortage of Indian trade goods. This prompted a desperate exchange between Mercer and his commanders. In early January he wrote to Forbes, begging him to send "a large quantity of Indian Goods." He added that "the Constant Sollicitations of all our friends obliges me again to repeat it, as a measure equally necessary to gain the Indian Interest, as a Body of Troops is to Secure the Country."[13] Sir William Johnson was equally concerned and warned Amherst that without a "plentiful & proper Supply of Goods, we shall . . . soon loose all those . . . favorable Dispositions."[14] Relations soured further when the few traders who did venture west sought to take advantage of the desperate need for goods and maximize their profits by selling substandard goods at high prices. Indeed, desperate for any trade, Mercer had encouraged the arrival of unlicensed traders. This, however, only enraged the Indians, for the unlicensed traders charged exorbitant rates for their goods. In response the Indians complained bitterly they had been promised an abundance of goods "as cheap as in Philadelphia."[15]

The Quaker Friendly Association again stepped into the fray. Hearing of the need for trade goods on the Ohio, the association saw a new opportunity to demonstrate its continuing support of the peace process. The acquisition of trade goods was easy, as many of the association's members were merchants or had ties to Philadelphia merchant families. In addition, the association was prepared to subsidize the goods as another way of demonstrating its determination to seek peace. Transporting the goods to the forks was more of a challenge, but Quaker meetings across western Pennsylvania and northern Virginia agreed to provide wagons and horses.[16] The association soon found itself in a more important role than simply that of a supplier of trade goods. Hearing of the impartiality and trustworthiness of the association from their brethren on the Susquehanna, the Ohio Indians soon began to confide in the association's agent at the forks, Samuel Lightfoot. Lightfoot soon proclaimed that the Indians had "put a singular confidence in Friends beyond others and . . . would hear them when they would not hear others without them."[17]

Within a few months, Lightfoot had established important contacts with many of the leading headmen of the region, and his presence became crucial in calming some of the Indians' fears. For much of the summer the Indians who came to Fort Pitt would trade with no one but Lightfoot. Amherst and Brig. Gen. John Stanwix, who assumed command in the west following Forbes's death, quickly came to rely on the Quakers to maintain an adequate supply of goods, Stanwix claiming that he knew of "no body that understands what goods are proper so much as your self or that I think I can depend on so well."[18] The premature death of Lightfoot in July curtailed but did not end these activities, as James Kenny continued to act as Pemberton's agent and to supervise the sale of goods. Indeed, Stanwix urged Pemberton to "continue to send down Indian goods with an agent to carry on the trade either for your self or the Friendly Society." The extent of the association's involvement was substantial. By the end of 1759 the Friendly Association had spent over three thousand pounds in gifts and presents for the Indians. Without such a lavish expenditure, the British influence at the forks would have been very weak indeed.[19]

The growing influence of the association, however, made negotiations with the Indians more complicated for George Croghan, who arrived at Fort Pitt in June 1759 carrying orders from Stanwix to confirm peace with the Ohio Indians and to invite them to a conference in Philadelphia in the summer. Croghan was a good choice to win over the support of the Ohio Indians. He had an extensive web of influence that stemmed from his widespread trading activities before the Seven Years' War. Lightfoot commented, "I have frequently heard the Indians ask for

George Croghan, as a man for whom they have some regard."[20] Over the summer Croghan held a continuous series of meetings with headmen from the different Ohio villages. However, he found them intransigent. They would not travel to Philadelphia. Not only were they suspicious of British intentions, but many were also afraid to travel so far into the colonies at a time when the Ohio Valley was being wracked by a series of epidemics of measles and smallpox.[21]

Croghan's meetings with the Ohio Indians did, however, uncover a new issue that would soon become another thorn in the side of Anglo-Indian relations: the continuing presence of white "captives" in the Ohio Valley. The issue of prisoners had come up in negotiations with the Susquehanna Delawares, but on the Ohio it had not previously been discussed in detail. Many headmen presumed that they would have to return a few prisoners but that they would be able to retain those whom they had adopted into their families. The issue of prisoners was raised in a meeting between Croghan and the Delawares in July. Croghan demanded that before any peace could be concluded the Delawares would have to return their prisoners. Delaware headman Tamaqua, hoping that others would follow his example, immediately handed over two prisoners, both adopted members of his family, stressing their importance by describing them as his "mother" and "sister." However, despite Tamaqua's lead, other Delawares remained reluctant.[22]

Croghan's demands began to raise additional concerns about British intentions and the extent to which the British would reestablish the traditional diplomatic protocols of the region. Indian concerns were heightened not only by events on the Ohio. In the east the wishes of their Susquehanna brethren were rapidly being swept aside, and news of their treatment soon came to the Ohio. As the war on the Ohio wound down, the Penns had stepped up their campaign to discredit the Delawares. The campaign had begun as early as 1756, when the Penns established a committee of the provincial council to investigate the Delawares' claims. In the wake of the 1758 Easton treaty the committee finally forwarded its report to London. The report was little more than a whitewash of the Penns' administration. Point by point it dismissed Teedyuscung's complaints, concluding that "there is not the least Shadow of Foundation for any part of the Complaint made by Teedyuscung . . . against the Proprietaries." Where had such complaints come from? The report concluded that "we must, therefore, attribute his exhibiting that false and groundless Charge

. . . to some undue Influence." Who else but the Quakers?[23] In one bold stroke the Penns tried to discredit both Teedyuscung and the Friendly Association.

However, the Penns found that they faced unexpected opposition. On February 2, 1759, Benjamin Franklin, who had traveled to London to argue the assembly's case against the proprietors, presented the Delawares' complaints directly to the Privy Council and the Board of Trade. Over the spring of 1759 the board considered the reports and petitions received from both sides. Their findings concluded that Indian concerns over the acquisition of their lands had been "one princl. Cause of . . . the Hostitiltys." However, rather than specifically naming the Walking Purchase, the Board of Trade blamed "the extensive purchases of Lands made not only by the Proprietaries of Pensilva. but in other Governments" and stressed that "the Frauds & Abuses, with Respect to Purchases, & Settlement of Indians Lands . . . are not confined to the Province of Pennsylva. nor to this particular Tribe of Indians, they have been as much practiced, complained of, & almost as severely felt in every other Province."[24] While the board did not directly accuse the Quakers of inventing the accusations of land fraud, they did maintain that the Susquehanna Delawares had been encouraged by "the irregular and unwarrantable Interferings . . . of particular Persons." The proprietors thus escaped with their reputations all but untarnished. The Quakers were rebuked, but not too severely. The Delawares suffered the greatest defeat. While the board recognized their complaint, they ruled that the only person who could adjudicate in the matter was Sir William Johnson. The Delawares would not get an impartial hearing in London, as they had been promised. When Johnson finally came to hear their concerns, the issue of fraud at the forks would finally be buried and Iroquois influence restored.[25]

News of the dismissal of the Delawares' claims came at the same time that increasing numbers of white hunters were trespassing into the upper Susquehanna Valley and unlicensed traders were flooding Delaware villages with liquor. Many of the Susquehanna Delawares saw their fate clearly outlined and moved to the Ohio. Their arrival served to underline the concerns of the Ohio headmen; they wondered how long it would be before their wishes were swept aside.

There were other reasons for the Ohio Indians to worry. On September 18 Quebec surrendered to the British. The British had captured the very heart of the French Empire. Across British North America the news was greeted with exultation. Philadelphia "was illuminated, Bonfires were lighted, and other Demonstrations of Joy shewn."[26] Yet even while the colonists celebrated, peace was beginning to unravel. Confident in their victory over the French, the British failed to realize the need to secure peace with their Indian neighbors. In the Ohio Valley that unraveling would take several more years, but in the backcountry of Virginia and the Carolinas peace had already proved very transitory, as Cherokee warriors now commenced a war against the British.

The Cherokee War

While Britons and colonists alike basked in victory in Canada, the backcountry of Virginia remained violent, as Anglo-Cherokee relations broke down and resulted in a new frontier war. The Cherokee War that descended upon the backcountry of the Carolinas and southwestern Virginia from 1759 to 1761 had many of its origins in the diplomacy of the Seven Years' War. Many Cherokees had long sought to free themselves from the stranglehold they felt that South Carolina had on the tribe's trade. Even before the war, Cherokee headmen had tried to open up trade with Virginia. As war broke out and Virginia looked for Indian allies, the Cherokees had approached the colony and encouraged it to construct Fort Loudoun in their territory. However, the construction of the fort led to difficulties. For the Cherokees a fort meant a "strong-house" that could store the goods of traders and protect them from theft and pilferage. For the Virginians the purpose of Fort Loudoun was to protect Cherokee towns from any French attack. Consequently the Virginians made little attempt to encourage the development of the fur trade, and when traders failed to arrive at the new fort, the Cherokees rapidly became annoyed. Cherokee resentment at Virginia's neglect grew when Cherokee warriors were encouraged to assist the colony in its fight with the Ohio Indians. Cherokee warriors expected to be rewarded for their services and were well aware of their importance to the British. When they returned from their forays toward Fort Duquesne to find not the rewards they expected but only paltry goods, they grew very restless. Shawnee raids into Bedford and Halifax Counties, along the routes traversed by Cherokee warriors, further complicated Anglo-Cherokee relations. Local inhabitants could not distinguish between Cherokee allies and Shawnee enemies and treated all Indians with similar enmity. Like their brethren in the Ohio Valley the Cherokees found their lands being overrun by white settlers as Indian raids on the Virginia backcountry compelled many to flee to the Carolinas and settle upon Cherokee lands.[27]

By 1759 Anglo-Cherokee relations were at crisis point. Nevertheless, it was still possible for both sides to compromise, for the Cherokees remained deeply divided, with a strong Anglophile faction led by Attakullakulla, or the Little Carpenter. Indeed, Governor Fauquier sent William Byrd to negotiate with Attakullakulla in an attempt to forestall war. Compromise was not found, however, because South Carolinians sought a war. South Carolina governor William Henry Lyttelton believed that the Cherokees were so weakened by divisions that South Carolina could gain a major victory and force the cession of substantial tracts of land. In October 1759, despite concerns from the provincial assembly at the costs of a war, Lyttelton prepared for an expedition against the Cherokees and seized several headmen sent to negotiate with him.[28]

Lyttelton's expedition marched into the heart of Cherokee country. However, smallpox soon broke out among the force. As the epidemic spread through his ranks, Lyttelton hurriedly declared Attakullakulla sole negotiator for the tribe, concluded a "peace treaty," and retreated. The expedition did not serve to pacify the Cherokees but merely stirred up a hornet's nest of hostility. This hostility was heightened when the Cherokees Lyttelton had seized were executed. The execution of the hostages pushed many wavering Cherokee warriors into open hostility, and a number of war parties descended upon the colonial frontier from southwestern Virginia to South Carolina. The backcountry was once more in a sorry state, although the Carolinas, rather than Virginia, bore the full brunt of the raids. A report from South Carolina claimed that "no Description can surpass it's Calamity.—What few escape the Indians . . . are seized with the Small-Pox." However, the fact that their fellow settlers further south were bearing an even heavier assault was no comfort to those Virginia backcountry residents in Augusta, Bedford, and Halifax Counties who were killed, captured, or fled their homes for safety.[29]

In the spring of 1760 the newly arrived South Carolina governor, William Bull, dispatched another expedition into Cherokee country. The expedition, which included fresh troops of the Royal Scots and the First Battalion of Highlanders and was commanded by Col. Archibald

Montgomery, marched quickly into Cherokee country. On June 27 it had reached the town of Echoe when it came under fierce fire. For once the technological advantage lay with the Cherokees, who "having many Rifles among them . . . did Execution at a greater Distance than our People could." Fiercely pressing their advantage, the Cherokees threatened Montgomery's supply train and forced him to beat a speedy retreat to Charleston, where he embarked for the northern colonies. Once more, an expedition had served merely to underline British weakness.[30]

The failure of Montgomery's expedition placed the backcountry inhabitants of Virginia in a dangerous position. In June Governor Fauquier had refused to prepare the militia to defend the region, believing that Montgomery would force the Cherokees to agree to terms and arguing that he would "not . . . put the Colony to the great and useless Expence of a Militia to ease a few people of their ill-grounded Fears."[31] However, as Montgomery's expedition achieved little, Cherokee raiding parties continued to attack the frontier. The backcountry residents of southwestern Virginia were not, however, those who had most to lose from the failure of Montgomery's expedition. Fauquier had been relying on Montgomery to relieve the besieged garrison of Fort Loudoun. When it was clear that his expedition had failed, Fauquier attempted to send a relief expedition to the fort. However, relief attempts were hampered by the parsimony of the House of Burgesses, which would provide little money for a recruiting bounty. When the expedition finally mustered at the Augusta County Court House in July, the expedition's commander, William Byrd, described it as no more than a "Mob."[32]

Fortunately for Byrd, the expedition never had to face the Cherokees, for on August 8 Fort Loudoun surrendered. The Virginia garrison believed the Cherokees would escort them to safety at Fort Prince George. However, soon after they left the safety of the fort, the Cherokees attacked, killing the fort's commander and twenty-five of his men and carrying the remainder away into captivity. This was almost certainly more than a mindless violation of the Cherokees' oath, for, as historian David Corkran has pointed out, the number of men killed at Fort Loudoun was almost the same as the number of Cherokee hostages executed by the South Carolinians at Fort Prince George. For many Cherokee warriors the capture of Fort Loudoun was sufficient compensation for the harsh treatment they had received from the British. When offered terms by the Virginians, the Cherokees accepted and delivered up most of the Virginia prisoners from Fort Loudoun, promising to negotiate a permanent peace with South Carolina.[33]

Once more, however, the South Carolinians remained the major hurdle to the negotiation of any peace treaty. Once more, they sought a military victory over the tribe, but this time not to seize land but to reassert the colony's influence. Many were jealous of Virginia's growing control over the tribe and wanted to reassert South Carolina's dominant position in Cherokee affairs. The opportunity to punish the Cherokees came when another detachment of British regulars arrived in the colony in January 1761. South Carolina's determination to continue the war placed the Virginians in an awkward position. Governor Fauquier in particular was concerned, since the Cherokees had kept the terms of the peace made with Virginia. As a result, the governor felt that "we cannot enter their Country with Fire and Sword, without a most notorious and infamous Breach of Faith." Yet it was clear that neither could Virginia conclude a separate peace with the Cherokees, for "we shall with Justice be represented at home by Carolina, as having deserted them." At the end of February Fauquier ordered the provincial negotiator with the Cherokees to inform them that Virginia sought peace with the tribe, but that any peace must include all parties—the South Carolinians as well as the Virginians, and the Anglophobe lower and middle Cherokee towns as well as the Anglophile upper towns.[34]

The South Carolinians, however, had the full support of the commander in chief, Jeffrey Amherst. Amherst felt frustrated at the inability of the colonies to bring the Cherokees into line. He wrote to Bull that "peace . . . must not be Granted 'till the Cherokees are properly Chastised."[35] Still, the Virginians were not in favor of the war, and the House of Burgesses openly expressed opposition to the planned expedition. Only when pressed hard by Amherst did the burgesses agree to provide for the expedition. However, they set the recruiting bounty at only five pounds, guaranteeing just a trickle of recruits. Once the men were assembled, the low pay led to a tide of desertions. In just eight days sixty-eight men, or one-tenth of the force, deserted. By the beginning of July the remains of the regiment had reached Fort Chiswell, still 220 miles from the regiment's target, Chota.[36]

While Byrd was slowly maneuvering his expedition toward Chota, Maj. James Grant marched boldly into Cherokee country. This third expedition against the Cherokees had few more concrete victories than the previous ones had. Grant advanced, burning all before him. However, the Cherokees were consistently well informed of the movements of Grant's men and were able to evacuate their settlements before the enemy arrived. Despite the destruction of their towns, Grant could not bring the Cherokees to a decisive battle; it was his men, rather than the Cherokees, who began to display signs of the fatigues of a prolonged campaign. When several Cherokee headmen arrived at Grant's headquarters on August 28 to negotiate a peace, the terms that Grant offered were more lenient than those offered *before* the expedition.[37]

Peace had been finally concluded, but in Virginia the Cherokee War left a legacy of deep popular resentment. While the bulk of the devastation caused by the war was on the Carolina frontier, Augusta, Halifax, and Bedford Counties in southwestern Virginia had all suffered from Cherokee raids, particularly major raids on Halifax County in the spring of 1758 and on Augusta and Halifax Counties in May and June of 1760. Population growth in southwestern Virginia had stalled, and in some areas population declined over the three years of war. Settlements in the Greenbrier and New River Valleys, reoccupied in 1757 and 1758, had soon been abandoned when the Cherokee raids commenced. While the devastation was not as great as that from the earlier Indian raids, the continuing destruction of the backcountry still caused widespread discontentment.[38]

The Fueling of Indian Unrest, 1760–1762

The Cherokee War distracted Virginia's attention from the Ohio Valley and made the provision of large numbers of troops for the west unthinkable. This occurred at a time when Bouquet desperately needed men to rebuild roads and construct blockhouses to rest troops and expresses. With inadequate numbers of regular troops and few Virginia troops available, Bouquet was solely reliant upon Pennsylvania to provide him with the men he needed. The province was forthcoming. After two months of continued bickering over the taxation of proprietary estates, the Pennsylvania Assembly agreed to raise twenty-seven hundred men for the campaign, believing that it would lead to the final conquest of Canada and the opening of the trans-Appalachian west for settlement, which would bring great advantages to the province.[39]

On the surface the Ohio Valley was relatively secure. It had been al-most two years since the French withdrawal from Fort Duquesne, and the French had been driven from Quebec, yet they still threatened British posts in the west, notably new posts such as Venango and Presque Isle. The French garrison at Detroit, though desperately short of supplies, was still able to count on the support of some remaining Indian allies. While the number of Indians who actively supported the French was much smaller than in previous campaigns, they were still capable of seriously disrupting the extended British supply lines. The Great Lakes Indians had valid reasons for continuing to support the French. The French commander at Detroit beseeched them to continue the struggle, warning that the British intended to seize their lands. Many Ohio Indians also listened to such warnings, for the British did nothing to ease their fears. When Forbes seized Fort Duquesne, many Ohio Indians had announced that they would only make peace if the British would "go back, after hav-ing drove away the *French,* and not settle there." Indeed, Tamaqua speci-fically warned the British "to go back over the Mountain & to stay there."[40] Over the winter of 1758–59 the British seemed to heed these warnings and stressed to the Ohio Indians that they intended merely to force the French from the region and had no intention of establishing perma-nent settlements. In the summer of 1760 Brig. Gen. Robert Monckton, who had assumed Stanwix's command in the west, attempted to assuage Indian concerns by promising that he "did not send an Army here against the Indians but against the French, neither did He build Forts in the In-dians Country with an Intent to take their Lands from them by Force, but to prevent the French from doing the same." However, even as Monckton spoke, the French were being driven from Canada and out of the Ohio. How, wondered the Ohio Indians, could the French still pose a threat to the British presence in the region?[41]

Such concerns seemed to be justified by events in Pennsylvania, where a group of Connecticut settlers organized by the "Susquehannah Com-pany" began settling Delaware lands in the Wyoming Valley. Connecticut's charter of 1662 had fixed its western boundary as the Pacific, and as its charter predated Pennsylvania's, the colony claimed the Wyoming Valley. At the Albany Conference in 1754 representatives of the Susquehanna Company had persuaded some Iroquois headmen to sign a deed for the lands around Wyoming. The company's attempts to develop the settle-ment had been postponed during the war, but now they recommenced.

In autumn of 1760 the first Connecticut settlers appeared, although it was not until 1762 that they began to settle the Wyoming Valley itself.[42]

A guarantee of the Wyoming lands had been a principal aim of the Delawares at the Easton conferences. The Iroquois, however, had refused to provide them with a deed for the lands, and now they were being overrun by settlers who themselves claimed to have a deed from the Iroquois. Teedyuscung stormed down to Philadelphia to meet Governor Hamilton, "full of anger and resentment."[43] However, he no longer carried the influence that he once had. Frustrated at his loss of power, and possibly egged on by the Iroquois, his drunken excesses had increased. To purchase liquor he sold the presents and even the wampum given to him by both Pennsylvania and the Indians in conducting diplomacy. When he finally met with the Ohio Indians in August 1760, Teedyuscung "did not speak in Council, being either too drunk, or not permitted by the other Indians," who "seem'd to be all ashamed of him." Dismayed at Teedyuscung's drunken antics, the headmen "Unking'd him & Unchief'd him."[44] Consequently, when Teedyuscung arrived in Philadelphia to complain about the activities of the Susquehanna Company, Governor Hamilton would provide him with no assistance. Faced with the theft of their lands by the Susquehannah Company, many Susquehanna Delawares abandoned their homes and migrated to the Ohio and Allegheny Rivers. As the refugees informed their Ohio brethren of the activities of the Susquehanna Company, the Ohio Indians can only have wondered how long it would be before the British attempted such settlements in the Ohio Valley. They soon had reason to suspect that it would not be long at all.[45]

As the British tightened their hold on North America, colonists regarded the western lands with increasing greed. All along the frontier, squatters and hunters poured onto Indian lands. In Cumberland County skirmishes broke out between Pennsylvania squatters and Indian hunters. Angus McDonald wrote from Fort Burd, on Pennsylvania's western frontier, "Here Comes Such Crowds of Hunters out of the Inhabitence as fills those woods at which the Indians seems very much disturbed and say the white people Kills all there Deer."[46] While these squatters and hunters may not have had official sanction, colonial governors did not necessarily disapprove of their actions. Indeed, Governor Fauquier complained to the Board of Trade that one of the main reasons "in driving the French from this Country, was I conceive . . . to get possession of the fertile Lands on the Ohio." He questioned why then he had been told not to allow settlers to cross the Appalachians. Fauquier's concerns were made more pressing because his predecessor, Robert Dinwiddie, had encouraged men to enlist in the Virginia Regiment in the early stages of the war by promising them lands around the forks of the Ohio. Now that the British had captured the Ohio, these veterans were clamoring for what they believed they had earned.[47]

The French surrender of Canada in September 1760 heightened tensions between the British and the Indians still further, particularly when Amherst decided to maintain and garrison all the French posts in the west. The Oneidas and Tuscaroras reminded Johnson that "at the commencement of this War, great promises were made us . . . that at the End thereof, you would demolish all your outposts & fortifications erected in our Country."[48] Now that the war had ended, they wondered, why were these promises not being kept? Headmen from almost "every Nation" complained to Johnson about "the hasty Steps . . . [that] we are taking towards getting possession of their severall Countrys."[49]

Nowhere were these tensions more apparent than around Fort Pitt, where the town of Pittsburgh was growing rapidly. By April 1761 there were 160 houses for the post's civilian population outside the fort, with several hundred inhabitants. Meanwhile the garrison continued to extend the fortification far beyond the limits of the French fort. Soon it covered over seventeen acres and had accommodation for over one thousand troops. It was more than ten times the size of Fort Duquesne. Yet, the French no longer posed a threat to its security. As Indians traveled to the fort to trade, they wondered if this was the future of all the British forts across the region. Increasingly, headmen questioned whether the British "designed to Build another Philadelphia on their Lands."[50]

The British still could have gained support among the Ohio Indians by using the traditional diplomatic protocol of gift exchanges to make important allies in the region. After several years of warfare, and with the French unable to provide the Ohio Indians with supplies from 1757 onward, the Ohio villages were desperately short of trade goods. In March 1760 Johnson reported to Amherst that "the Indians from almost all parts have been comeing in this winter to me, and all the Out Posts for Provisions, they and their Familys being . . . in a Starving Condition."[51] A few gifts and a growing trade could have secured allies for the British. However, many British officials viewed the Indians not as equals but as a conquered people and could not see any need to placate them. Amherst took a particularly imperious tone toward the Indians, maintaining that should they ever again rise against the British it was in his power "not only to frustrate them, but to punish the delinquents with Entire Destruction."[52]

Amherst's arrogance and confidence were matched by a new frugality in British policy. Victory in North America had rapidly changed the perspective of Whitehall. During the Seven Years' War Whitehall had been prepared to run up huge debts; now the costs of administering the empire had to be constrained. The death of King George II in October 1760 had undermined Pitt's position. The new king opposed a continuation of the war. The Duke of Newcastle, who had supervised the financing of the war, was worried that the massive expense had overstretched Britain's ability to pay. For a year Pitt faced growing opposition in the cabinet to the war. Finally, in October 1761 he resigned. The new administration sought to cut back on the expense of military operations on the Ohio, including a subsidy for Indian diplomacy—the distribution of gifts at conferences and other official meetings, as well as the day-to-day provision of small quantities of ammunition and powder for hunting. From the start several officials perceived that such frugality would lead to future problems. Sir William Johnson cautioned that "it is very necessary, and will always be Expected by the Indians that the Commanding Officer of Every Post have it in his power to supply them in Case of Necessity with a Little Cloathing, Some arms & ammunition to hunt with; also some provisions on their Journey homewards, as well as a smith to repair their arms & working utensils &ca."[53] Johnson's warning went unheeded, and as pressures to control expenditures grew, Amherst sought to halt the distribution of all gifts and presents to the Ohio Indians. Amherst singled out Croghan for particular criticism. Instead of Britain's newfound allies being provided with gifts and goods as a sign of good faith, Amherst argued, they "must be punished but not bribed."[54] By the summer of 1761 Amherst had determined that all gift giving should cease, and he wrote brusquely to Johnson that he should "avoid all presents in future."[55]

For the Indian peoples of the Ohio Valley the return of trade and traditional diplomatic protocols had been a central element in their acceptance of the British presence in the region. Following the disruption of years of continual warfare many of the Ohio Indians were desperate for trade goods. Shortly after assuming command at Detroit at the end of 1760, Capt. Donald Campbell, the new British commander at the post, wrote to Bouquet that the local Indians were "in great distress for want of Ammunition" and were "absolutely Starving."[56] Clearly, Amherst's new policy had had an instant effect. Almost immediately, Iroquois headmen reproached Johnson. They complained that they were "obliged to pay such exorbitant prices, that our hunting is not sufficient to purchase us more cloathing as is necessary to cover us, & our families, indeed, our hunting is not so great as usual—(altho there is more game) through the want of ammunition which we can by no means procure."[57]

Frustration with the new British administration soon began to manifest itself openly: settlers and Indian hunters skirmished; traders found their stores looted; the army's horses were stolen from their paddocks and stables. Matters came to such a head that in May 1761 Bouquet suspended all trade with the Shawnees at Fort Pitt in retaliation for the endemic theft of horses from the garrison. The unrest soon spread to other posts in the upper Ohio Valley. At Presque Isle, Gavin Cochrane, the fort's commander, was barely able to restrain his men from opening fire on some Mingo horse thieves. Across the upper Ohio Valley violence erupted between the Indian peoples and the British garrisons at the frontier posts. For many Indians "the illtreatment they generally met with at the Posts, induced them to imagine the English proposed to fall upon & destroy them."[58] From Fort Pitt, George Croghan reported that "the six Nations, are very uneassy And make great complaints of the usage they have met with from the General Since the reduction of Canada, and says it is True they have acquainted all those western indians of it, and Seems very jealous that the English have some bad designs Against them."[59]

In this atmosphere of distrust, not surprisingly, plots against the British began to emerge. In the spring of 1761 the Senecas sent "Deputys to all the nations from nova Scotia to the Illinois," urging them to prepare to take up arms against the British invaders of their homeland and to meet in the summer at Sandusky, where British influence was more limited than at Detroit. In June two Seneca messengers, Kiasuta and Tahiadoris, arrived in Detroit with an invitation to the Detroit Indians to attend the Sandusky conference. The Senecas promised that if the Detroit Indians could seize the post, they would fall on Forts Pitt and Niagara. They urged all the Ohio Indians to unite in resistance to the British forces now occupying their homelands, telling them that they were all "but one people, & had but one Voice"; together they could "dispossess the English of their Country."[60] However, possibly because of the traditional enmity between the Hurons and the Iroquois, but also because the Detroit Hurons resented the plan to hold a council at Sandusky, outside their influence, the Detroit Hurons immediately reported the Senecas' message to the British commander at Detroit, Donald Campbell. Campbell called all the Detroit Indians together to inform them of the Senecas' scheme. He then confronted Kiasuta and Tahiadoris and convinced them that now that the British knew of their plan they should abandon it, for they would not be able to surprise any of the British posts. Confronted with this betrayal, the two Senecas admitted their involvement in the conspiracy and abandoned the plan.[61]

As news of the Sandusky "conspiracy" spread, panic moved through western Pennsylvania. At Fort Pitt, Bouquet formed the inhabitants of the growing town into militia companies, while other frontier settlers fled for protection to Carlisle and Fort Loudoun. Alarmed by reports of unrest in the west, Johnson had already arranged to travel to Detroit before news of the "conspiracy" broke. Now his visit to Detroit took on a new significance. He arrived on September 3, 1761. On September 9 he convened a conference with representatives from all the western nations. Johnson intended to make any future conspiracies difficult to form. His policy at Detroit thus had two central elements: first, to placate the Great Lakes Indians by redressing their main complaints; second, to divide the Great Lakes and Ohio Indians from the Iroquois by promoting disputes between the nations. To placate the Great Lakes Indians he repeated his former pledge that the British had no intention of seizing Indian lands. More practically, in response to Indian complaints about the high cost of trade goods and other irregularities, he issued new and strict orders for regulation of the Indian trade in the west. He even went so far as to order that, to avoid any future disputes, whenever possible the men in the western posts should avoid "having much intercourse wth. the Inds. or rambling abroad among them."[62] To promote divisions between the Great Lakes and Ohio Indians and the Iroquois Johnson used all his guile in private meetings to develop personal jealousies between headmen and to create misunderstandings about the nature of the relationship of the different Ohio peoples with the British. Later, Johnson would maintain that he "did all in my power in private conferences to create a misunderstanding between the 6 Nations, & Western Indians, as also between the latter & those of *Ohio* so as to render them Jealous of each other."[63] However, Johnson's greatest stroke was to admit the western nations into the Covenant Chain. This, he hoped, would generate disputes between the Ohio Indians and the Iroquois. Indeed, upon hearing this news, Bouquet reported to Israel Pemberton that "a Separate Confederacy is made between the Shawanese, Delaware, Wyandots, and other Western Indians offensive & deffensive in which we are Included; The Petticoat is taken from the Delawares & they are now Men." This was a development, he noted, that "can not be very agreeable to the Six Nations."[64]

Johnson had succeeded in creating some divisions between the Great Lakes and Ohio Indians and the Iroquois, but this could not prevent peace from breaking down in the west, for the Iroquois were playing an increasingly unimportant role in the affairs of the Ohio Valley. Indeed, by 1761, in central Pennsylvania, along the Susquehanna and Delaware Rivers, the peace concluded at Easton in 1758 had already broken down. Angered by the failure of the Pennsylvanians to halt the activities of both the Susquehannah Company and the many hunters who flooded onto their lands across Pennsylvania's northern frontier, Indians frequently skirmished with white families. Pennsylvania trader Charles Brodhead, who was held hostage for some time at the Delaware town of Asinsink, on the Chemung River, a tributary of the Delaware, reported the repeated passage of messengers from the Susquehanna Delawares and the Iroquois. In this tense atmosphere rumors spread of the capture of a British fort near Fort Pitt and of seven hundred French canoes coming up the Ohio with supplies. While these rumors may have been ripples from the "Seneca conspiracy" of the summer, they also reflected a belief that would grow in strength among the Ohio Indians over the next two years: that the French would return to assist them, as they always had, in their struggle against the British.[65]

The antagonism surfaced at a conference between the Delawares and the Pennsylvanians at Easton in August 1761. As soon as the conference opened, a barrage of complaints from the Indians met Governor Hamilton. The Delawares complained bitterly about the settlers trespassing on their lands. In particular, they rebuked the Iroquois, from whom the Susquehannah Company claimed to have a grant for the Wyoming lands. Teedyuscung turned on the Iroquois and reminded them that they had told the Delawares "to go and live at Wyomink, for you gave me the Land there, where I might raise my bread & get my living."[66] Now the Iroquois seemed to expect the Delawares to move elsewhere. The Delawares demanded either compensation or a deed for the lands at Wyoming. Hamilton refused to give the Delawares a deed for their lands and asserted that any claims for compensation would have to come from Johnson, who had been appointed to look into the Delawares' complaints.[67]

The Delawares were incensed. Joseph Peepy, a Bethlehem Indian and one of the most Anglophilic of all the Delawares, now launched into a bitter attack on the entire conduct of British Indian diplomacy, presenting a long string of grievances. He complained about the conduct of both Sir William Johnson and Governor Francis Fauquier, who would "not speak or do right to us." He questioned the change in British policy toward supplying the Indians with gifts and complained that when they now visited Johnson to trade their skins "he does not give us the worth of our Skins, but only a handful of powder, and for that reason we think there is certain death coming upon us." Peepy remarked on the duplicity of British diplomacy. He asked pointedly, "How come it . . . that you do not all speak alike?"[68] However, the Pennsylvanians now saw little need to placate the Delawares, and Teedyuscung's and Peepy's concerns were dismissed.

It was not only on the Susquehanna that the actions of the colonists were raising the concerns of the natives. On the Ohio news of their repeated treaty violations in Pennsylvania seemed to augur the future on the Ohio. Indeed, white settlements seemed already to be spreading beyond the forks. In the summer of 1761, for instance, Christian Frederick Post began construction of a Moravian mission at Tuscarawas, in the Muskingum Valley, the new home of Tamaqua and Shingas. Many of the local headmen bitterly opposed the project, believing that the mission would provide a route both for the undermining of Indian culture and, more importantly, for white acquisition of Indian land.[69]

In response to these rising concerns Bouquet issued a proclamation at Fort Pitt at the end of October reminding settlers that the 1758 Treaty of Easton forbade any settlement or hunting west of the Allegheny Mountains. To the Ohio Indians such promises must have seemed empty, as British troops continued to occupy the abandoned French posts in the west. Indeed, Bouquet himself ordered the construction of a new fort at Sandusky, which had previously been only an unprotected trading post. First the British had made promises that they would leave the Ohio when the French were defeated. Then they had maintained that they needed to occupy the former French forts to defend their traders. Now they were constructing new forts. Many Ohio Indians must have wondered if their fate would follow that of their Susquehanna brethren, if settlers would soon overwhelm them and occupy their lands while the government claimed it was powerless to act.[70]

The concerns of the Susquehanna Delawares and the Seneca plot at Detroit should have alerted the British to a growing tide of discontent among the Ohio Indians. However, so confident were some British commanders of their military superiority that such warnings were ignored. Amherst in particular continued to maintain that the Ohio Indians were "incapable of doeing us any hurt."[71] Through the winter of 1761–62 his arrogance grew. Despite the necessity of containing the "Seneca conspiracy" among the Detroit Indians, Amherst bitterly attacked the "prodigious Expence" of Johnson's summer mission to Detroit. Amherst believed he could control the Indians by controlling trade: end the traditional gift giving, and the Indian peoples would have to spend their time hunting to acquire necessary trade goods; refuse to supply them with ammunition and powder, and they could pose no military threat to the new British posts in the west. Such a policy had failed miserably to bring the Cherokees into line. It would be even more disastrous on the Ohio.[72]

While initiated by the economic retrenchment instigated by Whitehall, Amherst's policy went beyond simply restricting the expenses of Indian diplomacy. Parsimony became an instrument of policy. At Niagara Maj. William Walters had provided the neighboring Indians with fish caught by the garrison, which "costs no Expence." Now Amherst forbade even this small act. Walters complained to Johnson: "You are sencible how necessary it is to give the Indians a Little Support, I have been at a great deal of trouble to Convince them of the good Intention that the English has towards them." He warned, "They are a jealous people and Should we hold our hand Intirely from them—they will be Easily made to beleive We Intend them Some hurt."[73]

Amherst's increasing parsimony reflected, in part, his anger at the growing reluctance of the colonies to provide any further military assistance. For most Pennsylvanians the war was over, yet the demands from the Crown continued. At the beginning of February 1762 Governor Hamilton received a request from the secretary of state, Charles Wyndham, the Earl of Egremont, to provide troops for the summer's campaign. It was not clear where the campaign would be nor what benefit Pennsylvania might gain from it. Consequently, the assembly was reluctant to provide men. This reluctance was only heightened by Amherst's arrogant demand that it encourage enlistment into the regular forces by providing an additional provincial bounty. Despite news that war on Spain had been declared, both assembly and governor were able to use their long-lasting animosity over the taxation of the proprietors' lands as an excuse not to fund any forces in 1762.[74]

Virginia was initially equally reluctant to raise men. With the Cherokee War over, the House of Burgesses ordered the Virginia Regiment disbanded. However, in Virginia the news of war against Spain was received with greater enthusiasm than in Pennsylvania. With the prospect of Caribbean booty and a chance to issue paper money to pay for any men raised, the burgesses agreed to recruit 1,000 men for the summer's campaign and to provide bounties for an additional 268 to be recruited into regular regiments. However, those Virginians who did venture to enlist were more interested in the proposed expedition against Havana than in garrison duty in the Ohio Valley. With few men at his disposal, Amherst needed to find alternative ways of controlling the Indian peoples of the Ohio Valley. With additional pressures from Whitehall to keep costs at a minimum, controlling trade provided a cheap alternative to maintaining a substantial military presence.[75]

As Indian concerns over British intentions mounted, opposition to the British began to take on a new dimension, for the first time incorporating a religious and spiritual element. Indian sachems began to urge their fellow villagers to cast off all aspects of European culture. In 1760 Munsee holy man Papoonan, from the upper reaches of the Susquehanna River, began to attack the impact of trade on the hunting practices of his young men, particularly the way in which they were now treating animals, arguing for a return to respect for the spirits of the animals. Papoonan's teachings influenced another Munsee holy man named Wangomend. Wangomend took Papoonan's teachings much further, arguing for a rejection of all European influences. In the early 1760s, as the stream of refugees from the Delaware and Susquehanna Rivers mounted, these ideas were transmitted to the Ohio Valley. In October 1762 James Kenny, the Pennsylvania agent at Fort Pitt, reported the spread of the teachings of another Delaware holy man named Neolin. Neolin argued that the Indians should reject all European influences and "learn to live without any Trade or Connections with ye White people, Clothing & Supporting themselves as their forefathers did."[76] For seven years the Indians were to brace themselves for a final struggle against the Europeans while their young men were "Train'd to ye use of the Bow & Arrow." After seven years they were "to quit all Commerce with ye White People & Cloth themselves with Skins."[77] Neolin's message quickly spread throughout the Ohio Valley, gaining strength from Indian fears about the new British presence in the region. Implicit in the message to reject trade was the rejection of all alliances with Europeans, for trade had formed the basis of the relationship between the Ohio Indians and the French. Resistance to British occupation had taken on a new significance.

Redeeming the Captives

There was another element in the growing resistance to British policy: British demands for the return of prisoners taken during the war. As early as April 1760 the flow of returned prisoners from the Ohio Indians had ceased. John Langdale, an agent of the Friendly Association, began to doubt whether any more prisoners would be returned. He reported back to the association that there were "certainly many [prisoners] amongst them especially children, but they do not seem to take kindly our inquisitiveness nor do I beleive they are in earnest in their promises to deliver them all up."[78] Headmen faced a problem in demanding that their increasingly suspicious kinfolk hand over any prisoners they held. Croghan himself reported that "they have no laws to Oblige their people but by preueassion and the prisnors by Adoption is a property of the Familys they live with." For many headmen forcing the return of captives was impossible, especially at a time when the traditional buttress of their authority, the distribution of gifts and reciprocal gift exchanges within and between clans, was breaking down because of the lack of trade goods in the west.[79]

The issue was further complicated by the fact that many prisoners, once "released," had no desire to return to their original homes. Croghan reported from Fort Pitt in July 1761 that many of the prisoners had "been at liberty Some time and I cannot prevaile on them to go Home."[80] Indeed, many "prisoners" remained in the Ohio Valley not as captives but because they had no wish to return to the colonies. The Detroit Hurons informed Johnson that they had freed "all such prisoners as were amongst us who were willing to return home." They added that those who still remained behind were "no Slaves with us, being at their free liberty to go anywhere, or act as they please, neither is it our Custom to Exercise any Authority over them, they having the same priviledges with ourselves." They concluded that they had not "detained them a moment longer than they chose to stay."[81] Christian Frederick Post reported in the summer of 1761 that the Shawnees still held over 150 captives but were "not willing to deliver them all . . . those they Love they will not part with."[82]

To families in Virginia and Pennsylvania whose loved ones remained among the Ohio Indians, the claims that "captives" were free to return to the colonies if they wished, no matter how true, seemed very hollow. Isom Barnett, for instance—who had himself been captured by the Indians on Smith's River in Halifax County, Virginia, in 1758 but had later been set free—sent an agent to the Ohio in an attempt to secure the release of his wife, Sarah, and son, Jesse, who were still living among the Indians. James McCullough petitioned Henry Bouquet to use all means possible to achieve the release of his two sons, John and James, captured in 1756. Yet despite Bouquet's efforts, and the Friendly Association's offer of a fifteen-pound reward for all prisoners brought in by the Indians, few were returned.[83]

There was another reason, however, why the Ohio Indians refused to return their prisoners. Increasingly, Ohio headmen saw Anglo-American prisoners as useful hostages in case the British should not live up to their promises. The idea of retaining prisoners as hostages may have originated with Teedyuscung. Governor Denny's successor, James Hamilton, reported that during the negotiations at Easton in 1758, "tho' it was not minuted in the Treaty," and after that "at sundry times to some members of the [Friendly] Association" Teedyuscung had pledged that "the prisoners would never be deliver'd up, till the Indians were satisfied about the Lands."[84]

Sir William Johnson was aware of these stirrings of unrest and sought to change the direction of British policy. In desperation, Johnson wrote to the Earl of Egremont in May 1762, informing him of his fears. Johnson warned that Indian concerns were fueled by "our growing power, which the Enemy . . . had always told them would prove their ruin, as we sho[ul]d by degrees Surround them on every side, & at length Extirpate them." He pointed out that the construction of posts in the west seemed only to confirm these fears. If further confirmation was needed, the change in diplomatic protocol provided this. The French, Johnson argued, "spared no labor, or Expence, to gain their friendship and Esteem . . . whilst we . . . not only fell infinitely short . . . in our presents &ca to the Indians, but have of late . . . been rather premature in our sudden retrenchment of some necessary Expences."[85]

Johnson's pleas were not heeded, for Egremont was one of the authors of Amherst's policy; his main concern seems to have been with the southern frontier. Indeed, Egremont sent out instructions that southern commanders should ensure the "opening & carrying on [of] so large a Traffic with . . . [the Indians] as will supply all their Wants."[86] British officials in general still saw the Ohio as conquered territory, and in the west Amherst continued to implement his policy of fiscal retrenchment. As George Croghan traveled early in 1762 to the newly occupied Illinois Country to hold councils with the Indians to convince them of the amity of the British, Johnson was compelled to send him strict orders to be as economical as possible in his distribution of gifts. Across the west British officers found that they were unable to distribute presents to influential headmen.[87]

The Breakdown of Anglo-Indian Relations, 1762–1763

All these underlying issues—the role of Anglo-American captives, the lands of the Susquehanna Delawares, the role of trade and diplomacy—came to the fore at two conferences held in the summer of 1762. In June a final conference with the Susquehanna Delawares convened at Easton. Johnson was to make a final hearing of the Delawares' claims of fraud, but there was already much scheming and chicanery. Hamilton hoped that he could engineer an end to the continuing impasse over Delaware compensation. The Delawares could be compensated for the damages inflicted by Connecticut settlers at Wyoming rather than at the forks. This would allow the proprietors to escape disgrace by avoiding any mention of fraud in the Walking Purchase. Teedyuscung would have to be persuaded to accept recompense, but not specifically for the loss of land in the Walking Purchase.

From the start it was apparent that the conference would be an acrimonious affair; rumors about the conduct of both Johnson and the Quakers would later fill Philadelphia coffeehouses. The Quakers sought to ensure that the Delawares received fair treatment at the conference, while Johnson was angered at what he saw as their unwarranted interference in Indian affairs and tried to maintain the influence of the Iroquois over the Susquehanna Delawares. When the proprietors' defense was finally read to the conference, it consisted of four hours of legal arguments and precedents with little mention of the Walking Purchase. When Teedyuscung demanded to have the defense translated, Johnson launched into an abusive attack on both Teedyuscung and the Quakers. As the attack grew more vitriolic Israel Pemberton "stood up, and speaking aloud with great warmth and Indecency" attacked Johnson's whole conduct, maintaining that he had deliberately "misrepresented" the Delawares' case.[88] Reports later circulated in Philadelphia that Johnson, swearing loudly, brandished his sword at Pemberton and asked "what right he had to interpose in this matter, and said that, *He* was, by the Royal order, to hear the Complaints of the Indians . . . and that no other person had any right to Intermeddle." He added snidely that "he plainly saw thro what Channel Teedyuscung conducted his Business, and had taken Notice that He was constantly nurs'd and Entertain'd at Pemberton's, or at the Lodgings of the Committee of the Assembly."[89]

Johnson then went on the offensive. In a series of closed meetings, from which the Quakers were specifically barred, he pressured Teedyuscung to accept Hamilton's offer of compensation for the activities of the Susquehanna Company. Teedyuscung initially replied that he was willing to settle, but for the Walking Purchase lands. Johnson repeatedly pressed Teedyuscung to abandon his claim to the forks of the Delaware, and Teedyuscung repeatedly dismissed him, informing him that "this is all I have to say to you . . . but I do not think your wanting to do things in the dark looks well."[90] Johnson now placed psychological pressure on Teedyuscung. He isolated him, threatening him and warning him of the dire consequences if he refused to settle. After several days the conference finally reconvened. Whatever Johnson had done, it had worked. Teedyuscung seemed a different person. Now cowed and subdued he formally withdrew his complaint. He admitted to the conference that his claim of fraud "was a Mistake." He continued simply that "as to the Walk, the Proprietary Commissioners insist, that it was reasonably performed; but we think otherwise. Which Difference in Opinion may happen without either of us being bad men. But this is a matter that Brethren ought not to differ about." He concluded, "wherefore, being desirous of living in Peace and Friendship with our Brothers the Proprietaries, and the good People of Pennsylvania, we bury under Ground, all Controversies about Land; and are ready . . . to sign a Release for all the Lands in Dispute." After six years of negotiations, Teedyuscung had accepted failure and was a broken man. Over the next few months he became increasingly paranoid, even accusing the Pennsylvanians of hatching a plot to poison him.[91]

Dealings at Easton had revealed that some imperial officials were prepared to ride roughshod over Indian concerns. News of Johnson's and the Penns' chicanery reached the Ohio Indians as they traveled to Lancaster for a conference with the British to conclude a final peace on the Ohio. The conference that convened at Lancaster only five weeks later would demonstrate, however, that unlike their Delaware brethren the Ohio Indians would not accept such treatment. At Lancaster provincial demands for the return of prisoners would override even the niceties of conference protocol and convince the Ohio Indians of the ill intentions of the British. The Ohio Indians had come to Lancaster specifically "to confirm our Friendship, & make a lasting peace."[92] However, after only the briefest of ceremonies, the Pennsylvanians opened the conference with forceful demands that the Ohio Indians hand over any remaining "prisoners." The Ohio Indians were appalled that this issue had been raised at the start of the conference. They had come to Lancaster expecting the full formalities of a peace ceremony. Tamaqua bluntly stated, "I suppose this matter of the prisoners to be the principal Business for which you invited us here"—rather than the conclusion of a general peace. Hamilton merely replied, "You judge right, in thinking that the affair of our Prisoners was a principal reason of our inviting you here."[93]

The Indians were incensed, and their anger only rose further when Hamilton brusquely informed them that he was sending provincial commissioners to Fort Pitt, where he expected them to immediately hand over all the remaining prisoners. Thomas King, the Oneida headman, informed Hamilton that many of the remaining "prisoners" had been accepted into Indian society; they were wives and children of Indian families. Hamilton, however, brusquely brushed aside King's concerns. He reminded him simply that "it was a positive Engagement between us, upon re-establishing the antient Chain of Friendship, that those Nations who had taken any of our people Prisoners, should deliver them all up; and this Brethren, I must insist upon."[94]

The Ohio Indians were furious at the Pennsylvanians' dismissal of their concerns. But the Pennsylvanians did nothing to assuage their anger; indeed, they did all they could to increase Indian resentment.

Hamilton now pressed the Ohio Delawares to acknowledge Teedyuscung's admission that there had been no fraud in the original acquisition of Delaware lands. If the Ohio Delawares would disavow the claim of fraud, this would give more weight to the proprietors' claims that the fraud was merely a creation of the Quakers. Tamaqua, the Ohio Delaware head-man, was enraged by Hamilton's guile. He had had little involvement in this issue. He merely informed the conference, "I must acknowledge that I know nothing about Lands upon the Delaware, & have no concern with Lands upon that river; We know nothing of the Delawares' claim to them."[95] To most Ohio Indians the self-interest of the Pennsylvanians, not the conclusion of a lasting peace, seemed to have become the sole issue of the conference. In anger Thomas King commenced a bitter attack on Pennsylvania's entire Indian policy, focusing particularly on their land hunger and their treatment of the Delawares. Summing up the thoughts of many of his compatriots, he informed Hamilton: "You are always long-ing after my Land: from the East to the West you seem to be longing after it. Now I desire you will not covet it any more; you will serve me as you have done our Cousins, the Delawares; you have got all their Land from them; all the Land hereabouts belonged to them once, and you have got it all."[96]

The conference dissolved on August 27. To demonstrate their ire with the proceedings, the Ohio Indians abandoned their presents at Fort Burd with a sarcastic comment on the parsimony of the British: Governor Hamilton, they said, "might send for them to give to the Indians the next Treaty."[97] As if to add insult to injury, mobs of frontiersmen at-tacked many of the delegates as they returned home through the back-country, stealing their horses and all their supplies and leaving them to make their way to the Ohio as best they could. They returned with tales of the arrogance and cupidity of the British.[98]

In many ways the conference at Lancaster marked the final stage in the breakdown of Anglo-Indian relations. As the Indians returned to the Ohio in September many had already determined that it was time to break with the British, and there was plenty of support for such action on the Ohio. When Thomas Hutchins traveled through the Illinois Country in the spring and summer of 1762, he found the villagers "much dissatisfy'd" with the British presence. They complained openly to Hutchins that the British were not supplying them with presents "as the french had always Accustomed themselves." Hutchins concluded, "They think it very Strange that this Custom should be so immediately broke off by the English, and the Traders not allowed even to take so much Ammunition with them as to enable those Indians to kill game sufficient for the Support of their families."[99]

Ironically, the ultimate element in the unraveling of Anglo-Indian relations in the Ohio Valley had nothing to do with British policy in the region. In January 1763 news of ongoing negotiations with France arrived in Philadelphia with the first details of the peace treaty. In the Ohio Valley news that the French intended to cede Canada to the British was met at first with disbelief by the Indian peoples. Alexander McKee broke the news to a group of Shawnee headmen at Lower Shawnee Town. They were horrified. They asked McKee if the French really had given up "their country," meaning the Ohio Valley, and "by what right they could pretend to do so." McKee reported that many of the Indians were now concerned that "the English would soon be too Great a People in this Country."[100] For three years the Ohio Indians had expressed fears that the British intended to eliminate them. Now they had done the unthinkable and eliminated the French. Onontio, the great father, had looked after the Indian peoples of the Ohio Valley for nearly a century. Many now feared that the British would turn on them. Following news of the peace treaty, the number of belts circulating in the Ohio Valley and Illinois Country increased rapidly. Rumors abounded of an impending Indian uprising. Yet such rumors had been circulating for so long that most British officials took little notice of them.[101] Amherst in particular dismissed all talk of an Indian uprising as ludicrous, for the Ohio Indians were a "Contemptible Figure . . . as it certainly is not in their Power to Effect any thing of Consequence against Us; But if, they are so Rash as to make an Attempt, the Mischief they Intend will certainly Recoil upon themselves."[102]

By the spring of 1763 it was apparent to some observers that war clouds were gathering in the west. George Croghan wrote to Johnson that if the Ohio Indians could overcome their internal differences, "we should Soon have an Indian Warr." The conference at Lancaster, Amherst's parsimonious policy, demands for the return of captives, the thousands of settlers heading west, and now news of the peace treaty in Paris all provided convincing proof that the British intended the Ohio Indians only harm. Even worse, by restricting trade Amherst had destroyed a means by which he could have continued to exercise some influence over the Ohio Indians. The inability of the French to supply them with goods had encouraged many to end the previous war in the late 1750s. Now, if the British were not going to supply them with the expected presents and trade goods, there was little to lose in commencing a new war.[103]

However, there was another essential element in the threat of war that Croghan alone seems to have recognized: the Indian peoples' "Success [at] ye beginning of this Warr on our fronteers."[104] The success of the Indian raids on the Virginia and Pennsylvania frontier from 1755 to 1758 had given the Ohio Indians a confidence in their abilities and convinced them that they could once more bring the British colonies to their knees. Without that prior experience and confidence many of the Ohio and Illinois peoples may have been reluctant to take up arms against so numerous and powerful an adversary. Despite their occupation of the Ohio Country, the British army in the west remained fundamentally the same "Old Women" that Shingas had dismissed in 1756. British garrisons, pitifully small and isolated in the west, offered tempting targets. During the Seven Years' War raiding parties had found it easy enough to destroy such garrisons. In addition the experience of raiding parties in capturing supplies and prisoners convinced many headmen that raids could provide an alternative source of supply of European trade goods. While they lacked ammunition, it could be obtained from the captured forts and from raids on the frontier, and all manner of trade goods were there for the taking from thousands of frontier plantations and farmsteads. When the headmen of villages across the Ohio and Illinois Country considered the choice of war, they were not motivated solely by greed and the lure of plunder; indeed, these played a distinctly secondary role to their anger with British trade and land policy. If Amherst had not imposed his embargo upon the Ohio Indians, the threatened loss of trade with the British might have restrained some headmen from participation in war; with trade embargoed, the lure of goods that could not now be obtained through the usual channels drew headmen instead to contemplate war.

While the Ohio Indians concluded from the warfare of the 1750s that they had little to fear from the British, British commanders drew the opposite conclusion. They saw a conquered people whose lands had just been surrendered to the British by a mighty European power. Amherst laughed at suggestions that there could be a new Indian war. He dismissed reports of Indian plots as "Meer *Bugbears.*" He claimed that if the

Ohio Indians attacked the frontier, it would have no other effect "than that of hurting themselves by making Us Treat them as Enemies and Withdraw Our Friendship from them; the Greatest Misfortune that can befall them."[105] Even as news of the first Indian attacks on British posts in the west arrived, he arrogantly claimed that any war would only "bring Certain & Inevitable Ruin on the Whole Race of the Indians."[106]

FROM THE fall of Fort Duquesne to the onset of the siege of Detroit, British officials struggled to define a new Indian policy for the upper Ohio Valley. Yet British policy contained too many conflicting aims. Pennsylvanians and Virginians sought the return of captives, British military commanders sought land for the construction of forts, and officials in Whitehall sought savings on the great expense of empire. The Penns sought to diffuse any suspicions that they might have defrauded the Delawares, while the Quakers sought to develop their close ties with the Indian peoples to ensure future peace. Policies that could have restored peace, such as the restoration of prewar diplomatic protocols, were abandoned as being too expensive. Policies bound to increase friction, such as demands for the return of captives and the decision to maintain garrisons in the west, were accepted with little thought. British policy failed because most people saw the Ohio Indians as a defeated and conquered enemy. Only a few who had close contacts in the Ohio Valley, such as George Croghan, accurately perceived that the Ohio Indians had not been defeated and that if their concerns were not heeded they would surely recommence their raids upon the backcountry.

Even as Pontiac and the Detroit Indians finally took up arms against the British, in Philadelphia celebrations of the peace with France were underway. At the city's new college, commencement on May 17 was accompanied by a "Dialogue on Peace," a eulogy on the success of British arms set to music. Peace had finally come to America, and Philadelphians celebrated in verse:

> Stern Chiefs no more their crimson'd Blades shall wield,
> Nor deadly Thunders bellow o'er the Field.[107]

However, in the Ohio Valley those crimsoned blades were once more being wielded with renewed ferocity.

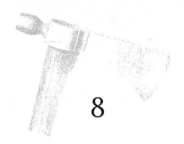

8

Denouement

"Pontiac's War," 1763–1765

THE WAR THAT BROKE OUT ON THE COLONIAL FRONTIER IN 1763 was the culmination of four years of British maladministration. At the root of the conflict was the perception by some British officials that the Ohio Indians were a weak and defeated people whose concerns they did not need to heed. As "Pontiac's War" broke out, however, it was the strength rather than the weakness of the Indians that became apparent to the British. The war revealed how far the Indians had been able to adapt their strategies and tactics to European warfare, for now they fought without European allies to guide and assist their war effort. In Pontiac's War the Ohio Indians demonstrated their ability to besiege and seize fortified positions, although where possible they preferred to take such positions by guile rather than force. Once more, raiding parties created a swathe of devastation through the backcountry; once more, backcountry inhabitants and colonial legislatures bickered; once more, the Ohio Indians would emerge from the conflict perceived as defeated, but in reality retaining much of their strength.

Pontiac's Uprising

At the end of April 1763 rumors of an Indian "conspiracy" began to circulate through the British post at Detroit. Such rumors were hardly new, but this rumor seemed to have some additional veracity. Indeed, the Indian villagers around the post had been considering their actions for some time. On April 27 a local Ottawa chief named Pontiac, after whom later historians would name the "uprising," called a meeting of the Ottawa, Potawatomi, and Huron bands living around Detroit. He showed the assembled conference wampum belts that he maintained he had received "from his Great Father, the King of France, to induce him to attack the English" and to avenge the "insults which he and his nation had received from the Commandant and the English officers."[1]

Over the next few days several hundred warriors massed around the fort, ostensibly to trade. The fort's commander, Maj. Henry Gladwin, believed the reports of Indian unrest and kept his men at the highest state of readiness. On May 1 Pontiac sought admission to the fort, but Gladwin was hesitant. When Pontiac finally persuaded Gladwin to admit him, it became all too apparent to him that the garrison was prepared for an attack. On May 5 Pontiac called the Hurons and Potawatomis to another council. Rather than abandoning his plans for an assault he urged the Indians to redouble their efforts and to prepare to "exterminate from our lands this nation which seeks only to destroy us." He provided the council with a long list of grievances against the British, focusing especially on Gen. Jeffrey Amherst's recent trade policy.[2] He stated: "The English sell us goods twice as dear as the French do, and . . . they do not want to give us credit. . . . When I go to see the English commander and say to him that some of our comrades are dead, instead of bewailing their death, as our French brothers do, he laughs at me and you. If I ask anything for our sick, he refuses with the reply that he has no use for us. From all this you can well see that they are seeking our ruin. Therefore my brothers, we must all swear their destruction and wait no longer. Nothing prevents us; they are few in numbers, and we can accomplish it."[3]

Pontiac's first move was to invite Gladwin and his aides to come to his camp to share a peace pipe and ostensibly diffuse the tension around the fort; judging by later events this was an attempt to lure Gladwin out of the fort to capture him. Gladwin, however, refused to leave the safety of the post. If Gladwin would not leave the fort, Pontiac would have to try to seize him in the fort. Consequently, on the morning of May 9 Pontiac and his men appeared outside the fort and demanded to speak with the commander. When Gladwin again refused, Pontiac's followers descended on some of the settlers outside the fort, killing six men, two women, and two children, an attack traditionally seen as the start of Pontiac's War. The following morning Pontiac requested another face-to-face meeting, this time with Gladwin's second in command, Capt. Donald Campbell. The fort was desperately short of supplies, and Gladwin decided to send Campbell to parley, planning to take advantage of the negotiations to send out other parties to round up cattle and supplies. While Gladwin's men were able to secure many vital supplies, enabling the fort to withstand the first few weeks of the siege, Campbell was not so fortunate, for Pontiac seized him and held him hostage.[4]

Pontiac forced Campbell to write to Gladwin with his demand that the garrison immediately withdraw to Niagara. To back up this demand, he massed his supporters around the post. By May 11 there were around 600 Indians encamped outside the fort. The fort's garrison was only about 120, even including the British traders who joined in its defense. However, Gladwin refused to surrender the post, and Pontiac thus prepared to take it by force. He compelled the French settlers who had not yet taken shelter inside the fort to provide ammunition and prepared his men for a direct assault. On the morning of May 12 the battle began.[5]

The attack on Detroit reveals the extent to which the Indians of the Great Lakes and upper Ohio Valley had adapted their tactics and strategy to European warfare. A direct assault upon a fortified position was not the kind of attack typically practiced by Indian warriors. However, this was what Pontiac intended. Tactics utilized during the battle also demonstrate how the traditional "skulking war" had been merged with European battlefield techniques. Pontiac's men used the outbuildings that surrounded the fort to provide cover for the attack and advanced to within only a few yards of the fort. In the fierce fighting that ensued even British commanders admitted that the Indian warriors "behaved extremely well." Gladwin himself believed that the fort was close to capture. In desperation he issued orders that as "defense [was] hopeless, and since to all appearances the expected assistance would not arrive on time, and as there was a lack of supplies of food and ammunition . . . everybody should hold himself in readiness to embark at the first signal in order to fall back upon Niagara." However, after several hours of fierce combat, Pontiac's men abandoned their assault. The fighting had cost the attackers heavy casualties, and Pontiac felt that it was more sensible to starve out the garrison.[6]

Pontiac knew that the fort was desperately short of supplies and that resupplying it would be extremely difficult. He had every reason to feel confident. If he could prevent the fort from receiving fresh supplies, it would have to surrender. A supply convoy was expected within a few days. Its fate could determine the fate of the fort. Gladwin knew that any convoy would be unaware of the siege and would need to be warned to take special care as it approached the fort. Consequently, on May 21 he dispatched the sloop *Michigan* to patrol the entrance to the Detroit River. As the *Michigan* appeared at the head of Lake Erie, Pontiac ordered his men to prepare to attack the vessel. On May 26 he sent Donald Campbell to talk to the sloop's crew, "hoping that the presence of this officer would lead the people of the vessel to surrender." However, Campbell refused to cooperate and instead warned the crew of Pontiac's intentions, allowing the sloop to slip away under cover of night into the safety of Lake Erie.[7] Still, while Pontiac had failed to capture the *Michigan,* it would not be on station to warn any incoming convoy of the danger they faced.

Two days later a supply convoy arrived. As Pontiac had hoped, the convoy's commander took no unusual precautions to protect his fleet. He beached it on the north shore of Lake Erie at Point Pelee to rest overnight before the convoy entered the Detroit River and made its way to the fort. Just before midnight the Indians stormed the encampment and captured eight of the nine bateaux carrying supplies. The following day the Indians rowed the bateaux past the fort and displayed their prisoners to the horrified garrison.[8]

The Spread of Unrest

The loss of the supply fleet had a devastating effect on the morale of the garrison, but even more demoralizing were the reports and the prisoners that came in from the surrounding posts. There is no evidence that Pontiac coordinated the attacks on British posts across the Great Lakes and the Ohio Valley. However, as soon as the siege of Detroit began he sent belts across the Great Lakes, Illinois country, and the Ohio Valley, informing the Indians of the actions of their Detroit brethren. Dissatisfied by four years of British mismanagement of Indian affairs, the

Indian peoples of the region needed little encouragement to eliminate the small British posts in their midst. As these belts arrived at villages across the region they sparked off a widespread Indian war, and the British posts fell like dominoes.[9]

The first to fall was Sandusky on May 16. The fort's commander, Ens. Christopher Pauli, allowed seven Indians into the fort. Once inside they seized and bound Pauli and overwhelmed the small guard. Most of the garrison and all the traders at the post were killed. Pauli himself was taken to the Indian settlements around Detroit, from which he escaped or, more likely, was allowed to escape, carrying the news of the fall of Sandusky to the beleaguered garrison. Nine days later, on the morning of May 25, the Indians captured Fort St. Joseph after a party of Detroit Potawatomis sought admittance to visit their relations. A French trader attempted to warn the fort's commander, Capt. John Joseph Schlosser, but he was too late. By the time he alerted the garrison the Indians had already broken into the barracks and killed everyone except for six men.[10] The next post to fall was Fort Miami. Unlike most of the other western forts, Fort Miami was prepared for a siege. On May 23 the garrison had received news that Detroit was under attack. The fort's commander, Ens. Robert Holmes, had ordered the garrison to remain alert and be prepared for trouble. However, only four days later Holmes himself received a message from his Indian mistress, informing him that she was desperately ill. Holmes rushed to her bedside. Unfortunately for Holmes, this was a ruse. No sooner had he stepped outside the fort than he was killed. The Indians then called upon the garrison to surrender, promising that their lives would be spared. With their commander butchered, and with only nine men remaining in the garrison, the men felt they had little choice.[11]

The largest western fort to fall to the Indians was Michilimackinac. Once more, a ruse was used to seize it. On June 2 a band of Chippewas arrived at the fort and invited the garrison to play baggataway, a version of lacrosse. There was nothing at all unusual in this request, as the garrison were accustomed to cordial relations with their Chippewa neighbors. The Chippewas, however, had received a belt from Pontiac a few days earlier, informing them of his plans at Detroit, and they had determined to seize the vital post. The garrison was unprepared for the sudden attack. Those men not playing in the game were watching over the stockade. Even the commanding officer was refereeing. Suddenly, at a prearranged signal, the Indians dropped their baggataway sticks and stormed into the fort, killing almost half the garrison.[12]

The revolt spread with equal speed to the east. News of the siege of Detroit seems to have reached the Indians around Fort Pitt about May 25, although it did not reach the garrison inside for several more days. On May 27 Thomas McKee, Pennsylvania's agent at the fort, reported that the Shawnees and Delawares around the fort seemed to be very restless. More worryingly, they had "sold 300 pounds worth of peltry very hastily with which they bought as much powder and lead as they could get." The following day McKee set off for the Indians' villages, but to his horror he found them all abandoned. On May 29 the Indians finally commenced their attacks, destroying small settlements around Fort Pitt and killing several settlers, including William Clapham, former commander of the Pennsylvania Regiment.[13] While the Shawnees and Ohio Delawares besieged Fort Pitt, the Detroit Indians proceeded to destroy the last British posts in the west. On June 19 two hundred Ottawas, Hurons, and Chippewas from Detroit appeared outside Fort Presque Isle, where they were soon joined by a body of Senecas from Chenussio. The garrison put up a brave fight for two days. However, the Indians used fire arrows to set the fort's bastions and wooden buildings alight. It soon became clear that prolonged resistance was impossible. With little hope of relief, and with Indian promises of safe passage to Fort Pitt, the garrison surrendered on June 21. Simultaneously, another party descended on the smaller posts of Venango and Le Boeuf, on the supply route between Fort Pitt and Presque Isle, and they fell with little struggle. By the end of June Fort Pitt and Detroit were the only remaining British posts west of the Appalachians.[14]

British military outposts were not alone in feeling the wrath of the Ohio peoples. Bands of angry villagers descended upon British traders. For months they had been denied ammunition and powder; now they would seize them and kill the traders. In the west and north, across the Great Lakes and in the Illinois Country, Indians killed and even tortured many of the traders they captured, blaming them for their dire straits—a fact suggested by the somewhat unusual manner in which many of the traders were put to death, "tied to stakes and shot . . . with arrows."[15] Nearer Fort Pitt, perhaps reflecting the influence of the trade goods supplied by the Friendly Association, the villagers gave the traders time to leave. At Tuscaroras, for instance, Tamaqua warned trader

Thomas Calhoon to flee, although he suggested that it might be sensible for Calhoon to leave his trade goods behind. By the beginning of June all British traders on the Ohio River and the Great Lakes had fled or been captured.[16]

At the beginning of June news of the attacks on the British forts reached the Indians settled on the upper Susquehanna. At Fort Augusta the Wyoming Indians hastily traded their skins before moving further up the east branch, nearer the security of the Iroquois. Within a few days many of them had also taken up arms. During late June and July bands of Indians descended on the reestablished frontier settlements, particularly on the Juniata River, wreaking havoc. By the end of July Col. Henry Bouquet was forced to evacuate the Juniata settlements and pull his forces further south.[17] Other parties began to disrupt communications between Fort Pitt and Carlisle. By mid-June, although Fort Pitt was not closely besieged, it was effectively cut off from the rest of Pennsylvania. Over the next few weeks raiding parties harassed convoys and expresses attempting to head west from Carlisle. Indian raiding parties engaged the garrisons of Forts Ligonier and Bedford in repeated skirmishes. On June 22 the Indians launched a full-scale assault on Fort Ligonier. The garrison fought desperately. After a fierce battle lasting one and a half days the attackers retired. While these assaults on the posts east of Fort Pitt failed to capture a single fort, they made communication across the Appalachians almost impossible. With Fort Pitt so isolated, many of the Ohio Indians were hopeful that the garrison would surrender or at least be evacuated, and they felt little need to tighten the siege. With this in mind, on June 24 Delaware headman Turtle Heart traveled to Fort Pitt to offer the garrison a chance to retire to safety. When the garrison refused, the Ohio Indians began to expand the scope of their raids.[18]

Raiding parties now increased their assaults upon the backcountry. Sherman's Valley in Cumberland County was devastated. Reports maintained that over one thousand families had fled from Cumberland County alone, and Carlisle became once more the westernmost point of settlement. By the end of July there were nearly fourteen hundred people sheltering in Shippensburg, "many of whom were obliged to lie in Barns, Stables, Cellars, and under old Leaky Sheds, the Dwelling houses being all crowded."[19] At Fort Bedford Capt. Lewis Ourry, the post's commander, reported that the post "was like a Fair. The mottled Crew of Women, Children, Drivers, Sorebacks, & Side Saddles, that flocked in, furnished thro' the Dust they kicked up, a diverting Scene." Families clamored to see Ourry begging for help, "and my Floor was Sprinkled partly with Mothers Tears, & partly with Children's P——ss—Distressfull Scene!"[20] Having devastated Cumberland County the raiders moved on. Soon they began to penetrate across the South Mountain into York County.[21]

Other raiding parties also descended upon Hampshire and Frederick Counties in Virginia. Thousands of settlers fled in terror before them. One report from Hampshire County claimed that "from the Face of Circumstances, the beginning of the last War was not so alarming or affecting."[22] A similar report from Maryland claimed that "never was Panic more general or forcible than that of the Back Inhabitants, whose Terrors at this Time, exceed what followed on the Defeat of General *Braddock*."[23] The attacks spread even further. By late July small raiding parties were attacking settlements in Augusta and Halifax Counties, and Governor Francis Fauquier wrote to Amherst, lamenting "the Devastation the Indians had made on our whole Frontier, from Potowmack almost as low as the Carolina Line."[24]

The number and composition of raiding parties operating on the colonial frontier in the summer of 1763 are impossible to determine exactly. However, the wide extent of the raids suggests a large number of separate parties, perhaps more than on any single occasion during the 1750s. During July 1763 raiding parties were active along the entire colonial frontier, from the Susquehanna River to the North Carolina line. Only Berks and Northampton Counties, east of the Susquehanna River, remained comparatively free from raids for the moment. The speed with which the war spread was extraordinary. In the 1750s Indian raiders had been supplied and, at least in part, directed by the French; during Pontiac's War, despite rumors of French involvement, the raiders were motivated solely by their own interests.

Other forces also accounted for the rapid spread of the war. There were four main centers of opposition to the British: Pontiac and his followers around Detroit; the Shawnees on the Scioto River; the Delawares on the Muskingum River and around Kuskuski; and the Chenussio Senecas. Outside these four groups opposition was more sporadic. Villages and bands were split, and these splits had been widened by the breakdown of the tradition of reciprocal gift giving caused by Amherst's trade policy. They were made yet worse because the traditional means of healing these divisions, mediation by the French, was no longer possible.

Across the Ohio Valley and the Great Lakes many Indian villages drifted toward what amounted to anarchy. Traditional leadership had always been weak, but by 1763 it was all but nonexistent.

If Indian leadership was weak, the British also failed spectacularly to provide leadership in their new regime in the west. At the small British posts scattered across the west, inexperienced commanders, young officers naive in the ways of their Native American neighbors, struggled to quell the growing unrest. Indeed, many Indian headmen may have been aware of the naivete of these commanders and taken pity on them, for a surprising number survived the onslaught on their posts. Had more experienced officers been in command, men who possessed a greater understanding of village life, they could perhaps have conciliated many of the Ohio Indians' concerns. Pontiac's War might then have been limited to localized unrest around Detroit and Fort Pitt. Instead it became a pan-Indian movement across the Ohio Valley and the Great Lakes, from the frontier of Virginia to Michilimackinac on Lake Superior, from the Illinois Country to Iroquoia.

By the end of June Bouquet had assembled his men in Carlisle, ready to march to Fort Pitt. He delayed, waiting for reinforcements from Pennsylvania. On July 4 Governor James Hamilton called the assembly into emergency session.[25] He hoped that it would re-form the Pennsylvania Regiment and allow him to send several companies to assist Bouquet in quelling the unrest on the Ohio. However, the assembly had rather different ideas. Instead of agreeing to provide men to serve alongside the regulars, the assembly would only agree to raise seven hundred men to serve in the backcountry over the summer. They could be deployed solely "within the purchased parts of the said Province, during the time of Harvest, or until the next Meeting of this House." They would not be allowed to serve on the Ohio under Bouquet, nor would they be of any use in garrisoning the forts protecting communications with Fort Pitt. Regular troops would have to be used, and they could scarcely be spared.[26]

To make matters even worse the assembly refused to provide a bounty for the new recruits. Governor Hamilton informed one recruiter, "If any of the people should be so unreasonable as to demand a Bounty for inlisting, you are to let them know, that the Government has done, and is doing all in its power at present for their assistance, & if they are not satisfied with being paid, to secure their own properties, without the addition of a Bounty, they must take the consequence." Not surprisingly, with few financial incentives for enlisting, recruiting was slow. Back-country settlers, who had everything to lose, were more interested in personally protecting their property than serving in the provincial forces, while the artisans and former servants who had enlisted in the 1750s could not be enticed into service without a bounty. Consequently the province's northern frontier remained all but unprotected throughout the summer.[27]

Virginia offered little more resistance. Governor Fauquier decided that by the time the assembly convened to consider raising the Virginia Regiment, any forces they might authorize would be too late to be of use in any campaign. He had not been in Virginia during the mid-1750s to witness the chaos of the early frontier raids. He thus decided to rely on the province's militia to provide at least a modicum of defense. Command of the militia forces was given to two experienced officers, Adam Stephen and Andrew Lewis, both of whom had seen considerable service on the frontier during the 1750s. The militia would be supplemented by small numbers of volunteers who agreed to range the frontier to detect incoming raiding parties. These volunteer parties had some success. However, their numbers were small, and since the militia once more proved itself of very limited capabilities, Virginia's frontier, like Pennsylvania's, remained relatively unprotected throughout the summer of 1763. Fortunately for the colonists, both Virginia and Pennsylvania were spared from further immediate devastation as the Indians increasingly focused their attentions on harassing the force Henry Bouquet was amassing in western Pennsylvania for the relief of Fort Pitt.[28]

The British Counteroffensive

Amherst found great difficulty in devising a military strategy to deal with the uprising. In mid-June Bouquet confided to him, "We are yet too much in the dark to form a Plan."[29] Amherst's initial plan called for Bouquet to march with elements of the Forty-second and Seventy-seventh Regiments to Fort Pitt, and then on to Presque Isle. From there he was to assist the relief expedition to Detroit. Amherst ordered that Bouquet was to do all in his power to wreak vengeance upon the Ohio Indians. He strongly suggested that Bouquet should take "no Prisoners, should any of the Villains be met with in Arms."[30] He also ordered Bouquet to ensure that no further frontier posts were abandoned and even attacked the demolition of outbuildings at Fort Pitt, for, he argued, these actions would only cause the Ohio Indians "to Imagine themselves more Formidable than they really are." He concluded, "There is no Doubt but it is in the Power of the Indians if they Exert their Utmost Force to Cutt off some of those Small Posts, before We can Send the Necessary Reinforcements . . . but an Attack on any fencd Post, tho' thinly Garrisoned, ought to Cost the Indians so Dear that they should not make a Second Attempt of the Kind."[31]

When Amherst later heard of the fall of not only Forts Le Boeuf and Venango but also Presque Isle, he was mortified. He spoke of little but "the Punishment of the Indians."[32] Deeply frustrated, he wrote to Bouquet suggesting a new stratagem. He asked whether Bouquet might be able to use blankets from the smallpox hospital in Fort Pitt to infect the Indians with the disease. "Could it not be contrived," Amherst asked, "to Send the *Small Pox* among those Disaffected Tribes of Indians? We must, on this occasion, Use Every Stratagem in our Power to Reduce them." While there is uncertain evidence that this strategy was ever seriously considered by Bouquet, or that it would have worked had it been tried, Amherst's message reflects the depths of despair to which he had sunk by August.[33]

The plight of Fort Pitt was growing more serious. During July the attackers began to tighten their siege. By the end of the month the Indians had built pits in the riverbank close to the fort, from which they sniped at exposed soldiers and shot fire arrows at the wooden buildings. While the fort was not under immediate threat, it was becoming apparent that it could not resist a siege indefinitely. However, Bouquet and his relief force could make only slow progress. At the beginning of August they arrived at Fort Ligonier. There Bouquet discovered that all communication with Fort Pitt had been cut for several weeks. He decided to push on in haste, to rush supplies to the beleaguered garrison. On August 4 he left Ligonier for the Ohio. In the middle of the following afternoon, when he had only advanced seventeen miles, his force was attacked by a body of four hundred Indians near Bushy Run. Bouquet's men fought bravely all day, but they soon found themselves surrounded and fired upon from all sides. The situation was desperate. It looked as if Bouquet's expedition might have an even worse fate than Braddock's.[34]

Bouquet was aware of many of the advantages that the Indians possessed. He later claimed that "their general ferocity of manners, and the

success where with they have often been flushed, have conspired to render their name terrible, and some times to strike pannic even into our
bravest and best disciplined troops."[35] Bouquet knew that his first task
was to prevent his troops from panicking and to utilize their superior
discipline to lure the Indians into a trap. The following morning the
Indians resumed their attack. As in 1755 they attempted to demoralize
the force "by Shouting and yelping" round the camp. However, Bouquet's
men held their ground. Realizing that his troops were exhausted, dehy-
drated, and could not maintain combat for another day nor gain victory
from a frontal assault on the Indian lines, Bouquet devised a new tactic.
He sent four companies of light infantry to take cover on a ridge, where
they could remain unseen by the enemy. Then he ordered his troops to
begin to move as if in retreat. His ploy succeeded. Thinking victory was
again theirs, the Indians rushed headlong at Bouquet's center. The fighting was fierce, but the Ohio warriors were lured further and further forward. Suddenly, the four hidden companies reappeared on their flanks.
This time there was panic among the Indian ranks. Within a few minutes they were in retreat. Victory was Bouquet's.[36]

News of the victory was met with jubilation. In Philadelphia church
bells were rung all night. However, Bushy Run was not the decisive victory that many colonists believed. While it allowed Bouquet to raise the
siege of Fort Pitt, it did not seriously undermine the military capability
of the Ohio Indians, and Bouquet's forces suffered substantial losses that
would prevent them from taking any major offensive action for another
year. Bouquet arrived in Fort Pitt with less than three hundred effective
troops. This hardly posed a threat to the Ohio Indians. Bouquet realized that he now had to take the war to the Ohio Indians' villages in order
to bring them to terms. Amherst certainly had no doubts. He wrote to
Sir William Johnson that only "when the Savages, who have been Concerned in the present Disturbances, are Sufficiently Punished for the
Depredations & Barbarities, they have Committed" would he think of
granting them peace. Before that they must "be Brought to such a State
as may give us Room to hope they will Remember the Engagements they
make with Us."[37]

The central problem was how to take the war to the Ohio Indians.
Bouquet's three hundred men were insufficient for that task. Amherst
suggested that some of the Virginia volunteers should attempt an attack
on the Shawnee settlements on the Ohio River. Perhaps mindful of the

fate of the Sandy Creek expedition, officers politely ignored this suggestion. Also mindful of his experiences during the 1750s, Col. John Armstrong attempted to recover some of the past glory poured on him following the raid on Kittanning. He organized an expedition to attack the Indian settlement at Great Island, on the west branch of the Susquehanna River. Armstrong set out at the beginning of October with 250 volunteers. He returned a few weeks later "half starved without any Success." While the expedition did destroy the settlement at Great Island, the Indians who lived there had already abandoned it for the safety of the Ohio.[38]

The problem of how to counterattack was underlined at Detroit. On the evening of July 28 a relief convoy from Niagara arrived at the mouth of the Detroit River and prepared to approach the fort the next morning. As dawn broke on July 29 a thick fog descended. Scarcely able to believe their good fortune, the members of the convoy made their way up the Detroit River undetected by Pontiac's men. Only as the expedition passed the Huron villages just downstream from the fort did the Indians realize that a relief convoy had arrived. In desperation they fired as it passed, killing two men and wounding fifteen. However, the attack was too late, and the convoy sailed safely into Detroit carrying several months' worth of supplies, 280 additional men, and six cannons.[39]

Having arrived safely, the expedition's commander, Capt. James Dalyell, was determined to strike a decisive blow against Pontiac to end the siege. He believed that the fresh troops he had brought with him should act before Pontiac might be able to call in reinforcements from the neighboring villages. Immediately upon his arrival he pressured Gladwin to authorize an offensive. At 2:00 A.M. on July 31, less than forty-eight hours after his arrival, Dalyell sallied out of Detroit with a force of 240 men. Quickly they marched to Pontiac's camp. However, Pontiac was not surprised, for French "spies" had informed him of Dalyell's intentions, and his men lay in ambush for the force. When the force reached a creek just short of the camp, Pontiac's men opened fire. The fighting was fierce and at close quarters. As day broke Dalyell reluctantly ordered his men to retreat. Pontiac, however, had already sent men to cut off the retreat. Dalyell now discovered that his force was surrounded. For a while it looked as if Pontiac would capture the entire expedition. Fortunately for the British troops, though, retreat was made possible through the determination of Robert Rogers and some of his rangers, who broke through

Indian lines and held off pursuing warriors for nearly an hour. In the early morning light the bedraggled remnants arrived back in Detroit. The expedition had been a disaster. Twenty-one men had been killed, including Dalyell himself, and another fifty seriously wounded, while the Indians had lost only five men killed, with eleven wounded. Once more Pontiac's men had demonstrated that they were quite capable of engaging British troops in regular combat.[40]

At the beginning of August the British hold on Detroit remained as precarious as ever. Even in the west Bouquet's relief of Fort Pitt did not threaten the Ohio Indians. However, the arrival of his force did make it apparent that they would not be able to seize the fort by a direct assault. The most successful strategy now appeared to be to expand the raids upon the frontier. Up until September the northern Pennsylvania frontier— Lancaster and particularly Berks and Northampton Counties—had remained relatively peaceful. At the end of September, however, a party of Ohio Delawares arrived on the Susquehanna to encourage their eastern brethren to join in the war. They found their task surprisingly easy. The remnants of the Susquehanna Delawares had every reason to wish to wreak vengeance upon the colonial frontier. On April 19, 1763, the final blow had befallen them. On that morning someone had burned and destroyed the Delaware settlement at Wyoming. All that remained of the town were the charred remains of the Indian cabins. Inside one of the ruins lay the burned body of Teedyuscung. The war on the Ohio would provide the Susquehanna Delawares with a final chance for revenge. In October, led by Captain Bull, Teedyuscung's son, they descended on the Susquehannah Company settlers and destroyed all their settlements before retreating to the Ohio. Other Delaware raiding parties, possibly from the Ohio, descended upon Northampton and Berks Counties. Once more the raids in this region were particularly brutal. One report maintained that many of the victims were horribly mutilated. A woman's body was found "roasted and had two Hinges in her Hands, supposed to be put in red hot; and several of the Men had Awls through their Eyes, and Spears, Arrows, Pitchforks, &c. sticking in their Bodies." While some of these stories could be the creation of overactive colonial minds, there is every reason to believe that the raiders who descended upon this region had particular motives to seek vengeance, especially the Susquehanna Delawares.[41]

The Breakup of Pontiac's Confederacy

The extension of the war to northern Pennsylvania reflected the difficulty that the colonies faced in containing the war. Indeed, even maintaining their current posts remained a difficult task. In particular, Detroit remained isolated. Despite the arrival of Dalyell's relief expedition, communication with the fort was at best uncertain. On September 3 another supply vessel arrived off Detroit, with a crew of only eleven men. Because of contrary winds it was forced to moor at the mouth of the Detroit River. Under the cover of night Pontiac's men attacked in canoes. In a fierce struggle the schooner's crew repulsed the attackers, but not without losing their captain. A fortuitous change in the wind allowed the vessel to reach Detroit, but it had been a close call. Worse news was to come. The cargo of the supply vessel the *Huron* had been improperly loaded in Niagara. It had not sailed far when it encountered rough weather and was wrecked. The loss of the *Huron* was a serious setback to British attempts to maintain the supply lines to Detroit. Already desperately short of vessels on the Great Lakes, now their supply capability was even more limited.[42] In October Gladwin wrote to Amherst in desperation: "The Enemy are Masters of the Country, the Season far Advanced, not a Stick of fire Wood in the Garrison, and but little provisions owing to the loss of the Sloop." The supply lines soon became even more tenuous when a party of Senecas attacked a wagon train on the Niagara portage, killing sixty-four men. If the Senecas had joined the rebellion, the resulting disruption of the Niagara portage would threaten communication with the Great Lakes.[43]

By the beginning of October Detroit had been under close siege for five months. Gladwin was desperately short of goods and had all but exhausted his supply of flour. The Indian besiegers, however, were also short of supplies. The siege had prevented them from hunting, and they were growing increasingly restless. They had hoped for assistance from the French, but the local French habitants were reluctant to provide supplies. Many of the Great Lakes Indians in particular desired to leave to hunt. Without French assistance, they wondered, what possibility was there of seizing the fort? There had also been substantial dissension between the different peoples about the treatment of captives. Instead of prisoners being distributed among Indian families to replace their losses in war, as was traditional, Pontiac had demanded that all prisoners be kept centrally, near Detroit, to be used specifically as hostages in his negotiations with the British. The adoption of prisoners was even more pressing as so many men, including many war captains, had been killed during the siege or had died from the epidemics now sweeping the Great Lakes.[44]

Pontiac's "confederacy" had always been a shaky creation. Indeed, in many ways it was more a creation of later historians such as Francis Parkman than of Pontiac himself.[45] Throughout the siege headmen from different villages across the Great Lakes had traveled to Detroit to assure Gladwin that they were not in arms against the British. However, in September the number of these visits increased, and on October 12 some of the Indian headmen encamped around Detroit sent messengers to Gladwin asking for a parley. Gladwin agreed, for, as he admitted to Amherst, he "was so circumstanced for want of flour that I must either abandon my post, or hear them. Of the two I chose the latter thinking it of the utmost consequence to keep possession of the country." Much to Gladwin's surprise the headmen asked for peace. Gladwin readily accepted. Although he would make no guarantees as to the future treatment the Detroit Indians would receive, he did assure them that once Amherst "was thoroughly convinced of their sincerity everything would be well again." During the latter half of October a stream of headmen, representing villages from across the Great Lakes, approached Gladwin seeking an end to the hostilities.[46]

Pontiac's sole hope now lay in receiving support from the French posts still on the Mississippi. However, when the French commandant at Fort Chartres, Maj. Pierre Joseph Neyon de Villiers, received word of the Treaty of Paris he hurriedly sent belts to his former allies, urging them to end the war. De Villiers bluntly informed Pontiac that he must "leave off . . . the spilling of the Blood of your Brethren the English. Our Hearts are now but one. You cannot strike at present the one without having the Other for an Enemy, so if you continue Hostilities you will have no Supplies, and it is from them you are to expect them."[47]

Pontiac's hopes of gaining victory had disappeared. On October 30 he dictated a letter to Gladwin, telling him bluntly: "The word which my Father sent me to make peace, I have accepted; all my young men have buried their hatchets: I think that you will forget all the evil things which have occurred for some time past. Likewise, I shall forget what you may have done to me, in order to think nothing but good."[48] By the beginning of November the siege of Detroit was over. Ironically, French intervention had effectively ended it.

Despite the lifting of the siege, the war was far from over. In five months of conflict the entire frontier had been set aflame, over six hundred people had been killed, and all the western posts except Fort Pitt and Detroit had been destroyed.[49] The only British "victory" had been Bouquet's relief of Fort Pitt. Around Detroit British forces had suffered two major defeats, and relief had only come from French diplomatic intervention. Amherst, in particular, was aware that the British had not won any decisive victory and was determined to bring the Ohio Indian peoples to their knees. He maintained that he would only consider concluding a peace "when the Savages, who have been Concerned in the present Disturbances, are Sufficiently Punished for the Depredations & Barbarities, they have Committed."[50] To many British officials it was all too apparent that he would have to wait a long time. George Croghan in particular was bitterly upset at Amherst's continuing arrogance toward the Indians. At the end of September he resigned his commission and denounced Amherst and many of his fellow officers, claiming that they "seem Nott to feel for ye Distress of thire fellow Creturs & Talk of Nothing Butt ye Country of ye Indians being Now Conquerd & Every B——T of p——e haveing a grant for a Large Tract of Land."[51]

Some matters were dealt with quickly. In November Amherst was recalled to England. He was replaced by Gen. Thomas Gage, who possessed a greater understanding of the predicament of the Indian peoples and of frontier warfare. Despite Amherst's departure, by the end of 1763 there was no sign of a conclusion to the war. While Pontiac may have raised the siege of Detroit, the Ohio Delawares and Shawnees remained hostile to the British, and convoys to Fort Pitt were still regularly ambushed. With insufficient troops to launch offensive operations on the Ohio, Bouquet's first task at Fort Pitt was simply to evacuate the several hundred civilians who were trapped there. Their plight had been made worse by a smallpox epidemic. Indeed, the only civilian deaths at the fort were caused not by Indian actions but by smallpox and dysentery.[52] Throughout the autumn Indian raiding parties continued to attack the Pennsylvania frontier. On October 8 a raiding party led by Captain Bull attacked a militia party returning to Fort Allen, killing the captain. James Burd reported that when he visited Northampton County he found "men,

Women, & Children, flying before the Enemy whom they said was . . .
killing all before them and burning the Houses."[53] Despite Bouquet's victory, the frontier remained in flames, and the plight of the backcountry settlers was as dire as it had been in 1756.

The Growth of Indian Hating

In Pennsylvania a new assembly met in mid-October. Hopes were high that it might approve new defense measures, but it was little different from its predecessor and no more prone to abandon its principals and approve a supply bill acceptable to the governor. Prospects for a compromise receded even further at the end of October, when Hamilton was recalled to England and replaced by John Penn, the nephew of the proprietors. Penn had been sent to Pennsylvania specifically to ensure that the proprietors' rights were not trampled upon any further. Any compromise with the assembly seemed more remote than ever.[54] The refusal of the governor and assembly to provide protection for the frontier angered many settlers there. They felt both abandoned by central government and betrayed by their Indian neighbors. For most people in the backcountry peace had been concluded on just terms with the Ohio Indians after the war. For several years the colonies had sought to develop trade, to provide them with gifts and homes. Now they had turned and bitten the hand that fed them.

Central to this disillusionment with government was the failure of both Virginia and Pennsylvania to raise adequate forces to protect the backcountry during Pontiac's War. In Pennsylvania, although the assembly agreed to raise one thousand men, Governor Penn and the assembly failed to find a compromise over the issue of the assessment and taxation of proprietary lands, just as during the late 1750s. Increasingly, members of the assembly used the governor's intransigence as evidence to support their claims that the Crown should intervene to protect the province and "royalize" its government.[55] With no secure funding to guarantee pay, it was not surprising that officers found recruiting difficult, and the frontiers remained relatively unprotected throughout the winter. The Virginia House of Burgesses was equally reluctant to provide men. The burgesses noted that in previous years they had been forced to pay large bounties in order to recruit the required number of troops. The bounties were funded by the emission of paper money that was to be paid off at a later date, avoiding the need to raise the funds immediately. Now that merchants in London were clamoring against paper money, the burgesses were reluctant to make any new emissions and were not prepared to raise new duties or taxes. Also, London was no longer prepared to recompense the colonies for expenses. Lacking funding, Governor Fauquier could not authorize a bounty for recruits. Without one it proved impossible to recruit many men, and the assembly simply urged Fauquier to rely on the militia, as he had done the previous year.[56]

Not only were the provincial governments failing to provide adequate protection for the backcountry, but the ministry in Whitehall seemed to be making concessions to the Ohio Indians. At the same time that raiders were devastating the backcountry of Virginia and Pennsylvania, news reached America of the Royal Proclamation of October 1763. This famous proclamation made the Appalachian Mountains the formal boundary between Anglo-American settlements and Indian lands. While neither Gage nor Johnson felt that the proclamation would end the current conflict, both felt that it addressed several central issues. Indeed, Gage described it as "a salutary measure" that "if fallen upon some years ago would have prevented the [current] Grievances."[57]

In Virginia the royal instructions limiting the expansion of settlement caused great concern. Fauquier wrote to the Board of Trade several times asking for clarification of the Royal Proclamation. In particular, it had caused unrest in areas that had been settled before 1755 but abandoned during the war. Fauquier was particularly concerned as to whether he should use force to drive off settlers in these areas, for he was aware that such an action would be deeply unpopular throughout Virginia. Indeed, it was not just backcountry settlers who were concerned at the Royal Proclamation. Many powerful Virginians had interests in the Ohio Company. If western settlement was to be halted to protect the Ohio Indians' interests, their investments would become worthless.[58]

Not only was the government in Whitehall apparently protecting the interests of the Ohio Indians, but to many backcountry settlers it also seemed that the government of Pennsylvania was doing its utmost to protect and support those responsible for the war. Angered by what they saw as a betrayal, backcountry settlers turned their vitriol toward the Quakers in particular. After several years of anti-Quaker rhetoric from the proprietors and their supporters, many backcountry settlers accused the Quakers of openly supporting the Indians. In particular, they attacked the role of the Friendly Association in subsidizing supplies for the Ohio and Susquehanna Indians, claiming that "under the Pretence of buying Peace" the association had supported their enemies and enabled them to recommence their war. They wondered, "Is it our hard Fate to be at War with a Tribe, while a Part of it is supported at the public Expence & furnishing their Brethren with constant Intelligence about the state of affairs amongst us?"[59]

Backcountry settlers looked with special disgust at the scattered groups of Anglophile Indians now being protected by Pennsylvania from the wrath of the Ohio Indians, particularly the Moravian Delawares, who lived at Nazareth and at Wyalusing, upstream from Wyoming. These Indian refugees were being not only protected but also clothed and fed at provincial expense, while frontier settlers driven from their homes had to fend for themselves. Soon incensed settlers decided to take matters into their own hands. In the middle of October a party of "Irish Volunteers" arrived in Nazareth seeking revenge for the raids. It was only with the greatest difficulty that the "volunteers" were persuaded that these pacifist Delawares, who had determined not to defend themselves if attacked, could not have committed any of the frontier hostilities.[60] In the wake of the visit the Moravian Delawares decided their only hope of survival was to seek protection from the government. Joined by their brethren from Wyalusing, they traveled to Philadelphia. There they received a hostile reception. The governor had intended that the refugees should be lodged in the city's barracks, but unfortunately no one had informed the British army of this fact. When the refugees arrived at the barracks' gates, the guards refused to admit them. While leading Quaker Joseph Fox hurriedly conferred with the governor, a mob assembled, demanding the execution of all the Delawares. Only with some difficulty were the refugees extracted to be lodged in the relative safety of the former smallpox hospital on Province Island, just outside the city.[61]

Hearing that the assembly was prepared to find the Wyalusing Delawares secure accommodation while backcountry families remained homeless in the bitter cold of winter, settlers were outraged. They argued that throughout this crisis the assembly had done little to defend the backcountry. While it had raised seven hundred men for defense, the settlers claimed that the restrictions placed on their service meant that "had the Design been to have sent so many men to have only looked on the Ravages that were committed amongst the back settlers without giving them the least assistance, it could not have been more effectually executed."[62] On December 14 their anger finally boiled over into violence. Unable to attack the Moravian Delawares, they turned their attention to the nearest available Indians, at Conestoga. A party of fifty-seven "volunteers," popularly called the Paxton Boys, rode from Paxton, in Lancaster County, to nearby Conestoga, where they butchered six Conestogas.[63]

The attack caused consternation throughout Pennsylvania. Penn called the assembly back into session on December 20 but was pessimistic about finding a compromise. The assembly had only been in session a week when more news arrived from Lancaster County. Not satisfied with killing the six Conestogas, the Paxton Boys had returned and killed all the survivors of the raid, who had taken shelter in the county jail. This action finally spurred the assembly into limited action, and they belatedly approved a bill for raising one thousand men.[64]

The assembly's actions did little more than temporarily dampen unrest in the backcountry. In an attempt to diffuse the crisis Penn determined to send the remaining Wyalusing refugees to New York, where they could be placed under the protection of Sir William Johnson. The refugees had only reached Trenton when they received news that the New York provincial authorities were not prepared to receive them and that they must return at once to Philadelphia. Their return to Philadelphia precipitated an even worse crisis. The Paxton Boys assembled a mob of seven hundred and began to march on the city. The city was thrown into chaos. Several of the leading Quaker families fled in terror to New Jersey, while the assembly hastily passed a riot act. In desperation Benjamin Franklin and Benjamin Chew organized five hundred volunteers into a local militia to defend the Delawares from the frontiersmen. For five days the city was in complete turmoil. Only an agreement negotiated by Franklin, allowing the mob's leaders, Matthew Smith and James Gibson, to present their grievances to the governor, prevented further bloodshed.[65]

The activities of these extralegal mobs demonstrate the extent to which settlers' hatred of their Indian neighbors had been increased by Pontiac's uprising. Their anger was fueled by the misconception that the colonies had "won" the struggle of the 1750s. The Ohio Indians had been given a just peace, but now were demonstrating their true colors. However, instead of seeking to crush them the government in London was making concessions, while in both Virginia and Pennsylvania the governments seemed unwilling to protect the backcountry from the renewed attacks. By the summer of 1764 antipathy to central authority had reached a peak on the frontier. Backcountry settlers had developed an inveterate hatred of all Indians that could not easily be assuaged. Unless matters changed quickly, affairs in the backcountry and the Ohio Valley would prove difficult to resolve.

The Dilemma of Securing Peace

The man who had the greatest responsibility for settling affairs in the Ohio Valley was Col. Henry Bouquet, who commanded the British forces in the Pennsylvania backcountry. Bouquet hoped to launch a major offensive into the Ohio Valley in the summer; however, the failure of both Virginia and Pennsylvania to provide men threatened to end his plans. At the end of February 1764 Gage wrote to Fauquier, bluntly telling told him that "as your Assembly decline giving their Assistance, and there is Reason to apprehend, the Assembly of Pennsylvania; tho' they have granted the Number of Men demanded, will offer such Supply Bills as the Governor can't Pass . . . We shall be again be reduced to a defensive War." He continued that such a war was "never advantageous, And must ever be particularly destructive, against such an Enemy, as we are now engaged with."[66] Without sufficient troops from Virginia and Pennsylvania there would be no easy military solution to the war.

Bouquet spent much of the winter of 1763–64 trying to requisition supplies for the summer's campaign and supervising the repair of Forts Pitt and Bedford. While he pondered the possibility of an offensive against the Ohio Indians in the summer of 1764, the Ohio Indians planned their own summer offensive against the colonies. Gershom Hicks, a "white Indian" captured spying for the Delawares outside Fort Pitt, reported that the Shawnees and Delawares were expecting reinforcements from the Wyandots and Ottawas. Hicks claimed that the Ohio Indians hoped to have eight hundred warriors in the field by the end of May and to attack Fort Pitt. If they discovered they could not take the post they planned to attack Forts Ligonier and Bedford, "which they knew they could easily destroy."[67] Without substantial colonial support it appeared that there was little Bouquet could do but maintain his hold on Fort Pitt.

Johnson suggested a partial solution. With the departure of Amherst, whose contempt for the Indians prevented any admission that their service might be useful to the British army, Johnson was finally encouraged to utilize the assistance of any Anglophile Indians, in particular the Iroquois. At the end of December the Iroquois had approached him seeking a rapprochement between the British and the Chenussio Senecas, who had been at the forefront of attacks on the British around Niagara and had encouraged their Ohio brethren to take up arms. As a means of proving their attachment to the British, and encouraged by Johnson's promise of an abandonment of Amherst's parsimony and a return to the old tradition of gift exchanges, many Iroquois warriors agreed to launch raids against the Shawnee and Delaware villages on the Ohio and to join in a larger expedition in the west. Launching raids against the Ohio Indians was not only a way for the Iroquois to prove their fealty to the British but also an opportunity to reassert their authority over their former "subjects."[68]

Johnson placed much faith, perhaps too much faith, in the ability of the Iroquois to halt the war. In April he promised the Pennsylvanians that raids would "free your Province from the Incursions of the Delawares, &c."[69] In reality the raids achieved little. There is no evidence that life on the Ohio was disrupted, while the Ohio Indian raids on Virginia and Pennsylvania continued unabated. Indeed, one report from Sandusky claimed that when some Onondaga raiders arrived at their village, the local headman told them to take "two old scalps that he had newly painted" and to "go home & tell Sir William you have Scalp'd some Shawanies. Upon which they return'd." By the summer of 1764 the Ohio Indians had little reason to change their perception of British military capability: the British were still Shingas's "Old Women." In June the Ohio Indians told a messenger from Sir William Johnson that "the English allways told them they had as many men as there was leaves on the Trees, but wee look upon Indians as good as a thousand of them."[70]

The number of raids declined throughout the winter, not because of Iroquois involvement but because winter snows made passage over the Appalachians difficult and also because many Ohio Indians wished to hunt. Most of the raids that took place over the winter were small and isolated. In western Pennsylvania raids continued to concentrate on disrupting the supply lines to Fort Pitt. On the Virginia frontier and between the Susquehanna and Delaware Rivers raiders struck civilian targets. As spring arrived the frequency of the raids increased. At the end of March 1764 a large party attacked Cumberland County near Carlisle and pressed on southward into Maryland and then into northern Virginia. Another large raiding party descended upon Augusta County and penetrated deep into the backcountry, leaving a trail of destruction. These parties were composed principally of Ohio Delawares and Shawnees from the villages of Salt Licks, Hockhocking, Wakatomica, and Scioto, exactly the locations that Johnson's Iroquois allies were supposed to be raiding.[71]

Johnson's parties did have some important victories, but not on the Ohio. On February 26 a party commanded by métis Henry Montour surprised a party of Delawares on the north branch of the Susquehanna. The whole party, including Captain Bull, son of Teedyuscung and leader of much of the opposition to the British on the Allegheny River, was captured and taken back in chains to New York. The capture of this party would provide useful hostages for the coming negotiations. Two other parties, chiefly of Oneidas, threatened the Chenussio Senecas. The threat succeeded in bringing the Senecas to terms. Within a month over three hundred Senecas were preparing to come to Fort Johnson to make peace.[72]

On the Ohio it was not military pressure from the British that was influencing the growth of a peace party, but diplomatic pressure from the French. Despite repeated reports from British traders on the Ohio and some of the Indian peoples themselves that the French had actively encouraged the Indians to rise against the British, during the spring of 1764 French officials sought to end hostilities as quickly as possible. French commanders seem to have been aware that prolonged hostilities might encourage the British to follow a much more repressive policy toward any French citizens living in British North America and to have sensed that the French Empire was not likely to reassert its presence in the near future. As the Illinois Country contained a substantial number of French habitants, it seemed to be in their best interest for the remaining French garrisons to end the conflict as quickly as possible.[73]

Despite previous messages urging him to make peace, Pontiac was still hopeful that he could encourage the French to intervene. In the early spring of 1764 he had traveled to Fort Chartres to seek assurances of assistance from the French. The fort's commander, de Villiers, had already grown exasperated with Pontiac's stubbornness and his refusal to make peace. When Pontiac repeatedly pressed him to accept a war belt he kicked it away, asking him "if he had not heard what he had said to him." He told the assembled Illinois headmen, watching in some astonishment, that "they saw him that day in the Fort, but perhaps they would see their Brothers the English the next day, and exhorted them to live in Amity with them."[74] As news traveled throughout the west of Pontiac's reception, it underlined the necessity for the Ohio Indians to come to terms. Opposition to the British quickly decreased around Detroit. Now the centers of hostility were focused in the Shawnee and Delaware towns on the Scioto and Muskingum Rivers.

Despite the growing pressure for peace, as summer approached the raids continued unabated. At the end of May one large raiding party attacked south through Berks County, and another attacked the Juniata, while yet another harassed communications between Fort Pitt and Fort Bedford. These parties then divided up into small groups spreading across the countryside to create as much devastation as possible, setting fire to abandoned farmhouses and outbuildings. The heaviest raids, however, fell on Virginia. In just three weeks at the end of May over one hundred people were killed or captured, mainly in Augusta County. The climax of these raids came on May 26, when raiders attacked workers in the fields outside Fort Dinwiddie, killing fifteen and capturing sixteen, and then proceeded to besiege the fort itself for six hours.[75]

While Gage was no Amherst, he still believed that there should be a summer offensive to ensure that the Ohio Indians would halt their raids and be unable to renew them. At the beginning of April he sent Bouquet orders to ready his forces for an expedition to the Ohio Country, while at Niagara Col. John Bradstreet was to prepare his forces to launch an expedition across Lake Erie. Both Bradstreet and Bouquet were handicapped by a lack of men. The Virginia Assembly refused to heed requests from Amherst and Gage to raise the Virginia Regiment and would not allow the militia to march outside the colony's boundaries. Even more frustrating for Bouquet, when several hundred Virginians volunteered to serve with him on the Ohio, the burgesses refused to pay their wages. In Pennsylvania there was better news. When the assembly reconvened at the beginning of May tensions continued to run high. A petition circulated through Philadelphia demanding the royalization of the colony, while settlers continued to clamor for increased protection and greater political representation for the frontier counties in the assembly. At the end of May the stalemate was finally broken when the assembly abandoned most of its claims and agreed to a supply bill that would provide for a regiment of one thousand men to serve with Bouquet.[76]

Even with one thousand recruits Bouquet was still disappointed. Before the Pennsylvania troops reached Fort Pitt their ranks had already been thinned by desertion. Nearly one-quarter of the men deserted in the first six weeks of their commissions. Bouquet hoped that the Virginia volunteers might be able to replace the deserters from the Pennsylvania ranks, but initially neither Virginia nor Pennsylvania would approve of such a step. The Virginia burgesses remained stubborn about raising men for the expedition without being able to emit paper money, while the Pennsylvania Assembly did not see why it should pay the wages of forces from another colony. Bouquet felt that he needed at least one thousand men to mount a successful expedition to attack the Delawares and Shawnees in their villages on the Muskingum and Scioto Rivers. With continuing raids on the frontier he had to leave substantial garrisons in the frontier forts, and it seemed impossible that he would be able to march such a force to the Ohio.[77]

Initially Bouquet had hoped that the expedition would depart in the late spring, when he could move his men and supplies by river. When it was clear that the expedition would be delayed into the summer, when river levels had dropped, Bouquet began to worry. If the expedition marched overland to the Shawnee and Delaware villages on the Muskingum and Scioto Rivers and was defeated, retreat might be difficult. Instead Bouquet suggested that he should merely launch a series of small raids on the Indians' towns to keep their warriors at home. Gage agreed with Bouquet that marching the entire army to the Muskingum would be dangerous. However, he felt that the alternative of launching a series of smaller raids from Fort Pitt would achieve little. Instead he proposed a compromise: march the army into the Ohio Country, some way toward the Indians' villages, but remain close enough to Fort Pitt to retreat if needed. From camp "Parties will be able to harass them to much greater Advantage . . . and your Approach will probably oblige them to leave some of their Habitations entirely exposed. And seeing you in motion towards their Country will naturaly make them fear for all their Settlements and incline them to Sue for Peace."[78]

While Bouquet was threatening the Shawnees and Delawares from Fort Pitt, Maj. John Bradstreet was to launch a simultaneous expedition from Fort Niagara. Accompanied by a substantial force of Iroquois warriors, he was to advance his army along Lake Erie to threaten the Shawnees and Delawares from the north. In particular it was hoped that if Bradstreet could destroy the settlement at Sandusky, on the southern shore of Lake Erie, the Shawnees and Delawares might be more inclined to come to terms with Bouquet in the south. Gage had high expectations for the expedition. He wrote to Johnson that "Bradstreet will doubtless make an Attempt upon the *Scioto* and the *Muskingham,* and give the Indians a fair opportunity to shew their Sincerity. Our Affairs should absolutely be finished this Campaign, which a good blow upon the Delawares &ca and particularly on the Tribes of that villain Pondiac would certainly bring about."[79] However, while Bouquet attempted to amass his force at Fort Pitt, Bradstreet was also delayed at Fort Niagara. He had intended to depart on April 10. At first he was frustrated by the slow march of some of the New England troops who were to join in the expedition. Then he had to wait for the Iroquois warriors that Johnson had persuaded to accompany him. It was not until the beginning of August that Bradstreet's expedition finally left Fort Niagara.[80]

The central purpose of Bradstreet's expedition was to threaten the Shawnees and Delawares from the north in order to strengthen Bouquet's position. However, Bradstreet proceeded timorously. A few days after setting out his force arrived at Presque Isle. Here, instead of making a display of force, he concluded a "peace" with several representatives of the Shawnees, Delawares, and Wyandots who had been sent to keep watch on his progress. The Indians assured Bradstreet that his expedition was unnecessary; they claimed they had already recalled all their warriors from the frontier and that the raids were at an end. They agreed to return in a few weeks to hand over all prisoners and promised to "relinquish their claims to the Forts and Posts the English now have in their Country" (as the British only held Fort Pitt and Detroit, this was hardly a major concession) and to allow the British "to build and erect as many Forts or Trading Houses as they may find necessary for carrying on Trade."[81] Bradstreet trumpeted his achievement. Other British commanders were less pleased. Bouquet was appalled. He wrote to Gage that "the Terms he gives them are such as fill me with Astonishment. After the massacres of our Officers and Garrisons, and of our Traders & Inhabitants, in Time of profound Peace: After the Immense Expence of the Crown, and some of the Provinces to punish those infamous Murders, not the least Satisfaction is obtained."[82] Nor had Bradstreet provided the slightest show of force to assist Bouquet.

This skepticism seems to have been justified. Unfortunately for Bradstreet, the main intention of the headmen who met with his force at Presque Isle seems to have been not to conclude a peace but merely to delay his expedition. Despite their promises that the raiding parties had already been withdrawn, the frontier raids continued unabated. At the end of July a large raiding party descended on Cumberland County. On July 26 the raiders attacked Enoch Brown's Schoolhouse in the Conococheague Valley, killing Brown and nine schoolboys and capturing another four pupils. Suspicion fell on the very Indians who had negotiated with Bradstreet when, at the beginning of September, the body of one of the schoolboys was found on the road between Presque Isle and Fort Pitt. Two weeks later there were two more raids. One again struck Cumberland County and moved on into York County. Another descended on Hampshire County and pushed through to Frederick County. Throughout July and August smaller raiding parties continued to harass communications westward to Fort Pitt.[83]

Unaware of the failure of his diplomacy, and of the furor that was brewing behind him, Bradstreet pushed on from Presque Isle toward Detroit. His intention was now to threaten the allies of Pontiac and force the residents of the Illinois Country to conclude a peace. He halted at the mouth of the Maumee River. There, instead of advancing his army toward the Illinois Country, he engaged in a fierce dispute with the Iroquois warriors who accompanied him. They urged Bradstreet to march up the Maumee River and attack the villages that formed the heart of Pontiac's support. Bradstreet refused. Instead he urged the Iroquois to launch raids against the villages while he remained with the army at Sandusky. The Iroquois were amazed. Why, they asked, should they risk their lives while the British remained in safety at Sandusky? With the Iroquois refusing to launch their own raids, Bradstreet determined to send Capt. Thomas Morris, accompanied by a small Iroquois escort, to the villages in the Illinois Country to encourage the Indians to travel to Detroit to negotiate peace, without exposing the army to any danger. He hoped that the presence of his army might intimidate Pontiac's confederates. He was very wrong.[84]

Morris did not get very far. Eighteen miles up the Maumee River the party was halted at Pontiac's village. There Miami warriors threatened to kill Morris, and it was only with great difficulty that his Iroquois escorts were able to save his life. After a face-to-face meeting between Pontiac and Morris's escorts, during which the Iroquois convinced Pontiac that their nation had no intention of supporting the war, Pontiac reluctantly allowed Morris to continue his journey to Fort Miami. At Miami he received an even more hostile reception and was forced into hiding for several days while the warriors debated his fate, eventually determining that he must return to Detroit. Morris had achieved nothing. Meanwhile Bradstreet had advanced his force to Detroit. There he intended to finalize the details of peace with Pontiac. However, instead of receiving peace envoys from Pontiac he received news that the Shawnees and Delawares, with whom he had negotiated at Presque Isle, still remained at war and now had promised that they would never make a peace with the British. Bradstreet had been duped.[85]

Bouquet's Expedition

The hopes of achieving peace in 1764 now rested with Bouquet, who arrived at Fort Pitt on September 18. The previous day several Delaware headmen, including The Pipe and Tamaqua, had come at the fort to discover Bouquet's intentions. Bouquet reminded the Delaware headmen that they had told Bradstreet that they desired peace; however, the behavior of Delaware war parties suggested otherwise. Bouquet issued them a warning: "As I must now consider You as a People whose Promises I can no more trust, I was determined to attack you, as soon as the rest of the Army joins me, which I expect immediately; But I will put it once more in your Power to prevent your total Destruction and save yourselves and your Familys, by giving us Satisfactions for the Hostilitys committed against us."[86]

Bouquet had with him twelve hundred men: four hundred regulars, four hundred Pennsylvanians, two hundred light horse, and a similar number of Virginia volunteers; he had also left sizeable garrisons on the frontier and at Fort Pitt. It remained to be seen whether such a force could finally bring the Shawnees and Delawares to terms before the onset of winter. On October 2, when the dense summer undergrowth of the woods was dying back and it was easier for his men to march through the Ohio forests, Bouquet set out for the Delaware villages on the Muskingum. The Delawares sensed that he was in earnest. Unlike Bradstreet, he would, they realized, press home his threat, and he had the military experience to inflict serious losses on them. Almost immediately the Delawares sent a delegation of Ohio Iroquois to Bouquet begging him to halt and to

allow them to gather all their prisoners to deliver them up. Bouquet refused. He informed the delegation that he had had enough of their false
promises, adding: "We know them & will Chastise them[.] [T]hey say
they are sorry for what they have done, and will make Peace; that is not
enough, nor any satisfaction to us. The General has sent me here with
an Army to take revenge of the Murders comitted by the Delawares &
Shawanese, & not to make Peace."[87] However, if the Delawares were truly
for peace, he promised, he would discuss preliminary terms with them
when he arrived at Tuscaroras.

The Delawares had every reason to seek peace. It was apparent that the
anticipated French support would not materialize, leaving the Delawares
desperately short of ammunition. On occasion Indian warriors had already been forced to resort to the use of bows and arrows in their attacks
on the frontier. Against an army such weapons would be of little use.
Since the start of the war smallpox had been ravaging the Ohio peoples.
The smallpox epidemics had not only weakened the physical capacity of
the Ohio peoples to resist the British but had also undermined their
morale. In addition, news had reached the Ohio of Johnson's meeting
with some of the western headmen at Niagara at the end of July. While
Johnson had failed to negotiate a definitive peace, since many western
headmen such as Pontiac refused to attend, he had made clear to those
who did attend what the prospect of peace might offer. In private negotiations, "at which more was done than at the publick ones," Johnson
convinced them that with peace the relationship between the British and
the Indians would return to the old patterns, including a return to the
prewar economic and diplomatic protocols and the abandonment of some
of the smaller posts.[88] These promises were especially attractive to the
Ohio Shawnees and Delawares. With such terms they could in many ways
justly feel that they were the "victors" of the war.

With the pressure for peace mounting, Bouquet arrived at Tuscaroras
on October 13. Two days later the Delawares began to arrive and "behaved
with the utmost Submission."[89] They sought forgiveness from Bouquet
and blamed the western nations for the war. Bouquet would hear none
of this. He informed the Delawares simply that "it is your fault." He reminded them that they were supposed to deliver their prisoners to Bradstreet at Sandusky but had not. Now they claimed once more that they
wanted peace, but they were still hesitating to hand over their prisoners

to Bouquet. They had assured Bradstreet that they had recalled all their warriors, but the frontier raids had continued. Bouquet even had intelligence that the Delawares had gathered together to see if they had enough men to attack his army. He informed them: "You must be sensible that you deserve the severest Chastisement. . . . It is . . . in our Power to destroy you."[90]

While the Delawares may have doubted the veracity of Bouquet's last statement, there was little doubt in their minds that any continuation of the war would bring them few benefits. Indeed, many of the prisoners now released by the Delawares claimed that most of them "have constantly been against the War, and have taken no Share in it; and that most of the Traders were killed by the Wyandots, Ottawas, and other Western Indians who compelled these Nations to join with them." The Delawares quickly agreed to return all prisoners to Bouquet and provided him with hostages as guarantee for their actions.[91]

While the Delawares may have been prepared to come to terms, the Shawnees still remained aloof. Bouquet now ordered his army to march from Tuscaroras to the Muskingum River. There he intended to receive prisoners from the Delawares and to treat with the Shawnees. In case the Shawnees should continue to prove reticent about negotiations, he ordered a party to be prepared to march to the Shawnee villages on the Scioto to destroy them. Bouquet's army marched from Tuscaroras on October 21 and arrived on the Muskingum on October 25. There Bouquet held a series of conferences, first with the Delawares and Ohio Senecas but then also with the Shawnees. At first the Shawnees treated Bouquet with some insolence. However, while meeting with Bouquet they received yet another message from the French urging them to make peace, and they reluctantly agreed to terms.[92]

The reluctance of the Shawnees, however, soon became apparent. On November 12 several Shawnee headmen met with Bouquet. They handed over a small number of prisoners but claimed they would not be able to return the rest until the following spring. Bouquet was furious. He raged at them: "You have at last thought proper to come with a small part of the Prisoners & You propose to deliver up the rest Next Spring. I have for a long time been a Wittness to the arrogant behaviour of Your Nation but I did not expect that You would dare to provoke us again by this new breach of Faith." He continued, "You have now Convinced me that you are still the same inconsiderate & light headed People as formerly & that it is impossible to Treat with You as a Nation as there is neither Faith nor Trust in You." He was convinced that they had "been equally perfidious at all Times. I must therefore take such Measures as will Compell You to perform your Promises and put it out of Your Power to deceive us again with Impunity."[93] Bouquet prepared detachments of his army to march to the Shawnee villages on the Scioto. The Shawnees were horrified. Threatened by Bouquet's army and abandoned by their traditional allies the Delawares, they knew they had to make concessions. Over two days of almost continual negotiations they gradually gave ground and agreed to hand over hostages as guarantee of their good behavior and to return to their towns to bring in the prisoners immediately. Convinced at last of the Shawnees' sincerity, the army returned to Fort Pitt on November 28, accompanied by six hostages and five peace envoys.[94]

Bouquet now gave the Shawnees and Delawares specific orders "to bring in all their Prisoners, even to Children born of white Women, and to tie those who were grown as Savage as themselves, and unwilling to leave them, and bring them bound to the Camp."[95] For many Indians and their captives such demands were especially difficult. Even Bouquet reported that "many of them have remained so many Years amongst them, that they part from them with the greatest Reluctance. We are obliged to keep Guards to prevent their Escape, and unless they are treated with Indulgence & Tenderness by their Relations, they will certainly return to their Savage Masters."[96] He reported to Sir William Johnson that he had "received upwards of 200 Captives including the Children Born from White Women married to Savages which I have obliged them to give up."[97] Many "captives" were so reluctant to return to the colonies that their adopted families were "obliged to tie them to bring them to us."[98] William Smith claimed that many of the children in particular "considered their new state in the light of a captivity." He continued: "It must not be denied that there were even some grown persons who shewed an unwillingness to return. The Shawnese were obliged to bind several of their prisoners and force them along to the camp; and some women who had been delivered up, afterwards found means to escape and run back to the Indian towns. Some, who could not make their escape, clung to their savage acquaintance at parting, and continued many days in bitter lamentations, even refusing sustenance."[99]

Victory for Whom?

Bouquet returned to Pittsburgh accompanied by nearly three hundred prisoners. He had finally negotiated peace on the upper Ohio. After his negotiations there were no more major raids on the backcountry. However, the peace in 1764 was essentially another truce. The proclamation of 1763 had recognized and protected Indian lands. The Board of Trade's "Plan for the Future Management of Indian Affairs," promulgated in July 1764, began the restoration of traditional gift exchanges and confined trade to licensed traders operating only from army posts. In addition, the cost of maintaining the western posts in a time of fiscal stringency meant that the army would soon abandon many of the smaller posts. While some of these points, particularly the abandonment of western posts, were never explicitly stated in open peace negotiations, they may well have been discussed in the many private sessions, and many Indians must have sensed the weakness of the British position. In essence the Ohio Indians had by the mid-1760s retained a redress of their grievances before Pontiac's War. They had emerged as victors in all but name.[100]

In the previous fifteen months of conflict, George Croghan estimated, the Indians had "killed or captivated not less than two thousand of His Majesty's subjects and drove some thousands to beggary and the greatest distress."[101] While Croghan's estimate may be rather high, it reflects the distress caused in the Virginia and Pennsylvania backcountry, which was no less than it had been during the Seven Years' War. In Pennsylvania much of Cumberland County was abandoned, as were parts of Berks and Northampton Counties. Raiders also hit Lancaster County, although with less severity than during the Seven Years' War. In Virginia, Augusta and Hampshire Counties suffered heavily and lost many inhabitants, a large number of whom had only recently returned to the region following the Seven Years' War and the Cherokee War. Frederick County also suffered, although probably less than during the Seven Years' War.

The British seemed to have learned few lessons from the Seven Years' War. Indeed, during Pontiac's War the colonies relied even more upon the protection of the British army than during the Seven Years' War. Continuing disputes between the colonial assemblies and governors hampered attempts at raising provincial troops. No effective strategy was developed for dealing with Indian raids, and, with the exception of the destruction of the abandoned settlement at Great Island and a few Iroquois-led raids on the upper Allegheny River, the British had destroyed no Indian towns. The difficulties of campaigning in the west were underlined by the failure of Bradstreet's expedition. Not only did Bradstreet fail to launch any attack upon the Ohio Indians, but his expedition returned in chaos. Johnson wrote to Gage that "the disperesed, distressed & confused State of the Army, exceeds that of most Armys who have been entirely routed, & had not the *Chenussios* been sincere in their engagements too me, I am certain that ten Men of the whole Army Scattered & distressed as they were, would never have reached Niagara."[102]

The weakness of the British position was reflected in the changing nature of the Crown's relationship with the Ohio Indians. Johnson appointed Croghan, who returned from London at the end of 1764, to finalize peace. At the beginning of May 1765 Croghan met with Shawnee, Delaware, and Seneca headmen at Fort Pitt. Croghan promised that trade would be reopened once a definitive peace had been concluded with Johnson. In addition, he agreed that the Crown itself would now assume from the colonial governors the role of protecting the Ohio Indians from the Anglo-American settlers pushing west over the Appalachians. This marked the beginning of a new relationship between the Crown and the Ohio Indians that in some ways resembled their old relationship with the French Crown. This was reflected in turn by the Ohio Indians' changing view of their metaphorical relationship with the Crown. After they had been informed of these promises, the Shawnees encamped around Fort Pitt and "came over the River with the English Prisoners, beating a Drum & singing their *Peace Song*." They entered the conference room, and one of their headmen addressed Croghan, informing him, "It gave us great satisfaction to be called the Children of the great King of England; it convinces us that your intentions towards us are upright, as we know a *Father* will be tender to his Children, and they more ready to obey him than a *Brother*."[103] The king of England was now their "father," not their "brother"; as such he had new duties and responsibilities to perform, most importantly to protect his "children" from any harm. For the next fifty years the relationship of the Crown to the Ohio Indians would parallel that of the French Onontio, while the colonies, and then the United States, would assume the role that the British had previously taken. Trade would be reestablished, gift exchanges would return, and the British army would attempt to protect the Ohio Indians from the ravages of frontier settlers.

Croghan had one more task to perform: concluding a peace with the Indians of the Illinois Country. Accompanied by an escort of Shawnee warriors, he set out for the west.[104] On June 8, 1765, he had neared the Wabash River when his party was ambushed by a party of eighty Kickapoos and Mascoutens. Three of the Shawnee deputies and two of Croghan's men were killed, and the rest of the party was captured. The attack on Croghan's party proved to be a blessing in disguise, for the western nations were deeply divided over the rationale for the attack. Many believed that it could only cause a war with the Shawnees, Delawares, and Iroquois. When, on July 11, two Frenchmen arrived with a message from the commanding officer at Fort Chartres instructing the Indians to release Croghan immediately and escort him to Illinois, the Indians complied. At Ouiatonon Croghan met with the western headmen and persuaded them to travel to Detroit. There he finalized peace with the western nations. In return for Croghan's promises that the British would "not look upon their taking possession of the posts the French formerly possessed, as giving them a title to their country," they agreed to terms.[105] The Indian peoples still at war with the British had finally agreed to terms, or, rather, the British had agreed to the Indians' terms.

PONTIAC'S WAR saw the backcountry of Virginia and Pennsylvania once more go up in flames. After little more than four years of peace, raiding parties again ravaged the frontier and Indian warriors once more demonstrated their military capabilities by driving the British from the Ohio Valley. Yet the Ohio Indians also demonstrated new abilities: to wage siege warfare and to counter the actions of European armies in "regular" battles. In 1763 the Ohio Indians lacked French support and guidance, yet the devastation of Pontiac's War was comparable with that of the Seven Years' War. British armies struggled for two years to bring the Ohio Valley back under their control, and without French intervention it would have taken them much longer to complete the task. British officers quickly sensed the military capability of the Ohio Indians and concluded that "experience has convinced us that it is not in our interest to be at war with them."[106]

Civilians, however, drew rather different conclusions. The devastation of Pontiac's War generated a deep animosity that could not easily be assuaged. Encouraged by the Penns' tales of their fabrication of Indian claims against Pennsylvania, and with clear evidence of their determination to protect and supply the Indians, many singled out the Friendly Association and the Quakers as enemies of the colony. The Shawnees and Delawares fared even worse. Many colonists viewed them as breaking agreements made after the end of the Seven Years' War. They failed to comprehend that it was the British who had not lived up to Indian expectations and that the Ohio Indians had never agreed to any peace terms. Now colonists turned their full vitriol against the Indians. The tide of Indian hating that emerged with the Paxton Boys would not easily be healed. In the postwar world Britain would struggle to protect the Ohio Indians and their lands from the rapacious and violent backcountry settlers. The struggle would fuel a wider conflict between Britain and her colonies that would ultimately deprive her of the much of the empire that she had struggled so hard to protect.

Conclusion

IT WAS AN EARLY MARCH MORNING IN 1765. THE CONVOY WOUND its way slowly toward Fort Loudoun over the notorious Sideling Hill. Suddenly, without warning, the attackers descended on the convoy whooping and hollering. In panic most of the wagoners fled for safety and were pursued to the very walls of Fort Loudoun. To celebrate their victory the attackers set fire to anything they could not drink or carry off. Yet these attackers were not Ohio Indians, but backcountry settlers. Frustrated at the continuing negotiations with the Ohio Indians, they had decided to take matters into their own hands to prevent supplies from reaching the Ohio.[1]

Two months later, as the sun again rose over the mountains, another mob descended on a small band of Indians and with shouts of delight butchered six of them. When news reached the local justices they set out to arrest the perpetrators of the murder. They managed to apprehend one of the ringleaders and confined him in the local jail. As if from nowhere, a mob of over one hundred men, led by a former captain in the provincial forces and terming themselves "the boys," descended on the tiny jail and broke it open to free the captives. The gang then threatened to march on the colonial capital unless the ringleaders were pardoned. Only the governor's advice to local justices to let the matter slip temporarily diffused the situation. This was not Lancaster County, Pennsylvania, and these were not the Paxton Boys; rather, these were the "Augusta Boys," in Virginia.[2]

Three thousand miles away a crowd assembled to stare and gawp at the confused Mohawks, Harmannus and Joseph, who had become celebrities in London taverns and coffeehouses. Kidnapped and now displayed to the public by a New York merchant, they drew a considerable crowd. News of the spectacle came to the ears of the House of Lords. Horrified, the House arrested the kidnapper and ordered the return of the Mohawks to New York, at public expense, ruling that "making a publick shew of Indians, Ignorant of such Proceedings is Unbecoming & Inhuman."[3]

The lessons learned from the preceding ten years of conflict were very different on either side of the Atlantic. In Whitehall officials sought to protect and heed the concerns of the new inhabitants of their empire. In the summer of 1765 officials drew up a new and grandiose plan for the management of Indian affairs. However, scarcely was the ink dry on their proposals than a new imperial crisis broke, as colonists protested the new taxes imposed upon them by a distant government. Instead of heeding Indian concerns, British policy during the late 1760s would be driven principally by a need to economize.[4]

If British officials believed that the Indian inhabitants of the Ohio Valley deserved to be protected, backcountry settlers had drawn rather different conclusions. The devastation wrought upon the backcountry during the war, the deaths of thousands of settlers between 1754 and 1764, the captivity of thousands more, and the flight of many thousands more created a deep animosity toward all Indians. This legacy of anger and violence would shape relations between settlers and Indians over the years following the Seven Years' War and Pontiac's War.[5] A further complication was the failure of many colonists to perceive the extent of the Indians' victories in the Seven Years' War. Many colonists rejoiced in the "successes" of British arms and viewed the Native American population of the Ohio Valley as crushed and defeated. Indeed, many seemed incapable of assessing the extent of Indian military prowess. At the end of September 1763 one correspondent in the *Pennsylvania Gazette* wrote with much bombast and equal amnesia that "since this War broke out, there has not been one Engagement in which the Indians got the better of our People, on any Part of the Frontier, that I can recollect."[6]

The Seven Years' War and Pontiac's War thus left conflicting legacies. The various Indian groups who had humiliated both British regulars and provincial troops, and who in the process had repeatedly devastated the backcountry, believed that they had demonstrated their ability to compel British imperial authorities to recreate the kind of empire of trade and alliance that France had previously supported; after all, the British were, in Shingas's words, no more than "Old Women."[7] The region's settlers, on the other hand, concluded on the basis of a decade of suffering and bloodshed that the only good Indian was a dead one. In 1767 Sir William Johnson reported that "Numbers of the Frontier Inhabitants of *Pensilvania, Maryland, Virginia,* &ca Animated with a Spirit of *Frenzy* under pretext of revenge for past Injuries tho' in Manifest Violation of *Brittish faith* and the Strength of the Late *Treatys* attacked, robbed, and Murdered Sundry Indians of Good Character, and Still continue to do so, Vowing Vengeance against all that come their Way."[8] With such behavior it is not surprising that imperial authorities reasoned that the only way to maintain order was to separate the two populations geographically. This policy, however, resulted in backcountry settlers asking what their victory in the Seven Years' War had meant and increased their suspicions of British treachery at the same time that the Indian raids seemingly illustrated the British Empire's inability to defend them. The empire's inability to enforce the separation that this policy had decreed—to enforce the Proclamation Line of 1763 and the later Treaty of Fort Stanwix, as Virginia settlers, and indeed Virginia's government, repeatedly invaded the Ohio Valley in the years following 1765—in turn led the Ohio Indians to suspect that their new Onontio was not a real protector and mediator. Despite British promises to restrain the land hunger of white settlers and to maintain lands over the Appalachians for the Indians, settlers continued to pour into the region, and land speculators continued to eye the west hungrily. Only slowly did the British assume the mantle of the French in protecting the interests of the Ohio Indians. As late as the War of 1812 British officials were still pressing to create a homeland for the Ohio Indians.[9]

The Ohio Indians were not the only people to conclude that the British army was composed of "Old Women." To most colonists the war on the frontier had been fought largely by provincial forces. Even Gen. John Forbes's expedition had consisted of many provincial forces. They had succeeded where British general Edward Braddock had failed so miserably.[10] For them, too, the British were little more than "old women." Provincial officers took great pride in their achievements. It was with great satisfaction that Capt. Robert Stewart would later write to George Washington, "I think without vanity we can assert that there never was and very probably never will be such another Provincial Regiment."[11] The experience of war had taught Virginia and Pennsylvania, once inexperienced, how to fight. By the end of the war both colonies were recruiting men into their regiments and maintaining armies in the field for years at a time. The assemblies had discovered that they could raise armies, pay for them, and supply them. All this was to prove central in the confidence that both colonies had in going to war in 1775. Had the two colonies not fought a bitter war from 1755 to 1765, they might have been much more ambivalent about supporting their New England cousins in their conflict with Great Britain.

Service in the Virginia and Pennsylvania Regiments provided many colonists with their first taste of military life, which would prove vitally important during the Revolutionary War. It was little wonder that once war with Britain loomed in 1775 the colonies should turn to their most experienced commander from the Seven Years' War, George Washington, to command the Continental Army. Indeed, Washington's experience with the Virginia Regiment would prove vitally important in equipping him to command the Continental Army in the later years of the Revolutionary War, when the initial fervor that encouraged many men to enlist had disappeared.[12]

The war may also have played a vital role in the "arming" of the backcountry. At the start of the Seven Years' War backcountry settlers lacked experience in using weapons and were reluctant to produce weapons for militia service even if they possessed them. Before the war many backcountry settlers had no need for arms. British and provincial military commanders repeatedly complained about the lack of experience in arms of the backcountry settlers. However, during the war, and then again during Pontiac's War, the descent of Indian raiding parties on the frontier meant that backcountry settlers needed to be armed. With every reason to possess arms for their own protection, backcountry settlers acquired guns and began the process of arming their communities. Indeed, by 1767 there were four gunsmiths operating in Berks County alone.[13]

The war also increased interest in the west. The thousands of colonial and provincial troops who served in the west returned home with tales of the fertility of the Ohio Country. Many, having been promised lands in the west as part of their enlistment bounty, found British prohibitions on westward expansion particularly rankling. Not surprisingly, in the years following the war many of these former soldiers would be actively involved in attempts to acquire lands in Kentucky and around Pittsburgh. Johnson reported bitterly that "the reduction of Canada raised the value of Lands, and those who thought they had not enough (who may be presumed to Amount to a very Large Number), now took every Step and employed every Low Agent who understood a little of the Indian Language to obtain Tracts for them."[14]

The removal of France as a continental power in North America also removed a threat to the colonists and allowed them to think about westward expansion while simultaneously giving them further self-confidence in seeking independence from the protection of Great Britain. The victory over France created a new sense of America's importance. Ministers and politicians alike noted the implications of America's expansion into the west and its victory in the war, and the rise of "civil millennialism" that accompanied the war increasingly stressed America's unique position in the world. These forces provided colonists with a degree of self-assurance, of identity, that would prove of vital importance in the coming conflict with Britain.[15]

Interest in the west also went hand in hand with an expansion of trade in the Ohio Valley. However, the trade that developed after the war was very different from the trade that had existed before. The carefully regulated and reciprocal trade of the French had disappeared, and the Pennsylvania traders who had opposed the French soon found themselves overwhelmed by a new tide of peddlers. The war had provided many ordinary backcountry settlers with experience of the west, and many of those who entered the peddling trade in the aftermath of the war were former soldiers. Indeed, in 1767 Sir William Johnson informed Whitehall that "the profits made by a few [traders] induced . . . [large] Numbers to embark in it, amongst Whom were the very Dregs of the people, such as discharged *Provincial Soldiers, Batteaumen* &ca."[16]

The growth of western trade helped to develop the backcountry economy, and the war further transformed it. Winchester and Carlisle became major provisions centers for the army and developed rapidly as important mercantile trading centers. Indeed, the most prominent merchants in

Frederick County in the late eighteenth century had all moved to Winchester from Philadelphia during the Seven Years' War.[17] Ironically, war also played a major role in shaping the development of the backcountry. The war had stalled and in some cases reversed the population growth of the backcountry. This, in turn, allowed the elite in the region to solidify their power. Wartime profits filled the coffers of backcountry gentlemen, and they were able to reinvest these profits in buying up lands abandoned by their less fortunate neighbors. Wartime commissions served to buttress the authority of backcountry gentlemen, and folktales about the exploits of local heroes and Indian atrocities would become a lasting feature of the region.

The war had demonstrated the fragility of backcountry society. Tensions emerged during the war that demonstrated the intense individualism and competitiveness of the region. Competition among settlers revealed the limitations of community networks shattered by migration and the diverse ethnic composition of the backcountry. The war, however, also began to shape new social structures. Shared wartime experiences provided one focus for community cohesion. Proven leadership during the war, whether in the militia, the provincial regiments, or during the Indian onslaught, provided some members of the elite with one means of validating their authority. Many who would lead the region during the Revolutionary War had proved their abilities during the Seven Years' War. Members of the elite also learned important lessons about how to cajole the "lower sort" into supporting unpopular policies. During the Revolutionary War backcountry leaders in Virginia and Pennsylvania made frequent concessions to popular and local feelings and carefully avoided espousing the same ideology as their eastern brethren. The lessons learned in the Seven Years' War were thus central in sparing the Pennsylvania and Virginia backcountry some of the horrific violence seen in the backcountry of the Carolinas during the Revolutionary War.[18]

The Seven Years' War played a major part in preparing Virginia and Pennsylvania for the Revolutionary War in a wide variety of ways. Many historians have noted this, but the impact of war in Virginia and Pennsylvania was very different from the impact of war in New England. The war did not generate identical tensions between the colonies and the mother country, serving instead to give the colonies a sense of their own self-importance. The tensions that it did raise were within the colonies themselves, and the lesson of how to control these conflicts was vitally important. The war also served to awaken the colonies' interest in the west, although giving the colonists a different perspective on the west than that held by British and imperial officials. Its conflicting results all prepared the frontier for the outbreak of an even more horrifying, general, and destructive war—the American Revolution.

Appendix: Composition of
the Provincial Regiments

Table 1. Birthplaces of Provincial Privates

	Massachusetts		Virginia		Pennsylvania	
Birthplace	N	%	N	%	N	%
Same Colony	2,013	82.4	635	41.2	171	18.8
Neighboring Colony	183	7.5	114	7.4	61	6.7
Other N. American Colony	22	0.9	24	1.6	15	1.7
Other G.B. Colony	12	0.5	1	0.1	4	0.4
British Isles	193	7.9	724	47.0	490	53.9
Continental Europe	19	0.8	42	2.7	168	18.5
	2,442		1,540		909	

Fred Anderson, *A People's Army: Massachusetts Soldiers and Society in the Seven Years' War* (Chapel Hill: University of North Carolina Press, 1984), 232; Size Rolls for the Virginia Regiment, Washington Papers, microfilm, (Washington, D.C.: Library of Congress, Manuscript Division, 1964), ser. 4, reels 29–31; *PA* 2d ser. 2:419–528.

Table 2. Preenlistment Occupations of Provincial Troops

	Massachusetts		Virginia		Pennsylvania	
Occupation	N	%	N	%	N	%
Farmer	—	19.8	652	45.2	14	2.1
Laborer	—	30.8	124	8.6	307	46.4
Artisan	—	35.8	548	38.0	300	45.4
Seafarer	—	3.5	72	5.0	33	5.0
Nonmanual	—	1.8	45	3.1	7	1.1
	2,309		1,441		661	

Fred Anderson, *A People's Army: Massachusetts Soldiers and Society in the Seven Years' War* (Chapel Hill: University of North Carolina Press, 1984), 237; Size Rolls for the Virginia Regiment, Washington Papers, microfilm (Washington, D.C.: Library of Congress, Manuscript Division, 1964), ser. 4, reels 29–31; *PA* 2d ser. 2:419–528. For a discussion of some of the problems involved in interpreting these figures, see Matthew C. Ward, "'An Army of Servants': The Pennsylvania Regiment during the Seven Years' War," *PMHB* 119 (1995): 75–93.

Table 3. The Most Common Preenlistment Occupations of Recruits

Pennsylvania Regiment			Virginia Regiment		
Laborer	304	45.99%	Planter	577	39.99%
Weaver	54	8.17%	Carpenter	124	8.59%
Mariner	31	4.69%	Shoemaker	93	6.44%
Carpenter	26	3.93%	Tailor	76	5.27%
Shoemaker	25	3.78%	Farmer	69	4.78%
Cooper	23	3.48%	Sailor	47	3.26%
Tailor	21	3.18%	Laborer	40	2.77%

PA 2d ser. 2:419–528; Size Rolls for the Virginia Regiment, Washington Papers, microfilm (Washington, D.C.: Library of Congress, Manuscript Division, 1964), ser. 4, reels 29–31.

Table 4. Age Distribution of Provincial Troops

	Massachusetts		Virginia		Pennsylvania	
Age Cohort	N	%	N	%	N	%
14–19	591	24.7	147	10.2	112	14.2
20–24	758	31.7	604	41.9	325	41.2
25–29	395	16.5	319	22.1	178	22.6
30–34	208	8.7	165	11.5	92	11.7
35–39	158	6.6	60	4.2	53	6.7
40–44	117	4.9	78	5.4	23	2.9
45–49	87	3.6	50	3.5	5	0.6
50+	77	3.2	18	1.2	0	0.0
	2391		1441		788	

Fred Anderson, *A People's Army: Massachusetts Soldiers and Society in the Seven Years' War* (Chapel Hill: University of North Carolina Press, 1984), 231; Size Rolls for the Virginia Regiment, Washington Papers, microfilm (Washington, D.C.: Library of Congress, Manuscript Division, 1964), ser. 4, reels 29–31; PA 2d ser. 2:419–528.

Abbreviations

The following abbreviations are used in the notes for sources frequently cited.

APS   American Philosophical Society Library, Philadelphia

BL   British Library, London

BOEHM   Randolph Boehm, ed. *Records of the British Colonial Office, Class 5.* Microfilm. Part 1, *Westward Expansion, 1700–1783.* 12 reels. Part 3, *The French and Indian War.* 8 reels. Frederick, Md.: University Microfilm, 1983

CRP   Samuel Hazard, ed. *Minutes of the Provincial Council of Pennsylvania* [*Colonial Records of Pennsylvania*]. 16 vols. Harrisburg: Theophilus Fenn, 1838–53

EJVC   H. R. McIlwaine, Wilmer Lee Hall, and Benjamin J. Hillman, eds. *Executive Journals of the Council of Colonial Virginia.* 6 vols. Richmond: Virginia State Library, 1925–66

FFP   George Henkle Reese, ed. *The Official Papers of Francis Fauquier, Lieutenant Governor of Virginia, 1758–1768.* 3 vols. Charlottesville: University Press of Virginia, 1980

GWP   W. W. Abbot and Dorothy Twohig, eds. *The Papers of George Washington, Colonial Series.* 10 vols. Charlottesville: University Press of Virginia, 1983–95

HBP   Louis Waddell, S. K. Stevens, Donald H. Kent, Autumn L. Leonard, and J. L. Tottenham, eds. *The Papers of Henry Bouquet.* 6 vols. Harrisburg: Pennsylvania Historical and Museum Commission, 1951–94

HSP   Historical Society of Pennsylvania, Philadelphia

IHC   *Collections of the Illinois Historical Library.* 34 vols. Springfield: The Trustees of the Illinois State Historical Library, 1915–40

JAH   *Journal of American History*

JHB   H. R. McIlwaine and John P. Kennedy, eds. *Journals of the House of Burgesses of Virginia.* 15 vols. Richmond: Everett Waddey Co., 1905–15

MVHR   *Mississippi Valley Historical Review*

NYCD	Edmund B. O'Callaghan and Berthold Fernow, eds. *Documents Relative to the Colonial History of the State of New York: Procured in Holland, England and France.* 15 vols. Albany: Parson's Weed, 1853–87
PA	Samuel Hazard, Thomas Lynch Montgomery, George Edward Reed, William Henry Egle, and John Blair Linn, eds. *Pennsylvania Archives.* 10 series. 107 vols. Philadelphia and Harrisburg: J. Severns, 1852
PMHB	*Pennsylvania Magazine of History and Biography*
PRO CO	Public Record Office, Kew, London, Colonial Office files
PRO WO	Public Record Office, Kew, London, War Office files
PSA	Pennsylvania State Archives, Harrisburg
RDP	Robert A. Brock, ed. *The Official Records of Robert Dinwiddie, Lieutenant-Governor of the Colony of Virginia, 1751–1758.* 2 vols. Virginia Historical Society Collection, 3–4. Richmond: Virginia Historical Society Collections, 1883–84
SWJP	James Sullivan et al., eds. *The Papers of Sir William Johnson.* 14 vols. Albany: University of the State of New York, 1921–65
VMHB	*Virginia Magazine of History and Biography*
VSAL	William Waller Henning, ed. *The Statutes at Large, Being a Collection of All the Laws of Virginia.* 13 vols. Richmond: Franklin Press, 1809–23
WMQ	*William and Mary Quarterly*
WPHM	*Western Pennsylvania Historical Magazine*

Notes

Notes to Introduction

1. "Project for Next Year's Campaign in N. America," Aug. 11, 1755, Additional Mss., 35,909 ff. 208–10, BL.

2. Where possible I have used the specific ethnic identity of individuals—Huron, Shawnee, and Delaware, for example. However, the Ohio Valley in the mid-eighteenth century was a collection of many polyglot peoples. Many villages were composed of numerous different tribal groups. I have chosen not to follow the lead of Richard White and label the Indians of the region the Ohio Algonquians. While most of the inhabitants of the Ohio Valley were members of a tribe speaking an Algonquian language and sharing common cultural traits, there were also many Iroquoian peoples, most notably the Hurons, and some members of the Iroquois themselves. It is thus difficult to refer to these peoples by the generic term "Algonquians." For a discussion of many of these problems, see Richard White, *The Middle Ground: Indians, Empires, and Republics in the Great Lakes Region, 1650–1815* (New York: Cambridge University Press, 1991). There is also a problem in naming the European participants in this conflict. Contemporaries generally referred to all members of the British Empire as "Englishmen." This, of course, is very misleading and certainly does not correspond with modern terminology. In addition, terming all members of the British Empire "Englishmen" does not effectively distinguish between the polyglot inhabitants of North America and the inhabitants of the British Isles. Irish immigrant George Croghan, who arrived in North America in 1741, and German immigrant Conrad Weiser, who arrived in North America in 1710, cannot be regarded as "English" and of the same ethnic and cultural identity as Maj. Gen. Edward Braddock. Thus, I have referred to those whose roots are in the British Isles as "British" and to those whose roots are in the North American colonies as "Anglo-American" or by the appropriate colonial appellation, "Pennsylvanian" or "Virginian." When referring to the empire as a whole I have referred to the "British." Thus, Brig. Gen. John Forbes led the "British" assault on the Ohio Valley in 1758, even though his forces were composed of many Anglo-Americans. I have used terminology similarly for the French, referring to French colonists as "Canadians," those whose origins were in metropolitan France as "French," and the empire as a whole as "French."

3. John E. Ferling, "School for Command: Young George Washington and the

Virginia Regiment," in *George Washington and the Virginia Backcountry,* ed. Warren R. Hofstra (Madison: Madison House, 1998), 195–222.

4. Eric Hinderaker, *Elusive Empires: Constructing Colonialism in the Ohio Valley, 1673–1800* (Cambridge: Cambridge University Press, 1997), 158–62.

5. James H. Merrell, *Into the American Woods: Negotiators on the Pennsylvania Frontier* (New York: W. W. Norton, 1999), 36.

6. See, for instance, Fred Anderson, *A People's Army: Massachusetts Soldiers and Society in the Seven Years' War* (Chapel Hill: University of North Carolina Press, 1984); and Harold E. Selesky, *War and Society in Colonial Connecticut* (New Haven: Yale University Press, 1990).

7. John Shy, *A People Numerous and Armed: Reflections on the Military Struggle for American Independence* (Ann Arbor: University of Michigan Press, 1990), 40. See also Peter Russell, "Redcoats in the Wilderness: British Officers and Irregular Warfare in Europe and America, 1740–1760," *WMQ* 3d ser. 35 (1978): 652.

8. Lawrence Henry Gipson, *The Great War for the Empire: The Years of Defeat,* vol. 6 of *The British Empire before the American Revolution* (New York: Alfred A. Knopf, 1946); and Lawrence Henry Gipson, *The Great War for the Empire: The Victorious Years, 1758–1760,* vol. 7 of *The British Empire before the American Revolution* (New York: Alfred A. Knopf, 1949).

9. Fred Anderson, *Crucible of War: The Seven Years' War and the Fate of Empire in British North America, 1754–1766* (New York: Alfred A. Knopf, 2000). For other military studies, see Ian K. Steele, *Betrayals: Fort William Henry and the "Massacre"* (New York: Oxford University Press, 1990); Douglas Edward Leach, *Arms for Empire: A Military History of the British Colonies in North America, 1607–1763* (New York: MacMillan, 1973); John Morgan Dederer, *War in America to 1775: Before Yankee Doodle* (New York: New York University Press, 1990); John E. Ferling, *A Wilderness of Miseries: War and Warriors in Early America* (Westport: Greenwood Press, 1980); Don Higginbotham, "The Early American Way of War," *WMQ* 3d ser. 44 (1987); John Shy, *Toward Lexington: The Role of the British Army in the Coming of the American Revolution* (Princeton: Princeton University Press, 1965).

10. Gary B. Nash, *The Urban Crucible: The Northern Seaports and the Origins of the American Revolution* (Cambridge: Harvard University Press, 1986).

11. For a discussion of the impact of the war in this region, see below. The Seven Years' War and Pontiac's War resulted in at least three thousand casualties when the population of Virginia and Pennsylvania was less than four hundred thousand. War-related deaths in the Revolution were approximately 1 percent of the population, in the Civil War 1.6 percent. See Allan R. Millet and Peter Maslowski, *For the Common Defense: A Military History of the United States of America* (New York: Free Press, 1984), 79; and U.S Bureau of the Census, *Historical Statistics of the United States, Colonial Times to 1970* (Washington D.C.: U.S. Government Printing Office, 1975), 2:1168.

12. For a discussion of backcountry society in this region and its importance in shaping later cultural patterns, see David Hackett Fischer, *Albion's Seed: Four British Folkways in America* (New York: Oxford University Press, 1989).

13. Turk McCleskey, "Rich Land, Poor Prospects: Real Estate and the Formation of a Social Elite in Augusta County, Virginia, 1738–1779," *Virginia Magazine of History and Biography* 98 (1990): 449–86.

14. Richard R. Beeman, *The Evolution of the Southern Backcountry: A Case Study of Lunenburg County, Virginia, 1746–1831* (Philadelphia: University of Pennsylvania Press, 1984), 455–76.

15. Albert H. Tillson Jr., *Gentry and Common Folk: Political Culture on a Virginia Frontier, 1740–1789* (Lexington: University Press of Kentucky, 1991), 37.

16. For studies of the backcountry, see James T. Lemon, *The Best Poor Man's Country: A Geographical Study of Early Southeastern Pennsylvania* (Baltimore: Johns Hopkins University Press, 1976); Jack P. Greene, "Independence, Improvement, and Authority: Toward a Framework for Understanding the Histories of the Southern Backcountry during the Era of the American Revolution," in *An Uncivil War: The Southern Backcountry during the American Revolution*, ed. Thad W. Tate, Ronald Hoffman, and Peter J. Albert (Charlottesville: University Press of Virginia, 1985), 3–36; Warren R. Hofstra, ed, *George Washington and the Virginia Backcountry* (Madison: Madison House, 1998); Gregory H. Nobles, "Breaking into the Backcountry: New Approaches to the Early American Frontier, 1750–1800," *WMQ* 3d ser. 46 (1989); Michael J. Puglisi, ed., *Diversity and Accommodation: Essays on the Cultural Composition of the Virginia Frontier* (Knoxville: University of Tennessee Press, 1997); Tillson, *Gentry and Common Folk*; Woody Holton, *Forced Founders: Indians, Debtors, Slaves and the Making of the American Revolution in Virginia* (Chapel Hill: University of North Carolina Press, 1999); David Hackett Fischer and James C. Kelly, *Bound Away: Virginia and the Westward Movement* (Charlottesville: University Press of Virginia, 2000).

17. Peter C. Mancall, *Valley of Opportunity: Economic Culture along the Upper Susquehanna, 1700–1800* (Ithaca: Cornell University Press, 1991); Robert D. Mitchell, *Commercialism and Frontier: Perspectives on the Early Shenandoah Valley* (Charlottesville: University of Virginia Press, 1977).

18. Richard Slotkin, *Regeneration through Violence: The Mythology of the American Frontier, 1600–1860* (Middletown: Wesleyan University Press, 1973).

19. Richard I. Melvoin, *New England Outpost: War and Society in Colonial Deerfield* (New York: W. W. Norton, 1988), 284.

20. For recent studies of Indian affairs during the middle of the eighteenth century, see Michael N. McConnell, *A Country Between: The Upper Ohio Valley and Its Peoples, 1724–1774* (Lincoln: University of Nebraska Press, 1992); White, *Middle Ground;* Hinderaker, *Elusive Empires;* Merrell, *Into the American Woods;* and Jane T. Merritt, "Metaphor, Meaning and Misunderstanding: Language and Power on the Pennsylvania Frontier," in *Contact Points: American Frontiers from the Mohawk Valley to the Mississippi, 1750–1830*, ed. Andrew R. L. Cayton and Fredrika Teute (Chapel Hill: University of North Carolina, 1998), 60–87.

21. Robert Orme, "Journal of General Braddock's Expedition," Kings Mss., BL, 212:84–88.

22. "Account of the Battle of the Monongahela," July 9, 1755, *NYCD* 10:303.

23. The difficulties of accurately identifying many Indian headmen and war captains can be immense. In part this reflects the difficulties with which colonists grappled in attempting to spell out names that to them were all but unpronounceable. Consequently, one Indian name can appear under widely variant spellings—Ohio

Delaware headman Keekyuscung, for example, was for many years thought to be a variation of Teedyuscung, whereas in reality they were two important, but very different, Delaware leaders. In addition to the problems of spelling, most Indian leaders had several different names in different Indian languages and in English; Scarouady was also known as Monacatoocha and the "Half King." To obfuscate matters even further, some Indians seem to have adopted the names of former leaders, not unlike European princes and popes. It seems probable that Delaware leader Captain Jacobs was killed in the Pennsylvania raid on Kittanning in 1756. Yet a Captain Jacobs features prominently in negotiations on the Ohio in the 1760s. Such difficulties have on occasion even confused otherwise distinguished historians. Richard White, for example, writes that "Keekyuscung appears to have been Delaware George since Hugh Mercer, who knew him well, later used the names interchangeably." Yet this cannot be the case, for Samuel Lightfoot, an agent at Fort Pitt who also knew Delaware George well, included both Keekyuscung and Delaware George as two of the major Delaware chiefs of the region. For confusion over Delaware George and Keekyuscung, see White, *Middle Ground,* 250n.; and Samuel Lightfoot to Israel Pemberton, Apr. 22, 1759, Friendly Association Records, 3:103, Quaker Collection, Collection 1250, Haverford College. For Shingas quote, see "Deposition of John Craig," Mar. 30, 1756, Penn Mss.: Indian Affairs, 2:78, HSP.

24. "Deposition of John Craig," Mar. 30, 1756, Penn Mss.: Indian Affairs, 2:78.

Notes to Chapter 1

1. Robert D. Mitchell, "'From the Ground Up': Space, Place, and Diversity in Frontier Studies," in *Diversity and Accommodation: Essays on the Cultural Composition of the Virginia Frontier,* ed. Michael J. Puglisi (Knoxville: University of Tennessee Press, 1997), 23–57.

2. Alfred Proctor James, *The Ohio Company: Its Inner History* (Pittsburgh: University of Pittsburgh Press, 1959); McConnell, *Country Between;* White, *Middle Ground.*

3. T. H. Breen, *Tobacco Culture: The Mentality of the Great Tidewater Planters on the Eve of the Revolution* (Princeton: Princeton University Press, 1985); Rhys Isaac, *The Transformation of Virginia, 1740–1790* (New York: W. W. Norton, 1988).

4. Mitchell, *Commercialism and Frontier,* 29–33.

5. Robert Dinwiddie to Board of Trade, June 16, 1753, BOEHM pt. 1, 11:788–89; Robert D. Mitchell, "'Over the Hills and Far Away': George Washington and the Changing Virginia Backcountry," in *George Washington and the Virginia Backcountry,* ed. Warren R. Hofstra (Madison: Madison House, 1998), 69; Warren R. Hofstra, "'A Parcel of Barbarian's and an Uncooth Set of People': Settlers and Settlements of the Shenandoah Valley," in *George Washington and the Virginia Backcountry,* ed. Warren R. Hofstra (Madison: Madison House, 1998), 93.

6. For a discussion of Pennsylvania society, see Sally Schwartz, *A Mixed Multitude: The Struggle for Toleration in Colonial Pennsylvania* (New York: New York University Press, 1987); Mancall, *Valley of Opportunity;* Lemon, *Best Poor Man's Country;* and Thomas M. Doerflinger, *A Vigorous Spirit of Enterprise: Merchants and Economic Development in Revolutionary Philadelphia* (Chapel Hill: University of North Carolina Press, 1986).

7. Thomas Slaughter, for instance, has claimed that in western Pennsylvania "poverty was the standard." See Thomas Slaughter, *The Whiskey Rebellion: Frontier Epilogue to the American Revolution* (New York: Oxford University Press, 1986), 66.

8. George W. Franz, *Paxton: A Study of Community Structure and Mobility in the Colonial Pennsylvania Backcountry* (New York: Garland Publishing, 1989), 184–85. For Berks County, see the 1767 tax list, *PA* 3d ser. 18:3–86.

9. Lemon, *Best Poor Man's Country*, 56; Terry G. Jordan and Matti Kaups, *The American Backwoods Frontier: An Ethnic and Ecological Interpretation* (Baltimore: Johns Hopkins University Press, 1989), 69; *CRP* 5:431, 5:440–49; Tillson, *Gentry and Common Folk*, 62.

10. Tillson, *Gentry and Common Folk*, 63.

11. Tillson, *Gentry and Common Folk*, 35–37; Warren R. Hofstra, "Ethnicity and Community Formation on the Shenandoah Valley Frontier, 1730–1800," in *Diversity and Accommodation: Essays on the Cultural Composition of the Virginia Frontier*, ed. Michael J. Puglisi (Knoxville: University of Tennessee Press, 1997), 59–81; A. G. Roeber, "'The Origin of Whatever Is Not English among Us': The Dutch-Speaking and the German-Speaking Peoples of Colonial British America," in *Strangers within the Realm: Cultural Margins of the First British Empire*, ed. Bernard Bailyn (Chapel Hill: University of North Carolina Press, 1991), 220–83; Isaac, *Transformation of Virginia*.

12. Tillson, *Gentry and Common Folk*, 20; Mitchell, "'Over the Hills and Far Away,'" 76; Richard R. Beeman, "Social Change and Cultural Conflict in Virginia: Lunenberg County, 1746 to 1774," *WMQ* 3d ser. 35 (1978): 455–76; *PA* 3d ser. 18:3–86.

13. Maldwyn A. Jones, "The Scotch-Irish in British America," in *Strangers within the Realm: Cultural Margins of the First British Empire*, ed. Bernard Bailyn (Chapel Hill: University of North Carolina Press, 1991), 284–313; Hofstra, "Ethnicity and Community Formation," 59–81; Fischer and Kelly, *Bound Away*, 107–21.

14. For the rise of the Baptists, see Isaac, *Transformation of Virginia*. For a general discussion about ethnic and religious diversity, see Joseph D. Illick, *Colonial Pennsylvania: A History* (New York: Scribners, 1976); Mitchell, *Commercialism and Frontier*, 104–6; Nobles, "Breaking into the Backcountry," 650–53; and Hofstra, "'Parcel of Barbarians,'" 87–114.

15. For mobility rates, see Franz, *Paxton*, 121–26. See also Abbot Emerson Smith, *Colonists in Bondage: White Servitude and Convict Labor in America, 1607–1776* (Chapel Hill: University of North Carolina Press, 1947); and Jerome H. Wood Jr., *Conestoga Crossroads: Lancaster Pennsylvania, 1730–1790* (Harrisburg: Pennsylvania Historical and Museum Commission, 1979).

16. Richard Peters to Thomas Penn, Feb. 22, 1763, Penn Mss.: Official Correspondence, 9:190; Mitchell, *Commercialism and Frontier*, 46; Kenneth W. Keller, "The Outlook of Rhinelanders on the Virginia Frontier," in *Diversity and Accommodation: Essays on the Cultural Composition of the Virginia Frontier*, ed. Michael J. Puglisi (Knoxville.: University of Tennessee Press, 1997), 104–5; Philip D. Morgan and Michael L. Nicholls, "Slaves in Piedmont Virginia, 1720–1790," *WMQ* 3d ser. 46 (1989): 211–51.

17. *PA* 3d ser. 18:3–86.

18. Chester Raymond Young, "The Effects of the French and Indian War on

Civilian Life in the Frontier Counties of Virginia, 1754–1763" (Ph.D. diss., Vanderbilt University, 1969), 333.

19. D. W. Meinig, *Atlantic America, 1492–1800*, vol. 1 of *The Shaping of America: A Geographical Perspective on Five Hundred Years of History* (New Haven: Yale University Press, 1986); Mitchell, *Commercialism and Frontier*, 16–36; Mitchell, "From the Ground Up," 23–57.

20. Mitchell, *Commercialism and Frontier*, 18; Mancall, *Valley of Opportunity*, 72–78.

21. Quoted in Young, "Effects of the French and Indian War," 11; Mitchell, *Commercialism and Frontier*, 36–37.

22. Mitchell, "'Over the Hills and Far Away,'" 72; Hofstra, "'Parcel of Barbarians,'" 97; Franz, *Paxton*, 101–4, 67–71; Lemon, *Best Poor Man's Country*, 45–47, 61–70.

23. James Kirby Martin, "The Return of the Paxton Boys and the Historical State of the Pennsylvania Frontier," *Pennsylvania History* 38 (1971): 117–33; Mitchell, "From the Ground Up," 28.

24. Isaac, *Transformation of Virginia*, 90–91.

25. Tillson, *Gentry and Common Folk*, 46.

26. Franz, *Paxton*, 28–29.

27. Greene, "Independence, Improvement, and Authority," 3–36.

28. *PA* 3d ser. 18:3–86; Hofstra, "'Parcel of Barbarians,'" 99; Greene, "Uncivil War," 12–13; Mitchell, *Commercialism and Frontier*, 1–8, 46; Young, "Effects of the French and Indian War," 211–14.

29. *PA* 3d ser. 18:3–86.

30. Hofstra, "'Parcel of Barbarians,'" 99; Jordan and Kaups, *American Backwoods Frontier*, 120.

31. *PA* 3d ser. 18:3–86.

32. Mancall, *Valley of Opportunity*, 54–70.

33. Proceedings of Criminal Court, 1750–1759, Cumberland County Historical Society, Carlisle, Pa., Box 6; *CRP* 5:628, 5:749, 6:149.

34. White, *Middle Ground*, 48; Mancall, *Valley of Opportunity*, 11–26.

35. For a discussion of the fur trade, see William Eccles, "The Fur Trade and Eighteenth Century Imperialism," *WMQ* 3d ser. 40 (1983): 341–62; White, *Middle Ground*, 50–93.

36. "Deposition of John Patton," Mar. 8, 1752, *IHC* 29:496.

37. "Abstract of Despatches from Canada," 1749, *NYCD* 10:200; Charles de Raymond to Jean Frederick Philippeaux, comte de Maurepas, Nov. 2, 1747, *IHC* 29:42–44; Maurepas, to Pierre de Rigaud de Vaudreuil, Feb. 23, 1748, *IHC* 29:49; Lawrence Henry Gipson, *Zones of International Friction: North America, South of the Great Lakes Region, 1748–1754*, vol. 4 of *The British Empire before the American Revolution* (New York: Alfred A. Knopf, 1936), 175; White, *Middle Ground*, 195.

38. William Eccles, *The Canadian Frontier, 1534–1760*, 2d ed. (Albuquerque: University of New Mexico Press, 1984), 151–53; Stephen H. Cutcliffe, "Indians, Furs and Empires: The Changing Policies of New York and Pennsylvania, 1674–1768" (Ph.D. diss., Lehigh University, 1976), 221; Lois Mulkearn, *George Mercer Papers: Relating to the Ohio Company of Virginia* (Pittsburgh: University of Pittsburgh Press, 1954), 476; "Accounts of Ohio Traders," Cadwallader Collection: George Croghan Papers, HSP.

39. De Raymond to La Jonquière, Jan. 5, 1750, *IHC* 29:154; "Reports to Raymond," Mar.–Apr. 1750, *IHC* 29:167; White, *Middle Ground,* 212.

40. De Raymond to La Jonquière, Sept. 4, 1749, *IHC* 29:105–6.

41. De Raymond to La Jonquière, Jan. 5, 1750, *IHC* 29:154; White, *Middle Ground,* 37, 187–88.

42. McConnell, *Country Between,* 25–27.

43. Richard Aquila, *The Iroquois Restoration: Iroquois Diplomacy on the Colonial Frontier, 1701–1754* (Detroit: Wayne State University Press, 1983), 184–86; Francis Jennings, *The Ambiguous Iroquois Empire: The Covenant Chain Confederation of Indian Tribes with English Colonies from Its Beginning to the Lancaster Treaty of 1744* (New York: W. W. Norton, 1984), 238–316; C. A. Weslager, *The Delaware Indians: A History* (New Brunswick: Rutgers University Press, 1972), 196–218; C. A. Weslager, *The Delaware Indian Westward Migration* (Wallingford: Middle Atlantic Press, 1978), 12–19.

44. Jennings, *Ambiguous Iroquois Empire,* 316–24; Richard S. Dunn and Mary Maples Dunn, *The World of William Penn* (Philadelphia: University of Pennsylvania Press, 1986).

45. "In Reference to the Walking Purchase," Friendly Association Records, 1:407; Jennings, *Ambiguous Iroquois Empire,* 330–32, 44; Aquila, *Iroquois Restoration,* 185–87.

46. "Report of Richard Peters on Proceedings at Albany," Aug. 5, 1754, Penn Mss.: Indian Affairs, 2:4–7; "Minutes of a Meeting of the Susquehannah Company," Sept. 6, 1753, and "Deed from Indians of the Six Nations to the Susquehannah Company," both in Julian P. Boyd and Robert Joseph Taylor, *The Susquehannah Company Papers,* 11 vols. (Ithaca: Cornell University Press, 1962), 1:40–41, 1:101–2.

47. "A Brief Account of the Travels of Peter Salley a German who Lives in the County of Augusta in Virginia," BOEHM pt. 1, 11:657, 11:659; *EJVC* 5:172–73, 5:191–95, 5:231–32, 5:295–98; James, *Ohio Company,* 9; Warren Hofstra, "'The Extension of His Majesties Dominions': The Virginia Backcountry and the Reconfiguration of Imperial Frontiers," *JAH* 84 (1998): 1281–312.

48. Governor William Gooch to Board of Trade, June 16, 1748, BOEHM pt. 1, 11:548–54; Mulkearn, *George Mercer Papers,* 1.

49. "Orders in Council," Nov. 24, 1748, BOEHM pt. 1, 11:550; Francis Jennings, *Empire of Fortune: Crowns, Colonies and Empires in the Seven Years War* (New York: W. W. Norton, 1988), 12–13.

50. Dinwiddie to Thomas Cresap, Jan. 23, 1752, *RDP* 1:17–18; Louis Knott Koontz, *Robert Dinwiddie: His Career in American Colonial Government and Westward Expansion* (Glendale: Arthur H. Clark Co., 1941), 159.

51. "Orders in Council," Feb. 9, 1749, BOEHM pt. 1, 11:551–53; Mulkearn, *George Mercer Papers,* 1–2.

52. "Petition of John Hanbury," Feb. 9, 1749, BOEHM pt. 1, 11:555–60; James, *Ohio Company,* 14.

53. "Deed of Release of Lands in Virginia, by the Six Nations at the Treaty of Lancaster, 1744," BOEHM pt. 1, 12:168–70; Jennings, *Ambiguous Iroquois Empire,* 359–62.

54. Mulkearn, *George Mercer Papers,* 5, 7–10, 142.

55. "Account of the Treaty of Logstown," 1752, BOEHM pt. 1, 11:752–53; "Case of the Ohio Company, 1762," in Mulkearn, *George Mercer Papers,* 53.

56. "Account of the Treaty of Logstown," 1752, and "Confirmation of the Lancaster Deed," both BOEHM pt. 1, 11:761–64, 11:766, 11;770, 11:774, 12:171–72; "Case of the Ohio Company, 1762," 56, 62–64; Jennings, *Empire of Fortune,* 43–44.

57. M. de Macarty Mactique to Antoine Louis de Rouillé, count de Souy, May 20, 1753, *IHC* 29:816.

58. Lord Halifax to the Duke of Newcastle, Aug. 15, 1753, Additional Mss., 33,029:96–100; "Ministerial Minute of the Attempts of the English to settle on the Ohio," Sept. 23, 1751, *NYCD* 10:239–40; Eccles, *Canadian Frontier,* 147, 59–60; Donald H. Kent and Sylvester K. Stevens, eds., *Wilderness Chronicles of Northwestern Pennsylvania* (Harrisburg: Pennsylvania Historical Commission, 1941), 25–26.

59. *CRP* 5:568–69, 5:570, 5:571.

60. "Detail of Indian Affairs," in Kent and Stevens, *Wilderness Chronicles,* 31; "Journal of William Trent," BOEHM pt. 1, 11:712–28; *CRP* 5:599–600, 5:674; Mactique to Vaudreuil, Dec. 7, 1752, *IHC* 29:748.

61. Dinwiddie to Board of Trade, Dec. 10, 1752, BOEHM pt. 1, 11:702–4.

62. Ange Duquesne du Menenville to Rouillé, Aug. 20, 1753, *NYCD* 10:255–57.

63. François-Marie le Marchand de Lignery to Vaudreuil, Oct. 3, 1752, *IHC* 29:730–33; Macarty to Vaudreuil, Dec. 7, 1752, *IHC* 29:761–63; Menenville to Rouillé, Oct. 27, 1753, *IHC* 29:843.

64. *CRP* 5:665–70, 5:685; Duquesne to Rouillé, Oct. 27, 1753, *IHC* 29:838–43.

65. "Narrative of What Happened on the River Ohio," Additional Mss., 15,874:208–11; *EJVC* 5:458–59; *CRP* 6:5–7.

66. J. Frederick Fausz, "'Engaged in Enterprises Pregnant with Terror': George Washington's Formative Years among the Indians," in *George Washington and the Virginia Backcountry,* ed. Warren R. Hofstra (Madison: Madison House, 1998), 124.

67. Dinwiddie to Board of Trade, Mar. 12, 1754, BOEHM pt. 1, 11:981; Dinwiddie to William Fairfax, Mar. 15, 1754, *RDP* 1:108; Dinwiddie to James Abercromby, July 24, [1754], *RDP* 1:236; *VSAL* 6:420–22.

68. *EJVC* 5:464; Dinwiddie to Lord Fairfax, [Jan. 1754], Dinwiddie to Earl of Holderness, Apr. 27, 1754, Dinwiddie to Earl of Halifax, Apr. 27, 1754, all *RDP* 1:48–50, 1:133–34, 1:134–35.

69. Dinwiddie to Lord Fairfax, Feb. 23, 1754, *RDP* 1:82; Dinwiddie to Colonel Innes, July 20, [1754], *RDP* 1:232; George Washington to Cresap, Apr. 18, 1754, *GWP* 1:82.

70. Dinwiddie to Joshua Fry, Mar. 18, 1754, *RDP* 1:109–10; "Deposition of Ensign Ward," [May 1754], BOEHM pt. 1, 1:693–97; Washington to Hamilton, Apr. [24], 1754, *GWP* 1:83–85; Washington to Dinwiddie, Apr. 25, 1754, *GWP* 87–90; Douglas Southall Freeman, *George Washington* (New York: Charles Scribner's Sons, 1948), 355.

71. Washington to Dinwiddie, May 29, 1754, *GWP* 110–11; Washington to John Augustine Washington, May 31, 1754, *GWP* 118; Dinwiddie to Washington, June 4, 1754, *GWP* 126–27; Fausz, "Engaged in Enterprises," 127–29; Anderson, *Crucible of War,* 50–65.

72. Dinwiddie to Washington, June 1, 1754, *GWP* 1:119.

73. "Minutes of Council of War, 28 June 1754," *GWP* 1:155–56; *CRP* 6:151.

74. Dinwiddie to Sir Thomas Robinson, July 24, 1754, BOEHM pt. 1, 1:712–14; Jean Victor Varin to François Bigot, July 24, 1754, *NYCD* 10:260–61; "Narrative of What Happened upon the River Ohio"; Anderson, *Crucible of War.*

Notes to Chapter 2

1. "Demandes de La Grande Bretagne et de La France, 1755," Additional Mss., 6,865:97–104; Duke of Newcastle to Dayrolle, Nov. 16, 1753, Additional Mss., 15,874:217; Robert D'Arcy, earl of Holderness, to Robert Keith, Mar. 11, 1755, Additional Mss., 15,874:286.

2. P. Collinson, "Some Thoughts on the French Scheme and the Ohio Country," Feb. 25, 1757, Additional Mss., 33,029:380–81.

3. Jean Baptiste de Machault d'Arnonville to Kerlérec, Feb. 17, 1755, *IHC* 29:925–26.

4. Anderson, *Crucible of War*, 66–73; Gipson, *The Years of Defeat*, 55–58.

5. Edward Braddock to Sir Thomas Robinson, Mar. 18, 1755, Additional Mss., 32,853:346–54; Dinwiddie to Board of Trade, Mar. 17, 1755, BOEHM pt. 1, 11:1021; "Instructions to General Braddock," Nov. 28, 1754, BOEHM pt. 3, 1:16–26; *CRP* 6:297, 6:300–301; W. A Speck, *Stability and Strife: England, 1714–1760* (London: Edward Arnold, 1977), 252.

6. Braddock to Duke of Newcastle, Mar. 20, 1755, Additional Mss., 32,853:388–91; *CRP* 6:332–33, 6:335–38.

7. "Account of the Battle of the Monongahela," *NYCD* 10:303–4; Vaudreuil to Machault, July 24, 1755, *NYCD* 10:307.

8. Dinwiddie to John Hanbury, Apr. 1755, Additional Mss., 32,854:378; "Minutes of a Council of War held at Alexandria," Apr. 14, 1755, Additional Mss., 33,029:174–77.

9. *CRP* 6:368; Orme, "Journal," King's Mss., 212:13, 212:23.

10. Robert Hunter Morris to Sir Thomas Robinson, Apr. 9, 1755, BOEHM pt. 1, 2:43; Braddock to Morris, Mar. 9, 1755, BOEHM pt. 3, 1:41–42; *CRP* 6:295–96, 6:387; *PA* 4th ser. 2:235, 8th ser. 5:3865; Dinwiddie to Lord Halifax, Feb. 24, 1755, *RDP* 1:512–17; Dinwiddie to Braddock, May 9, 1755, *RDP* 2:34.

11. *CRP* 6:404–6.

12. Washington to John Augustine Washington, May 14, 1755, *GWP* 1:277–78; "Instructions to General Braddock"; Orme, "Journal," King's Mss., 56–69.

13. Orme, "Journal," King's Mss., 11, 39–40; Dinwiddie to Sir Thomas Robinson, June 23, 1755, *RDP* 2:70; *Virginia Gazette*, May 23, 1755; *CRP* 6:398–99; "Speech of General Braddock to the Indians at Fort Cumberland," May 10, 1755, BOEHM pt. 1, 2:247–49.

14. *CRP* 6:588–89.

15. Beverly W. Bond Jr., ed., "The Captivity of Charles Stuart, 1755–1757," *MVHR* 13 (1926): 58–91.

16. Governor Horatio Sharpe to Sir Thomas Robinson, June 28, 1755, BOEHM pt. 1, 2:361; Orme, "Journal," King's Mss., 40, 77.

17. Orme, "Journal," King's Mss., 66; H. C. B. Rogers, *The British Army of the Eighteenth Century* (London: George Allen and Unwin, 1977), 68; Daniel J. Beattie, "The Adaptation of the British Army to Wilderness Warfare," in *Adapting to Conditions: War and Society in the Eighteenth Century*, ed. Maarten Ultee (University: University of Alabama Press, 1986), 56–59.

18. John Rutherford to Peters, Aug. 1755, Peters Papers, 4:41, HSP.

19. Orme, "Journal," King's Mss., 52, 67–69; Dinwiddie to Governor Dobbs, June 13, 1755, *RDP* 2:60; Guy Frégault, *Canada: The War of the Conquest*, trans. Margaret M. Cameron (Toronto: Oxford University Press, 1969), 94–95.

20. Orme, "Journal," King's Mss., 79, 84–88, 97–98; Washington to John Augustine Washington, June 28–July 2, 1755, *GWP* 1:322.

21. "Account of the Battle of the Monongahela," *NYCD* 10:303–4; Charles Swaine to Peters, Aug. 5, 1755, Peters Papers, 4:38; Orme, "Journal," King's Mss., 99–104.

22. "Account of the Battle of the Monongahela," *NYCD* 10:303.

23. Orme, "Journal," King's Mss., 102–7; Robert Orme to Morris, July 18, 1755, BOEHM pt. 1, 2:395–99; Swaine to Peters, Aug. 5, 1755; "A list of Officers who were present and of those killed and wounded in the action on the Banks of the Monongahila the 9th July 1755," Additional Mss., 33,046:330–35; Washington to Dinwiddie, July 18, 1755, *GWP* 1:399–40; Anderson, *Crucible of War*, 102.

24. Orme, "Journal," King's Mss., 107; *CRP* 6:514, 6:593, 6:595; Dinwiddie to Sir Thomas Robinson, Aug. 20, 1755, BOEHM pt. 1, 2:449.

25. Innes to Colonel Dunbar, Aug. 6, 1755, BOEHM pt. 1, 2:468; Dinwiddie to Board of Trade, Sept. 6, 1755, BOEHM pt. 1, 11:1027; *CRP* 6:602–3; Dinwiddie to Dunbar, July 26, 1755, *RDP* 2:118–20; Dinwiddie to Sir Thomas Robinson, Aug. 7, 1755, *RDP* 2:139–40.

26. *Pennsylvania Gazette*, Jan. 1, 1756; "Deposition of John Craig," Mar. 30, 1756, Penn Mss.: Indian Affairs, 2:78.

27. The Duke of Newcastle to Sir Benjamin Keene, Apr. 28, 1755, Additional Mss. 2,854:299–302.

28. J. R Jones, *Britain and the World, 1649–1815* (London: Fontana, 1980), 209–10; Speck, *Stability and Strife*, 262–63.

29. Vaudreuil to Machault, June 8, 1756, *NYCD* 10:413.

30. Eccles, *Canadian Frontier*, 139.

31. "Deposition of John Craig," Mar. 30, 1756, Penn Mss.: Indian Affairs, 2:78.

32. William Smith, *An Historical Account of the Expedition against the Ohio Indians in the Year 1764* (London: T. Jefferies, 1766), 39.

33. Washington to Dinwiddie, Apr. 7, 1756, *GWP* 2:332–35.

34. McConnell, *Country Between*, 49–50.

35. "Conference held at Fort Pitt," Apr. 6–12, 1760, *SWJP* 3:211.

36. William West to Thomas Penn, Nov. 8, 1755, BOEHM pt. 1, 2:769–70.

37. West to Penn, Nov. 8, 1755, BOEHM pt. 1, 2:770.

38. McConnell, *Country Between*, 48–50.

39. James E. Seaver, *A Narrative of the Life of Mrs. Mary Jemison . . .* (Canadaigua, N.Y.: J. D. Bemis and Co., 1824), 25–26; *Pennsylvania Gazette*, Aug. 19, 1756.

40. "Abstract of Despatches from America," Aug. 30, 1756, *NYCD* 10:486–87; *Virginia Gazette*, Sept. 19, 1755.

41. "Colo. Bradstreet's Thoughts upon the Indian Trade, etc.," Dec. 4, 1764, PRO CO 5/65, pt. 3:135–41; Leroy V. Eid, "'A Kind of Running Fight': Indian Battlefield Tactics in the Late Eighteenth Century," *WPHM* 71 (1988): 147–71.

42. *Pennsylvania Gazette*, Aug. 12, 1756.

43. "Depositions of those who had been taken prisoners by the Indians," June 20, 1757, Northampton County Records: Miscellaneous Papers, 1:253, HSP.

44. *CRP* 7:97–98; "Examination of John Baker," Mar. 31, 1756, Penn Mss.: Indian Affairs, 2:78; William S. Ewing, "Indian Captives Released by Colonel Bouquet," *WPHM* 39 (1956): 187–201; Matthew C. Ward, "'Redeeming the Captives': Pennsylvania Captives among the Ohio Indians, 1755–1765," *PMHB* 125 (2001): 161–89.

45. Adam Stephen to Washington, Oct. 4, 1755, *GWP* 2:72; "James Burd letter," Dec. 20, 1756, Edward Shippen Thompson Family Papers, Box 1, Folder 3, PSA.

46. For a more detailed discussion of the treatment of captives, see James Axtell, *The European and the Indian: Essays in the Ethnohistory of Colonial North America* (New York: Oxford University Press, 1981), 168–200; and James Axtell, *The Invasion Within: The Contest of Cultures in Colonial North America* (New York: Oxford University Press, 1985), 302–27.

47. *Maryland Gazette*, Apr. 1, 1756.

48. "Deposition of John Craig," Mar. 30, 1756, Penn Mss.: Indian Affairs, 2:78.

49. *Pennsylvania Gazette*, July 28, 1757; George Mercer to John Fenton Mercer, Apr. 15, 1756, *GWP* 2:354–55; Reuben Gold Thwaites, ed., *Early Western Travels, 1748–1846*, vol. 1 of *Two Journals of Western Tours, by Charles [sic] Frederick Post* (Cleveland: Arthur H. Clark, 1904), 190.

50. *Pennsylvania Gazette*, Sept. 9, 1756; *CRP* 7:241–45; Yves Goddard, "Delaware," in *Handbook of North American Indians: Northeast*, ed. Bruce G. Trigger (Washington, D.C.: Smithsonian Institution, 1978), 220; Charles Callender, "Shawnee," in *Handbook of North American Indians: Northeast*, ed. Bruce G. Trigger (Washington, D.C.: Smithsonian Institution, 1978), 628; James H. Howard, *Shawnee! The Ceremonialism of a Native Indian Tribe and Its Cultural Background* (Athens: Ohio University Press, 1981), 119–25.

51. "Examination of Daniel McMullen," Sept. 22, 1756, Penn Mss.: Indian Affairs, 2:101; Thwaites, *Early Western Travels*, 212, 14.

52. *Pennsylvania Gazette*, July 28, 1757; *Maryland Gazette*, Mar. 18, 1756; "Examination of John Hochtattler," [May 5(?), 1758], *HBP* 1:391–93.

53. *Pennsylvania Gazette*, Dec. 22, 1757.

54. Elvert M. Davis, ed., "History of the Capture and Captivity of David Boyd from Cumberland County Pennsylvania, 1756," *WPHM* 14 (1931): 39; John Ingles, *The Story of Mary Draper Ingles and Her Son Thomas Ingles* (Radford: Commonwealth Press, 1969), 27; *CRP* 6:147.

55. John Bard to Henry Bouquet, June 8, 1762, *HBP* 6:89.

56. *EJVC* 6:24; *Pennsylvania Gazette*, Jan. 15, 1756; *CRP* 7:341; Harry S. Douglas, "The Immortal Mary Jemison," *Historical Wyoming* 9 (1958): 33–46; Seaver, *Mary Jemison*, 25; Young, "Effects of the French and Indian War," 133.

57. "Account of the Battle of the Monongahela," *NYCD* 10:303–4; Orme, "Journal," King's Mss., 104–5.

58. "List of Inhabitants Killed in Northampton County," Dec. 19, 1755, Penn Mss.: Indian Affairs, 2:52; Gipson, *The Victorious Years,* 283.

59. *CRP* 6:768.

60. *CRP* 6:590; *Pennsylvania Gazette,* Aug. 28, 1755.

61. ["Memorandum"], [July 1756], William Preston Papers, Draper Manuscript Collection, 1QQ/132, University of Wisconsin, Madison; Jacques Fontaine, *Memoirs of a Huguenot Family,* trans. Ann Maury (New York: Putnam, 1907), 432.

62. James Burd to Edward Shippen, Aug. 24, 1755, Shippen Family Papers, vol. 2, HSP; Conrad Weiser to Morris, Nov. 18, 1755, Conrad Weiser Papers, 1:60, HSP; William Fairfax to Washington, May 20, 1756, *GWP* 3:167.

63. "Report of Chew, Stedman, West and Shippen," Apr. 21, 1756, Penn Mss.: Indian Affairs, 2:80; Earl P. Olmstead, *David Zeisberger: A Life among the Indians* (Kent: Kent State University Press, 1997), 96.

64. Joseph Turner to Mrs. Ann Barclay and Sons, Nov. 14, 1755, Allen and Turner Letterbook, HSP.

65. Louis M. Waddell, "Defending the Long Perimeter: Forts on the Pennsylvania, Maryland, and Virginia Frontier, 1755–1765," *Pennsylvania History* 62 (1995): 179–80.

66. Washington to John Robinson, Nov. 9, 1756, *GWP* 4:16–17.

67. *PA* 4th ser. 2:284; Jennings, *Empire of Fortune.*

Notes to Chapter 3

1. Tillson, *Gentry and Common Folk,* 20–43; McCleskey, "Rich Land, Poor Prospects," 449–86.

2. Weiser to Morris, Nov. 19, 1755, Conrad Weiser Papers, 1:34.

3. Dinwiddie to William Shirley, Oct. 18, 1755, *RDP* 2:245; Morris to Thomas Penn, Nov. 28, 1755, BOEHM pt. 1, 2:794–800.

4. Dinwiddie to Richard Pearis, Aug. 2, [1754], *RDP* 1:266–68; Menenville to Rouillé, May 31, 1755, in Kent and Stevens, *Wilderness Chronicles,* 89–90.

5. *Pennsylvania Gazette,* July 3, 1755; *CRP* 6:402, 6:455–58, 6:464; Edward Shippen to William Allen, July 4, 1755, Shippen Family Papers, vol. 1; Dinwiddie to Sharpe, July 5, 1755, *RDP* 2:85.

6. Dinwiddie to Thomas Bryan Martin, July 4, 1755, *RDP* 2:84–85; Dinwiddie to David Stewart, July 16, 1755, *RDP* 100–101; Dinwiddie to John Buchanan, Aug. 11, 1755, *RDP* 154–55; "A Register of Persons who have been either Killed, Wounded or taken Prisoners by the Enemy in Augusta County, as also of such as have made their Escape," William Preston Papers, 1QQ/83; *Maryland Gazette,* Sept. 11, 1755, Sept. 22, 1755, Oct. 2, 1755; "Journal of Occurrences in Canada from October 1755 to June 1756," *NYCD* 10:401; *CRP* 6:465–67, 641–42.

7. Washington to Warner Lewis, Aug. 14, 1755, *GWP* 1:360–63; "Instructions of Dinwiddie to Washington," Aug. 14, 1755, 2:4–6; *VSAL* 6:521–44; *JHB 1752–1755, 1756–1758,* 297–98; James Titus, *The Old Dominion at War: Society, Politics, and Warfare in Late Colonial Virginia* (Columbia: University of South Carolina Press, 1991), 79–80.

8. Stephen to Washington, Oct. 4, 1755, *GWP* 2:72–73; Washington to William Vance, Oct. 10, 1755, *GWP* 2:93; "Register of Persons," William Preston Papers, 1QQ/83; *CRP* 6:641–43.

9. Washington to Dinwiddie, Oct. 11, 1755, *GWP* 2:101–7; *Pennsylvania Gazette*, Oct. 30, 1755.

10. Washington to Dinwiddie, Oct. 11, 1755, *GWP* 2:101–7; "Memorandum and Advertisement," Oct. 13, 1755, *GWP* 2:109–10.

11. Washington to Dinwiddie, Jan. 14, 1756, *RDP* 2:317.

12. Dinwiddie to Stephen, Oct. 3, 1755, *RDP* 2:233–34; *JHB 1752–1755, 1756–1758,* 319–20.

13. *Pennsylvania Gazette,* July 31, 1755.

14. *PA* 8th ser. 5:3932–39; *Pennsylvania Gazette,* Aug. 14, 1755; *CRP* 6:517–43.

15. *CRP* 6:683; "Examination of John Schmick and Henry Fry," Nov. 15, 1755, Horsfield Papers, 1:51–54, APS.

16. *CRP* 6:659–60, 6:672–73.

17. "Petition of the Inhabitants of Penn's Creek," Oct. 20, 1755, Penn Mss.: Indian Affairs, 2:32; William Buchanan and John Armstrong to James Burd, Oct. 27, 1755, Shippen Family Papers, vol. 2.

18. Weiser to Morris, Nov. 18, 1755, Conrad Weiser Papers, 1:60; *CRP* 6:705.

19. *CRP* 6:673–76, 6:706–7; "Meeting of Residents of Cumberland County," Nov. 3, 1755, Lamberton Scotch-Irish Collection, 1:23, HSP.

20. *CRP* 6:673–76, 6:703–5, 6:736–37; Weiser to Morris, Nov. 18, 1755, Conrad Weiser Papers, 1:60; Timothy Horsfield to William Parsons, Nov. 25, 1755, BOEHM pt. 1, 2:736–37; *Pennsylvania Gazette,* Nov. 27, 1755, Dec. 4, 1755; Olmstead, *David Zeisberger,* 89–92.

21. *CRP* 6:667.

22. *CRP* 6:680; "Meeting of the General Council of Cumberland County," Oct. 30, 1755, Lamberton Scotch-Irish Collection, 1:23.

23. "Remonstrance by the Mayor, Aldermen, etc. to the Assembly of Pennsylvania," Nov. 25, 1755, BOEHM pt. 1, 2:714–17; Morris to Thomas Penn, Nov. 28, 1755, BOEHM pt. 1, 2:794–800; *CRP* 6:693–96.

24. Dinwiddie to Allen, Jan. 2, 1756, *RDP* 2:313; Morris to Thomas Penn, Nov. 28, 1755, BOEHM pt. 1, 2:794–800.

25. *CRP* 6:756–61; *Pennsylvania Gazette,* Dec. 18, 1755, Dec. 25, 1755, Jan. 1, 1756.

26. "List of Inhabitants Killed in Northampton County," Dec. 19, 1755, Penn Mss.: Indian Affairs, 2:52.

27. "Deposition of John Craig," Mar. 30, 1756, Penn Mss.: Indian Affairs, 2:78; "List of People Killed or Captured in Berks County," Conrad Weiser Papers, 2:117; *Pennsylvania Gazette,* Mar. 11, 1756, Mar. 18, 1756, Apr. 1, 1756.

28. "Instructions to Ensign Douville," Mar. 23, 1756, *NYCD* 10:396.

29. Edward Shippen to James Burd, Mar. 24, 1756, Shippen Family Papers, vol. 2; *Maryland Gazette,* Apr. 8, 1756; *Pennsylvania Gazette,* Apr. 8, 1756, Apr. 29, 1756, May 6, 1756.

30. Washington to Dinwiddie, Apr. 7, 1756, *GWP* 2:332–35.

31. Washington to Dinwiddie, Apr. 16, 1756, *GWP* 3:1–3; Washington to John Robinson, Apr. 24, 1756, *GWP* 48–51; *Maryland Gazette,* May 6, 1756.

32. Washington to Dinwiddie, Apr. 24, 1756, *GWP* 3:46; Dinwiddie to Washington, Apr. 29, 1756, *GWP* 3:65–67; Dinwiddie to Andrew Lewis, May 5, 1756, *RDP* 2:403–4; *Maryland Gazette*, May 13, 1756.

33. "Memorandum respecting the Militia," May 14, 1756, *GWP* 3:127–28; "Register," William Preston Papers, IQQ/83; *Pennsylvania Gazette*, June 17, 1756, June 24, 1756, Aug. 19, 1756.

34. Robert Stewart to Washington, July 31, 1756, *GWP* 3:303–5; *Pennsylvania Gazette*, July 29, 1756, Sept. 2, 1756; "List of People Killed or Captured in Berks County," Conrad Weiser Papers, 2:117; *CRP* 7:241–45.

35. Dinwiddie to Shirley, Oct. 18, 1755, *RDP* 2:244.

36. Matthew C. Ward, "Fighting the 'Old Women': Indian Strategy on the Virginia and Pennsylvania Frontier, 1754–1748," *VMHB* 103 (1995): 297–320.

37. Vaudreuil to Machault, June 8, 1756.

38. Washington to Dinwiddie, Apr. 24, 1756.

39. Quoted in Frégault, *Canada*, 155.

40. *CRP* 7:97–98.

41. "Abstract of Dispatches received from Canada," June 4, 1756, *NYCD* 10:408; "Abstract of Despatches from America," Aug. 30, 1756, 10:484.

42. Particularly useful for estimating the numbers of casualties are "Register," William Preston Papers, IQQ/83; "Memorandum of Persons Killed and Captured on the Frontier of Lancaster County," Conrad Weiser Papers, 2:89; "List of People Killed or Captured in Bethel Township, Lancaster County," Conrad Weiser Papers, 2:107; "List of People Killed or Captured on South-West side of Schuylkill," Conrad Weiser Papers, 2:109; "List of People Killed or Captured eastwards of River Lecky," Conrad Weiser Papers, 2:115; "List of People Killed or Captured in Berks County," Conrad Weiser Papers, 2:117; and "List of People Killed or Captured in Heidelburg Township," Conrad Weiser Papers, 2:117. In addition, the *Pennsylvania Gazette* and the *Maryland Gazette* carried frequent details of frontier raids (copies of the *Virginia Gazette* are not extant for much of this period). There are also numerous accounts and casualty statistics in *CRP*, vols. 6–8.

43. Washington to Dinwiddie, Apr. 24, 1756, *GWP* 3:45; *VSAL* 7:67; *JHB 1758–1761*, 110; Young, "Effects of the French and Indian War," 207.

44. Millet and Maslowski, *For the Common Defense*, 79; U.S Bureau of the Census, *Historical Statistics of the United States, Colonial Times to 1970*, 2:1168.

45. "Abstract of Despatches from America," Aug. 30, 1756, *NYCD* 10:484.

46. Joseph Turner to David Barclay and Sons, Sept. 10, 1757, Allen and Turner Letterbook.

47. Gough and Carmault to William Neate, July 30, 1757, Gough and Carmault Letterbook, HSP; *Pennsylvania Gazette*, Dec. 23, 1756.

48. Thomas Willing to Mayne, Burns, and Mayne, Dec. 2, 1756, Thomas Willing Letterbook, 241, HSP; Washington to John Augustine Washington, May 28, 1755, *GWP* 1:289–92.

49. Joseph Turner to John and William Halliday, Nov. 11, 1758, Allen and Turner Letterbook; Willing to Charles Digby, May 16, 1757, Willing and Morris Letterbook, 280–81, HSP; Willing to Robert Scott, Aug. 19, 1755, Thomas Willing Let-

terbook, 115; Willing to John Franks, Dec. 31, 1757, Thomas Willing Letterbook, 400; Doerflinger, *A Vigorous Spirit of Enterprise,* 70–71.

50. Receipt Book of John Harris II, 1749–69, Harris-Fisher Family Papers, Box 1, PSA; Nash, *Urban Crucible;* Sheila L. Skemp, "A World Uncertain and Strongly Checker'd," in *Adapting to Conditions: War and Society in the Eighteenth Century,* ed. Maarten Ultee (University: University of Alabama Press, 1986), 99.

51. Young, "Effects of the French and Indian War," 235–36.

52. Washington to Dinwiddie, Oct. 9, 1757, *GWP* 5:12; "James Burd letter," Apr. 23, 1757, Shippen Family Papers, vol. 2; William Denny to James Burd, Oct. 19, 1757, Shippen Family Papers, vol. 3; Hofstra, "'Parcel of Barbarian's,'" 91.

53. Joseph Shippen to Robert Thompson, Apr. 22, 1757, Shippen Family Papers: Military Letter Book of Joseph Shippen, 1756–58; Parsons to Horsfield, July 14, 1756, Horsfield Papers, 1:225.

54. Bouquet to John Forbes, July 11, 1758, *HBP* 2:180; Bouquet to Forbes, Aug. 26, 1758, *HBP* 2:424; "Evening Orders," May 26, 1756, *GWP* 3:177–78; Robert Stewart to Washington, June 20, 1756, *GWP* 3:207–9; Robert Stewart to Washington, Sept. 27, 1757, *GWP* 4:423–24; Washington to Dinwiddie, Oct. 9, 1757, *GWP* 4:10–13.

55. John Billings to Bouquet, June 9, 1758, *HBP* 2:57; Stephen to Bouquet, Aug. 18, 1758, *HBP* 2:386–87; Orme, "Journal," King's Mss., 212:44; "Advertisement sent to Harrisons, & Harrises" Apr. 23, 1757, Shippen Family Papers, vol. 2; "Orders: Carlisle," July 5, 1758, Shippen Family Papers: Orderly Book of Joseph Shippen's Company, 1758.

56. Edward Shippen to Bouquet, June 9, 1758, *HBP* 2:63; "Bouquet Orderly Book," July 2, 1758, *HBP* 2:661; Washington to Thomas Walker, [Jan. 10, 1756], *GWP* 2:269–70.

57. Weiser to Morris, Oct. 26, 1755, BOEHM pt. 1, 2:831; *JHB 1752–1755, 1756–1758,* 350; Charles Smith to Washington, Aug. 15, 1758, *GWP* 5:392.

58. Dinwiddie to Clement Read, Sept. 8, 1756, *RDP* 2:504; Bouquet to Forbes, June 11, 1758, *HBP* 2:73.

59. Tillson, *Gentry and Common Folk,* 20; Mitchell, "'Over the Hills and Far Away,'" 76; Beeman, "Social Change and Cultural Conflict in Virginia," 455–76.

60. Dinwiddie to Board of Trade, Feb. 23, 1756, BOEHM pt. 1, 11:1050.

61. *VSAL* 6: 527, 7:9, 7:14–18; *JHB 1752–1755, 1756–1758,* 381, 397; "Council of War of Officers of Militia of Augusta County," May 20, 1756, William Preston Papers, 1QQ/130; Washington to Lord Loudoun, Jan. 10, 1757, *GWP* 4:79–90; Young, "Effects of the French and Indian War," 56.

62. Bouquet to Forbes, June 3, 1758, *HBP* 2:18; Bouquet to George Stevenson, June 3, 1758, *HBP* 2:27–29; John Ingles to James Burd, July 2, 1756, Shippen Family Papers, vol. 2; *CRP* 6:368; Braddock to Sir Thomas Robinson, Apr. 19, 1755, BOEHM pt. 3, 1:47–56; Orme, "Journal," King's Mss., 212:13, 23.

63. Stevenson to Bouquet, May 30, 1758, *HBP* 1:398.

64. Stephen to Washington, Dec. 23, 1755, *GWP* 2:226–27; Robert Stewart et al. to Washington, Nov. 5, 1756, *GWP* 3:454–55; Gabriel Jones to Washington, Oct. 6, 1757, *GWP* 5:7–8.

65. Washington to Dinwiddie, Oct. 9, 1757, *GWP* 5:10–13.

66. Bouquet to Lt. Col. John Young, Dec. 15, 1756, *HBP* 1:37.

67. "A Report of the Behaviour of the Battoemen," May 1757, Shippen Family Papers, vol. 2.

68. "Deposition of Robert Brown," Aug. 1756, Conrad Weiser Papers, 1:79.

69. "Court Martial," June 19, 1757, *GWP* 4:230; William Taliaferro to Charles Lewis, Sept. 22, 1757, *GWP* 4:419.

70. Armstrong to James Burd, Sept. 13, 1757, Shippen Family Papers, vol. 2.

71. "Orders," Oct. 23, 1755, *GWP* 2:135; Washington to Stephen, Oct. 29, 1755, *GWP* 2:146–47.

72. Washington to Thomas Waggener, [Sept. 6, 1756], *GWP* 3:393; Parsons to Weiser, [Jan.] 1757, Conrad Weiser Papers, 2:67.

73. Alan Rogers, *Empire and Liberty: American Resistance to British Authority, 1755–1763* (Berkeley: University of California Press, 1974); Leach, *Arms for Empire.*

74. Quoted in Charles Brodine, "Civil-Military Relations in Pennsylvania, 1758–1760: An Examination of John Shy's Thesis," *Pennsylvania History* 62 (1995): 215.

75. Bouquet to Young, Dec. 10, 1756, *HBP* 1:32–33; *CRP* 7:358; Joseph Shippen to Edward Shippen, Jan. 19, 1757, Shippen Family Papers, vol. 2; *PA* 8th ser. 4448–96.

76. *CRP* 8:282, 8:285; Weiser to Peters, Nov. 17, 1757, Conrad Weiser Papers, 2:105.

77. Washington to Henry Woodward, May 5, 1756, *GWP* 3:96.

78. Weiser to Bouquet, [June 1758(?)], Conrad Weiser Papers, 2:71.

79. *CRP* 8:282.

80. Bouquet to Edward Shippen, June 3, 1758, Shippen Family Papers, vol. 3.

81. Washington to Dinwiddie, Oct. 11–12, 1755, *RDP* 2:237.

82. "Address of Robert Dinwiddie to the Assembly," Oct. 27, 1755, *RDP* 2:254; Dinwiddie to Earl of Halifax, Nov. 15, 1755, *RDP* 2:272–74; Dinwiddie to Washington, Aug. 19, 1756, *RDP* 2:479–83; Dinwiddie to Henry Fox, May 10, 1756 BOEHM pt. 1, 3:12–15.

83. Washington to Dinwiddie, Oct. 11–12, 1755, *RDP* 2:237.

84. Stephen to Washington, Dec. 23, 1755; Washington to Dinwiddie, Oct. 9, 1757.

85. Edmund Pendleton to [William Preston(?)], May 12, 1756, William Preston Papers, 1QQ:126–28; *PA* 4th ser. 2:552; Morris to Thomas Penn, Nov. 28, 1755, BOEHM pt. 1, 2:794–800; Tillson, *Gentry and Common Folk,* 39–40.

86. For a discussion of some of the problems related to "class" consciousness in Virginia, see Allan Kulikoff, *The Agrarian Origins of American Capitalism* (Charlottesville: University Press of Virginia, 1992); Allan Kulikoff, *From British Peasants to Colonial American Farmers* (Chapel Hill: University of North Carolina Press, 2000). For the classic definition of "class consciousness" see E. P. Thompson, *The Making of the English Working Class* (London: Victor Gollancz, 1965).

87. Weiser to James Burd, June 7, 1757, Shippen Family Papers, vol. 2.

88. William Smith, *A Brief State of the Province of Pennsylvania* (London: R. Griffiths, 1755), 40.

89. William Smith, *Brief State*, 41–42.

90. Quoted in Theodore Thayer, *Pennsylvania Politics and the Growth of Democracy, 1740–1776* (Harrisburg: Pennsylvania Historical and Museum Commission, 1953), 36.

91. *CRP* 6:503, 6:533.

92. *CRP* 6:599.

93. *CRP* 6:705; Weiser to Morris, Nov. 18, 1755, Conrad Weiser Papers, 1:60.

94. Shippen Letter, Oct. 29, 1755, Horsfield Papers, 1:31; Jacob Orndt to Weiser, Aug. 24, 1756, Horsfield Papers, 2:302–3; George Reynolds to Weiser, Aug. 26, 1756, Horsfield Papers, 2:308.

95. Parsons to Weiser, Jan. 28, 1757, Conrad Weiser Papers, 2:30; R. S Stephenson, "Pennsylvania Provincial Soldiers in the Seven Years' War," *Pennsylvania History* 62 (1995): 201.

96. "Lt. Schlosser's Advertisement for Recruits," July 2, 1756. Horsfield Papers, 1:157; *CRP* 7:180.

97. Dinwiddie to Abercromby, July 1, 1756, *RDP* 2:457.

98. Dinwiddie to Abercromby, July 24, 1756, *RDP* 2:466.

99. Dinwiddie to Loudoun, Sept. 8, 1756, *RDP* 2:498.

100. *EJVC* 5:449–52, 6:68–69.

101. Washington to Dinwiddie, [Sept. 28, 1756], *GWP* 3:421.

102. Dinwiddie to Washington, Oct. 24, 1757, *RDP* 2:710; Washington to Dinwiddie, Oct. 5, 1757, *GWP* 5:4; *Maryland Gazette*, Dec. 15, 1757.

103. Washington to Dinwiddie, June 25, 1756, *GWP* 3:222–24; Dinwiddie to Washington, June(?) 1756, *RDP* 2:434.

104. Washington to Dinwiddie, Aug. 4, 1756, *GWP* 3:315.

105. Dinwiddie to Washington, Aug. 19, 1756, *RDP* 2:481.

Notes to Chapter 4

1. Forbes to William Pitt, Sept. 6, 1758, in Alfred Proctor James, ed., *The Writings of General John Forbes Relating to His Service in North America* (Menasha: Collegiate Press, 1938), 205.

2. Jennings, *Ambiguous Iroquois Empire*, 145–60.

3. William L. Shea, *The Virginia Militia in the Seventeenth Century* (Baton Rouge: Louisiana State University Press, 1975); Lawrence Delbert Cress, *Citizens in Arms: The Army and Militia in American Society to the War of 1812*, Studies on Armed Forces and Society (Chapel Hill: University of North Carolina Press, 1982).

4. Dinwiddie to County Lieutenants, June 17, 1755, *RDP* 2:67; Washington to Dinwiddie, Oct. 11, 1755, *RDP* 2:239.

5. Dinwiddie to Sir Thomas Robinson, July 23, 1755, *RDP* 2:112.

6. Dinwiddie to William Wright, July 8, 1755, *RDP* 2:92; "Memorandum respecting the Militia," May 7, 1756, *GWP* 3:97; "Memorandum respecting the Militia," May 12, 1756, *GWP* 3:119; Washington to Lord Fairfax, Aug. 29, 1756, *GWP* 3:380–381; *VSAL* 6:541, 6:548; *JHB 1752–1755, 1756–1758*, 161, 449.

7. Washington to Dinwiddie, Nov. 9, 1756, *GWP* 4:1; "Forum: Historians and

Guns," *WMQ* 59 (2002): 203–68; Michael Bellesiles, *Arming America: The Origins of a National Gun Culture* (New York: Alfred A. Knopf, 2000).

8. Dinwiddie to Sharpe, July 30, 1757, *RDP* 2:677; Dinwiddie to Board of Trade, Feb. 23, 1756, BOEHM pt. 1, 11:1049.

9. Washington to Dinwiddie, Apr. 16, 1756, *GWP* 2:385.

10. Parsons to Morris, July 14, 1756, Northampton County Records: Miscellaneous Papers, 1:209, HSP.

11. Washington to Loudoun, Jan. 10, 1757, *GWP* 4:87.

12. Washington to Dinwiddie, June 26, 1757, *GWP* 4:2; Washington to Dinwiddie, Nov. 9, 1756, *GWP* 264–66; Dinwiddie to Captain Hogg, Nov. 1, 1756, *RDP* 2:537.

13. Dinwiddie to Colonel Patton, July 16, 1755, *RDP* 2:101; Dinwiddie to William Byrd, July 22, 1755, *RDP* 2:110.

14. Dinwiddie to John Buchanan, Aug. 11, 1755, *RDP* 2:155.

15. "Memorandum respecting the Militia," May 8, 1756, *GWP* 3:99.

16. Washington to Dinwiddie, May 23, 1756, *GWP* 3:171.

17. Christopher Wilson and John Hunt letter, Nov. 4, 1755, Additional Mss., 33029:355; Weiser to Peters, Oct. 2, 1755, Conrad Weiser Papers, 1:56.

18. *PA* 8th ser. 5:4096–109.

19. "Remonstrance by the Mayor, Aldermen, etc. to the Assembly of Pennsylvania," Nov. 25, 1755, BOEHM pt. 1, 2:714–17; *CRP* 6:695.

20. James T. Mitchell and Henry Flanders, eds., *The Statutes at Large of Pennsylvania from 1682 to 1809*, 18 vols. (Harrisburg: C. M. Busch, 1896), 5:197–201.

21. Peters to Thomas Penn, Feb. 17, 1756, Penn Mss.: Official Correspondence, 8:29; *Pennsylvania Gazette*, Jan. 8, 1756; "The Organization of John Van Etten's Company," Jan. 12, 1756, in Leonard Woods Labaree, William Bradford Willcox, and Barbara Oberg, eds., *The Papers of Benjamin Franklin*, 35– vols. (New Haven: Yale University Press, 1959–), 6:355.

22. Mitchell and Flanders, *Statutes of Pennsylvania*, 5: 219–21, 5:266–68.

23. "General Instructions for Recruiting," Sept. 1–3, 1755, *GWP* 2:13; Washington to Dinwiddie, Nov. 9, 1756, *GWP* 4:4; Dinwiddie to Shirley, Jan. 24, 1756, *RDP* 2:328–31.

24; *VSAL* 6:527, 7:9, 7:14–18, 7:61–63, 7:70; *JHB 1752–1755, 1756–1758*, 381, 397; "Council of War of Officers of Militia of Augusta County," May 20, 1756, William Preston Papers, 1QQ/130; Dinwiddie to Loudoun, Oct. 28, 1756, *RDP* 2:532; Dinwiddie to Colonel Bland, Aug. 24, 1757, *RDP* 2:688; Washington to Loudoun, Jan. 10, 1757, *GWP* 4:79–90.

25. Washington to Loudoun, Jan. 10, 1757, *GWP* 4:81.

26. Titus, *Old Dominion at War*, 122; Jennings, *Empire of Fortune*, 334.

27. Robert Strettell to Shirley, Jan. 24, 1756, Penn Mss.: Official Correspondence, 8:25; *CRP* 7:39–40; Mitchell and Flanders, *Statutes of Pennsylvania*, 5:219–21, 5:266–68.

28. Peters to Thomas Penn, Feb. 18, 1756, Penn Mss.: Official Correspondence, 8:43.

29. *CRP* 7:45.

30. Benjamin Franklin to Isaac Norris, May 30, 1757, in Labaree, Willcox, and Oberg, *The Papers of Benjamin Franklin,* 7:227–28; "List of Servants Belonging to the Inhabitants of Penna. & Taken into His Majesty's Service for whom Satisfaction has not been made by Officers according to act of Parliament," Apr. 1757, HSP (photocopy of original in Huntington Library, Ca.).

31. *PA* 4th ser. 2:764–67, 8th ser. 6:4555; Joseph Turner to David Barclay and Sons, Sept. 22, 1756, Allen and Turner Letterbook; Sharon Salinger, *To Serve Well and Faithfully: Labor and Indentured Servants in Pennsylvania, 1682–1800* (Cambridge: Cambridge University Press, 1987), 73.

32. Joseph Turner to Jacob Bosanquet, Sept. 1756, Allen and Turner Letterbook; Salinger, *To Serve Well,* 128.

33. *CRP* 7:153.

34. Morris to Washington, Feb. 2, 1756, *GWP* 2:316–17; Stephen to Washington, Aug. 1, 1756, *GWP* 3:309–10; Robert Stewart to Washington, Dec. 12, 1758, *GWP* 6:168; Roy Bird Cook, "Virginia's Frontier Defenses, 1719–1795," *West Virginia History* 1 (1940): 119–20; Waddell, "Defending the Long Perimeter," 171–95.

35. Washington to Waggener, Jan. 9, 1756, 2:265–66; Andrew Lewis to Preston, Feb. 26, 1757, William Preston Papers, 1QQ/150–51; "Meeting of the General Council of Cumberland County," Oct. 30, 1755, Lamberton Scotch-Irish Collection, 1:23; William Hunter, *Forts on the Pennsylvania Frontier, 1753–1758* (Harrisburg: Pennsylvania Historical and Museum Commission, 1960), 548–64; Chester Raymond Young, "The Effects of the French and Indian War on Civilian Life in the Frontier Counties of Virginia, 1754–1763" (Ph.D. diss., Vanderbilt University, 1969), 205.

36. Dinwiddie to Washington, Aug. 19, 1756, *RDP* 2:479–83; "Council of War," July 10, 1756, *GWP* 3:243–46; Washington to Dinwiddie, Aug. 4, 1756, *GWP* 3:312–16; Waddell, "Defending the Long Perimeter," 180.

37. Bouquet to Forbes, May 22, 1758, May 25, 1758, June 7, 1758, all *HBP* 1:351, 1:361, 2:47–51.

38. Bouquet to Forbes, June 21, 1758, and July 11, 1758, both *HBP* 2:121–22, 2:180–81.

39. Bouquet to Sir John St. Clair, June 30, 1758, *HBP* 2:149; "Proceedings of Court Martial at Raystown," Aug. 30, 1758, Shippen Family Papers, vol. 3.

40. William Smith, *Historical Account,* 44.

41. Orme, "Journal," King's Mss., 212:23–90; Dinwiddie to Sir Thomas Robinson, June 23, 1755, BOEHM pt. 1, 2:314; *CRP* 8:59; King Lawrence Parker, "Anglo-American Wilderness Campaigning, 1754–1764: Logistical and Tactical Developments" (PhD. diss., Columbia University, 1970), 79.

42. There is no extant copy of the *Virginia Gazette* for this date. The editorial was reprinted in the *Maryland Gazette,* Nov. 25, 1756.

43. Dinwiddie to Dobbs, Dec. 13, 1755, *RDP* 2:290; Dinwiddie to Andrew Lewis, Jan. 15, 1756, *RDP* 2:320–22; Dinwiddie to Preston, Dec. 15, 1755, and "William Preston's Diary of the Sandy Creek Expedition," both William Preston Papers, 1QQ/90, 1QQ/96–97; "Negotiations of Governor Dinwiddie with the Cherokees," Oct. 1, 1755, BOEHM pt. 1, 2:493–98.

44. Dinwiddie to John Smith, Jan. 15, 1756, *RDP* 2:322–23; Dinwiddie to Obadiah Wilson, Jan. 15, 1756, *RDP* 2:323; Dinwiddie to Pearis, Jan. 15, 1756, *RDP* 2:324–25; "William Preston's Diary," William Preston Papers, QQ/96–123.

45. "William Preston's Diary," William Preston Papers, QQ/96–123.

46. Peter Hog to Washington, Apr. 3, 1756, *GWP* 2:330; *JHB 1752–1755, 1756–1758,* 368, 385; *Maryland Gazette,* May 6, 1756.

47. *Maryland Gazette,* May 6, 1756, June 10, 1756; Stephen to Washington, May 29, 1756, *GWP* 3:182–83.

48. Morris letter, Sept. 1756, Gratz Collection, Case 15, Box 18, HSP; *CRP* 6:781, 7:230–33.

49. Armstrong to Denny, Sept. 14, 1756, Penn Mss.: Indian Affairs, 2:100; James P. Myers Jr., "Pennsylvania's Awakening: The Kittanning Raid of 1756," *Pennsylvania History* 66 (1999): 399–420.

50. *Maryland Gazette,* Nov. 25, 1756.

51. "Col. Burd's Journal at Ft. Augusta," Mar. 1757, Edward Shippen Thompson Family Papers, Box 2, Folder 13; Dinwiddie to Sir Thomas Robinson, Aug. 20, 1755, BOEHM pt. 1, 2:449–51; "Captain Widerhold Letter," Aug. 12, 1756, Horsfield Papers, 2:253–54.52. "Col. Burd's Journal," Mar. 1757, Edward Shippen Thompson Family Papers; Joseph Shippen to James Burd, Jan. 21, 1760, Shippen Family Papers, vol. 5; Anderson, *People's Army.*

53. Washington to Denis McCarty, Nov. 22, 1755, *GWP* 2:176; Washington to Dinwiddie, Nov. 9, 1756 *GWP* 4:1–6; Washington to Sharpe, July 20, 1757, *GWP* 4:318–19.

54. Joseph Shippen to James Burd, May 31, 1757, and Joseph Shippen to James Burd, June 7, 1757, both Shippen Family Papers, vol. 2.

55. "Petition of John Catlet," [1759(?)], *FFP* 1:140–41; Robert Carter Nicholas to Washington, Aug. 18, 1756, *GWP* 3:356–57.

56. Lewis Ourry to Bouquet, Dec. 20, 1758, *HBP* 2:638; Edward Biddle to James Burd, Aug. 5, 1759, Shippen Family Papers, vol. 4; *Virginia Gazette,* Sept. 5, 1755.

57. Reynolds to Weiser, Aug. 1756, Northampton County Records: Miscellaneous Papers, 1:187; "Captain Widerhold Letter," Aug. 12, 1756, Horsfield Papers, 2:253–54.

58. "Orders: Carlisle," July 5, 1758, Orderly Book of Joseph Shippen's Company, 1758, Shippen Family Papers; "Orderly Book," Sept. 22, 1758, *GWP* 6:32; "Orderly Book," Nov. 24, 1758, *GWP* 6:156–57; "Orderly Book of Captain Thomas Hamilton's Company," Sept. 30, 1759, Cumberland County Historical Society; "Bouquet Orderly Book," July 3, 1758, *HBP* 2:662.

59. "Orders: Carlisle," July 5, 1758, Orderly Book of Joseph Shippen's Company, 1758, Shippen Family Papers; "Orders," July 2, 1759, and Sept. 30, 1759, both in "Orderly Book of Captain Thomas Hamilton's Company," Cumberland County Historical Society.

60. Bouquet to Forbes, May 25, 1758, *HBP* 1:361.

61. Selesky, *War and Society in Colonial Connecticut;* Anderson, *People's Army.*

62. Mitchell and Flanders, *Statutes of Pennsylvania,* 5:197–201, 5:219–21, 5:266–68; Stephenson, "Pennsylvania Provincial Soldiers in the Seven Years' War," 196–213.

63. Washington to Dinwiddie, Oct. 11, 1755, *GWP* 2:102–3; *JHB 1752–1755, 1756–1758*, 319–20.

64. Anderson, *People's Army*, 127–28.

65. Washington to John Stanwix, July 15, 1757, *GWP* 4:306–7; Washington to Dinwiddie, Aug. 3, 1757, *GWP* 4:360; "Orderly Book of Captain Thomas Hamilton's Company," July 19, 1759, Cumberland County Historical Society.

66. "Court Martial," May 3, 1756, *GWP* 3:77–79; Washington to Dinwiddie, May 3, 1756, *GWP* 3:84; "After Orders," May 18, 1756, *GWP* 3:154.

67. "Orders," July, 6, 1756, July 7, 1756, July 8, 1756, *GWP* 3:238:41; Stephen to Washington, July 25, 1756, *GWP* 3:294.

68. Anderson, *People's Army*, 33–35, 38.

69. Anderson, *People's Army*, 39.

70. Anderson, *People's Army*, 67.

71. Dinwiddie to Shirley, Apr. 28, 1756, *RDP* 2:395; Dinwiddie to Washington, Aug. 19, 1756, *RDP* 2:481; Joseph Shippen to James Burd, May 19, 1757, Shippen Family Papers, vol. 2.

72. Selesky, *War and Society in Connecticut*, 173.

73. See table 1 in the appendix.

74. Anderson, *People's Army*, 239; John E. Ferling, "Soldiers for Virginia: Who Served in the French and Indian War?" *Virginia Magazine of History and Biography* 94 (1986): 307–28; Titus, *Old Dominion at War*, 78–88.

75. *PA* 2d ser. 2:419.

76. "Size Rolls for the Virginia Regiment," Washington Papers, microfilm (Washington, D.C.: Library of Congress, Manuscript Division, 1964), ser. 4, reels 29–31.

77. See table 2 in the appendix.

78. See table 3 in the appendix.

79. See table 4 in the appendix.

80. Anderson, *People's Army*, 161–64.

81. Ferling, "School for Command," 202.

82. Edward Shippen to Peters, July 22, 1756, Shippen Family Papers, vol. 2.

83. Dinwiddie to Captain Mercer, Jan. 15, 1755, *RDP* 1:463

84. Dinwiddie to Washington, Jan. 26, 1757, *RDP* 2:584–85; "Orders," July 12, 1756, *GWP* 3:251–53, 3:319.

85. "Dinwiddie's Instructions to Washington," May 16, 1757, *RDP* 2:622; Washington to Dinwiddie, May 24, 1757, *GWP* 4:162.

86. Washington to Loudoun, Jan. 10, 1757, *GWP* 4:87; James Burd to Armstrong, Sept. 6, 1758, in "Letter Book of Col. James Burd," 1756–58, 176–78, Shippen Family Papers.

87. Forbes to Bouquet, Sept. 4, 1758, in James, *Writings of Forbes*, 199; Washington to John Robinson, Aug. 5, 1756, *GWP* 3:323–31; Washington to John Robinson, Nov. 9, 1756, *GWP* 4:11–18; Washington to John Robinson, Dec. 19, 1756, *GWP* 4:67–69; Dinwiddie to Washington, Nov. 16, 1756, *RDP* 2:551–53.

88. "Memorandum respecting the Militia," May 8, 1756, *GWP* 3:99.

89. Bouquet to Forbes, Aug. 30, 1758, *HBP* 2:450; Washington to Dinwiddie, Jan.

14, 1756, *GWP* 2:283–84; Washington to Charles Lewis, Jan. 27, 1756, *GWP* 2:297–98; Washington to Joshua Beall, Nov. 1, 1757, *GWP* 5:37–38.

90. Edward Shippen to James Burd, June 29, 1756, and John Ingles to James Burd, July 2, 1756, both Shippen Family Papers, vol. 2; Armstrong Starkey, *European and Native American Warfare, 1675–1815* (London: UCL Press, 1998), 45–47; Don Higginbotham, *George Washington and the American Military Tradition* (Athens: University of Georgia Press, 1985), 15.

91. Washington to Dinwiddie, May 24, 1757, *GWP* 4:161–63.

92. Quoted in Higginbotham, *Washington and the American Military Tradition*, 31.

Notes to Chapter 5

1. Dinwiddie to Capel Hanbury, May 10, 1754, *RDP* 1:153; John Richard Alden, *Robert Dinwiddie: Servant of the Crown* (Charlottesville: University Press of Virginia, 1973), 26–37.

2. Dinwiddie to Abercromby, Sept. 1, 1754, *RDP* 1:298–300; Jack P. Greene, ed., *The Diary of Colonel Landon Carter of Sabine Hall, 1752–1778*, 2 vols. (Charlottesville: University Press of Virginia, 1965), 1:111–14.

3. Dinwiddie to Halifax, Feb. 24, 1755, *RDP* 1:512–17; Dinwiddie to Dobbs, Nov. 13, 1755, *RDP* 2:265–66; *VSAL* 7:9, 7:14–18; *JHB* 6:397; Jack P. Greene, *The Quest for Power: The Lower Houses of Assembly in the Southern Royal Colonies, 1689–1776* (Chapel Hill: University of North Carolina Press, 1963), 121–22.

4. G. B. Warden, "The Proprietary Group in Pennsylvania, 1754–1764," *WMQ* 3d ser. 21 (1964): 367–89.

5. *CRP* 6:206–11, 6:237–40, 6:244–46, 6:307; Morris to Sir Thomas Robinson, Dec. 24, 1754, BOEHM pt. 1, 2:6–12.

6. William Smith, *Brief State*, 10–11.

7. *An Answer to an Invidious Pamphlet, Intituled,* a Brief State of the Province of Pennsylvania (London: S. Bladon, 1755), 62–63.

8. Thayer, *Pennsylvania Politics and the Growth of Democracy*, 40–42.

9. *CRP* 6:525–26, 6:691–92, 6:695, 6:731; *PA* 8th ser. 6:4101, 6:4102–3; Peters to Weiser, Oct. 14, 1755, Conrad Weiser Papers, 1:57; *PA* 8th ser. 6:4431–33, 6:4641, 6:4590; Mitchell and Flanders, *Statutes of Pennsylvania*, 5:197–201.

10. Mitchell and Flanders, *Statutes of Pennsylvania*, 5:219–21; Ralph L. Ketcham, "Conscience, War and Politics in Pennsylvania, 1755–1757," *WMQ* 3d ser. 20 (1963): 427–29.

11. Thayer, *Pennsylvania Politics*, 54–55; Marc Egnal, *A Mighty Empire: The Origins of the American Revolution* (Ithaca: Cornell University Press, 1988), 80.

12. "The Petition of the Inhabitants of Pennsylvania Considered," Additional Mss., 15,489:47–56; Benjamin H. Newcomb, *Franklin and Galloway: A Political Partnership* (New Haven: Yale University Press, 1972), 28–30.

13. James Read letter, Oct. 7, 1756, Northampton County Records: Miscellaneous Papers, 1:229, HSP; "Members of the House of Assembly in Philadelphia as they stood October 14 1756," Additional Mss., 33,029:354; Ketcham, "Conscience, War and Politics," 432.

14. Denny to Thomas Penn, Nov. 4, 1756, Penn Mss.: Official Correspondence, 8:197; *Pennsylvania Gazette*, Sept. 23, 1756.

15. Peters to Thomas Penn, Sept. 16, 1756, Penn Mss.: Official Correspondence, 8:157; *PA* 8th ser. 6:4320–27, 6:4496–4504; *CRP* 7:249–57, 7:401–3, 7:409–10.

16. Ketcham, "Conscience, War and Politics," 416–39; Illick, *Colonial Pennsylvania*, 222–24.

17. Jennings, *Empire of Fortune*, 359–60.

18. *PA* 8th ser. 5:4102; *CRP* 6:693.

19. "Deposition of David Zeisberger," Nov. 22, 1755, BOEHM pt. 1, 2:718–19; Israel Spangenburg to Horsfield, Dec. 17, 1755, Horsfield Papers, 1:97; *PA* 4th ser. 2:562–65.

20. *CRP* 7:64–69; "Speech of Sir William Johnson to the Iroquois," Dec. 7, 1755, and "Indian Treaty at Fort Johnson," Feb. 1756, both Penn Mss.: Indian Affairs, 2:65, 2:66–68.

21. *PA* 4th ser. 2:591–92; *CRP* 7:83–94; "Minutes of the Friendly Association," 5, HSP.

22. *CRP* 7:103–5.

23. "Message of Governor Morris to Susquehanna Indians," Apr. 26, 1756, Penn Mss.: Indian Affairs, 2:81; "Minutes of the Friendly Association," 7–8; *CRP* 7:117.

24. "Minutes of Council with Indians," Apr. 23, 1756, Friendly Association Records, 1:123.

25. Letter to Thomas Penn, Apr. 29, 1756, Penn Mss.: Indian Affairs, 2:83; Anthony F. C Wallace, *King of the Delawares: Teedyuscung, 1700–1763* (Philadelphia: University of Pennsylvania Press, 1949), 87–97.

26. "Indian Intelligence," 1756, Horsfield Papers, 324; "Report of Capt. Newcastle, Jagrea, and William Lacquis," May 31, 1756, and "Minutes of Council in Easton," July 25, 1756, both Penn Mss.: Indian Affairs, 2:87, 2:97; *CRP* 7:64–67; Olmstead, *David Zeisberger*, 80.

27. *CRP* 7:163–64, 7:169, 7:198–201; *PA* 4th ser. 2:638–39.

28. "Minutes of the Friendly Association," 11–12, 25.

29. *CRP* 7:190–92.

30. Parsons to Morris, July 14, 1756, Northampton County Records: Miscellaneous Papers, 1:209; "Minutes of the Council at Easton," July 26, 1756, Penn Mss.: Indian Affairs, 2:97.

31. Wallace, *King of the Delawares*, 1–2; *CRP* 7:216.

32. "Minutes of the Friendly Association," 12; *CRP* 7:204–6.

33. "Minutes of the Treaty of Easton," Friendly Association Records, 1:155; "Minutes of the Friendly Association," 12b.

34. "Treaty held at Easton," July 1756, Friendly Association Records, 1:143; "Minutes of a Council at Easton," July 29, 1756, Penn Mss.: Indian Affairs, 2:97; *PA* 2d ser. 2:640–45.

35. "Minutes of the Friendly Association," 14.

36. Morris to Board of Trade, [Sept.] 1756, Gratz Collection; "Minutes of the Friendly Association," 14b; *Pennsylvania Gazette*, Oct. 21, 1756; *CRP* 7:222, 7:278, 7:284–89; *PA* 4th ser. 2:7729–34, 2:7742.

37. "Minutes of the Friendly Association," 15.

38. "Minutes of the Friendly Association," 16–17.

39. "Minutes of the Friendly Association," 19–20.

40. *PA* 4th ser. 2:743–45.

41. *CRP* 7:323–25.

42. "Minutes of the Friendly Association," 20–21.

43. "In Reference to the Walking Purchase," Friendly Association Records, 1:407; "Minutes of the Friendly Association," 20.

44. Charles Thomson, *An Enquiry into the Causes of the Alienation of the Delaware and Shawanese Indians from the British Interest* . . . (London: J. Wilkie, 1759); *CRP* 7:325; "Interview of Tatamy, Pamshire, and Teedyuscung, with Conrad Weiser," Nov. 26, 1756, Penn Mss.: Indian Affairs, 2:106.

45. For a discussion of the Walking Purchase see Jennings, *Ambiguous Iroquois Empire*.

46. "Petition of the Inhabitants of Pennsylvania Considered," Additional Mss., 15,489:47–56; *CRP* 7:394–98.

47. "Proprietors of Pennsylvania's Observations on Sir William Johnson's Letter," Dec. 11, 1756, Penn Mss.: Indian Affairs, 2:108.

48. *CRP* 7:354–55.

49. *PA* 4th ser. 2:847–48; "Pennsylvania Assembly Committee: Report on the Easton Conference," Jan. 29, 1757, in Labaree, Willcox, and Oberg, *The Papers of Benjamin Franklin*, 7:111–14.

50. *CRP* 7:326–27.

51. *PA* 4th ser. 2:758.

52. "Deposition of Andrew Lewis on negotiations with Cherokees," July 1756, BOEHM pt. 1, 3:123–27; Andrew Lewis to Dinwiddie, July 23, 1756, BOEHM pt. 1, 3:128–35; David H. Corkran, *The Cherokee Frontier: Conflict and Survival, 1740–1762* (Norman: University of Oklahoma Press, 1962), 71–101; Tom Hatley, *Dividing Paths: Cherokees and South Carolinians through the Revolutionary Era* (New York: Oxford University Press, 1995), 108–11; John Oliphant, *Peace and War on the Anglo-Cherokee Frontier, 1756–63* (Basingstoke: Palgrave, 2001).

53. Vaudreuil to Machault, Apr. 19, 1757, *NYCD* 10:539–40; Washington to Stanwix, June 28, 1757, *GWP* 4:270; *EJVC* 6:33.

54. George Mercer to Washington, Apr. 24, 1757, *GWP* 4:139–41; Gregory Evans Dowd, "Gift Giving and the Cherokee-British Alliance in the Seven Years' War," in *Contact Points: American Frontiers from the Mohawk Valley to the Mississippi*, ed. Andrew R. L. Cayton and Fredrika Teute (Chapel Hill: University of North Carolina Press, 1998), 114–50.

55. Dinwiddie to Andrew Lewis, Aug. 23, 1756, *RDP* 2:486–88; George Mason to Washington, Sept. 13, 1756, *GWP* 3:406–7.

56. *VSAL* 7:61–63, 7:116–18; *JHB 1752–1755, 1756–1758*, 401–3; *EJVC* 6:28–33.

57. Montcalm to Marc Pierre de Voyer, count d'Argenson, Apr. 24, 1757, *NYCD* 10:548; William Fairfax to Washington, Mar. 31, 1757, *GWP* 4:124–25; James Baker to Washington, June 10, 1757, *GWP* 4:200.

58. *EJVC* 6:44–46; Washington to Dinwiddie, May 30, 1757, *GWP* 4:171–73; Washington to Andrew Lewis, June 3, 1757, *GWP* 4:179.

59. "George Croghan's Journal," May–June 1757, Penn Mss.: Indian Affairs, 3:11–13.

60. *CRP* 7:600, 7:630–32; Washington to Stanwix, July 15, 1757, *GWP* 4:306–7.

61. *EJVC* 6:39–40, 6:45; Dinwiddie to Clement Read, Apr. 12, 1757, *RDP* 2:609–10; Dinwiddie to Clement Read, Apr. 15, 1757, *RDP* 2:612–13; Corkran, *Cherokee Frontier*, 115–27.

62. George Mercer to Washington, Apr. 24, 1757, *GWP* 4:139–41; George Mercer to Washington, Apr. 26, 1757, *GWP* 4:142–43.

63. Montcalm to d'Argenson, Apr. 24, 1757, *NYCD* 10:547–50; M. Doreil to d'Argenson, May 5, 1757, *NYCD* 10:563–64.

64. D. Peter MacLeod, "Microbes and Muskets: Smallpox and the Participation of the Amerindian Allies of New France in the Seven Years' War," *Ethnohistory* 39 (1992): 42–64; Steele, *Betrayals*, 80–81.

65. *Pennsylvania Gazette*, Nov. 11, 1756; *CRP* 7:302–4, 7:357; Vaudreuil to Rouillé, July 12, 1757, in Kent and Stevens, *Wilderness Chronicles*, 98–104.

66. *Pennsylvania Gazette*, Apr. 28, 1757, May 5, 1757, May 26, 1757; "Col. Burd's Journal," Mar. 1757, Edward Shippen Thompson Family Papers; Bartram Galbreath to James Burd, May 23, 1757, Shippen Family Papers, vol. 2; Montcalm to Antoine René de Voyer d'Argenson, marquis de Paulmy, July 11, 1757, *NYCD* 10:580–83; Vaudreuil to François Marie Peirenne de Moras, July 11, 1757, *NYCD* 10:589–90; Denny to Thomas Penn, Apr. 8, 1757, BOEHM pt. 1, 3:215–17; *CRP* 7:492–94.

67. Washington to Dinwiddie, June 16, 1757, *GWP* 4:217–18; "Memorandum," June 16, 1757, *GWP* 4:220–21; Montcalm to de Paulmy, July 11, 1757, *NYCD* 10:580–581; Dinwiddie to William Henry Lyttleton, May 26, 1757, *RDP* 2:632–33.

68. "Council of War," June 16, 1757, *GWP* 4:219–20.

69. Washington to Andrew Lewis, June 16, 1757, *GWP* 4:221–22.

70. John Dagworthy to Washington, June 17, 1757, *GWP* 4:226; Montcalm to de Paulmy, July 11, 1757, *NYCD* 10:581–83.

71. William Withers to Andrew Lewis, Aug. 15, 1757, *RDP* 2:686; *EJVC* 6:59–60; Clement Read to Preston, Aug. 9, 1757, William Preston Papers, 1QQ/154–57.

72. Washington to Dinwiddie, Sept. 17, 1757, *GWP* 4: 408; Lewis Stephens to Washington, Sept. 20, 1757, *GWP* 4:416–17; Robert Rutherford to Washington, Nov. 22, 1757, *GWP* 5:57; *Maryland Gazette*, Oct. 13, 1757.

73. Peters to Weiser, Dec. 7, 1756, Conrad Weiser Papers, 1:91; *CRP* 7:384, 7:434–35; "Instructions to George Croghan," Feb. 16, 1757, Penn Mss.: Indian Affairs, 3:2; *PA* 4th ser. 2:770.

74. William Penn to Peters, Mar. 8, 1757, Penn Mss.: Indian Affairs, 3:3; "Minutes of the Friendly Association," 30–32; *CRP* 7:392–97.

75. *CRP* 7:465–66, 7:474–77, 510; George Croghan to James Burd, Apr. 3, 1757, Shippen Family Papers, vol. 2.

76. "George Croghan's report on proceedings with the Iroquois at Lancaster," Apr. and May 1757, Penn Mss.: Indian Affairs, 3:5–9; *CRP* 7:484–88.

77. John Harris to James Burd, June 6, 1757, Shippen Family Papers, vol. 2; *CRP* 7:498–99, 7:513.

78. *CRP* 7:518–28, 7:540.

79. *CRP* 7:540–41.

80. *CRP* 7:542.

81. Vaudreuil to Rouillé, July 12, 1757, in Kent and Stevens, *Wilderness Chronicles*, 98–104; Montcalm to de Paulmy, July 11, 1757, *NYCD* 10:582.

82. *CRP* 7:465; Vaudreuil to de Moras, July 13, 1757, *NYCD* 10:582, 10:589–90.

83. Montcalm to de Paulmy, July 11, 1757, *NYCD* 10:583.

84. "Extract from Conrad Weiser's Journal," Conrad Weiser Papers, 2:77; *PA* 4th ser. 2:835.

85. "Minutes of the Friendly Association," 38.

86. *PA* 4th ser. 2:837.

87. "Address of the Friendly Association to Denny," July 14, 1757, Penn Mss.: Indian Affairs, 3:17–18; *PA* 4th ser. 2:837–38.

88. *CRP* 7:683.

89. *CRP* 7:677.

90. *CRP* 7:677; "Minutes of a Council at Easton," July and Aug. 1757, Penn Mss.: Indian Affairs, 3:19–22.

91. *CRP* 7:677–78, 7:683; *PA* 4th ser. 2:853–54.

92. *CRP* 7:687–91; *PA* 4th ser. 2:855–61; "Minutes of a Council at Easton," July and Aug. 1757, Penn Mss.: Indian Affairs, 3:19–22.

93. "Minutes of a Council at Easton," July and Aug. 1757, Penn Mss.: Indian Affairs, 3:19–22; "Minutes of the Treaty at Easton," *NYCD* 7:305–9; *CRP* 7:687–714; *PA* 4th ser. 2:863–64.

94. *CRP* 7:710.

95. Edward Shippen to James Burd, Aug. 23, 1757, Shippen Family Papers, vol. 3; *Pennsylvania Gazette*, July 14, 1757, Aug. 18, 1757, Sept. 1, 1757, Sept. 15, 1757; *CRP* 7:705–7, 7:735.

96. *Pennsylvania Gazette*, Aug. 4, 1757, Oct. 6, 1757; *PA* 4th ser. 2:870–72; *CRP* 7:757.

97. *Pennsylvania Gazette*, Sept. 8, 1757; Thomas Lloyd to James Burd, Oct. 8, 1757, Shippen Family Papers, vol. 3.

98. Washington to Dinwiddie, Oct. 5, 1757, *GWP* 5:4.

Notes to Chapter 6

1. Howard H. Peckham, *The Colonial Wars, 1689–1762* (Chicago: University of Chicago Press, 1962), 165; Frégault, *Canada*, 112–13, 37.

2. McConnell, *Country Between*, 128.

3. "Plan of Operation on the Mississippi, Ohio, & Ca," Feb. 1, 1758, in James, *Writings of General John Forbes*, 33–35; Peckham, *Colonial Wars*, 175; Forbes to Pitt, May 1, 1758, in James, *Writings of Forbes*, 76–77.

4. Joseph Shippen to James Burd, Apr. 30, 1758, Shippen Family Papers, vol. 3; *CRP* 8:52; Francis Fauquier to Board of Trade, June 11, 1758, *FFP* 1:23–24; *JHB 1752–1755, 1756–1758*, 495–506; *VSAL* 7:463–70; Titus, *Old Dominion at War*, 120–22.

5. "Plan of Operation on the Mississippi, Ohio, & Ca," Feb. 1, 1758, in James, *Writings of General John Forbes*, 35.

6. *CRP* 8:59.

7. Morris to Sir Thomas Robinson, Sept. 24, 1755, BOEHM pt. 1, 2:642; H.C. B. Rogers, *British Army of the Eighteenth Century*, 68, 71–73.

8. Forbes to Bouquet, June 27, 1758, in James, *Writings of Forbes*, 124; J. F. C Fuller, *British Light Infantry in the Eighteenth Century* (London: Hutchinson and Co., 1925), 54, 87; Lewis W. G Butler, *Annals of the King's Royal Rifle Corps*, 5 vols. (London: Smith Elder, 1913), 1:31; H. C. B. Rogers, *British Army of the Eighteenth Century*, 68–72.

9. "Bouquet Orderly Book," July 2, 1758, *HBP* 2:661.

10. "Forbes Advertisement for Wagons, Horses, Drivers, etc," in James, *Writings of Forbes*, 88–89; *CRP* 8:59–60; "Notice to Wagoners," May 28, 1758, *HBP* 1:378.

11. Bouquet to Forbes, May 29–30, 1758, *HBP* 1:386.

12. Bouquet to Edward Shippen, June 3, 1758, Shippen Family Papers, vol. 3.

13. Bouquet to Forbes, June 3, 1758, *HBP* 2:18; Bouquet to Forbes, July 11, 1758, *HBP* 2:181.

14. Forbes to Pemberton, May 31, 1758, Friendly Association Records, 1:513.

15. "Report of Charles Thomson and Christian Frederick Post," June 18, 1758, Friendly Association Records, 2:15–27; Forbes to Bouquet, Aug. 9, 1758, *HBP* 2:344–45; Walter T. Champion Jr., "Christian Frederick Post and the Winning of the West," *PMHB* 104 (1985): 308–25.

16. Abercromby to Forbes, May 4, 1758, PRO WO 34/44, 213; Sir William Johnson to Abercromby, Apr. 28, 1758, PRO CO 5/50, 147–149; Forbes to Abercromby, July 9, 1758, in James, *Writings of Forbes*, 134–40.

17. "Memorial of the Freemen of Pennsylvania," July 12, 1758: Penn Mss.: Indian Affairs, 3:55; "Minutes of Conference with Indians," Friendly Association Records, 2:111–23; Pemberton to Forbes, July 19, 1758, Friendly Association Records, 2:135; *CRP* 8:187.

18. Thwaites, *Early Western Travels*, 198–201, 207, 209, 213–14.

19. Thwaites, *Early Western Travels*, 195, 224–25; McConnell, *Country Between*, 131.

20. Bouquet to Forbes, June 3, 1758, *HBP* 2:18; Byrd to Loudoun, Mar. 21, 1758, in Marion Tinling, ed., *The Correspondence of the Three William Byrds of Westover Virginia, 1684–1776*, 2 vols. (Charlottesville: University Press of Virginia, 1977), 2:640–41.

21. "Speech of Attakullakulla [the 'Little Carpenter'] to William Byrd," May 27, 1758, and George Turner to Byrd, Aug. 4, 1758, both in Tinling, *Correspondence of the Three William Byrds*, 2:656, 2:664–65.

22. Washington to John Blair, Apr. 24, 1758, *GWP* 5:139–41; Washington to Blair, May 4–10, 1758, *GWP* 5:156–60; *Maryland Gazette*, May 4, 1758, May 18, 1758; *EJVC* 6:95.

23. William Callaway to Washington, May 15, 1758, *GWP* 5:183–84; *EJVC* 6:94; Lachlin Mackintosh to Byrd, May 12, 1758, in Tinling, *Correspondence of the Three William Byrds*, 2:653.

24. Washington to Stanwix, Apr. 10, 1758, *GWP* 5:117; Washington to Francis Halkett, May 11, 1758, 5:176–77.

25. Washington to Stanwix, Apr. 10, 1758, *GWP* 5:117; Forbes to Pitt, May 19, 1758, in James, *Writings of Forbes*, 92.

26. Forbes to Stanwix, May 29, 1758, and Forbes to Abercromby, June 7, 1758, both in James, *Writings of Forbes,* 102–3, 109.

27. Johnson to Abercromby, Apr. 28, 1758, PRO CO 5/50, 149.

28. Forbes to Abercromby, Apr. 20, 1758, in James, *Writings of Forbes,* 65–66.

29. Bouquet to Forbes, June 3, 1758, *HBP* 2:18; William Trent to Bouquet, June 5, 1758, *HBP* 2:36–37; Forbes to Fauquier, Aug. 16, 1758, *FFP* 1:59–60; Bouquet to James Burd, Oct. 16, 1758, Shippen Family Papers, vol. 3.

30. Forbes to Abercromby, Apr. 22, 1758, in James, *Writings of Forbes,* 68–69; Forbes to Abercromby, June 7, 1758, in James, *Writings of Forbes,* 68–69; Abercromby to Forbes, May 4, 1758, PRO WO 34/44, 213.

31. Abercromby to Forbes, July 10, 1758, PRO WO 34/44, 157–58; Forbes to Abercromby, June [27], 1758, PRO WO 34/44, 221; "Minutes of the Friendly Association," 11–12, 25. Theodore Thayer, *Israel Pemberton: King of the Quakers* (Philadelphia: Historical Society of Pennsylvania, 1943), 97–102.

32. Forbes to Bouquet, May 29, 1758, *HBP* 1:379; St. Clair to Bouquet, May 31, 1758, *HBP* 1: 403; *EJVC* 6:87–88; *CRP* 8:79–84.

33. John Hughes to Commissioners, May 8, 1758, Shippen Family Papers, vol. 3; Washington to Blair, May 28, 1758, *GWP* 5:199–203; Bouquet to Stevenson, June 3, 1758, *HBP* 2:27–29; Washington to Fauquier, June 17, 1758, *FFP* 1:30–31.

34. "Forbes Advertisement about Deserters," June 1, 1758, in James, *Writings of Forbes,* 104–5; *Pennsylvania Gazette,* June 1, 1758; Bouquet to Forbes, May 29–30, 1758, *HBP* 1:386–90.

35. Forbes to Bouquet, July 23, 1758, *HBP* 2:264; Forbes to Bouquet, Aug. 20, 1758, *HBP* 2:398; Stephen to Washington, July 20, 1758, *GWP* 5:363; Washington to Walker, Sept. 2, 1758, *GWP* 5:446.

36. Peter Burd to James Burd, July 20, 1758, Shippen Family Papers, vol. 3; "Washington's Orders," June 13, 1758, *FFP* 1:32; Washington to Fauquier, Aug. 5, 1758, *FFP* 1:57–58; Bouquet to Washington, June 27, 1758, *GWP* 5:246; Forbes to Abercromby, July 18, 1758, PRO WO 34/44, 170–71.

37. Bouquet to Forbes, May 22, 1758, and June 7, 1758, both *HBP* 1:351, 2:47; Armstrong to Bouquet, July 25, 1758, *HBP* 2:272.

38. Bouquet to Forbes, June 21, 1758, and July 11, 1758, both *HBP* 2:121–22, 2:180–81.

39. Ourry to Bouquet, July 4, 1758, HBP 2:180–81.

40. Forbes to Bouquet, July 14, 1758, *HBP* 2:207–8; Bouquet to Forbes, Aug. 26, 1758, *HBP* 2:423.

41. Stephen to Bouquet, Aug. 26, 1758, *HBP* 2:430–31.

42. Stephen to Bouquet, Aug. 26, 1758, *HBP* 2:432; St. Clair to Bouquet, Aug. 27, 1758, Bouquet to St. Clair, Aug. 28, 1758, *HBP* 2:434, 2:435–36.

43. Forbes to Jeffrey Amherst, Jan. 30, 1759, in James, *Writings of Forbes,* 288.

44. John Kirkpatrick to Washington, July 21, 1758, *GWP* 5:314; Washington to Bouquet, Aug. 2, 1758, *GWP* 5:353–60; Bouquet to Forbes, July 21, 1758, *HBP* 2:251–52; Forbes to Bouquet, July 23, 1758, *HBP* 264–65; *EJVC* 6:107–8.

45. Washington to John Robinson, Sept. 1, 1758, *GWP* 5:432.

46. Forbes to Bouquet, Sept. 4, 1758, in James, *Writings of Forbes,* 199.

47. John Hite to Washington, July 2, 1758, *GWP* 5:254; *Pennsylvania Gazette,* July 27, 1758.

48. Bouquet to Forbes, Aug. 8, 1758, Sept. 11, 1758, Oct. 20, 1758, all *HBP* 2:335, 2:492–94, 2:578–80.

49. Forbes to Bouquet, Sept. 2, 1758, *HBP* 2:462; Bouquet to Forbes, Sept. 4, 1758, *HBP* 2:471–74.

50. Bouquet to Forbes, Sept. 4, 1758, *HBP* 2:472.

51. Bouquet to Washington, Aug. 17, 1758, *GWP* 5:394–95; Forbes to Bouquet, Sept. 2, 1758, *HBP* 2:461; "Journal of Occurrences in Canada, October 20, 1757, to October 20, 1758," *NYCD* 10:835–55.

52. Bouquet to Washington, July 14, 1758, *GWP* 5:286–86; Washington to Bouquet, July 16, 1758, *GWP* 5:291–93.

53. James Grant to Forbes, [ca. Sept. 14, 1758], *HBP* 2:499–504; James Burd to Bouquet, Sept. 16, 1758, in "Letter Book of Col. James Burd," 1756–1758, 182–183, Shippen Family Papers; M. Daine to Marshall de Bell Isle, Nov. 3, 1758, *NYCD* 10:884–85.

54. Grant to Forbes [ca. Sept. 14, 1758], *HBP* 2:499–504; "List of Killed & Wounded at Ft. Duquesne," Sept. 14, 1758, Shippen Family Papers: Military Notebook No. 7.

55. Bouquet to Forbes, Sept. 17, 1758, *HBP* 2:520; Edward Shippen to James Burd, Sept. 20, 1758, Shippen Family Papers, vol. 3.

56. Forbes to Abercromby, Sept. 21, 1758, and Forbes to Bouquet, Sept. 23, 1758, both in James, *Writings of Forbes,* 215–16, 218–21.

57. James Burd to Sarah Burd, Oct. 14, 1758, Shippen Family Papers, vol. 3; James Burd to Bouquet, Oct. 12, 1758, *HBP* 2:552–53; Bouquet to Forbes, Oct. 15, 1758, *HBP* 2;560.

58. Fauquier to Washington, Sept. 16, 1758, *FFP* 1:72–73; Fauquier to Board of Trade, Sept. 23, 1758, BOEHM pt. 1, 12:66.

59. Fauquier to Washington, Nov. 4, 1758, *FFP* 1:99–100; Bouquet to Forbes, Oct. 28, 1758, *HBP* 2:588–89.

60. *CRP* 8:224–25; *PA* 4th ser. 2:959.

61. "Council of War," Nov. 11, 1758, *HBP* 2:600–601; Forbes to Bouquet, Nov. 22, 1758, *HBP* 2:606–7; Forbes to The Beaver and Shingas, Nov. 9, 1758, in James, *Writings of Forbes,* 252–53.

62. Montcalm to Marshal de Belle Isle, Nov. 15, 1758, *NYCD* 10:900–901.

63. Forbes to Pitt, Sept. 6, 1758, in James, *Writings of Forbes,* 203; Forbes to Pemberton, May 31, 1758, and July 9, 1758, both Friendly Association Records, 1:513, 2:99; Abercromby to Forbes, June 4, 1758, and June 24, 1758, both PRO WO 34/44m 218, 219.

64. Forbes to Pemberton, Aug. 18, 1758, Friendly Association Records, 2:211.

65. See Friendly Association Records, especially vol. 2.

66. "Minutes of the Friendly Association," 12b; "Minutes of the Treaty of Easton," Friendly Association Records, 1:155.

67. Forbes to Pemberton, Aug. 18, 1758, Friendly Association Records, 2:211.

68. Charles Thomson to Franklin, Dec. 10, 1758, in Labaree, Willcox, and Oberg, *The Papers of Benjamin Franklin,* 8:201; *CRP* 8:178; Denny to Johnson, Oct. 24, 1758, *SWJP* 3:10–11.

69. Pemberton to Franklin, Dec. 11, 1758, in Labaree, Willcox, and Oberg, *The Papers of Benjamin Franklin,* 8:212;

70. Thomson to Franklin, Dec. 10, 1758, in Labaree, Willcox, and Oberg, *The Papers of Benjamin Franklin,* 8:207–11; Pemberton to Forbes, Oct. 26, 1758, Friendly Association Records, 2:179; *CRP* 8:199, 8:218–19.

71. *CRP* 8:190–92.

72. *CRP* 8:203–5.

73. Pemberton to Franklin, Dec. 11, 1758, in Labaree, Willcox, and Oberg, *The Papers of Benjamin Franklin,* 8:211–12.

74. *CRP* 8:221.

75. Pemberton to Franklin, Dec. 11, 1758, in Labaree, Willcox, and Oberg, *The Papers of Benjamin Franklin,* 8:211–12.

76. *CRP* 8:212.

77. *CRP* 8:219–23.

78. Forbes to Abercromby, Nov. 17, 1758, in James, *Writings of Forbes,* 255–56.

79. Thwaites, *Early Western Travels,* 256.

80. Bouquet to Stanwix, Nov. 25, 1758, *HBP* 2:609; Bouquet to Allen, Nov. 25, 1758, *HBP* 2:610; Daine to de Belle Isle, Nov. 3, 1758, *NYCD* 10:884–85.

81. Forbes to Amherst, Feb. 7, 1759, in James, *Writings of Forbes,* 289–90.

82. Forbes to Denny, Nov. 26, 1758, PRO CO 5/54, 37

83. *Pennsylvania Gazette,* Dec. 14, 1758.

Notes to Chapter 7

1. "Observations on certain Peculations in New France," Apr. 5, 1761, *NYCD* 10:1132; *CRP* 8:391–93.

2. Gipson, *The Victorious Years,* 118–38; Anderson, *Crucible of War,* 297–310.

3. Lloyd to James Burd, Apr. 14, 1759, Shippen Family Papers, vol. 4; Hugh Mercer to Bouquet, Dec. 19, 1758, *HBP* 2:635–36.

4. Fauquier to Byrd, Jan. 23, 1759, in Tinling, *Correspondence of the Three William Byrds,* 2:669–70; Fauquier to Board of Trade, Apr. 14, 1759, *FFP* 1:207–9.

5. Amherst to Denny, Apr. 11, 1759, Penn Mss.: Official Correspondence, 9:85.

6. Richard Hockley to Thomas Penn, Apr. 21, 1759, Penn Mss.: Official Correspondence, 9:89.

7. David Jameson to James Burd, May 14, 1759, Shippen Family Papers: General Correspondence, vol. 4; Illick, *Colonial Pennsylvania,* 179–80, 200–204.

8. Lloyd to Stanwix, May 23, 1759, *HBP* 3:309–11; Stephen to Stanwix, May 25, 1759, *HBP* 3:318–19; Adam Hoops to Bouquet, May 30, 1759, *HBP* 3:334.

9. *CRP* 8:282, 8:285.

10. Croghan to Bouquet, July 11, 1759, *HBP* 3:398; Croghan to Stanwix, July 23,

1759, *HBP* 3:450–51; Nicholas N. Wainwright, ed., "George Croghan's Journal, April 3, 1759, to April 1763," *PMHB* 71 (1947): 322, 334–35.

11. Croghan to Stanwix, July 15, 1759, *HBP* 3:416–17; Johnson to Stanwix, July 25, 1759, *SWJP* 3:111–13; Johnson to Amherst, Apr. 22, 1759, PRO WO 34/39, 87; Anderson, *Crucible of War*, 330–38; Gipson, *The Victorious Years*, 342–57; Frégault, *Canada*, 257–58.

12. John W. Jordan, ed., "Journal of James Kenny, 1761–1763," *PMHB* 37 (1913): 437; Hugh Mercer to Stanwix, Aug. 15, 1759, *HBP* 3:568.

13. Hugh Mercer to Forbes, Jan. 8, 1759, *HBP* 3:26.

14. Johnson to Amherst, Feb. 22, 1759, PRO WO 34/39, 77–80.

15. Lightfoot to Pemberton, July 7, 1759, Friendly Association Records, 3:199.

16. [Pemberton] to Commissioners of Indian Affairs, Jan. 16, 1759, and Lightfoot to [Pemberton], Jan. 27, 1759, both Friendly Association Records, 2:365, 2:395.

17. Lightfoot to Friends at Opecon, Jan. 19, 1759, Friendly Association Records, 2:383.

18. Stanwix to Pemberton, July 2, 1759, Friendly Association Records, 3:195.

19. James Kenny to Pemberton, Aug. 1, 1759, Friendly Association Records, 3:247; Stanwix to Pemberton, Sept. 8, 1759, Friendly Association Records, 3:339; Friendly Association to Thomas and Richard Penn, Mar. 20, 1760, Penn Mss.: Indian Affairs, 3:89.

20. Lightfoot to Pemberton, June 18, 1759, Friendly Association Records, 3:179; Wainwright, "George Croghan's Journal," 316–17.

21. Wainwright, "George Croghan's Journal."

22. *CRP* 8:389, 8:429–31.

23. *CRP* 8:246–59.

24. "Board of Trade Report on Benjamin Franklin's Petition," June 1, 1759, Penn Mss.: Indian Affairs, 3:78.

25. "Board of Trade Report on Benjamin Franklin's Petition," June 1, 1759, Penn Mss.: Indian Affairs, 3:78; Orders of Council on Benjamin Franklin's Petition, Aug. 29, 1759, Penn Mss.: Indian Affairs, 3:80.

26. *Pennsylvania Gazette*, Oct. 18, 1759; *PA* 4th ser. 2:982; *CRP* 8:416–17; Nathaniel Holland to Pemberton, Dec. 7, 1759, and Jan. 1, 1760, both Friendly Association Records, 3:403, 3:407.

27. Andrew Lewis to Dinwiddie, July 23, 1756, BOEHM pt. 1, 3:123–27; "Deposition of Andrew Lewis on negotiations with Cherokees," July 1756, BOEHM pt. 1, 3:128–35; *EJVC* 6:61; William L. McDowell, *Documents Relating to Indian Affairs*, 2 vols., Colonial Records of South Carolina, Ser. 2: Indian Books (Columbia: South Carolina Archives Dept., 1958), 463–70. For discussions of the Cherokee War, see Hatley, *Dividing Paths;* Corkran, *Cherokee Frontier;* and Oliphant, *Peace and War on the Anglo-Cherokee Frontier.*

28. Fauquier to Board of Trade, Aug. 30, 1759, BOEHM pt. 1, 12:96–97; *Maryland Gazette*, Nov. 8, 1759, Dec. 6, 1759.

29. *Maryland Gazette*, Feb. 7, 1760, Feb. 14, 1760, Mar. 13, 1760, Apr. 10, 1760, Apr. 17, 1760; "Treaty with the Cherokees," Dec. 26, 1759, *FFP* 1:292–93; *EJVC* 6:154,

6:156; Byrd to [Robert Monckton(?)], July 16, 1760, Papers of Byrd, Virginia Historical Society (photocopies of original in Canadian Public Archives).

30. *Maryland Gazette*, Aug. 7, 1760; Arbhibale Montgomery to Amherst, June 4, 1760, and July 2, 1760, both PRO WO 34/47, 14–15, 17–18.

31. Fauquier to Preston, June 24, 1760, *FFP* 1:381–82.

32. Byrd to Abercromby, Sept. 16, 1760, in Tinling, *Correspondence of the Three William Byrds*, 2:703–5; Byrd to [Monckton(?)], July 16, 1760, Papers of Byrd; Fauquier to William Bull, May 24, 1760, *FFP* 1:365.

33. Byrd to Abercromby, Sept. 16, 1760, in Tinling, *Correspondence of the Three William Byrds*, 2:703; Fauquier to Board of Trade, Sept. 17, 1760, BOEHM pt. I, 12:140–41, *EJVC* 6:170–71, 6:174–175; *Maryland Gazette*, Dec. 18, 1760; Corkran, *Cherokee Frontier*, 193–223.

34. Fauquier to Byrd, Feb. 16, 1761, *FFP* 2:475; Fauquier to Richard Smith, Feb. 21, 1761, *FFP* 2:480–81; *EJVC* 6:181–83; Hatley, *Dividing Paths*, 134–35.

35. Amherst to Byrd, May 11, 1761, in Tinling, *Correspondence of the Three William Byrds*, 2:730.

36. Byrd to Amherst, Mar. 10, 1761, in Tinling, *Correspondence of the Three William Byrds*, 2:717–19; "Enclosure: Address from the Burgesses," Mar. 1761, *FFP* 2:487; Fauquier to Byrd, Apr. 18, 1761, *FFP* 2:515–16; Amherst to Fauquier, Aug. 2, 1761, *FFP* 2:554–55.

37. *Maryland Gazette*, Aug. 13, 1761, Oct. 1, 1761, Nov. 5, 1761; Hatley, *Dividing Paths*, 139–40.

38. Young, "The Effects of the French and Indian War," 143–44.

39. Bouquet to Stanwix, Apr. 26, 1760, *HBP* 4:541; Hamilton to Pitt, Apr. 15, 1760, Penn Mss.: Official Correspondence, 9:132.

40. Tamaqua to Forbes, [Nov. 1758], Friendly Association Records, 2:291; Thwaites, *Early Western Travels*, 272; Bouquet to Stanwix, Oct. 9, 1760, *HBP* 5:63–64.

41. John Langdale to Pemberton, Aug. 18, 1760, Friendly Association Records, 3:515; "A Narrative of what hath passed between the King's Generals, Governors etc. and the Indians in relation to Lands," [June 1761], BOEHM pt. I, 12:173–78; Denny to Indians at Wyoming, Apr. 24, 1759, *NYCD* 3:33–36.

42. "Minutes of a Meeting of the Susquehannah Company," Sept. 6, 1753, and "Deed from Indians of the Six Nations to the Susquehannah Company," both in Boyd and Taylor, *Susquehannah Company Papers*, 1:40–41, 1:101–2; Anderson, *Crucible of War*, 529–30.

43. Hamilton to Thomas Penn, Nov. 21, 1760, Penn Mss.: Official Correspondence, 9:184–86.

44. "Heads of Indian Treaty," Aug. 15, 1760, Penn Mss.: Indian Affairs, 3:92; Christian Frederick Post to Pemberton, Oct. 5, 1760, Friendly Association Records, 4:39.

45. Hamilton to Penn, Nov. 21, 1760, Penn Mss.: Official Correspondence, 9:184–86; Boyd and Taylor, *Susquehannah Company Papers*, 2:180–83; Wallace, *King of the Delawares*, 257.

46. Angus McDonald to Bouquet, Oct. 25, 1761, *HBP* 5:840; Peters to Weiser, Feb. 21, 1760, Conrad Weiser Papers, 2:169.

47. Fauquier to Board of Trade, Mar. 13, 1760, and May 7, 1760, both BOEHM pt. I, 12:107, 12:145–46.

48. "Niagara and Detroit Proceedings," July–Sept. 1761, *SWJP* 3:432; Monckton to Robert Rogers, Oct. 19, 1760, *HBP* 5:78–81.

49. Johnson to Amherst, July 19, 1761, *SWJP* 10:321.

50. Edward Shippen to Thomas Penn, Nov. 20, 1759, Penn Mss.: Official Correspondence, 9:126–28; "List of House and Inhabitants at Fort Pitt," Apr. 14, 1761, *HBP* 5:407–11; Anderson, *Crucible of War*, 328–29.

51. Johnson to Amherst, Mar. 24, 1760, *SWJP* 3:201.

52. Amherst to Johnson, Aug. 9, 1761, *SWJP* 3:514.

53. Johnson to Amherst, Feb. 12, 1761, *SWJP* 3:330–33; Richard Middleton, *The Bells of Victory: The Pitt-Newcastle Ministry and the Conduct of the Seven Years' War, 1757–1762* (Cambridge: Cambridge University Press, 1985), 178–94; Anderson, *Crucible of War*, 476–86.

54. Amherst to Johnson, Feb. 22, 1761, *SWJP* 3:343–47.

55. Amherst to Johnson, Aug. 9, 1761, *SWJP* 3:515.

56. Donald Campbell to Bouquet, Dec. 23, 1760, *HBP* 5:196

57. "Journal of Indian Affairs," Mar. 8–15, 1761, *SWJP* 10:238.

58. "Niagara and Detroit Proceedings," July–Sept. 1761, *SWJP* 3:459; "Order Limiting Trade with Shawnees," May 13, 1761, *HBP* 5:477; Gavin Cochrane to Bouquet, June 1, 1761, *HBP* 5:518–21; Holland to Pemberton, Dec. 29, 1760, Friendly Association Records, 4:63.

59. Croghan to Johnson, July 25, 1761, *SWJP* 10:316.

60. Donald Campbell to Bouquet, June 16, 1761, and July 7, 1761, both *HBP* 5:555–56, 5:618–20.

61. "Niagara and Detroit Proceedings," July–Sept. 1761, *SWJP* 3:450–53; "Report of Indian Council," June 18, 1761, *HBP* 5:561–64; McConnell, *Country Between,* 174.

62. "Niagara and Detroit Proceedings," July–Sept. 1761, *SWJP* 3:468–503; "Instructions to officers at Western Posts," Sept. 16, 1761, *SWJP* 3:527; Bouquet to Monckton, June 30, 1761, *HBP* 5:598–99; Ourry to Bouquet, July 13, 1761, *HBP* 5:633; "Indian Trade Regulations, Fort Pitt," Sept. 18, 1761, *HBP* 5:762–63.

63. Johnson to Thomas Gage, Jan. 12, 1764, *SWJP* 4:296.

64. Bouquet to Peters, Oct. 5, 1761, *HBP* 5:803.

65. "Affidavit of Charles Brodhead," Sept. 2, 1761, Horsfield Papers, 2:437–39; Horsfield to Hamilton, Sept. 3, 1761, Horsfield Papers, 2:441–43.

66. *CRP* 8:651.

67. *CRP* 8:653.

68. *CRP* 8:641–42.

69. *CRP* 8:654, 8:659–61; Olmstead, *David Zeisberger,* 108.

70. "Bouquet: Orders for Meyer," Aug. 12, 1761, *HBP* 5:691; "Bouquet: Proclamation against Settlers," Oct. 31, 1761, *HBP* 5:844.

71. Donald Campbell to Bouquet, Sept. 17, 1761, *HBP* 5:758.

72. Amherst to Johnson, Dec. 30, 1761, *SWJP* 3:597.

73. William Walters to Johnson, Apr. 5, 1762, *SWJP* 10:427.

74. *CRP* 8:678, 8:686, 8:695–97, 8:710–11, 8:715–19.

75. Fauquier to Amherst, Feb. 3, 1762, and Apr. 7, 1762, both *FFP* 2:672–73, 2:709–10.

76. Jordan, "Journal of James Kenny," 171; *CRP* 8:488–89; Gregory Evans Dowd, *A Spirited Resistance: The North American Indian Struggle for Unity, 1745–1815* (Baltimore: Johns Hopkins University Press, 1992), 31–33; White, *Middle Ground,* 280; McConnell, *Country Between,* 222.

77. Jordan, "Journal of James Kenny," 188.

78. Langdale to Pemberton, Aug. 2, 1760, Friendly Association Records, 3:499; "Conference held at Fort Pitt," Apr. 6–12, 1760, *SWJP* 3:214; Wainwright, "George Croghan's Journal," 369.

79. Croghan to Johnson, July 25, 1761, *SWJP* 10:316; "Indian Conference at Detroit," Dec. 3–5, 1760, *HBP* 5:151.

80. Croghan to Johnson, July 25, 1761, *SWJP* 10:318.

81. "Niagara and Detroit Proceedings," July–Sept. 1761, *SWJP* 3:486.

82. Post to Pemberton, Aug. 8, 1761, Friendly Association Records, 4:167.

83. Pemberton to Langdale, Feb. 10, 1761, Friendly Association Records, 4:67; "Petition of McColoch," June 3, 1761, *HBP* 5:525–26.

84. Hamilton to Penn, Nov. 21, 1760, Penn Mss: Official Correspondence, 9:184–86.

85. Johnson to Earl of Egremont, May 1762, *SWJP* 10:461–62.

86. Egremont to Amherst, Mar. 16, 1763, Jeffery Amherst Papers, vol. 1, William L. Clements Library, Ann Arbor, Mich. *Note:* Amherst's first name is most commonly spelled "Jeffrey." However, the Clements library collection uses the spelling "Jeffery"; that is the spelling that will be used in all subsequent references to this collection.

87. "[Enclosure] Johnson to Croghan," Jan. 8, 1762, *HBP* 6:70–71; Croghan to Johnson, Mar. 31, 1762, and May 10, 1762, both *SWJP* 3:662–63, 3:732–34; Donald Campbell to Johnson, June 9, 1762, *SWJP* 3:758; *CRP* 8:702.

88. "Meeting At Easton with the Delawares," June 18, 1762, *SWJP* 3:771–72; Committee of Assembly to Johnson, June 22, 1762, Penn Mss.: Indian Affairs, 3:105.

89. "Meeting At Easton with the Delawares," June 18, 1762, *SWJP* 3:773; Croghan to Johnson, July 3, 1762, *SWJP* 3:822–23.

90. "Teedyuscung's Message to Johnson," June 24, 1762, Penn Mss.: Indian Affairs, 3:105.

91. "Teedyuscung's Speech to Johnson," June 28, 1762, Penn Mss.: Indian Affairs 3:104; Johnson to Lords of Trade, Aug. 1, 1762, *SWJP* 3:837–51; *CRP* 8:729–32, 8:749.

92. *CRP* 8:740.

93. *CRP* 8:735, 8:737; "Minutes of Treaty of Lancaster," Aug. 1762, *SWJP* 10:498; Wainwright, "George Croghan's Journal," 427.

94. *CRP* 8:737–38, 8:743–44, 8:760.

95. *CRP* 8:740.

96. *CRP* 8:747–48; Wainwright, "George Croghan's Journal," 427.

97. Thomas McKee to Johnson, Nov. 1, 1762, *SWJP* 3:921.

98. Wainwright, "George Croghan's Journal," 426–27, 429.

99. "Journal and Report of Thomas Hutchins," Apr. 4–Sept. 24, 1762, *SWJP* 10:521–29; Croghan to Johnson, Dec. 10, 1762, *SWJP* 3:964–66.

100. "[Enclosure] McKee to Croghan," Apr. 12, 1763, *HBP* 6:181; *CRP* 9:12.

101. "Correspondence Concerning Western Indians," Apr. 20–May 29, 1763, *SWJP* 4:95–100.

102. Amherst to Johnson, May 29, 1763, *SWJP* 10:689.

103. Croghan to Johnson, Dec. 10, 1762, *SWJP* 3:965.

104. Croghan to Johnson, Dec. 10, 1762, *SWJP* 3:965.

105. Amherst to Johnson, Apr. 3, 1763, *SWJP* 10:648–49.

106. Amherst to Johnson, June 16, 1763, *SWJP* 4:149.

107. *Pennsylvania Gazette*, May 26, 1763.

Notes to Chapter 8

1. Milo Milton Quaife, *The Siege of Detroit in 1763: The Journal of Pontiac's Conspiracy, and John Rutherfurd's Narrative of a Captivity* (Chicago: Lakeside Press, 1958). The most detailed, if rather dated, account of Pontiac's Uprising is still Howard H. Peckham, *Pontiac and the Indian Uprising* (Princeton: Princeton University Press, 1947).

2. Jehu Hay, "Journal of Pontiac's Conspiracy," 82, William L. Clements Library, Ann Arbor, Mich.

3. Quaife, *Siege of Detroit*, 22.

4. Quaife, *Siege of Detroit*, 53–58; Hay, "Journal," 83–85; Amherst to Gage, June 24, 1763, Jeffery Amherst Papers, vol. 6; James McDonald to Croghan, July 12, 1763, *SWJP* 10:736–45.

5. McDonald to Croghan, July 12, 1763, *SWJP* 10:739–40; Quaife, *Siege of Detroit*, 65–67.

6. McDonald to Croghan, July 12, 1763, *SWJP* 10:739–40.

7. Quaife, *Siege of Detroit*, 91, 104–5; Hay, "Journal," 96–100.

8. McDonald to Croghan, July 12, 1763, *SWJP* 10:742–43; Henry Gladwin to Amherst, May 28, 1763, Jeffery Amherst Papers, vol. 2.

9. Jean Baptiste de Couagne to Johnson, June 6, 1763, *SWJP* 4:137–38.

10. "Court of Inquiry," July 6, 1763, *SWJP* 10:730–31; Amherst to Gage, Aug. 5, 1763, Jeffery Amherst Papers, vol. 6.

11. "Court of Inquiry," July 6, 1763, *SWJP* 10:731–732; Peckham, *Pontiac*, 160.

12. Daniel Claus to Johnson, Aug. 6, 1763, *SWJP* 10:777–78; Peckham, *Pontiac*, 163.

13. Simeon Ecuyer to Bouquet, May 29, 1763, *HBP* 6:193; *Pennsylvania Gazette*, June 16, 1763.

14. G. Price to Bouquet, June 26, 1763, *HBP* 6:266–67; John Christie to Bouquet, July 10, 1763, *HBP* 6:301–3; Amherst to Gage, July 18, 1763, Jeffery Amherst Papers, vol. 6; "Court of Inquiry," July 10, 1763, *SWJP* 10:734–36.

15. Gladwin to Amherst, July 26, 1763, Jeffery Amherst Papers, vol. 2.

16. "Thomas Colhoon: Indian Intelligence from Tuscarawas," June 1, 1763, *HBP* 6:197–99; *Pennsylvania Gazette*, June 16, 1763.

17. Samuel Hunter to James Burd, June 7, 1763, Shippen Family Papers, 6:13; Bouquet to Amherst, July 26, 1763, *HBP* 6:325–26.

18. Ourry to Armstrong, June 18, 1763, Shippen Family Papers, 6:23; Ourry to Bouquet, June 20, 1763, *HBP* 6:243–44; "[Enclosure] Discourse between Delawares and Simeon Ecuyer," June 24, 1763, *HBP* 6:261–63.

19. *Pennsylvania Gazette,* July 21, 1763, July 28, 1763.

20. Ourry to Bouquet, Aug. 27, 1763, *HBP* 6:371–74.

21. *Pennsylvania Gazette,* Aug. 4, 1763.

22. *Maryland Gazette,* July 14, 1763.

23. *Maryland Gazette,* July 28, 1763.

24. Fauquier to Amherst, Aug. 2, 1763, *FFP* 2:1001; William Ingles to Preston, Sept. 13, 1763, William Preston Papers, 2QQ43.

25. Bouquet to Amherst, June 29, 1763, *HBP* 6:270–71; Bouquet to Hamilton, July 1, 1763, *HBP* 6:279–82; *CRP* 9:31–33.

26. *CRP* 9:36; Edward Shippen to James Burd, July 15, 1763, Shippen Family Papers: General Correspondence, 6:35.

27. Hamilton to Horsfield, July 11, 1763, Horsfield Papers, 2:456–57.

28. Fauquier to Amherst, Aug. 2, 1763, *FFP* 2:1001; Ourry to Bouquet, Aug. 27, 1763, *HBP* 6:371–74; *Maryland Gazette,* Oct. 6, 1763.

29. Bouquet to Amherst, June 16, 1763, *HBP* 6:225–26.

30. Amherst to Bouquet, June 25, 1763, and June 29, 1763, both *HBP* 6:255–56, 6:277.

31. Amherst to Bouquet, June 16, 1763, and June 19, 1763, both *HBP* 6:227, 6:239–41.

32. Amherst to Johnson, Sept. 10, 1763, *SWJP* 4:201.

33. "[Enclosure] Amherst: Memorandum," [July 7, 1763], *HBP* 6:301; Elizabeth A. Fenn, "Biological Warfare in Eighteenth-Century North America: Beyond Jeffrey Amherst," *JAH* 86 (1999–2000): 1552–80.

34. Bouquet to Amherst, Aug. 5, 1763, and Aug. 11, 1763, both *HBP* 6:338–40, 6:361–62.

35. William Smith, *Brief State,* 38.

36. Bouquet to Amherst, Aug. 6, 1763, *HBP* 6:342–45; *Pennsylvania Gazette,* Sept. 1, 1763.

37. Amherst to Johnson, Aug. 20, 1763, *SWJP* 4:192–93; Joseph Shippen to James Burd, Aug. 25, 1763, Shippen Family Papers: General Correspondence, 6:51; "[Enclosure] Casualty Return: Battle of Bushy Run," Aug. 6, 1763, *HBP* 6:371–74.

38. "[Enclosure] Amherst to Stephen," Aug. 31, 1763, *HBP* 6:380–81; Cederic Graydon to James Burd, Oct. 12, 1763, Shippen Family Papers: General Correspondence, 6:53; *Pennsylvania Gazette,* Oct. 27, 1763.

39. Gladwin to Amherst, Aug. 8, 1763, Jeffery Amherst Papers, vol. 2; Quaife, *Siege of Detroit,* 199–200.

40. Alexander Duncan to Johnson, July 31, 1763, *SWJP* 10:762–66; de Couagne to Johnson, Aug. 24, 1763, *SWJP* 10:790–91; Gladwin to Amherst, Aug. 8, 1763, Jeffery Amherst Papers, vol. 2; Hay, "Journal," 170–71.

41. *Pennsylvania Gazette,* Oct. 27, 1763; Johnson to Cadwallader Colden, Oct. 13,

1763, *SWJP* 4:215–16; Boyd and Taylor, *Susquehannah Company Papers*, 2:276–78; Wallace, *King of the Delawares*, 258, 261.

42. Gladwin to Amherst, Sept. 9, 1763, Jeffery Amherst Papers, vol. 2; Amherst to Gage, Oct. 6, 1763, Jeffery Amherst Papers, vol. 6.

43. Gladwin to Amherst, Oct. 7, 1763, Jeffery Amherst Papers, vol. 2; Couagne to Johnson, Sept. 16, 1763, *SWJP* 10:815.

44. Gladwin to Amherst, Nov. 1763, Jeffery Amherst Papers, vol. 7; Quaife, *Siege of Detroit*, 70; Hay, "Journal," 105.

45. For a recent edition of this often republished work, see Francis Parkman, *The Conspiracy of Pontiac and the Indian War after the Conquest of Canada*, ed. Michael N. Mc-Connell (Lincoln: University of Nebraska Press, 1994).

46. Gladwin to Amherst, Nov. 1763, Jeffery Amherst Papers, vol. 7; Gage to the Earl of Halifax, Dec. 23, 1763, Thomas Gage Papers, British Series, vol. 1, William L. Clements Library, Ann Arbor, Mich.

47. "Instructions of Villiers to Indian Nations," Sept. 27, 1763, *SWJP* 10:820; Pierre Joseph Neyon de Villiers to Sieur de Dabbadie, Dec. 1, 1763, *IHC* 10:50–51.

48. Gladwin to Amherst, Nov. 1, 1763, *HBP* 6:446–47; "[Enclosure] Pontiac to Gladwin and the reply," Nov. 1, 1763, *HBP* 6:448–49; Quaife, *Siege of Detroit*, 260; Pontiac to Gladwin, Oct. 30, 1763, Jeffery Amherst Papers, vol. 7.

49. Bouquet to Hamilton, Sept. 12, 1763, *HBP* 6:390.

50. Amherst to Johnson, Aug. 20, 1763, *SWJP* 4:193.

51. Croghan to Johnson, Sept. 28, 1763, *SWJP* 10:827.

52. Allan Campbell to Bouquet, Sept. 4, 1763, *HBP* 6:346–49; *Pennsylvania Gazette*, Nov. 24, 1763.

53. James Burd to Allen, Jan. 10, 1764, Shippen Family Papers: General Correspondence, 6:77; Hamilton to Horsfield, Oct. 10, 1763, Horsfield Papers, 2:491; *Pennsylvania Gazette*, Dec. 8, 1763.

54. *CRP* 9:58–59, 9:71.

55. John Penn to Richard Penn, Mar. 17, 1764, Penn Mss.: Official Correspondence, 9:216–18; *CRP* 9:149–74.

56. "Enclosure: Address of the House of Burgesses," ca. Jan. 17, 1764, *FFP* 3:1070–71.

57. Gage to Johnson, Jan. 12, 1764, *SWJP* 4:290.

58. Fauquier to Board of Trade, Feb. 13, 1764, PRO CO 5/1, 12:219–24.

59. "Apology of the Paxton Volunteers," HSP (AM 283).

60. Bernard Grube to Horsfield, Oct. 13, 1763, Horsfield Papers, 2:503–4.

61. John Penn to Richard Penn, Dec. 18, 1763, Penn Mss.: Official Correspondence, 9:210–14; Harris to James Burd, Dec. 2, 1763, Shippen Family Papers: General Correspondence, 6:65; Olmstead, *David Zeisberger*, 121–24.

62. "Apology of the Paxton Volunteers," HSP.

63. *CRP* 9:89–90, 9:100, 9:104–5; Martin, "Return of the Paxton Boys," *Pennsylvania History* 38 (1971): 117–33.

64. Joseph Shippen to James Burd, Jan. 3, 1764, Shippen Family Papers: General Correspondence, 6:73; *CRP* 9:104–5.

65. Joseph Shippen to James Burd, Feb. 9, 1764, Shippen Family Papers: General

Correspondence, 6:87; Harris to James Burd, Mar. 1, 1764, Shippen Family Papers, General Correspondence, 6:95; *CRP* 9:119–20, 9:131–32, 9:138–42; John Penn to Johnson, Jan. 5, 1764, *SWJP* 11:1–2.

66. Gage to Fauquier, Feb. 28, 1764, *FFP* 3:1089–90.

67. "[Enclosure] Re-examination of Gershom Hicks," Apr. 19, 1764, *HBP* 6:524.

68. Johnson to Gage, Jan. 12, 1764, *SWJP* 4:294–97; Johnson to John Stuart, Mar. 18, 1764, *SWJP* 11:103–4.

69. "Johnson Letter," Apr. 6, 1764, *SWJP* 11:123.

70. Hay, "Journal," 37.

71. *Maryland Gazette,* Apr. 12, 1764; *Pennsylvania Gazette,* Apr. 5, 1764, May 3, 1764; "[Enclosure] Re-examination of Gershom Hicks," Apr. 19, 1764, *HBP* 6:522–526; John Brown to Preston, June 8, 1764, William Preston Papers, 2QQ49.

72. Johnson to Henry Montour, Feb. 21, 1764, *SWJP* 4:336–37; Johnson to John Bradstreet, Mar. 2, 1764, *SWJP* 4:349–50; Johnson to Stuart, Mar. 18, 1764, *SWJP* 11:103–4; "Journal of Indian Affairs," Mar. 5–23, 1764, *SWJP* 11:105–15.

73. Gregory Evans Dowd, "The French King Wakes up in Detroit: 'Pontiac's War' in Rumor and History," *Ethnohistory* 37 (1990): 254–78.

74. "Indian Intelligence," June 9–11, 1764, *SWJP* 11:226; *IHC* 10:242.

75. *Pennsylvania Gazette,* June 7, 1764, June 14, 1764, June 21, 1764.

76. *CRP* 9:184–88; Fauquier to Thomas Rutherford, July 9, 1764, *FFP* 3:1109; Gage to Bouquet, Apr. 4, 1764, *HBP* 6:506–8; Bouquet to Johnson, May 31, 1764, *HBP* 6:551–53.

77. Bouquet to Gage, July 12, 1764, *HBP* 6:587–91; Bouquet to Franklin, Aug. 10, 1764, *HBP* 6:600–601; Bouquet to Gage, Aug. 10, 1764, *HBP* 6:601–2.

78. *IHC* 10:251–53; Bouquet to Gage, May 31, 1764, *HBP* 6:549–51.

79. Gage to Johnson, July 15, 1764, *SWJP* 4:483; Bouquet to Gage, May 31, 1764, *HBP* 6:549–51.

80. Johnson to Gage, May 17, 1764, *SWJP* 11:194–95.

81. "Minutes of Treaty Held at Lake Erie, 12 Aug. 1764," Penn Mss.: Official Correspondence, 9:246; *CRP* 9:193–97; Helen Hornbeck Tanner, ed., *Atlas of Great Lakes Indian History* (Norman: University of Oklahoma Press, 1987), 51.

82. Bouquet to Gage, Aug. 27, 1764, *HBP* 6:621.

83. *Pennsylvania Gazette,* Aug. 9, 1764, Sept. 20, 1764; Bouquet to Gage, Aug. 27, 1764, *HBP* 6:621; "[Enclosure] John Reid to Bouquet," Sept. 16, 1764, *HBP* 6:640–41.

84. "Johnson's Remarks on the Conduct of Colonel Bradstreet," Nov. 24, 1764, *SWJP* 4:599–604; "Indian Proceedings," Dec. 2–16, 1764, *SWJP* 11:500–509.

85. Johnson to Gage, Oct. 17, 1764, *SWJP* 11:382–84; Gage to Earl of Halifax, Oct. 12, 1764, and Nov. 9, 1764, both Thomas Gage Papers, British Series, vol. 2.

86. Bouquet to Gage, Sept. 16, 1764, *HBP* 6:646–48; "[Enclosure] Bouquet: Speech to the Delawares," *HBP* 6:650; Alexander McKee to Johnson, Oct. 21, 1764, *SWJP* 11:385–86.

87. "Enclosure: Onondaga and Oneida Indians: Speech to Bouquet," Oct. 2, 1764, *HBP* 6:653–56; *Pennsylvania Gazette,* Oct. 25, 1764.

88. "An Indian Congress," July 17–Aug. 4, 1764, *SWJP* 11:278–328; *Pennsylvania*

Gazette, Mar. 8, 1764; "[Enclosure] Deposition of Gershom Hicks," Apr. 14, 1764, *HBP* 6:514–16.

89. Bouquet to Gage, Oct. 21, 1764, *HBP* 6:675–77.

90. "Henry Bouquet, Speech to the Mingos, Delawares, and Shawanese, 19 Oct. 1764," Penn Mss.: Indian Affairs, 3:108.

91. Bouquet to Gage, Oct. 21, 1764, *HBP* 6:677; *CRP* 9:216–23.

92. Francis Turnbull to John Penn, Oct. 20, 1764, Penn Mss.: Official Correspondence, 9:280; Alexander McKee to Johnson, Nov. 17, 1764, *SWJP* 11:474–75.

93. "Minutes: Conference with Shawnees," Nov. 12, 1764, *HBP* 6:694–96; "Bouquet: Speech to the Shawnees," Nov. 13, 1764, *HBP* 6:698–99.

94. "Minutes: Conference with Shawnees," Nov. 14, 1764, *HBP* 6:700–703; Bouquet to Gage, Nov. 30, 1764, *HBP* 6:711–15.

95. Gage to Earl of Halifax, Dec. 13, 1764, Thomas Gage Papers, British Series, vol. 3.

96. *CRP* 9:207.

97. Bouquet to Johnson, Nov. 15, 1764, *SWJP* 4:586.

98. Bouquet to Gage, Nov. 15, 1764, *HBP* 6:704.

99. William Smith, *Brief State,* 29.

100. "[Enclosure] Plan for the Future Management of Indian Affairs," July 10, 1764, *NYCD* 7:637–41; Earl of Halifax to Gage, Jan. 14, 1764, Thomas Gage Papers, British Series, vol. 1.

101. Quoted in Peckham, *Pontiac,* 214.

102. Johnson to Gage, Nov. 20, 1764, *SWJP* 11:473.

103. *IHC* 11:9–19; McConnell, *Country Between,* 204–5.

104. Croghan to Johnson, May 12, 1765, *SWJP* 11:736–37.

105. Croghan to Johnson, July 12, 1765, *SWJP* 11:836–41; "An Indian Congress," July 13, 1765, *SWJP* 11:847–50; Croghan to Johnson, Aug. 17, 1765, *SWJP* 11:899–902.

106. William Smith, *Historical Account,* 40.

Notes to Conclusion

1. Nathaniel McCulloch to Croghan, Mar. 12, 1765, *SWJP* 11:635–36; John Penn to Johnson, Mar. 21, 1765, *SWJP* 11:643–45.

2. Andrew Lewis to Fauquier, May 9, 1765, *FFP* 3:1234–35; Andrew Lewis to Fauquier, June 3, 1765, *FFP* 3:1248–49; "Proclamation of the Augusta Boys," BOEHM pt. 1, 12:310–11; Fauquier to Andrew Lewis, June 14, 1765, BOEHM pt. 1, 12:312–13.

3. "Extract of a Minute of the House of Lords," Mar. 6, 1765, PRO CO 5/66, 27; Lords of Trade to Colden, Mar. 16, 1765, *NYCD* 7:708.

4. "Plan for the Future Management of Indian Affairs," [July 1765], PRO CO 5/65, pt. 3, 123–35.

5. For a broader discussion of the rise of "Indian hating," see Slotkin, *Regeneration through Violence.*

6. *Pennsylvania Gazette,* Sept. 29, 1763.

7. "Deposition of John Craig," Mar. 30, 1756, Penn Mss.: Indian Affairs, 2:78.

8. "Review of the Trade and Affairs in the Northern District of America," Sept. 22, 1767, *IHC* 14:43; Hinderaker, *Elusive Empires*, 162–69.

9. McConnell, *Country Between*, 303–4; Donald Hickey, *The War of 1812: A Forgotten Conflict* (Urbana: University of Illinois Press, 1990), 238.

10. For the classic statement of the role of the Seven Years' War in fomenting the Revolution, see Lawrence Henry Gipson, "The American Revolution as an Aftermath of the Great War for the Empire," *Political Science Quarterly* 65 (1950) 86–104; for a more recent restatement, see Anderson, *Crucible of War*. For a broader discussion of the role of these conflicts in the coming of the Revolution, see John Shy, *Toward Lexington;* Douglas Edward Leach, *Roots of Conflict: British Armed Forces and Colonial Americans, 1677–1763* (Chapel Hill: University of North Carolina Press, 1986); and Ferling, *Wilderness of Miseries.*

11. Quoted in Don Higginbotham, *George Washington and the American Military Tradition* (Athens: University of Georgia Press, 1985), 31.

12. Ferling, "School for Command."

13. For gunsmiths in Berks County, see *PA* 3d ser. 18:3–86. For a recent discussion of this topic, see "Forum: Historians and Guns." For Bellesiles's original comments, see Bellesiles, *Arming America.*

14. "Review of the Trade and Affairs in the Northern District of America," Sept. 22, 1767, *IHC* 14:38–39.

15. Ruth Bloch, *Visionary Republic: Millennial Themes in American Thought, 1756–1800* (Cambridge: Cambridge University Press, 1985); Kerry Trask, *In the Pursuit of Shadows: Massachusetts Millennialism and the Seven Years War* (New York: Garland, 1990).

16. "Review of the Trade and Affairs in the Northern District of America," Sept. 22, 1767, *IHC* 14:38. For a discussion of the role of the liquor trade, see Peter C. Mancall, *Deadly Medicine: Indians and Alcohol in Early America* (Ithaca: Cornell University Press, 1995); and Hinderaker, *Elusive Empires.*

17. Mitchell, "'Over the Hills and Far Away,'" 77–78.

18. Tillson, *Gentry and Common Folk;* Ronald Hoffman, Thad W. Tate, and Peter J. Albert, eds., *An Uncivil War: The Southern Backcountry during the American Revolution* (Charlottesville: University Press of Virginia, 1985); Holton, *Forced Founders.*

Selected Bibliography

Manuscript Collections

American Philosophical Society, Philadelphia: Indian and Military Affairs of Pennsylvania; Horsfield Papers.

British Library, London: Additional Manuscripts, Duke of Newcastle Papers; King's Manuscripts, Robert Orme, "Journal of General Braddock's Expedition."

William L. Clements Library, University of Michigan, Ann Arbor: Jeffery Amherst Papers; Thomas Gage Papers, British Series; Jehu Hay, "Journal of Pontiac's Conspiracy."

Cumberland County Historical Society, Carlisle, Penn.; Papers Relating to Provincial Affairs; "Orderly Book of Captain Thomas Hamilton's Company"; Cumberland County Court Records.

Haverford College, Haverford, Penn.: Friendly Association Records, Quaker Collection, Collection #1250.

Historical Society of Pennsylvania: "Apology of the Paxton Voluntiers"; Cadwallader Collection: George Croghan Papers; Conarroe Collection; Conrad Weiser Papers; Etting Collections; Gratz Collection; Lamberton Scotch-Irish Collection; "Minutes of the Friendly Association"; Northampton County Records; Penn Manuscripts, Proprietary Records: Indian Affairs; Penn Manuscripts: Official Correspondence; Peters Papers; Shippen Family Papers: General Correspondence; Shippen Family Papers: Military Letterbooks; Charles Willing and Sons Letterbook; Thomas Willing Letterbook; Willing and Morris Letterbook; Letterbook of William Allen and Joseph Turner, 1755–1774.

Library of Congress, Washington, D.C.: George Washington Papers. Microfilm.

Pennsylvania State Archives, Harrisburg: Edward Shippen Thompson Family Papers; Burd-Shippen Papers; Receipt Book of John Harris II, 1749–1769.

Public Record Office, Kew, London: Colonial Office Records, Class 5; War Office Records, Series 34, Baron Jeffrey Amherst, Commander in Chief: Papers.

University of Wisconsin, Madison: William Preston Papers, Draper Manuscript Collection. Microfilm.

Virginia Historical Society, Richmond: Preston Family Papers; Papers of William Byrd III.

Library of Virginia, Richmond: William Flemming Papers; Colonial Papers, Augusta County Records, Frederick County Records.

"Narrative of Marie Le Roy and Barbara Leininger." In *Pennsylvania Archives,* edited by Samuel Hazard, Thomas Lynch Montgomery, George Edward Reed, William Henry Egle, and John Blair Linn, 2d ser. 7:403–12. Philadelphia and Harrisburg: J. Severns, 1852.

"The Captivity of Peter Looney." *Mississippi Valley Historical Review* 15 (1928–29): 95–96.

Abbot, W. W., Dorothy Twohig, and Philander D. Chase, eds. *The Papers of George Washington.* 10 vols. Colonial Series. Charlottesville: University Press of Virginia, 1983–1995.

Alden, Timothy. "An Account of the Captivity of Hugh Gibson among the Delaware Indians . . ." *Massachusetts Historical Society Collections,* 3d ser. 6 (1837): 141–53.

An Answer to an Invidious Pamphlet, Intituled, a Brief State of the Province of Pennsylvania. London: S. Bladon, 1755.

Boehm, Randolph. *Records of the British Colonial Office, Class 5.* Microfilm. Part 1. *Westward Expansion, 1700–1783.* 12 reels. Part 3. *The French and Indian War.* 8 reels. Frederick, Md.: University Microfilm, 1983.

Bond, Beverly W., Jr., ed. "The Captivity of Charles Stuart, 1755–1757." *Mississippi Valley Historical Review* 13 (1926): 58–81.

Boyd, Julian P., and Robert Joseph Taylor. *The Susquehannah Company Papers.* 11 vols. Ithaca: Cornell University Press, 1962.

Brock, Robert A., ed. *The Official Records of Robert Dinwiddie, Lieutenant-governor of the Colony of Virginia, 1751–1758.* 2 vols. Virginia Historical Society Collection, 3–4. Richmond: The Virginia Historical Society, 1883–84.

Butler, Lewis W. G. *Annals of the King's Royal Rifle Corps.* 5 vols. London: Smith Elder, 1913.

Collections of the Illinois Historical Library. 34 vols. Springfield: The Trustees of the Illinois State Historical Library, 1915–40.

Ewing, William S. "Indian Captives Released by Colonel Bouquet." *Western Pennsylvania Historical Magazine* 39 (1956): 187–201.

Fontaine, Jacques. *Memoirs of a Huguenot Family.* Translated by Ann Maury. New York: Putnam, 1907.

Frazier, Jane. *Narrative of the Captivity of Mrs. Jane Frazier.* Vol. 109 of *The Garland Library of Narratives of North American Indian Captivities.* New York: Garland Publishing, 1977.

Greene, Jack P., ed. *The Diary of Colonel Landon Carter of Sabine Hall, 1752–1778.* 2 vols. Charlottesville: University Press of Virginia, 1965.

Hazard, Samuel, ed. *Minutes of the Provincial Council of Pennsylvania: From the Organization to the Termination of the Proprietary Government [Colonial Records of Pennsylvania].* 16 vols. Harrisburg: Theophilus Fenn, 1838–53.

Hazard, Samuel, Thomas Lynch Montgomery, George Edward Reed, William Henry Egle, and John Blair Linn, eds. *Pennsylvania Archives.* 10 series, 107 vols. Philadelphia and Harrisburg: J. Severns, 1852–56.

Heckewelder, John. *History, Manners, and Customs of the Indian Nations Who Once Inhabited*

Pennsylvania and the Neighbouring States. Vol. 11 of *Memoirs of the Historical Society of Pennsylvania.* Philadelphia: Historical Society of Pennsylvania, 1876.

Henning, William Waller, ed. *The Statutes at Large, Being a Collection of All the Laws of Virginia.* 13 vols. Richmond: Franklin Press, 1809–23.

Hulbert, Archer Butler, and William Nathaniel Schwarze. "David Zeisberger's History of the Northern American Indians." *Ohio State Archaeological and Historical Society* 19 (1910): 1–189.

James, Alfred Proctor, ed. *The Writings of General John Forbes Relating to His Service in North America.* Menasha: Collegiate Press, 1938.

Johnson, Susanna. *A Narrative of the Captivity of Mrs. Johnson. Containing an account of her sufferings during four years with the Indians and French.* Glasgow: R. Chapman, 1797.

Jordan, John W., ed. "Journal of James Kenny, 1761–1763." *Pennsylvania Magazine of History and Biography* 37 (1913): 1–47, 152–201.

Kent, Donald H., and Sylvester K. Stevens, eds. *Wilderness Chronicles of Northwestern Pennsylvania.* Harrisburg: Pennsylvania Historical Commission, 1941.

Labaree, Leonard Woods, William Bradford Willcox, and Barbara Oberg, eds. *The Papers of Benjamin Franklin.* 35– vols. New Haven: Yale University Press, 1959–.

McDowell, William L. *Documents Relating to Indian Affairs.* 2 vols. Colonial Records of South Carolina. Ser. 2: Indian Books. Columbia: South Carolina Archives Dept., 1958.

McIlwaine, H. R., Wilmer Lee Hall, and Benjamin J. Hillman, eds. *Executive Journals of the Council of Colonial Virginia.* 6 vols. Richmond: Virginia State Library, 1925–56.

McIlwaine, H. R, and John P. Kennedy, eds. *Journals of the House of Burgesses of Virginia.* 15 vols. Richmond: Everett Waddey Co., 1905–15.

Mitchell, James T., and Henry Flanders., eds. *The Statutes at Large of Pennsylvania from 1682 to 1809.* 18 vols. Harrisburg: C. M. Busch, 1896.

Mulkearn, Lois. *George Mercer Papers: Relating to the Ohio Company of Virginia.* Pittsburgh: University of Pittsburgh Press, 1954.

O'Callaghan, Edmund B., and Berthold Fernow, eds. *Documents Relative to the Colonial History of the State of New York: Procured in Holland, England and France.* 15 vols. Albany: Parsons Weed, 1853–87.

Quaife, Milo Milton. *The Siege of Detroit in 1763: The Journal of Pontiac's Conspiracy, and John Rutherfurd's Narrative of a Captivity.* Chicago: Lakeside Press, 1958.

Reese, George Henkle. *The Official Papers of Francis Fauquier, Lieutenant Governor of Virginia, 1758–1768.* 3 vols. Charlottesville: University Press of Virginia, 1980.

Rogers, Robert. *A Concise Account of North America.* London: J. Millan, 1765.

Seaver, James E. *A Narrative of the Life of Mrs. Mary Jemison . . .* Canadaigua, N.Y.: J. D. Bemis and Co., 1824.

Smith, William. *A Brief State of the Province of Pennsylvania.* London: R. Griffiths, 1755.

———. *An Historical Account of the Expedition against the Ohio Indians in the Year 1764.* London: T. Jefferies, 1766.

Stewart, Irene, ed. *Letters of General John Forbes relating to the expedition against Fort Duquesne in 1758.* Pittsburgh: Allegheny County Committee, 1927.

Sullivan, James, et al., ed. *The Papers of Sir William Johnson.* 14 vols. Albany: University of the State of New York, 1921–65.

Thomson, Charles. *An Enquiry into the Causes of the Alienation of the Delaware and Shawanese Indians from the British Interest . . .* London: J. Wilkie, 1759.

Thwaites, Reuben Gold, ed. *Early Western Travels, 1748–1846.* Vol. 1 of *Two Journals of Western Tours, by Charles [sic] Frederick Post.* Cleveland.: Arthur H. Clark, 1904.

Tinling, Marion, ed. *The Correspondence of the Three William Byrds of Westover Virginia, 1684–1776.* 2 vols. Charlottesville: University Press of Virginia, 1977.

Waddell, Louis M., ed. "New Light on Bouquet's Ohio Expedition: Nine Days of Thomas Hutchinson's Journal, October 3–October 11, 1764." *Western Pennsylvania Historical Magazine* 66 (1983): 271–79.

Waddell, Louis M., S. K. Stevens, Donald H. Kent, Autumn L. Leonard, and J. L. Tottenham, eds. *The Papers of Henry Bouquet.* 6 vols. Harrisburg: Pennsylvania Historical and Museum Commission, 1951–94.

Wainwright, Nicholas N., ed. "George Croghan's Journal, April 3, 1759, to April 1763." *Pennsylvania Magazine of History and Biography* 71 (1947): 305–444.

Books

Alden, John Richard. *Robert Dinwiddie: Servant of the Crown.* Charlottesville: University Press of Virginia, 1973.

Anderson, Fred. *Crucible of War: The Seven Years' War and the Fate of Empire in British North America, 1754–1766.* New York: Alfred A. Knopf, 2000.

———. *A People's Army: Massachusetts Soldiers and Society in the Seven Years' War.* Chapel Hill: University of North Carolina Press, 1984.

Aquila, Richard. *The Iroquois Restoration: Iroquois Diplomacy on the Colonial Frontier, 1701–1754.* Detroit: Wayne State University Press, 1983.

Axtell, James. *The European and the Indian: Essays in the Ethnohistory of Colonial North America.* New York: Oxford University Press, 1981.

———. *The Invasion Within: The Contest of Cultures in Colonial North America.* New York: Oxford University Press, 1985.

Beeman, Richard R. *The Evolution of the Southern Backcountry: A Case Study of Lunenburg County, Virginia, 1746–1831.* Philadelphia: University of Pennsylvania Press, 1984.

Bellesiles, Michael. *Arming America: The Origins of a National Gun Culture.* New York: Alfred A. Knopf, 2000.

Bloch, Ruth. *Visionary Republic: Millennial Themes in American Thought, 1756–1800.* Cambridge: Cambridge University Press, 1985.

Breen, T. H. *Tobacco Culture: The Mentality of the Great Tidewater Planters on the Eve of the Revolution.* Princeton: Princeton University Press, 1985.

Brumwell, Stephen. *Redcoats: The British Soldier and War in the Americas, 1755–1763.* Cambridge: Cambridge University Press, 2002.

Butler, Lewis W.G. *Annals of the King's Royal Rifle Corps.* 5 vols. London: Smith Elder, 1913.

Calloway, Colin. *New Worlds for All: Indians, Europeans and the Remaking of Early America*. Baltimore: Johns Hopkins University Press, 1997.

Cayton, Andrew R.L., and Fredericka J. Teute, eds. *Contact Points: American Frontiers from the Mohawk Valley to the Mississippi, 1750–1830*. Chapel Hill: University of North Carolina Press, 1998.

Colley, Linda. *Britons: Forging the Nation, 1707–1837*. New Haven: Yale University Press, 1992.

——. *Captives: Britain, Empire and the World, 1600–1850*. London: Jonathan Cape, 2002.

Corkran, David H. *The Cherokee Frontier: Conflict and Survival, 1740–1762*. Norman: University of Oklahoma Press, 1962.

Cress, Lawrence Delbert. *Citizens in Arms: The Army and Militia in American Society to the War of 1812, Studies on Armed Forces and Society*. Chapel Hill: University of North Carolina Press, 1982.

Dederer, John Morgan. *War in America to 1775: Before Yankee Doodle*. New York: New York University Press, 1990.

Doerflinger, Thomas M. *A Vigorous Spirit of Enterprise: Merchants and Economic Development in Revolutionary Philadelphia*. Chapel Hill: University of North Carolina Press, 1986.

Dowd, Gregory Evans. *A Spirited Resistance: The North American Indian Struggle for Unity, 1745–1815*. Baltimore: Johns Hopkins University Press, 1992.

Dunn, Richard S., and Mary Maples Dunn. *The World of William Penn*. Philadelphia: University of Pennsylvania Press, 1986.

Eccles, William. *The Canadian Frontier, 1534–1760*. 2d ed. Albuquerque: University of New Mexico Press, 1984.

Egnal, Marc. *A Mighty Empire: The Origins of the American Revolution*. Ithaca: Cornell University Press, 1988.

Ferling, John E. *A Wilderness of Miseries: War and Warriors in Early America*. Westport: Greenwood Press, 1980.

Fischer, David Hackett. *Albion's Seed: Four British Folkways in America*. New York: Oxford University Press, 1989.

Fischer, David Hackett, and James C. Kelly. *Bound Away: Virginia and the Westward Movement*. Charlottesville: University Press of Virginia, 2000.

Franz, George W. *Paxton: A Study of Community Structure and Mobility in the Colonial Pennsylvania Backcountry*. New York: Garland Publishing, 1989.

Freeman, Douglas Southall. *George Washington*. New York: Charles Scribner's Sons, 1948.

Frégault, Guy. *Canada: The War of the Conquest*. Translated by Margaret M. Cameron. Toronto: Oxford University Press, 1969.

Fuller, J. F. C. *British Light Infantry in the Eighteenth Century*. London: Hutchinson and Co., 1925.

Gipson, Lawrence Henry. *The Great War for the Empire: The Victorious Years, 1758–1760*. Vol. 7 of *The British Empire before the American Revolution*. New York: Alfred A. Knopf, 1949.

————. *The Great War for the Empire: The Years of Defeat.* Vol. 6 of *The British Empire before the American Revolution.* New York: Alfred A Knopf, 1946.

————. *Zones of International Friction: North America, South of the Great Lakes Region, 1748–1754.* Vol. 4 of *The British Empire before the American Revolution.* New York: Alfred A. Knopf, 1936.

Greene, Jack P. *The Quest for Power: The Lower Houses of Assembly in the Southern Royal Colonies, 1689–1776.* Chapel Hill: University of North Carolina Press, 1963.

Hatley, Tom. *Dividing Paths: Cherokees and South Carolinians through the Revolutionary Era.* New York: Oxford University Press, 1995.

Hickey, Donald. *The War of 1812: A Forgotten Conflict.* Urbana: University of Illinois Press, 1990.

Higginbotham, Don. *George Washington and the American Military Tradition.* Athens: University of Georgia Press, 1985.

Hinderaker, Eric. *Elusive Empires: Constructing Colonialism in the Ohio Valley, 1673–1800.* Cambridge: Cambridge University Press, 1997.

Hoffman, Ronald, Thad W. Tate, and Peter J. Albert, eds. *An Uncivil War: The Southern Backcountry during the American Revolution.* Charlottesville: University Press of Virginia, 1985.

Hofstra, Warren R., ed. *George Washington and the Virginia Backcountry.* Madison: Madison House, 1998.

Holton, Woody. *Forced Founders: Indians, Debtors, Slaves and the Making of the American Revolution in Virginia.* Chapel Hill: University of North Carolina Press, 1999.

Howard, James H. *Shawnee! The Ceremonialism of a Native Indian Tribe and Its Cultural Background.* Athens: Ohio University Press, 1981.

Hunter, William. *Forts on the Pennsylvania Frontier, 1753–1758.* Harrisburg: Pennsylvania Historical and Museum Commission, 1960.

Illick, Joseph D. *Colonial Pennsylvania: A History.* New York: Scribners, 1976.

Ingles, John. *The Story of Mary Draper Ingles and Her Son Thomas Ingles.* Radford: Commonwealth Press, 1969.

Isaac, Rhys. *The Transformation of Virginia, 1740–1790.* New York: W. W. Norton, 1988.

James, Alfred Proctor. *The Ohio Company: Its Inner History.* Pittsburgh: University of Pittsburgh Press, 1959.

Jennings, Francis. *The Ambiguous Iroquois Empire: The Covenant Chain Confederation of Indian Tribes with English Colonies from Its Beginning to the Lancaster Treaty of 1744.* New York: W. W. Norton, 1984.

————. *Empire of Fortune: Crowns, Colonies and Empires in the Seven Years War.* New York: W. W. Norton, 1988.

Jones, J. R. *Britain and the World, 1649–1815.* London: Fontana, 1980.

Jordan, Terry G., and Matti Kaups. *The American Backwoods Frontier: An Ethnic and Ecological Interpretation.* Baltimore: Johns Hopkins University Press, 1989.

Koontz, Louis Knott. *Robert Dinwiddie: His Career in American Colonial Government and Westward Expansion.* Glendale: Arthur H. Clark Co., 1941.

Kulikoff, Allan. *The Agrarian Origins of American Capitalism.* Charlottesville: University Press of Virginia, 1992.

———. *From British Peasants to Colonial American Farmers.* Chapel Hill: University of North Carolina Press, 2000.

Leach, Douglas Edward. *Arms for Empire: A Military History of the British Colonies in North America, 1607–1763.* New York: MacMillan, 1973.

———. *Roots of Conflict: British Armed Forces and Colonial Americans, 1677–1763.* Chapel Hill: University of North Carolina Press, 1986.

Lemon, James T. *The Best Poor Man's Country: A Geographical Study of Early Southeastern Pennsylvania.* Baltimore: Johns Hopkins University Press, 1976.

Mancall, Peter C. *Deadly Medicine: Indians and Alcohol in Early America.* Ithaca: Cornell University Press, 1995.

———. *Valley of Opportunity: Economic Culture along the Upper Susquehanna, 1700–1800.* Ithaca: Cornell University Press, 1991.

McConnell, Michael N. *A Country Between: The Upper Ohio Valley and Its Peoples, 1724–1774.* Lincoln: University of Nebraska Press, 1992.

Meinig, D. W. *Atlantic America, 1492–1800.* Vol. 1 of *The Shaping of America: A Geographical Perspective on Five Hundred Years of History.* New Haven: Yale University Press, 1986.

Melvoin, Richard I. *New England Outpost: War and Society in Colonial Deerfield.* New York: W. W. Norton, 1988.

Merrell, James H. *Into the American Woods: Negotiators on the Pennsylvania Frontier.* New York: W. W. Norton, 1999.

Middleton, Richard. *The Bells of Victory: The Pitt-Newcastle Ministry and the Conduct of the Seven Years' War, 1757–1762.* Cambridge: Cambridge University Press, 1985.

Millet, Allan R., and Peter Maslowski. *For the Common Defense: A Military History of the United States of America.* New York: Free Press, 1984.

Mitchell, Robert D. *Commercialism and Frontier: Perspectives on the Early Shenandoah Valley.* Charlottesville: University of Virginia Press, 1977.

Nash, Gary B. *The Urban Crucible: The Northern Seaports and the Origins of the American Revolution.* Cambridge: Harvard University Press, 1986.

Newcomb, Benjamin H. *Franklin and Galloway: A Political Partnership.* New Haven: Yale University Press, 1972.

Oliphant, John. *Peace and War on the Anglo-Cherokee Frontier, 1756–63.* Basingstoke: Palgrave, 2001.

Olmstead, Earl P. *David Zeisberger: A Life among the Indians.* Kent: Kent State University Press, 1997.

Parkman, Francis. *The Conspiracy of Pontiac and the Indian War after the Conquest of Canada.* Edited by Michael N. McConnell. Bison Books. Lincoln: University of Nebraska Press, 1994.

Peckham, Howard H. *The Colonial Wars, 1689–1762.* Chicago: University of Chicago Press, 1962.

———. *Pontiac and the Indian Uprising.* Princeton: Princeton University Press, 1947.

Puglisi, Michael J., ed. *Diversity and Accommodation: Essays on the Cultural Composition of the Virginia Frontier.* Knoxville: University of Tennessee Press, 1997.

Rogers, Alan. *Empire and Liberty: American Resistance to British Authority, 1755–1763.* Berkeley: University of California Press, 1974.

Rogers, H. C. B. *The British Army of the Eighteenth Century.* London: George Allen and Unwin, 1977.

Salinger, Sharon. *To Serve Well and Faithfully: Labor and Indentured Servants in Pennsylvania, 1682–1800.* Cambridge: Cambridge University Press, 1987.

Schwartz, Sally. *A Mixed Multitude: The Struggle for Toleration in Colonial Pennsylvania.* New York: New York University Press, 1987.

Selesky, Harold E. *War and Society in Colonial Connecticut.* New Haven: Yale University Press, 1990.

Shea, William L. *The Virginia Militia in the Seventeenth Century.* Baton Rouge: Lousiana State University Press, 1975.

Shy, John. *A People Numerous and Armed: Reflections on the Military Struggle for American Independence.* Ann Arbor: University of Michigan Press, 1990.

———. *Toward Lexington: The Role of the British Army in the Coming of the American Revolution.* Princeton: Princeton University Press, 1965.

Slaughter, Thomas. *The Whiskey Rebellion: Frontier Epilogue to the American Revolution.* New York: Oxford University Press, 1986.

Slotkin, Richard. *Regeneration through Violence: The Mythology of the American Frontier, 1600–1860.* Middletown: Wesleyan University Press, 1973.

Smith, Abbot Emerson. *Colonists in Bondage: White Servitude and Convict Labor in America, 1607–1776.* Chapel Hill: University of North Carolina Press, 1947.

Sosin, Jack M. *Whitehall and the Wilderness: The Middle West in British Colonial Policy, 1760–1775.* Lincoln: University of Nebraska Press, 1961.

Speck, W. A. *Stability and Strife: England, 1714–1760.* London: Edward Arnold, 1977.

Starkey, Armstrong. *European and Native American Warfare, 1675–1815.* London: UCL Press, 1998.

Steele, Ian K. *Betrayals: Fort William Henry and the "Massacre."* New York: Oxford University Press, 1990.

———. *Warpaths: Invasions of North America.* Oxford: Oxford University Press, 1994.

Szasz, Margaret Connell. *Between Indian and White Worlds: The Cultural Broker.* Norman: University of Oklahoma Press, 1994.

Tanner, Helen Hornbeck, ed. *Atlas of Great Lakes Indian History.* Norman: University of Oklahoma Press, 1987.

Thayer, Theodore. *Israel Pemberton: King of the Quakers.* Philadelphia: Historical Society of Pennsylvania, 1943.

———. *Pennsylvania Politics and the Growth of Democracy, 1740–1776.* Harrisburg: Pennsylvania Historical and Museum Commission, 1953.

Thompson, E. P. *The Making of the English Working Class.* London: Victor Gollancz, 1965.

Tillson, Albert H., Jr. *Gentry and Common Folk: Political Culture on a Virginia Frontier, 1740–1789.* Lexington: University Press of Kentucky, 1991.

Titus, James. *The Old Dominion at War: Society, Politics, and Warfare in Late Colonial Virginia.* Columbia: University of South Carolina Press, 1991.

Trask, Kerry. *In the Pursuit of Shadows: Massachusetts Millennialism and the Seven Years War.* New York: Garland, 1990.

Wallace, Anthony F. C. *King of the Delawares: Teedyuscung, 1700–1763.* Philadelphia.: University of Pennsylvania Press, 1949.

Weslager, C. A. *The Delaware Indians: A History.* New Brunswick: Rutgers University Press, 1972.

———. *The Delaware Indian Westward Migration.* Wallingford: Middle Atlantic Press, 1978.

White, Richard. *The Middle Ground: Indians, Empires, and Republics in the Great Lakes Region, 1650–1815.* New York: Cambridge University Press, 1991.

Wood, Jerome H., Jr. *Conestoga Crossroads: Lancaster Pennsylvania, 1730–1790.* Harrisburg: Pennsylvania Historical and Museum Commission, 1979.

Chapters in Edited Books

Beattie, Daniel J. "The Adaptation of the British Army to Wilderness Warfare." In *Adapting to Conditions: War and Society in the Eighteenth Century,* edited by Maarten Ultee, 56–83. University: University of Alabama Press, 1986.

Callender, Charles. "Shawnee." In *Handbook of North American Indians: Northeast,* edited by Bruce G. Trigger, 622–35. Washington, D.C.: Smithsonian Institution, 1978.

Dowd, Gregory Evans. "Gift Giving and the Cherokee-British Alliance in the Seven Years' War." In *Contact Points: American Frontiers from the Mohawk Valley to the Mississippi,* edited by Andrew R. L. Cayton and Fredrika Teute, 114–50. Chapel Hill: University of North Carolina Press, 1998.

Fausz, J. Frederick. "'Engaged in Enterprises Pregnant with Terror': George Washington's Formative Years among the Indians." In *George Washington and the Virginia Backcountry,* edited by Warren R. Hofstra, 115–55. Madison: Madison House, 1998.

Ferling, John E. "School for Command: Young George Washington and the Virginia Regiment." In *George Washington and the Virginia Backcountry,* edited by Warren R. Hofstra, 195–222. Madison: Madison House, 1998.

Goddard, Yves. "Delaware." In *Handbook of North American Indians: Northeast,* edited by Bruce G. Trigger, 213–39. Washington, D.C.: Smithsonian Institution, 1978.

Greene, Jack P. "Independence, Improvement, and Authority: Toward a Framework for Understanding the Histories of the Southern Backcountry during the Era of the American Revolution." In *An Uncivil War: The Southern Backcountry during the American Revolution,* edited by Thad W. Tate, Ronald Hoffman, and Peter J. Albert, 3–36. Charlottesville: University Press of Virginia, 1985.

Hofstra, Warren R. "Ethnicity and Community Formation on the Shenandoah Valley Frontier, 1730–1800." In *Diversity and Accommodation: Essays on the Cultural Composition of the Virginia Frontier,* edited by Michael J. Puglisi, 59–81. Knoxville: University of Tennessee Press, 1997.

Hofstra, Warren R. "'A Parcel of Barbarian's and an Uncooth Set of People': Settlers and Settlements of the Shenandoah Valley." In *George Washington and the Virginia Backcountry,* edited by Warren R. Hofstra, 87–114. Madison: Madison House, 1998.

Jones, Maldwyn A. "The Scotch-Irish in British America." In *Strangers within the Realm: Cultural Margins of the First British Empire,* edited by Bernard Bailyn, 284–313. Chapel Hill: University of North Carolina Press, 1991.

Keller, Kenneth W. "The Outlook of Rhinelanders on the Virginia Frontier." In *Diversity and Accommodation: Essays on the Cultural Composition of the Virginia Frontier,* edited by Michael J. Puglisi, 99–133. Knoxville.: University of Tennessee Press, 1997.

Merritt, Jane T. "Metaphor, Meaning and Misunderstanding: Language and Power on the Pennsylvania Frontier." In *Contact Points: American Frontiers from the Mohawk Valley to the Mississippi, 1750–1830,* edited by Andrew R. L. Cayton and Fredrika Teute, 60–87. Chapel Hill: University of North Carolina Press, 1998.

Mitchell, Robert D. "'From the Ground Up': Space, Place, and Diversity in Frontier Studies." In *Diversity and Accommodation: Essays on the Cultural Composition of the Virginia Frontier,* edited by Michael J. Puglisi, 23–57. Knoxville: University of Tennessee Press, 1997.

———. "'Over the Hills and Far Away': George Washington and the Changing Virginia Backcountry." In *George Washington and the Virginia Backcountry,* edited by Warren R. Hofstra, 63–86. Madison: Madison House, 1998.

Roeber, A. G. "'The Origin of Whatever Is Not English among Us': The Dutch-Speaking and the German-Speaking Peoples of Colonial British America." In *Strangers within the Realm: Cultural Margins of the First British Empire,* edited by Bernard Bailyn, 220–83. Chapel Hill: University of North Carolina Press, 1991.

Skemp, Sheila L. "A World Uncertain and Strongly Checker'd." In *Adapting to Conditions: War and Society in the Eighteenth Century,* edited by Maarten Ultee, 84–103. University: University of Alabama Press, 1986.

Articles

Beeman, Richard R. "Social Change and Cultural Conflict in Virginia: Lunenberg County, 1746 to 1774." *William and Mary Quarterly* 3d ser. 35 (1978): 455–76.

Brodine, Charles. "Civil-Military Relations in Pennsylvania, 1758–1760: An Examination of John Shy's Thesis." *Pennsylvania History* 62 (1995): 213–33.

Champion, Walter T., Jr. "Christian Frederick Post and the Winning of the West." *Pennsylvania Magazine of History and Biography* 104 (1985): 308–25.

Cook, Roy Bird. "Virginia's Frontier Defenses, 1719–1795." *West Virginia History* 1 (1940): 110–32.

Davis, Elvert M., ed. "History of the Capture and Captivity of David Boyd from Cumberland County Pennsylvania, 1756." *Western Pennsylvania Historical Magazine* 14 (1931): 28–32.

Douglas, Harry S. "The Immortal Mary Jemison." *Historical Wyoming* 9 (1958): 33–46.

Dowd, Gregory Evans. "The French King Wakes up in Detroit: 'Pontiac's War' in Rumor and History." *Ethnohistory* 37 (1990): 254–78.

Eccles, William. "The Fur Trade and Eighteenth Century Imperialism." *William and Mary Quarterly* 3d ser. 40 (1983): 341–62.

Eid, Leroy V. "'A Kind of Running Fight': Indian Battlefield Tactics in the Late Eighteenth Century." *Western Pennsylvania Historical Magazine* 71 (1988): 147–71.

Ewing, William S. "Indian Captives Released by Colonel Bouquet." *Western Pennsylvania Historical Magazine* 39 (1956): 187–201.

Fenn, Elizabeth A. "Biological Warfare in Eighteenth-Century North America: Beyond Jeffery Amherst." *Journal of American History* 86 (1999–2000): 1552–80.

Ferling, John E. "Soldiers for Virginia: Who Served in the French and Indian War?" *Virginia Magazine of History and Biography* 94 (1986): 307–28.

"Forum: Historians and Guns." *William and Mary Quarterly* 59 (2002): 203–68.

Gipson, Lawrence Henry. "The American Revolution as an Aftermath of the Great War for the Empire." *Political Science Quarterly* 65 (1950): 86–104.

Higginbotham, Don. "The Early American Way of War." *William and Mary Quarterly* 3d ser. 44 (1987): 230–73.

Hofstra, Warren. "'The Extension of His Majesties Dominions': The Virginia Backcountry and the Reconfiguration of Imperial Frontiers." *Journal of American History* 84 (1998): 1281–312.

Ketcham, Ralph L. "Conscience, War and Politics in Pennsylvania, 1755–1757." *William and Mary Quarterly* 3d ser. 20 (1963): 416–39.

MacLeod, D. Peter. "Microbes and Muskets: Smallpox and the Participation of the Amerindian Allies of New France in the Seven Years' War." *Ethnohistory* 39 (1992): 42–64.

Martin, James Kirby. "The Return of the Paxton Boys and the Historical State of the Pennsylvania Frontier." *Pennsylvania History* 38 (1971): 117–33.

McCleskey, Turk. "Rich Land, Poor Prospects: Real Estate and the Formation of a Social Elite in Augusta County, Virginia, 1738–1779." *Virginia Magazine of History and Biography* 98 (1990): 449–86.

McConnell, Michael N. "Kuskusky Towns and Early Western Pennsylvania Indian History, 1748–1778." *Pennsylvania Magazine of History and Biography* 116 (1992): 33–58.

Merritt, Jane T. "Cultural Encounters along a Gender Frontier: Mahican, Delaware and German Women in Eighteenth-Century Pennsylvania." *Pennsylvania History* 67 (2000): 503–32.

Morgan, Philip D., and Michael L. Nicholls. "Slaves in Piedmont Virginia, 1720–1790." *William and Mary Quarterly* 3d ser. 46 (1989): 211–51.

Myers, James P., Jr. "Pennsylvania's Awakening: The Kittanning Raid of 1756." *Pennsylvania History* 66 (1999): 399–420.

Nobles, Gregory H. "Breaking into the Backcountry: New Approaches to the Early American Frontier, 1750–1800." *William and Mary Quarterly* 3d ser. 46 (1989): 641–70.

Richter, Daniel. "A Framework for Pennsylvania Indian History." *Pennsylvania History* 57 (1990): 236–61.

Russell, Peter. "Redcoats in the Wilderness: British Officers and Irregular Warfare in Europe and America, 1740–1760." *William and Mary Quarterly* 3d ser. 35 (1978): 629–52.

Stephenson, R. S. "Pennsylvania Provincial Soldiers in the Seven Years' War." *Pennsylvania History* 62 (1995): 196–213.

Vaughan, Alden T. "Frontier Banditti and the Indians: The Paxton Boys' Legacy 1763–1765." *Pennsylvania History* 51 (1984): 1–29.

Vaughan, Alden T., and Daniel K. Richter. "Crossing the Cultural Divide: Indians and New Englanders, 1605–1763." *Proceedings of the American Antiquarian Society* 90 (1980–81): 23–99.

Waddell, Louis M. "Defending the Long Perimeter: Forts on the Pennsylvania, Maryland, and Virginia Frontier, 1755–1765." *Pennsylvania History* 62 (1995): 171–95.

Ward, Matthew C. "'An Army of Servants': The Pennsylvania Regiment during the Seven Years' War," *Pennsylvania Magazine of History and Biography* 119 (1995): 75–93.

———. "Fighting the 'Old Women': Indian Strategy on the Virginia and Pennsylvania Frontier, 1754–1748." *Virginia Magazine of History and Biography* 103 (1995): 297–320.

———. "'Redeeming the Captives:' Pennsylvania Captives among the Ohio Indians, 1755–1765." *Pennsylvania Magazine of History and Biography* 125 (2001): 161–89.

Warden, G. B. "The Proprietary Group in Pennsylvania, 1754–1764." *William and Mary Quarterly* 3d ser. 21 (1964): 367–89.

Unpublished Dissertations

Cutcliffe, Stephen H. "Indians, Furs and Empires: The Changing Policies of New York and Pennsylvania, 1674–1768." Ph.D. diss., Lehigh University, 1976.

Merritt, Jane T. "Kinship, Community, and Practicing Culture: Indians and the Colonial Encounter in Pennsylvania, 1700–1763. Ph.D. diss., University of Washington, 1995.

Parker, King Lawrence. "Anglo-American Wilderness Campaigning, 1754–1764: Logistical and Tactical Developments." Ph.D. diss., Columbia University, 1970.

Parmenter, Jon William. "At the Wood's Edge, Iroquois Foreign Relations, 1727–1768." Ph.D. diss., University of Michigan, 1999.

Young, Chester Raymond. "The Effects of the French and Indian War on Civilian Life in the Frontier Counties of Virginia, 1754–1763." Ph.D. diss., Vanderbilt University, 1969.

Index

de Villiers, Pierre Joseph Neyon, 234, 242–43

Dinwiddie, Robert, 11, 26, 60, 76–77, 89, 124–25, 168, *ill;* and Indian allies, 40–41, 104; and military, 31–32, 38–39, 44, 63, 85–86, 104–6, 118; and recruitment, 77, 202; relations with Indians, 30, 143, 145; and Virginia militia, 69, 92–95; and Washington, 34, 119

diseases, 193; among Indians, 24, 229, 234; among troops, 83, 110–11, 169, 188, 196, 235; smallpox, 83, 146, 150, 155, 229, 248

Dumas, Jean-Daniel, 43, 68

Dunbar, Thomas, 44, 60, 83

Easton, Pennsylvania, 75

Easton, Treaty of (1758), 164, 206, 207

Easton conferences, 201; in 1756, 134–41, 146; in 1757, 152; in 1758, 165, 178–82; in 1761, 206–7; in 1762, 212–14

economy, 5, 114; colonial, 72–73, 73–76, 189; and cost of war, 98–100, 124–29; individualism in at expense of communities, 20–22; and trade in Ohio Valley, 259–60; value of captives in Indian, 54–55

Egremont, Charles Wyndham, Charles, earl of, 208, 211–12

elite: backcountry's and eastern, 5–6, 13; eastern, 11, 13; as large landholders, 10–13; and military, 62, 86, 92, 94, 117–18; solidifying power during wars, 260; tensions with yeoman farmers, 12–13, 59; weakness of leadership by, 16, 59–60, 77, 85–86; wealth of, 6, 11–13

ethnic groups: divisiveness among, 13–15, 60, 87–89; segregation in provincial forces, 115–16

Fauquier, Francis, 120, 168, 188–89, 207; on expanding settlements, 201–2, 237; in Pontiac's War, 226, 228, 237, 240; relations with Cherokees, 196–98; and Virginia's military, 176, 197

Fleming, William, 52–53

food. *See* provisions

Forbes, John, 103, 184, 188; army commanded by, 157, 257; and attack on Fort Duquesne, 160, 168–78, 182–83; contrasted to Braddock, 177, 185,

258; on diplomacy with Indians, 2, 157–58, 162–65, 183–85; effectiveness of, 161, 183–84, 257–58; frustration with settlers, 83, 85; and peace negotiations with Indians, 163, 178, 182; and provincial armies, 91, 110–11, 119, 159, 161; and relations with Indians, 165–68, 191

Fort Allen, 88, 110, 133–34, 136

Fort Augusta, 100–101, 132–33, 225, *ill;* discipline at, 74–75, 108, 117–18; skeleton garrison at, 169–70

Fort Bedford, 225–26, 240, 243

Fort Cumberland, 44, 63, 101; attacks on, 49, 147–48; campaigns launched from, 40–42, 106; Indian raids around, 61–62, 68–69, 146, 174; problems at, 108, 119, 170

Fort Detroit, 220–21. *See also* Detroit

Fort Duquesne, 33, 103, 144, 202; Braddock's campaign against, 43–44; British route to, 170–74, 188; fall of, 183, 187; Forbes's campaign against, 160, 168–78, 182–83; French forces at, 38–39, 165, 177–78, 183; Indian raids sent out from, 48, 146–47; Washington's campaign against, 33–35

Fort Granville, 50–51, 69, 106

Fort Le Boeuf, 191, 224, 229

Fort Ligonier, 110, 225, 229, 240

Fort Loudon, 141–42, 255; and Cherokees, 195, 197; in Forbes's campaign, 160, 171–72; vulnerability of, 170, 197

Fort Miami, 30, 223, 247

Fort Michilimackinac, 223–24

Fort Necessity, 34–35

Fort Niagara, 48, 190. *See also* Niagara

Fort Pitt, 190, 205, 235; communication with, 225, 243, 246; Indian attacks on, 187, 240; and peace negotiations with Indians, 250, 252; in Pontiac's War, 224, 227–30, 240; supply lines to, 188–89, 235, 241; trade with Indians at, 192, 204. *See also* Pittsburgh

Fort Presque Isle, 30, 200, 204, 224, 228, 245–47

Fort Stanwix, Treaty of, 257

Fort Vause, 50, 56, 69

Fort Venango, 30, 190–91, 200, 224, 229

Fort William Henry, 57, 146, 152

France. *See* French

Franklin, Benjamin, 87, 97, 99, 127–28, 194, 239

Frederick County, Virginia, 10–11, 18, 69, 71–72, 86, 260; Indian raids in, 49, 61, 70, 172, 226, 246; militia of, 69, 92–93; in Pontiac's War, 226, 251

French, 52, 54, 69–71, 146, 226–27; and Anglophile Indians, 29–30, 64; Britain replacing in relations with Indians, 252, 257; British attempts to weaken Indians' alliance with, 2, 163, 182; British campaigns against, 36, 173–76, 200; British policy on, 159, 184; and Cherokees, 142, 145, 165–66; decline of North American empire, 1, 190–91, 194–95, 200, 216, 259; Delawares' relations with, 64–65, 132–33, 135, 151–52; and Forbes's campaign against Fort Duquesne, 168, 177–78, 183; forts of, 30–31, 33, 207–8; Indian allies of, 30–31, 158, 183, 187, 211–12, 220; and Indian raids, 42–44, 47–48, 68–69, 147, 187; and Indians in Pontiac's War, 226, 233–34, 242, 253; and Ohio Indians, 23–24, 206, 216; in Ohio Valley, 23–24, 27–29, 32, 35, 37–38, 57–58, 190; provisions for Indians from, 155, 164–65, 173; in Seven Years' War, 45–46, 70–71, 187–88; shipping by, 72–73, 158; trade by, 10, 22–24, 217; Washington skirmishing with, 33–35

Friendly Association, 134, 178, 224; animosity toward, 152, 194, 238, 254; providing trade goods for Ohio Indians, 191–92; and return of captives, 210–11. See also Quakers

Fry, Joshua, 32–33

fur trade, 9–10, 143, 195, 207; competitiveness over, 22–23, 35, 191; settlers in, 21–23

Gage, Thomas, 161, 235, 237, 240, 243–45
George II, king of Great Britain, 187, 203
Germans, 14, 60, 87, 109, 115–16
gifts, 28, 48, 76, 215; British cutting off, 207–8, 186, 202–3, 210, 212, 215–17; British reinstating, 241, 251–53; from French to Indians, 151–52, 158; importance in Indian diplomacy, 24, 207, 226; at peace negotiations, 41, 134, 136–37; Virginia not giving to Cherokees, 142–45, 165–67, 195
Gladwin, Henry, 220–21, 231, 233–35
Gnadenhütten, 66, 133

government, 26; civil, vs. military, 79–85; effects of excessive individualism on, 76–77. See also colonial assemblies
Grant, James, 174–76, 198–99
Great Britian. See British
Greenbrier River, 50, 62

Halifax, George Montagu Dunk, earl of, 26, 152
Halifax County, Virginia: Cherokees vs. Shawnees in, 195–96; Indian raids on, 61, 148, 166, 199, 226
Hamilton, James, 29, 206–7, 214; and Delawares, 201, 212; as governor, 189, 236; in Pontiac's War, 227–28
Hamilton, John, 79–80
Hampshire County, Virginia, 18, 69, 93; Indian raids on, 49, 61, 71, 172, 226, 246; in Pontiac's War, 226, 251
Hanover, 45, 188
Harris, John, 65, 74
Harris's Ferry, Pennsylvania, 65, 72, 74, 76, 130–31, 147
Holston River Valley, 17, 60
House of Burgesses, Virginia, 19, 105, 112, 118–19; on defense, 32, 228; and Dinwiddie, 32, 85, 124–25; funding for wars, 39–40, 124, 176, 197–98; issuing paper money, 124–25; relations with Indians, 104, 123, 143, 156, 166; reluctance to provide troops, 209, 228, 240, 243–44; on use of militia, 93, 228; and Virginia Regiment, 61–62, 97–98. See also colonial assemblies
hunting, 105, 208, 209; on Indian lands, 194, 201, 206; Indians' lack of ammunition for, 203–4, 216; wars interfering with, 104, 241
Hurons, 23, 48, 159, 205, 210–11, 224, 231
Hutchins, Thomas, 215–16

Illinois Country, 212, 242, 246–47
Illinois Indians, 31, 48–49, 242–43, 253
immigrants, 14, 115–16; and politics, 14, 87
Indian raids, 17, 76, 89, 195–96; aided by French, 36–37, 47–48; casualties of, 61, 67, 70; in Cherokee War, 196–97; colonies' expectation of success against, 46–47; defenses against, 101, 119, 126–27, 144, 227–28, 258; effectiveness of, 8, 57–58, 61–62, 68–69, 71–72, 217; effects of, 5, 56–57, 59, 74;

Venango. *See* Fort Venango
Virginia, 4–5, 9, 26, 47, 63, 92, 168, 237;
    backcountry of, 16–19, 31; in Chero-
    kee War, 195–99; conflict over route
    to Fort Duquesne, 171–72, 188; and
    control of Ohio Valley, 35–36, 184,
    188; defense of frontier, 100–102;
    effects of wars on, 2–3, 251; elite of,
    10, 60; ethnic and religious divisive-
    ness in, 88–90; and Indian allies,
    29–30, 141–45, 165; Indian raids on,
    60–61, 68–73, 146–47, 226, 242, 243;
    land claimed by, 27–28; and military,
    31–32, 85, 157, 159–60, 199, 228;
    militia of, 92–95; profiteering in,
    74–77, 94, 110; targets of Indian raids
    on, 49–50, 60, 187, 241. *See also specific
    counties;* colonial assemblies; House of
    Burgesses
Virginia Regiment, 32–33, 61–62, 68–69,
    84, 118, 143, 209, 243, 258; composi-
    tion of, 89–90, 113–16; creation of,
    95–99; effectiveness of, 91, 103–4,
    120–22; First, 176; in Forbes's expe-
    dition, 170, 172; recruitment for, 78,
    109, 202; Second, 160–61; supplies
    for, 75, 85; tensions with militia, 95,
    119, 172. *See also* armies, provincial

Walking Purchase, 25, 138–40, 181, 212–14
Washington, George, 3, 32–33, 86, 89, 98,
    117, 156, 188, *ill;* campaigns involved
    in, 61–62, 147–48; and conflict over
route to Fort Duquesne, 172–74; on
    effectiveness of Indian raids, 57,
    68–69, 71; and French, 32–35, 37;
    and frontier defenses, 62–63, 69;
    frustration with settlers, 62, 71, 83,
    85; frustration with troops, 75, 86,
    94, 98, 112–13, 118–19; military skills
    of, 120–21, 258; recruitment by,
    89–90, 109; relations with Indians,
    47, 166–67; and supplies, 79–80, 82
wealth: of backcountry elites, 6, 11–13, 16,
    77, 260; sources of, 11, 22
weapons, 23, 258; of Indians, 51, 54, 158;
    militia's lack of, 61, 93–94; quality of,
    42, 46–47, 197; shortages of, 29, 158,
    168–69, 187
Weiser, Conrad, 12, 56, 60, 65, 67, 87, 96;
    and causes of war, 138, 140–41; and
    military authority, 84–85; and peace
    negotiations, 135, 182
Welsh, in backcountry, 14
Winchester, Virginia, 40–41, 147–48, 259;
    Cherokees at, 144, 145, 167; military
    in, 75, 79–80
Wyalusings. *See* Delawares, Moravian
Wyandots, 43, 190, 240, 245, 249
Wyoming Indians. *See* Delawares, Wyoming
Wyoming Valley: Connecticut settlers in,
    200–201; Delawares' land in, 180–81,
    206–7, 212–13; Delawares moving
    into, 25–26

York County, Pennsylvania, 18–19, 226, 246